THE CULTURE OF CURSILERÍA

The Culture of

CURSILERÍA

Bad Taste, Kitsch, and Class in Modern Spain

NOËL VALIS

Duke University Press   Durham & London   2002

© 2002 Duke University Press
All rights reserved
Printed in the United States
of America on acid-free paper ∞
Designed by Rebecca Giménez
Typeset in Monotype Fournier
by Keystone Typesetting, Inc.
Library of Congress Cataloging-
in-Publication Data appear on the
last printed page of this book.
This book has been supported
generously by the Program for
Cultural Cooperation between
Spain's Ministry of Education
and Culture and United
States Universities.

FOR CAL

CONTENTS

A C K N O W L E D G M E N T S

This book has been a long time in coming. Over the years I have felt a debt of gratitude to many people and institutions. My deepest thanks go to Carolyn Richmond, Susan Kirkpatrick, Benedict Anderson, Monroe Z. Hafter, Dolores O'Connor, David Herzberger, Richard Kagan, Tamar Herzog, Eva Teba Fernández, Andrés Fuentes, Curtis Wasson, Nil Santiáñez-Tió, Russell Sebold, Gustavo Pellón, David Gies, Andrew Anderson, Teresa Vilarós, Robert Fedorchek, Manuel García Castellón, Marie García-Abrines, María Teresa Zubiaurre, Rodrigo Díaz-Pérez, Francesco Fiumara, José Manuel González Herrán, Hazel Gold, Angel Loureiro, Roberto González Echevarría, Edward Baker, Wayne Valis, Harriet Turner, Stephanie Sieburth, Milad Doueihi, Meriwynn Grothe, Ross Chambers, Reynolds Smith, Leigh Anne Couch, Sharon Parks Torian, Eduardo González, Pier Massimo Forni, Lincoln Lambeth, the wonderful graduate students in seminars at the University of Michigan, Johns Hopkins University, Duke University, and Emory University, the interlibrary loan staff at the University of Michigan, Johns Hopkins University, and Yale University, the Biblioteca Nacional of Madrid, the Instituto Internacional, and the Hemeroteca Municipal and Hemeroteca Nacional of Madrid.

I have benefited greatly from the lively discussions coming out of the Johns Hopkins University / Ford Foundation Seminar on Gender in the spring of 1992, the special seminars given at Duke University and Emory University in 1995 and 1996, the Johns Hopkins University Departmental Seminar in 1997, the Women's Study Colloquia at Colby College in 1998, and, above all, the initial support provided in 1986 by the generous funding of a postdoctoral research fellowship under the Treaty of Friendship between the United States and Spain, when what I thought was going to be one book turned out to be another.

An earlier version of chapters 5 and 7 appeared as "Fabricating Culture in Galdós's *Cánovas*," *MLN* 107 (1992); and as "Two Ramóns: A View from the Margins of Modernist *Cursilería*," *Anales de la literatura española contemporánea* 17.3 (1992). Passages from "Romanticism, Realism, and the Presence of the Word," *Letras peninsulares* 3.2–3.3 (1991), "Pardo Bazán's *El Cisne de Vilamorta* and the Romantic Reader," *MLN* 101 (1986), and "Nostalgia and Exile," *Journal of Spanish Cultural Studies* 1.2 (2000), appear in chapters 3 and 6.

All translations are my own, except where otherwise noted. In most instances, original language quotations are located in the notes. Additionally, unless stated otherwise, emphasis in quotations is true to the original.

THE CULTURE OF CURSILERÍA

Cursi: 1. Dícese de la persona que presume de fina y elegante sin serlo. 2. Aplícase a lo que, con apariencia de elegancia o riqueza, es ridículo y de mal gusto. 3. Dícese de los artistas y escritores, o de sus obras, cuando en vano pretenden mostrar refinamiento expresivo o sentimientos elevados.—*Diccionario de la Real Academia Española* (DRAE), 1984 (orig. 1869)

El ser *cursi* o parecerlo no es una cosa esencial, ni una idea absoluta, sino una cualidad derivada, una idea de relación que varía según los términos con que se compare.—SANTIAGO DE LINIERS AND FRANCISCO SILVELA, *La filocalia o arte de distinguir a los cursis de los que no lo son,* 1868

La invención de la palabra 'cursi' complicó horriblemente la vida. Antes existía lo bueno y lo malo, lo divertido y lo aburrido. . . . Ahora existe lo cursi; que no es lo bueno ni lo malo, ni lo que divierte ni lo que aburre; es . . . una negación: lo contrario de lo distinguido; es decir, una cosa cada día; porque en cuanto hay seis personas que piensan o hacen lo mismo, ya es preciso pensar y hacer otra cosa para ser distinguido; y por huir de lo cursi se hacen tonterías, extravagancias . . ., hasta maldades.—JACINTO BENAVENTE, *Lo cursi,* 1901

Si se analizase, lupa en mano, el significado de cursi se vería en él concentrada toda la historia española de 1850 a 1900. La cursilería como endemia, sólo puede producirse en un pueblo anormalmente pobre que se ve obligado a vivir en la atmósfera del siglo diecinueve europeo, en plena democracia y capitalismo. La cursilería es una misma cosa con la carencia de una fuerte burguesía, fuerte moral y económicamente. Ahora bien, esa ausencia es el factor decisivo de la historia de España en la última centuria.—JOSÉ ORTEGA Y GASSET, "Intimidades," 1929

Cursi: 1. Said of a person with pretensions to refinement and elegance. 2. Applied to that which, appearing to be elegant or luxurious, is ridiculous or in bad taste. 3. Said of artists and writers, or of their works, when they vainly attempt to show expressive refinement or elevated feelings. — *Diccionario de la Real Academia Española* (DRAE), 1984 (orig. 1869)

Being or appearing to be *cursi* is not an essential thing, or an absolute idea, but a derived quality, an idea of relationship that varies according to the terms with which it is compared. — SANTIAGO DE LINIERS AND FRANCISCO SILVELA, *La filocalia o arte de distinguir a los cursis de los que no lo son,* 1868

The invention of the word *cursi* complicated life horribly. Before, you had the good and the bad, the entertaining and the boring. . . . Now you have *lo cursi,* which is neither good nor bad, neither entertaining nor boring; it is . . . a negation: the opposite of distinguished; that is, plain old everydayness. Because the minute there are six people who think or do the same thing, it's time to think and do something else in order to be different; and to avoid what is *cursi,* sometimes foolish, outlandish, even bad things are done. — JACINTO BENAVENTE, *Lo cursi,* 1901

If one analyzes in close detail the meaning of *cursi,* one sees concentrated in it the entire history of Spain from 1850 to 1900. *Cursilería* as something endemic can only come about in a nation abnormally impoverished, obliged to live in the air of nineteenth-century Europe, in the midst of democracy and capitalism. *Cursilería* signifies the absence of a strong bourgeoisie, strong morally and economically. Now, this absence is the deciding factor in the history of Spain during the last century. — JOSÉ ORTEGA Y GASSET, "Intimidades," 1929

No hay cuestiones pequeñas; las que lo parecen son
cuestiones grandes no comprendidas.

There are no small questions. What seems small are
large questions which are not understood.

—SANTIAGO RAMÓN Y CAJAL, *Los tónicos de la voluntad*

WHEN DOES A book begin? The beginnings for this book go back to a
very specific date, although at the time I was not aware of it: 21 January
1986. I had just arrived in Madrid, all set to work on a project I thought
was going to be about the persistence of romanticism in modern Spanish
literature. At Barajas Airport I dropped exhausted into a taxi. The radio
was on, and from the announcer's solemn voice I could tell that something significant had happened. "What's going on?" I asked. "The
mayor died," the taxi driver told me. This was Enrique Tierno Galván,
the most popular mayor Madrid had ever seen, though an odd choice for
such a role: an academic and intellectual, he had founded the clandestine
Socialist Party of the Interior (Partido Socialista del Interior) in 1967,
which then became the Partido Socialista Popular, merging in 1976 with
the more powerful Socialist Workers Party (PSOE) of Felipe González.

I knew Tierno Galván. He had been a visiting professor at Bryn Mawr
College in 1969, when he gave a seminar on the philosophy of Ortega y
Gasset. In those days he was a wandering scholar since the Franco
regime had expelled him from the University of Salamanca for supporting student protests. I was a second-year graduate student, too full of
myself to be properly awed by Tierno's presence. The political atmosphere on American campuses was very tense in the late 1960s; I remember heated exchanges about Nixon and the Chicago Democratic Convention in my class on Spanish poetry. The ideological clash I experienced in
Tierno's seminar, in our complete disagreement over Ortega y Gasset's
relationship to fascism, was no less intense if more cerebral. Tierno, or

1. Funeral coach for the mayor of Madrid, Enrique Tierno
Galván (21 January 1986). Courtesy of Vimagen.

the Old Professor ("el viejo profesor") as he was affectionately called, never gave an inch in his belief that Ortega y Gasset had fascist tendencies. Tierno was low-keyed, almost priestly in demeanor, but like steel in his convictions and in his arguments, always finely honed and subtle.

Years later, in 1985, we were in contact again, and on much friendlier terms. I wrote asking him if he would be interested in speaking at a symposium on Leopoldo Alas (Clarín). Amazingly, he said he would. But he never did. He was by then dying, only I didn't know that. There was something strange in arriving on the day of his funeral. He had always been admirable in his opposition to the Franco regime, but now I felt that my respect for him, which had grown over the years, had taken on a poignancy I couldn't altogether explain to myself.

I dumped my bags in the *pensión* and rushed back into the streets, joining the hundreds of thousands gathered to pay homage to Tierno. The winding funeral procession, which by some accounts approached half a million, was ten kilometers long, the silence of that immense crowd almost total. As we came to the Calle Mayor, the funeral coach slowly passed into view (fig. 1). Tierno was going in style. The carriage, of a late nineteenth-century French design, was pulled by six black horses, which I later learned had been borrowed from the Spanish film industry. The coach itself came from a Museum of Funerary Carriages (Museo de Carruajes Fúnebres) in Barcelona.[1] It was resplendently rococo, gorgeously fake-looking, and with an outrance that produced an odd sensation of the sentimentally incongruous and the obsolete. It was, in a word, *cursi*.[2] Not kitsch, not camp, but simply: *cursi*.

This word is hard to define since all the English synonyms typically given in dictionaries to explain it—"in bad taste, vulgar," "showy, flashy," or "pseudo-refined, affected"—merely point to its symptoms, not to its underlying condition, cause, or context. Tierno, however, would have understood immediately. He had written one of the classic studies on *cursilería* in 1952. The horse-drawn funeral coach is traditional for royalty and figures of state, but Tierno Galván, as a socialist-Marxist (with libertarian leanings!), was unimpressed with rank. The elaborate funeral carriage is a sign of distinction, yet of an obsolete sort. Still, I suspect Tierno, who appreciated and on more than one occasion exploited a sense of the theatrical, would have enjoyed the faint whiff of absurdity in this scene, which seemed like something out of a movie, *de película*, like the six movie horses used to draw the carriage. Tierno held a highly ambivalent position toward tradition himself. His political writings were often cryptic and difficult to decipher because of the quasi-baroque style he adopted to elude Franco's censors. As mayor, he issued edicts, written in elegant, if ironic, seventeenth-century Castilian. Even as he modernized transport and reduced pollution, he also revived popular street festivals and courtyard theater in working-class neighborhoods.

Tierno was a thorough modern, yet strongly tied in his affections to tradition. Just as he had incarnated the opposition to Franco in an earlier period, as mayor of Madrid in the 1980s he symbolized the odd marriage of modernity and tradition that seemed to characterize the years of the transition toward democracy. His funeral was no different. The element of cursilería I detected was a sign of that shift from the traditional to the modern, in which pieces of an older culture survive, holding on nostalgically or even ironically. If the funeral coach seemed to me cursi in some respects, it served, in a positive sense, as an example of *lo cursi bueno,* to use Ramón Gómez de la Serna's expression.

It took me a while to see that my initial object of study, the persistence of romanticism in modern Spanish literature, was really an entry into lo cursi, that romanticism and lo cursi were, in a word, linked. Romantic literature and culture not only came on the scene belatedly in Spain, but continued long past their vogue elsewhere. This out-of-synch sense of obsolescence often was translated into images of cursilería—whether embodied as affectation, imitation, or triteness—in the manners of individuals or classes, or in the language of literary and nonliterary texts alike. But cursilería as cultural inadequacy survived even romanticism, suggesting the persistence of some underlying cause or condition. Both romanticism and lo cursi arise out of middle-class aspirations (and frustrations). While cursilería in particular is expressive of economic and cultural belatedness, that dyssynchronicity has to be understood at the same time as a sign of emergent modernity in Spain. Thus, the phenomenon of cursilería is not a "small question." It is, as Ramón y Cajal explains in a different context, one of those "large questions which are not understood."

Over the years, whenever I explained that I was working on the subject of middle-class cursilería, invariably someone would raise an eyebrow or do a mild doubletake. For some, cursilería just did not appear important or serious enough as research. It hardly seemed literary and only marginally historical. It was a subject that, until fairly recently, fell into the cracks as either unclassifiable or illegitimate (and often both) in academic circles. Then, suddenly, in the late 1980s and 1990s of post-Franco, postmodern Spain, there was a flurry of interest in cursilería and other related phenomena such as kitsch and camp. In 1988, for example, a collection of pieces, profusely and wildly illustrated, came out on the subject of *El kitsch español* [Spanish kitsch] (fig. 2). In 1992 Espasa-Calpe promoted Margarita Rivière's *Lo cursi y el poder de la moda* ["Lo cursi" and the power of fashion]; and in 1995, Carlos Moreno Hernández published his *Literatura y cursilería* [Literature and "cursilería"], the most serious of these studies.

The first two books are illuminating as extensions of the Madrid

4

movida, a youthful, postmodern yet curiously local movement of equal doses of artistic and anarchistic impulses in the late 1970s and 1980s. *El kitsch español* is subtitled *Aproximación al ansia de aparentar en nuestro país* [An approximation to the anxiety over appearances in our country], in which kitsch seems to be a postmodern form of cursilería, seasoned with several dashes of camp. Rivière, too, modernizes what is originally a nineteenth-century phenomenon, turning lo cursi into an all-pervasive (and oxymoronic) norm of bad taste, especially in the fashion industry, a much vaunted touchstone of Spain's coming-of-age in the late twentieth century. It is not coincidental or surprising that lo cursi should reemerge as kitsch or even camp in the post-Franco era, for the movida years more often than not vamped as pastische or parody the culture of Francoism (*franquismo*) itself (or its remains) as quintessentially cursi. Enrique Costus's 1979 camp portrait of Carmen Polo, Franco's widow, is a funny example of what I mean. Costus shows a jewelry- and hat-bedecked Carmen Polo, with excessive teeth, a mouth stretched in an artificial smile, and one hand held up in recognition of her public (fig. 3). The painting highlights the regime's affectation and concern with appearances; Polo is cursi. The portrait itself, with its ironic and parodistic citation of a public and political icon, is camp, while the acrylic medium suggests an intentional kitsch effect.[3]

Nineteenth-century cursilería persisted during the Franco period in part because post–civil war economic hardships and material shortages brought out more sharply the gap between appearances and reality, in part because the ideology of Francoism demanded it, in the sense that the regime's values were self-consciously modeled on an obsolescent code of behavior and beliefs. Behind the shield of "National Catholicism," a facade of national, political, and religious unity, Francoism defensively drew up barriers against both the outside world and internal dissent, stressing Spain's exceptionality and uniqueness. Ironically, the result was often far less grandiose and much more banal, indeed cursi, than intended, as a warped and retrograde, Victorian-style mentality suffocatingly took over. While Franco himself was depicted as the noble warrior triumphant in historical paintings and speeches, the vision that Francoism projected in reality was pompously and unremittingly middle-class.

Middle-class cursilería, filled as it is with social pretensions and affectations, does not jibe well with the image of Spain as a nation set apart in

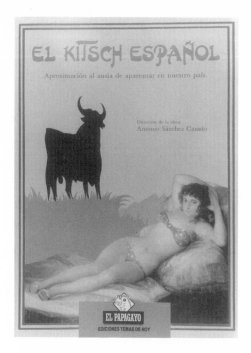

2. Txomin Salazar's cover for *El kitsch español*, edited by Antonio Sánchez Casado. Madrid: Temas de Hoy, 1988. Courtesy of Temas de Hoy.

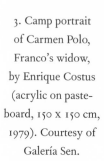

3. Camp portrait of Carmen Polo, Franco's widow, by Enrique Costus (acrylic on pasteboard, 150 x 150 cm, 1979). Courtesy of Galería Sen.

6

spirit and history from other Western countries. This view of Spain as different has led to some rather narrow and simplistic versions of its exceptional position and character. Inside and outside the country, the myth of Spain has proliferated over the centuries, from the Black Legend of the Conquest and Inquisition to the "eternal Catholic Spain" of the Franco regime. Under Franco the official company line—and tourist grabber—was, "Spain is different" (*España es diferente*). It was not exactly a lie. But neither was such myth propaganda based on historical realities. Indeed, what Franco and his supporters most desired was to obliterate history, at least modern history, and return to an earlier myth of Spain, the Spain of imperial grandeur and Catholic tradition, the Spain of Isabel and Ferdinand, Saint Theresa of Avila, and Saint Ignatius of Loyola (see Labanyi, *Myth and History*). But, of course, that Spain was not altogether mere myth either.

Between the end of empire and the start of dictatorship lies a period that can roughly be called modern (or contemporary, depending on usage). Although Spain did not lose most of her overseas colonies until the early nineteenth century (Cuba, Puerto Rico, and the Philippines were held until 1898), the process of imperial disintegration had begun well before, with what historians have generally viewed as the slow but implacable decay of the country's economic, social, and demographic fabric. Spanish decadence has served as the predominant leitmotiv for a good number of historians, essayists, and writers of fiction. Indeed, not so long ago, most historians of the nonapologetic variety, Spanish and non-Spanish alike, saw Spain as a kind of aberration from the European model of industrial-social development. Decadence appeared as intrinsic to the course of Spanish history, as was resistance to any non-Spanish influences. Recent scholarship has challenged this vision of an exceptional Spain, of a backward, closed-off former imperial power, however (see Kagan, Ringrose, Cruz). Ringrose, for example, has argued that "we can now see various events and crises in Spanish history not as failures but as Spanish variants of the general European movement toward modernity" (24; also Molinas and Prados de la Escosura 396–97).

Spain's historical and cultural position is of course far more complicated than a much needed corrective swing in historical scholarship can indicate. It could be argued that the Franco regime's identification with the so-called founding myths of the Spanish nation—the Catholic Kings, a unifying, larger-than-life religion, an imperial destiny—was in part a defensive response to the homogenizing tendencies of the modern era, a trend that has only intensified and become global in the last two decades. The argument for distinctiveness is especially crucial—and strikingly problematic—in the case of Spain. Within both the historiography and the myth-making capacities of Spain as nation-state, the narrative of exceptionality has played a major role. With the loss of empire, modern Spain became, as it were, the quintessential emblem of decadence. Thus marginalized, however, Spain was also shown to be no different than any number of other countries, particularly those of southern or Mediterranean character. Subsequent political messianism, linked to the wished-for restoration of Spain and most recently reenacted by Franco, has highlighted by contrast the weak sense of nationhood characteristic of modern Spain, offering similarities with Italy and Latin America.

In the nineteenth and twentieth centuries, national distinctiveness became associated with a form of tradition seen as backward and often identified with Andalusian, or southern, culture. The dilemma for those with more forward-looking views became entangled in an apparently unresolvable either/or proposition: to be modern seemed to mean *not* to be Spanish, that is, to be modern was to give up that which was traditional, in other words, what was seen simultaneously as both backward and authentic (see Torrecilla, *La imitación colectiva* 11–45). Unamuno attempted to circumvent the contradiction by emphasizing what he called "the eternal tradition" ("la tradición eterna"), that which remained most vital and enduring in Spanish culture, and "inner history" ("la intra-historia"), the constant undertow of ordinary lives and time, as opposed to the external history of monarchy, wars, and governments (Torrecilla, *El tiempo y los márgenes* 143–84). To complicate matters, from romanticism on, non-Spaniards often superficially valorized the traditional in Spain, associated with Andalusian culture, as quaint and picturesque, but underneath they disdained it as insignificant, as something open for the projection of all sorts of otherwise unacceptable traits and images, as the representative Other apparently needed to define oneself and others. As Peter Sahlins has observed, national identity "is contingent and relational: it is defined by the social or territorial boundaries drawn to distinguish the collective self and its implicit negation, the other" (271; see also Colley 5–6). That Spaniards themselves reappropriated these

8

romantic images, making them their own and, in the process, creating their own identity, is also true, as Diego Saglia has pointed out.

The presence of cursilería not only in the Spanish middle classes but in the national culture as well from the mid-nineteenth century on suggests two seemingly contradictory things. First, that Spain appeared to contemporary outsiders (and to many insiders such as Larra and Clarín) as backward, hence both different *and* cursi. And second, that Spanish culture and the middle classes in particular were perceived as cursi precisely for *not* being different, that is, for imitating the comportment and ideas of other national cultures, especially the English and the French. Both views are two sides of the same coin, and they demonstrate the sort of cultural bind in which Spain found itself.

That feeling of being caught in between two ways of existence is precisely what characterizes modernity in Spain. In that sense, Spain was and is like other developing Western countries. Its middle classes, too, are like those of other nations, emerging out of the changing character of earlier social formations and demonstrating the same insecurity and acute class consciousness. The middle classes in Spain are as hard to define as elsewhere since they signified for more clearly delineated groups such as the aristocracy a perturbing class confusion and social indeterminacy. Even more problematic than defining the middle classes is assessing their relative impact on, and role in, the power structure of their respective nations. In America, they were the "middling orders" or "the middling sort," and not until the 1830s did the term *middle class* come into use (Leverenz 75). For Arno Mayer, the United States, if it is anything, is the product of the lower middle class in the first half of the nineteenth century ("Lower Middle Class" 422). In England, *middle classes* (and *working classes*) were commonly heard expressions by the 1840s (Williams, *Keywords* 64). But Whig aristocrats still dominated in English politics of the 1840s; and the landed elite in general held both social and political sway (Colley). France, on the other hand, had had a solid bourgeoisie for some time and could even boast of a "bourgeois monarchy" in 1830. As Jerrold Seigel observes, such "political prominence [the July Revolution] made the French bourgeoisie unique in Europe: nowhere else did government rule in the name of that class"

(22). This did not, however, make it any easier to say who exactly made up the bourgeoisie in France. Seigel suggests that the artistic bohemian type emerged in part as counterpoint "to outline the bourgeoisie more clearly" (6). But there were many levels and kinds of bourgeois, a point which an early 1840s pamphlet, *Bourgeois Physiology*, drives home: "My bourgeois is not yours, nor your neighbor's" (qtd. in Seigel 6). If this was the case in France, consider the problems in assessing the character, visibility, and impact of the middle classes in Spain.

Whether one can also speak of a nineteenth-century Spanish bourgeoisie is still debated in historical circles.[4] The truth is, throughout Europe, the terms *bourgeoisie* and *middle class* were often used synonymously for practical purposes, since both occupy the same indeterminate ground between rank and the common people. In Spain, the term *clase media* does not appear officially until 1884 in the Royal Academy's *Diccionario de la lengua castellana*, but both the name and the reality existed well before that.

If, as Peter Goldman observes, in literature "the appearance of the word *clase* to replace *calidad, condición, categoría*, and *estado* is infrequent until the 1820s" (11), that does not mean that nothing had changed in eighteenth-century Spanish society.[5] Indeed, as Goldman says, the "*perception* of change" was evident. Jovellanos, for example, remarked in 1780 that the Marqués de los Llanos de Alguazas was disturbed to see at his son's university "a mass of young men born of varying social condition and provenance" heaped together indiscriminately (he uses the word "confundidos").[6] Such familiarity, Jovellanos says, was only too often pernicious. And he continues, "[the Marqués] knew how important it was for the monarchy to show its opposition to the mixing together [or confusion] of different orders and classes" (284–85).[7] Were these university students future bureaucrats, part of that new salaried class which was beginning to appear by then?

By the 1830s the expression *clase media* was assuming a modern, if somewhat tenuous, shape. But that class, says Larra in 1834, existed only in Barcelona and Cádiz, not in the capital: "if there is in Spain a middle class, of industry, manufacturing and commerce, don't look for it in Madrid, but in Barcelona, in Cádiz" ("Jardines públicos" 161).[8] As I discuss later, however, some of Larra's other writings belie his claim that Madrid has no middle class (see chapter 2). By the 1840s, the increasing use of the term *clase media* serves as something of an indication of a growing economic and political visibility of this class. Bretón de los Herreros declared in 1843 that "what we call *the lower orders* has diminished in quality and quantity, just as the wealth and authority of the aristocracy have also declined. The middle classes are visibly absorbing the extremes; a phenomenon which is due in part to the progress of civilization, in part to the influence of political institutions" ("La castañera" 504).[9]

Sometimes there is a disparity between the perception of middle-classness and the economic, material conditions required to produce it. Here, however, it is necessary to stress that awareness of being middle class and the adoption of certain life styles and attitudes can and do exist even when the economic structure lags behind, that is, when there is a perception of being modern despite insufficient modernization. This, I think, is the case for Spain in the nineteenth century.[10]

But what sort of middle class do I mean, and what is its relationship to cursilería? This issue proves more difficult to pin down. Cursilería is the effect produced when there are insufficient means (economic, cultural, social) to achieve desired ends: hence, for example, the now classic image of the *señorita cursi*. Roberto Robert (1871) describes her sartorial appearance in these terms: "the cursi par excellence always dresses behind the times, with respect to the fashions of the day; observe that she never follows a past fashion but rather decks herself out with objects of adornment that belong to different periods of time, and among them there is usually one which has never been fashionable: it is the exclusive and sole creation of the person using it."[11] Robert goes on to say that *la señorita cursi* is strictly middle class: "[her type] first spread through the lower ranks of the middle class, and later through the upper levels. . . . The cursi is a product of class confusion" ("La señorita cursi," 84–85).[12]

Lo cursi is, more than anything else, particularly lower middle class, reflecting the need to keep up appearances and the inability to do so in a satisfactory way. The lower middle class everywhere in the nineteenth century is especially vulnerable to feelings of "*individual anxiety* and *collective fear* of downward mobility," as Arno Mayer puts it ("Lower Middle Class" 434; also Felski 35). The first documented appearance of cursilería in 1830s Cádiz clearly points to its lower middle-class origins. An early commentary by Francisco de Paula Madrazo suggests the same:

there is in Cádiz, he says, "a class of people genteel in appearance, and no doubt at heart, but of less noble condition and of more mechanical occupations, who are distinguished with the unusual name of *cursis* in Andalusia" (*Dos meses en Andalucía* 41–42) (see chapter 1; fig. 4).[13] Madrazo describes this class of indeterminate social background as obscure, the young women literally stepping out of the evening shade of green bowers and foliage.

This social group is an especially complex and unstable category of analysis, as Mayer points out, adding that the "word concept 'lower middle class' can be assigned no fixed meaning for all times and places" (411). The lower middle class is usually, however, associated with negative, undesirable traits such as inauthenticity and insecurity. Rita Felski suggests that "what is particularly interesting about the lower middle class is that it does not constitute a class for itself, [there is not] usually . . . a group consciousness around that status. Instead, they think of themselves as middle-class. In this sense lower-middle-classness is a negative rather than positive identity. It is a category usually applied from outside" (41). Madrazo's outsider commentary on the cursis from Cádiz is pertinent here. But is there an absence of class consciousness in this social group, as Felski maintains? Sharply felt class awareness is a generalized condition among the middle classes in the nineteenth century. Whether the lower middle classes felt they belonged more properly to the middling ranks can only be appreciated subjectively. Similarly, whether people regarded as cursi knew that they were cursi is probably impossible to ascertain, although one of Galdós's more memorable character creations, Abelarda, certainly thought she and her sisters were fatally cursi in *Miau* (1888): "We are nothing but pathetic cursis. Cursis are born that way, and there is no human force on earth that can remove that stamp. I was born this way, and I will die that way. I will marry a cursi man, and I will have cursi children" (453).[14]

The fear of being perceived as cursi is voiced so insistently in nineteenth- and early twentieth-century Spain that it cannot be disregarded as inconsequential to understanding the period. The constant allusions to cursilería suggest that, whatever the realities, in the social imaginary of the times the subjective perception of lo cursi loomed large. While much of my book focuses on the relationship between lo cursi and the lower middle class, or petite bourgeoisie, it is clear that by the end of the

DOS MESES EN ANDALUCIA

EN

EL VERANO DE 1849,

POR

D. F. DE PAULA MADRAZO.

MADRID:
IMPRENTA DE LA BIBLIOTECA DEL SIGLO,
Calle de las Huertas, núm. 44.
1849.

4. Cover page of *Dos meses en Andalucía en el verano de 1849*, by Francisco de Paula Madrazo.

nineteenth century, cursilería was also associated with other social ranks, even the aristocracy, as Benavente's 1901 play, *Lo cursi*, suggests (see chapter 6). Thus the fear that the lower middle class had of falling back into the lower orders, or working class, is echoed in the fear of the middle and upper middle classes of slipping into lower middle-classness (or that of the aristocracy into the middle class).

Why should this be so? Social marginality is part and parcel of the lower middle class, as Crossick, Mayer, Felski, and others have observed. This is not the marginality of victimized or oppressed groups with a strong identity (or today's identity politics), but rather the marginality of a far less cohesive group with a weak identity, one which Felski even calls a "non-identity" (34).[15] What is intriguing to me is why this particular lower middle-class anxiety and feeling of inadequacy as expressed through cursilería should trickle upward, affecting the middle and upper middle class in Spain as well. If the social indeterminacy of middle-

13

classness in general is anxiety-producing, it is insufficient as an explanation. To posit a non-identity for the lower middle class, as Felski claims, may also go too far. This is a group always in the process of establishing its identity, a precondition perhaps to moving out of a social category that is precarious at best. While we generally think of this class as socially and politically conservative, historically the lower middle class has not always been so. Their participation in the French Commune and the Spanish *cantonalista* movement springs readily to mind. Even more germane to this study, the fragility of their social position led to dissatisfaction, a desire to move forward and upward. (Not surprising then are the petit bourgeois origins of many intellectuals.)

In this sense, cursilería in particular becomes an expression of a social and psychological drive, directed at the future and fueled by desire, as seen, for example, both in Rosalía de Bringas's passion for dress and for the social advancement of her children in Galdós's 1884 novel, *La de Bringas* [That Bringas woman] (see chapter 4). Yet, are Rosalía and her family lower middle class? As a minor palace bureaucrat, Rosalía's husband certainly would not figure as such. What makes them so, rather, is their particular relationship with the social and material realities of their culture, which, in turn, depends on a larger national frame (in *La de Bringas*, it is the Royal Isabeline Palace itself standing in for the nation). That is, the very presence of cursilería—or the threat of it—seems to define the Bringas's family as lower middle class, as though they (or any other representative example) had internalized anxiety-producing values issuing out of another social category. By placing this family within a national context, moreover, Galdós also suggests the problem of uncertain social status and an attendant cursilería as a national preoccupation.

Thus the feeling of marginality in the lower middle class appears to intersect at different moments with a parallel sense of collective marginality, coinciding with a weakly developed national identity in the nineteenth and early twentieth centuries. Spain's relatively minor role in international politics during this period contributed to the perception of national weakness. I am not, of course, at all suggesting that Spain was fatally or inherently stricken with cursilería. What concerns me here, rather, is how the perception of cursilería reflects, on the one hand, an individual and collective identity crisis and, on the other, the process of modernity redefining Spanish society in this period. Cursilería becomes then a metaphor of cultural change. The marginal and the feeling of being marginal as embodied in lo cursi are central to understanding nineteenth- and early twentieth-century Spain. This is, of course, only one image of modern Spain's self-representation, but its importance to the development of Spanish middle-class culture is indisputable.

The word itself is unique to the culture; it exists nowhere else, outside of being transplanted to some other Hispanic zones like Cuba, Mexico, and Argentina.[16] The term appears in print by the 1840s, and references to it proliferate from the late 1860s on. Nor is there an exact translation for it. Lo cursi is really a form of disempowered desire, since no one wanted to be cursi. No one wanted to be seen as imitative, in bad taste, pretentious, or cheaply sentimental. It is this language of middle-class desire I want to explore. Clearly, social pretensions are endemic to this group and may be found everywhere. But the particular circumstances of middle-class development vary considerably. The French, for example, could point to the *style pompier* as somewhat related to Spanish cursilería, but the aristocratic ideal of *civilisation* and *l'homme civilisé*, while adapted to the bourgeoisie's needs, prevailed as a counterinfluence. In Germany, while the Biedermeier style was stolidly middle class, the university-educated intelligentsia espoused the values of *Kultur*.[17]

Neither of these ideals or social groups figured prominently in nineteenth-century Spain. The aristocracy may have held on to its social, economic, and political power, but the *hombre de pro*, a political and economic opportunist who rose to the top in the 1860s and 1870s of fevered speculation, perhaps better defines that middling ground, that which so lends itself to the charge of cursilería for its social pretensions and cultural shallowness.[18] Social conservative Pereda somewhat mockingly put this group of bankers, lawyers, businessmen, and landowners into the category of "the modern bourgeoisie" (he uses the French term) in his 1876 novel *Los hombres de pro* [The honest men].[19] Like the lower middle class, this social group was not immune either to the condition of cursilería, thus pointing to the unstable, fragile status of such groups who lacked the aura that *civilisation* or *Kultur* could bestow on them.

Given that potentially anyone, not just the lower middle class, could be labeled cursi, marks lo cursi as a slippery category by its very social indeterminacy. Some critics view cursilería as another form of kitsch (see Moreno Hernández; Gibbs; Sánchez Casado). For Moreno Hernández, lo cursi appears on the one hand to refer essentially to a form of imitation based on class (the middle classes aping the aristocracy). This he ties to a particular period of Spain's social, political, and economic history, from the mid-nineteenth century on and culminating in the post-1875 Restoration era. On the other hand, he also maintains, first, that cursilería eventually comes "into contact" with kitsch by the end of the nineteenth century in Spain and, under both Francoist and postmodern conditions, is finally swallowed up by something called *neo-kitsch* (13).

There are serious problems in conceptualizing lo cursi within this apparently evolutionary framework. Cursilería and kitsch (as well as camp) are undoubtedly members of the same family of related cultural signifiers, but historically they are quite specifically situated and produced. The word *kitsch,* as far as I have been able to ascertain, does not enter Spanish vocabulary until the late 1960s and early 1970s. This is not a trivial observation. It suggests that the cultural, social, and economic conditions that make the awareness and existence of kitsch a possibility were apparently not present in Spain until then, certainly not at the turn of the century or even during the 1940s Falangist years, as Moreno Hernández maintains. While it is sometimes difficult to distinguish clearly between kitsch and cursi, it is *not* difficult to assert that, economically, Spain had not undergone sufficient industrialization or evolved into a consumerist mass society in the earlier part of the twentieth century enough to produce kitsch—a product of advanced industrialization and mass consumerism—in any significant way. Postmodern observers often view aspects of the Franco era as kitsch, but awareness of kitsch in Spain seems to have been limited at first to the vanguard of the Barcelona intelligentsia in the late 1960s. Thus characterizing the 1940s and 1950s as kitsch may be a reflection of the 1980s, a sort of retroactive naming that reveals more about the awareness and presence of kitsch in that decade than anything else (see *El kitsch español* for examples). That much of the Franco period could be called cursi, however, seems pretty evident (see chapter 9).

By throwing kitsch and lo cursi together indiscriminately, Moreno Hernández distorts the historical basis of cursilería, which is produced in the shift from a traditional to a more modern society, moving toward increasing industrialization and consumerism. Lo cursi is still associated with objects that primarily the human hand, and not the machine, produces (fans, albums, adornments) and to personal forms of private behavior whose inadequacies have been subjected to the public domain. Mixing up kitsch and lo cursi, without marking sufficient distinctions, makes it impossible for Moreno Hernández to see the implications for change that the presence of lo cursi suggests, since for him cursilería, like kitsch, constitutes an almost exclusively negative category—"an undesirable excrescence" (12)—limited to imitativeness and inauthenticity. But lo cursi also marks a sliding signifier of change, heralding and producing modernity through the agency of the Spanish middle classes. Like many other intellectuals, Moreno Hernández doesn't see what's good about the middle classes, or that the critique of the middle classes could only have come from the very heart of the beast itself. He notes that lo cursi is "a very vague concept today" (*borroso*) (12). It was always indeterminate, because it emerged out of the conflictive, insecure, unstable middle classes who have never managed to define themselves satisfactorily.

Any definition of lo cursi is bound to be inadequate or reductive. Andrew Ross remarks of kitsch that it "is no more of a *fixed* category than either schlock or camp. These categories are constantly shifting ground, their contents are constantly changing" (145). The same is true of lo cursi. Moreno Hernández valiantly tries to define the term by situating it within the frame of literary history, but the notion continually slips out of his grasp by refusing to remain within the limits (and limitations) of such an ordering principle.

Lo cursi can be found in all kinds of literary texts, as this study shows. It is not, however, primarily literary by nature, but rather cultural and social-historical. For this reason not all of the texts studied here are literary works of quality or part of the canon. Some of these writings are third-rate and cursi in themselves. Literary texts are especially appropriate for approaching the culture of cursilería because they provide windows into the underlying feelings that fuel lo cursi. You don't find allusions to cursilería in legal documents, death registries, or statistics. You find it in other kinds of texts—in literature certainly, but also in objects like fans and albums, social practices like the recitation of poetry at social gatherings (or *tertulias*) and salons, or the columns of a society reporter, and comportment both at home and in public places. With few exceptions, these are practices of a middle-class society or texts written by middle-class writers about middle-class characters and concerns. Some caution should be taken in not overgeneralizing on the basis of the opinions and perceptions found in these texts, but it is safe to say that at least some middle-class persons shared some of the views expressed in them. Because I deal with the subjective space of social perceptions in which historical change may not be self-evident, a history either of the Spanish middle classes or of cursilería itself, let alone of the nation, does not fit the indeterminate borders of this subject. Nor am I a historian. Coming primarily from literary studies, my analysis privileges the literary-aesthetic text, but in so doing, my aim is also to shed more light on a particular historical-cultural experience.

Many years ago, Theodore Zeldin remarked about the study of French clerks and shop assistants that "they need to be dealt with through a different approach, which involves studying not institutions or catastrophes, but largely silent ambitions, which take one out of the realm of economics or politics, beyond quantity or conflict in its simple forms, to the search for satisfactions which were seldom clearly formulated" (qtd. in Crossick 53).[20] Likewise, the presence of cursilería reveals a generally unstated search for satisfactions, not the smugness typically assigned to the middling orders. This is the space of sentiment, often of feelings all mixed up together: insecurity, anxiety, desire, ambition, loss, and need. It is very difficult to categorize the kinds of feelings that lo cursi both incarnates and elicits from those affected and unaffected by its name. Yet paradoxically, and despite this indeterminateness, once one is given the name of cursi, one has also received an identity. How, then, to approach this subject that is so visible yet so elusive in its significance?

The images of cursilería explored in these pages are merely the remnants of a vanished and forgotten society. If "culture [is] an assemblage of texts," as Clifford Geertz maintains (*Interpretation* 448), then what I analyze and reconstruct here are the metaphors of a particular society. As a metaphor of identity and change, lo cursi is, however, deeply embedded in the historical processes of modernity and modernization in Spain. The first appearances of cursilería in the 1830s and 1840s indicated a new social class coming into existence. Later expressions of this social phenomenon, beginning in the 1860s and 1870s and culminating in the post-1875 Restoration period, reveal to what extent cursilería was not simply perceived as middle-class, but as a national occurrence, as Galdós in particular brilliantly demonstrated. Lo cursi hangs on well into the twentieth century, with special intensity at the *fin de siglo* in the arts and in society. By the 1930s, as a subject from the past now seen through the lens of nostalgia, lo cursi continues to make appearances in artistic forms (in Lorca's *Doña Rosita la soltera*, or Gómez de la Serna's creative essay, "Lo cursi," for example). With the Franco regime, cursilería erupts once again into the social body. And finally, a reevaluation of lo cursi in light of such postmodern phenomena as kitsch and camp is undertaken in the 1980s and 1990s.

Lo cursi, I would suggest, persists partly because it is a recurring (and unstable) historical sign of the uneven processes of modernity that have characterized nineteenth- and twentieth-century Spain. At the same time, lo cursi also stands as an internalized marker of inadequacy and insecurity in periods when class distinctions were evolving or breaking down, or when advances in modernization stimulated social transformations. This internalized sense of inadequacy has, however, its own dynamic of desire attached to it, projecting individuals forward in their aspirations and ambitions, as Rosalía de Bringas beautifully illustrates.

Cursilería, then, is part and parcel of the developing narrative of middle-class and national identity in nineteenth- and early twentieth-century Spain. The language that appears in this complex narrative of identity, however, has to be conceived of in a broad enough analytical frame to encompass it (see chapter 1). Reliance on a psychoanalytical mode alone, which lends itself readily to issues of identity, would not only prove insufficient but even misleading on occasion, for at least two reasons. First, what may be valid in psychoanalytic terms for the individual may not be useful for a reading of national or collective realities. And second, there is some reason to doubt that critics can really speak psychoanalytically of what are not materially substantive realities but merely images, or metaphors, of a dead culture found in different kinds of texts—whether verbal, visual, or physical—texts that have turned into artifacts. Psychoanalysis in this instance can only be justified as an extended metaphor itself, an *imagined* understanding of the past. I have not hesitated in using such an approach in some of this book, especially in the last four chapters, but I have done so not only with the awareness of its limitations, but in tandem with other approaches and resources: namely, historical and literary interpretations of texts whose language is, on the one hand, intrinsically social, wedded to history, and, in that sense, capable of being analyzed. On the other hand, this language of cursilería also remains private and intimate, thus posing serious difficulties in grasping its nature and meanings. For, as I have noted before, lo cursi brings us into the realm of sentiment. How exactly is sentiment analyzed; how are the role and relationship it has with respect to historical change evaluated? Before those questions can be addressed, we first have to recognize that sentiment does have a part to play in the development of societies. That may seem obvious. But how exactly is sentiment gauged and interpreted? Much is said of key dramatic moments of great passion and heated emotions in historical events, or of the "mood" of a country, but how are those smaller emotions in past societies traced, emotions like the "silent ambitions" of French shop assistants whom Theodore Zeldin eloquently described?

I cannot pretend to give a completely satisfactory answer to these questions. To provide support for an analysis of something so indeterminate as cursilería, I have relied on a notion that Raymond Williams offered years ago when he spoke of an underlying "structure of feeling" in societies, which for him signified a kind of practical consciousness, "what is actually being lived" in contemporary life (*Marxism and Literature* 131). He was keenly interested in the formative conditions that went into producing social changes. Cultural anthropologists have also explored the role of feeling in social interactions as it transforms not only the inner but the outer worlds of individuals and groups. In the process a structure of feeling is created, which is most often (appropriately) expressed through metaphor, since metaphor already bears within itself the idea of transformation. Despite the evident differences—ideological, theoretical—between these approaches, what they do share in common is this: the recognition that sentiment functions as both knowledge and social practice. In drawing on these insights, and with no claims to being either a Marxist or an anthropologist, I have tried to interpret, to reimagine, those small indications of change, the moments of transition in attitudes and self-awareness of social identity. I have sought out those generally unstated structures of feeling that precede or accompany changes in the larger structures of family, community, and nation. No less than any other approach, this one is an imagined understanding of the past, in which I can only deal with the spectral traces of what is left behind in texts and objects.

It struck me that to understand more fully the significance of cursilería, what is needed is this kind of broad view that recognizes the "polymorphously perverse" nature of the phenomenon (with apologies to Freud for the deliberate misuse of his phrase). In truth, many of the words that I have blithely bandied about here—*culture, metaphor, sentiment, middle class* (to which I will add *home* in a moment)—are also polymorphously perverse, in the sense that they mean different things to different people, they are not fixed categories, and their symbolic import is so laden with diverse and changing significance that no definition of these terms would ever prove satisfactory.

The most vexing of these words is *culture* itself, which is, above all, "a process, not a fixed condition" (Levine 33).[21] Moreover, as anthropologist Anthony Cohen observes, there exists "an almost irresistible inclination to explain behavior by treating it as the product of culture. . . . There is a fundamental confusion here between culture as a body of substantive fact (which it is not) and as a body of symbolic form which provides means of expression but does not indicate what is expressed or the meaning of what is expressed. In this respect, culture is insubstantial: searching for it is like chasing shadows . . . it has no ontology: it does not exist apart from what people *do*" (206–7). He concludes by saying: "Culture is a matter less for documentation than for interpretation; it is more faithfully and sensitively depicted in metaphor than in museums" (207).

Culture as a "body of symbolic form" governs the conception of this book. The various explanations for the origins of the word *cursi* are illustrative of what I mean. As I discuss more fully in chapter 1, the story most often told about this term centers on two (sometimes three) young ladies of the lower middle class whose father is a French tailor and whose last name "Sicur" is mockingly transposed to "Cursi" by some medical students after seeing them on the street, dressed in shabby yet pretentious clothes.[22] The misses Sicur pretend to be something they are not. Thus, on the one hand, cursilería is clearly a form of social behavior. But it is also, as the linguistic transformation sicur > cursi indicates, a symbolic metaphor of social change.

In another version of the word's origins, Tierno Galván suggested

that *cursi* derived from *cursivo,* or cursive, referring to the English running hand used in commerce and accounting and identified with the
Spanish middle classes by the 1840s. Again, here we have a social practice
that becomes metaphorized in Tierno's explanation as the symbolic signature of a particular social class.

I take both explanations as true in their metaphoric sense, for their
capacity to transmit the underlying metaphorized nature and process of
culture itself. These explanations also show how much the culture of
cursilería, as seen in the misses Sicur and in a form of handwriting, is
conveyed as embodied metaphor. Cohen suggests that a " 'metaphorization' of culture [occurs] as a response to such historical circumstances as
demographic and economic change, secularization, integration, and vul-
nerability to new kinds of information" (204). Similarly, the perception
of cursilería from the 1830s on in Spain arises from a changing society
moving toward modernity, signaled in part by the awkward arrival of
new social classes, whose very existence could not be properly defined
and whose behavior and culture tended to blur social distinctions between classes. Cursilería provided an image, or metaphor, for such indeterminacy, but in the process also furthered the sense of social uncertainty amid changing circumstances.

This awareness of cursilería at first remained quite local, indeed
provincial, found in the 1830s and early 1840s apparently only in the
southern port city of Cádiz. By mid-century, use of the term, according
to Madrazo, spread throughout Andalusia. From the 1870s on, cursilería
existed everywhere. Galdós (and many others) associated it largely with
the middle classes of Madrid. This movement from periphery to center
indicates a more complex relationship between provinces and capital
than is usually observed, suggesting not the imposition of Madrid's
values and culture on the provinces, but the reverse in the absorption of
provincial traits within the capital.[23] Of course, much of Madrid's population came from somewhere else, as the exodus from countryside to city
intensified from around 1860 on (see Reher 190, 196–99). But more
importantly, the sense of the local as embodied in provincial life did not
simply fade away in this period, despite administrative and political
centralization. It is the connection between the local, or the provincial,
and cursilería that proves central to this book. The provincialism of
cursilería, even in the capital, meant backwardness, and was often de-

rided. But it also meant "home," as Ramón Gómez de la Serna brilliantly intuited in 1934. Home was domestic, associated with the feminine as well as with a specific localness.

The sense of datedness, or obsolescence, that cursilería represented appeared to bind local life, home, to a more traditional social structure, but it did so self-consciously, with the awareness that that structure was changing, that there was a disparity between old ways and something new appearing on the horizon (often identified as foreign). Lo cursi embodied that disparity. Thus in Cádiz, the Sicur sisters, though of French origin, are also Spanish, but they appear as socially hybrid and awkward to others. The mixed nature of their appearance points to an emergent modernity in which social identity is more constructed than inherited, analogous to the way the Sicur sisters fashion themselves with patchwork adornments of different periods and styles. This social and cultural bricolage is cursi in two ways: it is both provincial yet, significantly, also modern. The modernness of the Sicur sisters comes through precisely in the small ways they deviate from the traditional model of feminine behavior and appearance. Going against the norm of feminine invisibility, or *recato*, they call attention to themselves on the streets of Cádiz because of the incongruous nature of their dress. They appear dated (out of fashion) and, at the same time, curiously ahead of their time in the creation of at least one feature of their wardrobe which is uniquely theirs. That bit of inventiveness becomes a sign of individuality, that characteristic so highly prized by the middle classes everywhere in the nineteenth and early twentieth centuries. But the net effect of the Sicur sisters' appearance reveals them to be out of place in their world.

For Marshall Berman, modernism in the broadest sense of the word is the "struggle to make ourselves at home in a constantly changing world," and he adds that "no mode of modernism can ever be definitive" (6). Modernity, then, is shaped by the way a society adapts to unceasing flux and evolution. It *is* this continual adaptation to change. The pervasiveness of cursilería in nineteenth- and early twentieth-century Spain suggests a particular kind of tension, which occurs when a traditional social structure, here identified with provincial life, begins losing its familiar contours. An ironic—and fascinating—paradox, however, haunts the subject of cursilería: The more the society that produces lo cursi diverges from its traditional past, advancing industrially and economically and supporting change, the more persons and things once mocked for their cursi behavior and nature are now embraced as yearned-for remnants of a vanished past. By the early twentieth century, lo cursi becomes more and more nostalgically attached to the complex meanings of home, underlining an incipient and unstated loss. Modernists like Valle-Inclán and Llanas Aguilaniedo and vanguardists like Gómez de la Serna and Lorca end up aestheticizing cursilería as a feminine space of home. Home and the feminine are, in truth, variations on a theme, the theme of local life, which has been the consistently prevailing form of social habitus in Spanish society until recently.

To situate lo cursi within its early nineteenth-century context, chapter 1, "On Origins," deals with the initial appearances of the term in print and the nexus between lo cursi and the historical growth of the Spanish middle classes. As I hope to show, explanations of lo cursi's origins in Spain are as problematic as the status of the middle classes themselves. The chapter ends with a discussion of the southern port city of Cádiz, where the term seems to have originated and where the links between middle-class development, commerce, and lo cursi first appear within a provincial setting.

In chapter 2, "Adorning the Feminine, or the Language of Fans," I pursue further the commercial image of lo cursi through its hypothesized links with a particular form of handwriting used extensively in business and accounting among the middle classes. A generalized economics of circulation and exchange appears as a pervasive metaphor in an early text like Larra's "El álbum" [The album] (1835), just as it does in a much later one like Leopoldo Alas's story, "Album-abanico" [The autograph fan] (1898), where this language of circulation and exchange is not only clearly associated with middle-class cursilería and women in particular, but with a key component attached to lo cursi: cultural datedness. In these texts, things end up being used as metaphors, or adornments, of the self. A cursi language of fans, albums, flowers, and other, usually feminine objects associated with the middle classes, develops, which is exploited in works such as Galdós's *La de Bringas,* Alas's "Album-abanico," and Lorca's *Doña Rosita la soltera* [Doña Rosita the spinster].

The relationship between lo cursi and cultural obsolescence is further

Introduction

explored in chapter 3 ("Salon Poets, the Bécquer Craze, and Romanticism") through the cultural impact of a belated romanticism on the development of self in middle-class individuals. The social practice of romanticism, visible in salons and tertulias, poetry recitations and competitions, albums and almanacs, becomes a form of cursilería, which is nonetheless significant as a structure of feeling in the changing external expression of the inner life.

In "Textual Economies: The Embellishment of Credit," the social and psychological drive behind cursilería becomes the focus of this fourth chapter, centering in particular on Benito Pérez Galdós's 1884 novel *La de Bringas* as an expression of the culture of credit that dominated the 1850s and 1860s in the explosion of financial speculation, credit societies, and foreign investment in Spain. In the dynamic played out between credit, social behavior, and the expression of personality, a different kind of capital, known as cultural capital, is produced. The product of the interplay between personality and inadequate cultural capital is cursilería. There is, at the same time, a particular kind of future-directed, social and economic imagination at work here, which figures the material world as the "child" of one's imagination. This figure of the child, fundamental to Galdós's novel, also plays a role in a real story centered on politician Pascual Madoz's daughter Francisca and her significance as a sign of emotional and economic investment in the future.

The cursi society found in *La de Bringas* is also brilliantly reconstructed in one of Galdós's late historical novels, *Cánovas* (1912). This is the subject of my fifth chapter, "Fabricating History." The objects of culture, which have formed part of my discussion up to this point, appear to be insufficient in themselves as vehicles of new identities for a social class lacking the aristocracy's aura of distinction. As the Spanish middle classes assumed more visibility in politics and business, they also created a new language to stamp the seal of approval on themselves. What the middle classes needed was history. What Galdós shows us in *Cánovas* is how the discourse of history was used to legitimize the existence and impact of a particular social class.

But since society of the post-1875 Restoration period is itself characterized as quintessentially cursi, the history that Galdós recreates is written out as a cursi text. History becomes a form of rhetoric; language is perceived as adornment, or mere historical "style." Thus history turns into a kind of cursi performance, in which everything is played out in public as though already written out beforehand in a preexistent script. Significantly, cursilería is no longer seen simply as a middle-class phenomenon, but as a national one.

Chapter 6 ("The Dream of Negation") focuses on the turn-of-the-century period, when cursilería becomes once again an obsession, as it had after the revolution of 1868. Nationally, having fought a disastrous war with the United States in 1898, Spain found itself in a shambles. A sense of things falling apart, a crisis of values and identity, pervaded and found partial expression as an apparent loss of distinction. Socially, the increased blurring of class differences confirmed this perception of loss. The playwright Benavente called it lo cursi. "Now you have lo cursi, which is neither good nor bad, neither entertaining nor boring; it is . . . a negation: the opposite of distinguished" (79).[24] Aesthetically, however, in texts like Llanas Aguilaniedo's *Alma contemporánea* [Contemporary character] (1899) and Benavente's *Lo cursi* (1901), cursilería as a form of negation is turned on its head and converted into a subversive critique of modernity in Spain, which heralds, at the same time, a dream of something new.

It is here where, in my analysis, the notion of identity making, both individually and nationally, and that of a structure of feeling increasingly and more explicitly converge. The first three chapters concentrate on cursilería as a structure of feeling shaping middle-classness in Spain. In chapters 4 and 5, the emotions fueling cursi behavior and attitudes in 1860s and 1870s Spain start to take on a more national configuration. The predominant practical consciousness under which Restoration society operated, in Galdós's finely intuitive analysis, is encapsulated in the notion of *fabrication*, constructing what is needed, individually or collectively, to make an identity. Statesman-politician Cánovas del Castillo's fabrication of a workable form of governance is put together in the same way the Sicur sisters combine their disparate sartorial adornments. It's making do with the limited resources available, whether material or other, to project a different persona (the Sicur sisters) or political reality (*el turno pacífico*, in the case of Cánovas). Cánovas sincerely thought he was emulating (with a difference) the English system of representative government in the form of a constitutional monarchy. The Sicur sisters imagined themselves as different because of their distinct form of dress.

Whatever the actual consequences or realities may have been, the results appear as incongruous and incommensurate with the desires, illusions, and ambitions driving such comportment.

By 1900 the prospects of fabricating, patchwork-style, a nation or anything else seemed far less rosy. A keenly felt sense of loss infuses the writings of many *fin de siglo* Spaniards. They do not always make explicit or identify this loss, but one of the affective forms it takes is nostalgia. Chapter 6 centers around feeling out of place in a changing world. Nostalgia, in the broadest sense, is the yearning for home, for the sense of centeredness needed in individual lives and societies. By 1900 it had become clear to many that Cánovas's dream of political harmony, achieved through local bossism, electoral manipulation, and the use of a preexistent network of families and patronage, was inoperable. By then too, regionalistic differences were heating up, leading to demands for greater local autonomy. Class tensions in the form of strikes, protests, and emergent political movements like socialism and anarchism grew significantly. Economically, however, Spain had experienced sustained growth throughout the nineteenth century, even if industrialization lagged behind that of other countries. While rural life still prevailed around 1900, people were also pouring into the cities.[25]

In 1900 Spain was no more immune to the discontinuities, tensions, and confusion of modern life than any other country. Nostalgia and the feelings of loss examined in "The Dream of Negation" (chapter 6) and "The Margins of Home: Modernist Cursilería" (chapter 7) can also be regarded as expressions of mourning in reaction to Spain's modernization, which was especially visible in the dramatic growth of cities during the last quarter of the nineteenth century (Magnien 107–29). Even though traditional, provincial life had by no means disappeared, many of the voices heard at this time display a sharpened awareness of the swifter passage of things in comparison to an earlier period. Thus, for instance, Angel Ganivet disliked intensely the modernization of his hometown Granada, whose old center was rapidly disappearing under the impact of real estate speculation and urban expansion (see chapter 8). At times it seems almost as if some of these voices—Valle-Inclán in his *Sonatas*, for example—were mourning the death of local life (here Galicia) *before* it had actually happened in history. This obscurely perceived loss reflects, I would suggest, a structure of feeling in the process of coming to the

27

surface of consciousness in such writings, one that has shaped—and been shaped by—the forms modernity assumed in early twentieth-century Spain. Thus one encounters such strange, if delightful, incongruities as Ramón Gómez de la Serna's highly experimental, self-conscious prose wedded to a vision of bourgeois, feminine domesticity as symbolized in lo cursi in his 1934 essay of the same name. One of the things Gómez de la Serna loves about lo cursi is its marginal status, its belonging largely to the past, to the realm of the feminine and to the provincial. This image of marginality is central to Gómez de la Serna's vision of things here because it represents the image of home itself.

In a word, lo cursi has become home. Federico García Lorca's 1935 play, *Doña Rosita la soltera*, the subject of chapter 8, "The Culture of Nostalgia, or the Language of Flowers," makes this same identification. As in Gómez de la Serna's essay, nostalgia here plays a key role as a structure of feeling that converts cursilería, once considered a sign of a weak culture, into the central image of local life, symbolized in the Granadine figure of Doña Rosita.

Lorca's feelings toward his hometown of Granada were, however, decidedly mixed, and he pours this ambivalence into the loving yet critical portrayal of Granadine society, at once provincial and poignant, in his play. I read Granada's resistance toward modernity and modernization, its social and economic stagnation, allegorically into Doña Rosita's desire not to move forward in time, even as the action of the play progresses from 1885 to 1910. At the same time, Granada, because it is identified so intimately with the figure of Doña Rosita, represents for Lorca the domestic, the feminine, the interior, and, especially, the diminutive. This symbolic Granadine space transmits metaphorically the value that Lorca placed on the experience of local life. On the one hand, like Galdós, he pokes fun at middle-class cursi behavior. But on the other, he also makes lo cursi bear a heavy symbolic and emotional weight: the weight of memory and loss. For embedded in Lorca's aesthetic recreation of lo cursi—seen in the quintessentially clichéd, cursi image of the language of flowers developed throughout the play—is the process of mourning, that mourning which is part and parcel of the experience of modernity.

Lorca himself participated significantly in the localist fervor toward Granadine culture, one of several regionalist movements that had originated in the previous century, intensifying at the fin de siglo. Partly reformist, partly conservationist, such localism reflected a split identity between wanting to open up to modernity and wanting to retain some of the traditional features of provincial life. Lorca's complicated, love-hate response to Granadine culture thus does not enthrone local life as an ideal but, rather, signals, through his ambivalent presentation of lo cursi as a metaphor of the local, a conflicted view not only of provincial society and middle-classness but of modernity as well. Doubtless, many middle-class *granadinos* did not share his views, but Lorca's personal vision also reflects the very real social and economic difficulties of adjusting provincial life to modernity and modernization in early twentieth-century Spain.

This dream of the local, of retaining a sense of home or identity in the midst of continual change, persists. One of its latest permutations, the movida of the late 1970s and 1980s, is the subject of my last chapter, "Coda: The Metaphor of Culture in Post-Franco Spain." The Madrid movida emerged as a paradoxical blend of local themes and postmodern displacement. With the movida participants, the residual effects of Francoism were translated into self-consciously obsolescent images of kitsch and cursilería, thus suggesting both continuity and rupture with the earlier regime.

The movida turned marginalia—cursilería, kitsch, and camp—into a central metaphor for modern Spanish culture itself. Thus, for example, in Francisco Umbral's 1990 novelized memoir, *Y Tierno Galván ascendió a los cielos* [And Tierno Galván ascended to heaven], the cynicism that the author casts equally over historical events and his shallow love life reduces both to minor narratives of kitsch. Narrative detachment, however, also masks a deep sense of loss, which is symbolized in the death of Madrid's mayor, Enrique Tierno Galván, whose reputation by that time far exceeded the local boundaries of the capital. His death is seen as signifying the "end of Utopia," the political dream of the left. Franco's death meant the loss of oppositionality, signaling a void for many, but Tierno's pointed to a different kind of loss. Franco represented a repressive paternalistic order, Tierno a liberation.

Both were pivotal in expressing, in radically different ways, Spain's relationship within modernity, marked in the shifting balance between tradition and change and worked out historically through the dynamic between provinces and capital. Partly because so much of Spain's social and cultural habitus has been concentrated in the provinces until recently, national identity has seemed weak with respect to the building of a modern nation-state. The presence of lo cursi in provincial life reinforced that perception, but it also took on new configurations as Spanish society, and in particular the middle classes, entered more fully into the modern age. Lo cursi was provincial; it was intensely local, but it was also home. In this respect, it is not surprising that Madrid and other large cities could also harbor cursilería. The ambivalence felt by the middle classes in particular toward the provinces and their own middle-classness is the same ambivalence exhibited toward cursilería.[26] Encapsulated in lo cursi, in its awkward manners, airs of pretension, and graceless anxieties, is Spain's coming of age, its unresolved relationship with the forces of modernity.

Tierno Galván understood very well this conflicted relationship with the past, this clinging to provincial roots. When he was asked what it took "to be a successful mayor of a big city," he replied, "you have to act like the mayor of a small town" (Darnton A2). To be modern in 1980s Spain, he seems to suggest, means to assume the hybrid role of provincial cosmopolitan. But which role is more real: the big city or the small town mayor? I have now come full circle to my initial point of departure — Tierno Galván, my exemplary conundrum of Spanish modernity. You will meet him again at the end of this book.

CHAPTER ONE

On Origins

AN ENGLISH OBSERVER of Spanish middle-class life in 1910 remarked,

> Now is the time for a little diplomatic deception of the kind that is
> so often associated with poverty and long descent in Spain. The
> *cursis*, as these harmless pretenders are called in Spain, announce
> that they are going to some fashionable seaside place and invite
> their friends to attend their departure at the railway station. After
> affectionate leave-taking the train moves off, and the *cursi*, alight-
> ing at the first village at which the train stops . . . lies *perdu* until the
> close of the summer season brings rank and fashion back to the
> capital. . . . A strange snobbery indeed, but not without a certain
> element of pathos as a device which is one of the last laps in the
> desperate race to keep up appearances, and to hide poverty from
> curious eyes and cruel tongues. These are to be found in Spain as
> elsewhere. (Bensusan 147–48)

This commentary, coming from an outsider to Spanish society, is of
interest on comparative grounds alone. Bensusan, who was an English
Jew, understood marginalization particularly well, and the cursi was a
peripheral figure if he was anything. Rightly or wrongly, Bensusan also
sees these cursis as emblematic of the Spanish nation and history, that is,
as synonymous with decadence ("poverty and long descent"). Finally,
he notes that such persons are part of the landscape of modern life
everywhere.

Lo cursi is one of the most pervasive cultural phenomena of nine-
teenth- and early twentieth-century Spain. An untranslatable term, *cursi*
comes closest in meaning to *kitsch*, but encompasses much more than
trash, cheap sentimentality, or tackiness, traits commonly associated with
kitsch. In dictionaries, one who pretends to refinement and elegance

without possessing them is cursi. Popular imagination explains it more tersely as "querer y no poder" (wanting and not being able to). Lo cursi is a form of disempowered desire, frustrated in its aspiration to a higher order of things in life.[1]

The pervasiveness of lo cursi provides a significant key to an understanding of modern Spanish culture and literature. From mid-nineteenth century on, the Spanish middle classes were nervously obsessed with their appearance, their representation publicly and privately as the newest (and most unstable) symbol of success and power. These same middle classes, with interests and values tied to a burgeoning national identity, had also to contend with the realities of cultural, social, and economic dyssynchronicity, a sharply felt sense of inferiority (in relation to powers like France and England), and insufficiency. As a metaphor for the times, lo cursi symbolically captures the sense of inadequacy that a marginalized society in transition experiences when moving from a traditional economy to an industrialized, consumer-oriented economic organization. In literature, and especially in the realist novel, the fear of being called cursi surfaces repeatedly as one of the underlying obsessions of the period. In focusing on the multiple manifestations of lo cursi, I approach Spanish literature and culture from below, metaphorically speaking, aiming at the underbelly of repressed anxieties, desires, and fears that propelled nineteenth- and early twentieth-century Spanish society both forward and backward between the apparently anachronistic remains of romantic ideology and the uncertainties of problematic modernity.

Spain in the early nineteenth century was about to lose its old Catholic, kingly face and acquire a split personality. The Napoleonic invasion of 1808 simultaneously reinforced traditionalism with a defense of monarchy and stimulated liberal reform with the creation of the Cádiz Cortes. Fernando VII's return to the throne in 1814 initiated a period of misrule, followed by the liberal parenthesis of 1820 to 1823, and a new wave of antiliberal repression under Fernando afterward. Following his death in 1833, civil war erupted. His daughter Isabel II's reign (1833–68) saw significant administrative, economic, and constitutional reforms, which included the reorganization of the provinces into a more centralized state, the abolition of entail, the disentailment of lands held in mortmain, and the weakening of privilege. But royal scandal, incompetence in governance, an economic crisis, and other forms of disorder eventually made Isabel very unpopular, leading to her dethronement in 1868 and attempts at a constitutional monarchy and then a republic. Civil war and political and military upheaval finally brought about the return of the Bourbon dynasty under Isabel's son, Alfonso XII, in 1875. This period, known as the Restoration, inaugurated an era of relative tranquility and order, accomplished in part through manipulation and corruption of the parliamentary system and an entrenched *caciquismo* (local bossism), and in part through growth of industry, trade, and commerce (Catalonian textiles especially and Basque mining and banking, for example). By the early twentieth century (and after the disastrous war of 1898 in Cuba), however, it had become evident that the surface calm of Restoration life concealed deep ideological, economic, and religious divisions, which the increasing use of strikes, anarchist acts of terrorism, anticlericalism, liberal and radical opposition, and new political parties disclosed. Regional demands also grew.

Thus the country seemed to sway alarmingly between the poles of retrograde smugness and progressive confusion—pressured by the gradual breakup of traditional institutions and ways of being—and the arrival of ill-defined social classes and new political and economic demands for greater democratization and commercial expansion. Political and socioeconomic histories of Spain explain this crisis as a function of institutions and ideologies, on the one hand, and social classes and economic forces, on the other. Important as these organizing principles of written histories are, they need to be situated as well within the context of the culture's own self-representations. How did Spanish culture of this period perceive itself? What language did people find to represent change and difference, to express their anxieties, desires, and fears over such changes? More specifically, how did the Spanish middle classes, whose development is crucial to the making of modern Spain and of national identity in the nineteenth and twentieth centuries, see themselves?

For a long time historians claimed that there was no significant middle class in Spain, that Spain was an exception in Western development. Ortega y Gasset, for example, associated cursilería with the absence of a strong middle-class base. But much of our understanding of this period of Spanish history and culture needs to be revised, as Adrian Shubert, David Ringrose, Jesús Cruz, and others have amply demonstrated. As in the rest of Europe, Spain's middle classes, especially the upper middle class and *haute bourgeoisie*, functioned symbiotically in alliance with a centuries-old aristocratic oligarchy based on land and close political and familial ties with the governing structures at hand. Politically, the Spanish middle classes generally fell far short of revolutionary reforms, but socially this hard-to-define and amorphous class exercised considerable cultural influence on Spanish society. The perception of cursilería, which one would expect to see mostly in the lower echelons of the middle classes or petite bourgeoisie, is also increasingly projected onto all levels of middle-class Spanish society by the end of the nineteenth century. While Ortega y Gasset's thesis that the presence of cursilería disclosed a weak middle class is valid in some respects, it could also be argued that cursilería, especially in its perceived pervasiveness, pointed to an underlying anxiety and fear in both middle-class and non–middle-class persons. For the first group, which still looked to the aristocracy as its social role model, cursilería indicated cultural inferiority and pretentiousness. For the second, to be accused of cursilería meant a loss of distinction, the distinction of class itself. In either case, the omnipresent feeling that cursilería was difficult to escape suggests, first, that middle-class society, as a cultural entity, counted much more than Ortega's comment would indicate. Second, it implies that the fuzzy borders of lo cursi both represented and promoted the breakdown of differences in social classes.

I am dealing here, then, with perceptions, and not necessarily with empirical realities. What interests me particularly is the role that feeling plays in contributing to an understanding of social-historic changes and identities. If, as cultural anthropologists have maintained, there is a structure of feeling that reveals itself through the very transformations moving emotions into the sphere of the felt and the visible, how does that structure *feel* historically and culturally?[2] How does one talk about dead emotions? An emotion cannot be known except as it is expressed, and once expressed, it becomes something else; it becomes a representation of feeling. "Emotion," writes Jean Starobinski, "is not a word, but it can only be spread abroad through words" (81).

Most significantly, "the verbalization of emotion is intertwined with the structure of that which is experienced" (Starobinski 82). Even when feeling is communicated nonverbally, there is a language that must already exist or be created to make that feeling known. In any event, it is difficult to separate emotion from language because language—understood in its broadest context as communicative, culturally inflected discourse—profoundly shapes the contours, direction, and purpose of all human feelings. This is, of course, the as yet unreached revelation toward which psychoanalysis as a discipline moves. Unreached because the gap between emotion and language ultimately remains an open conundrum. It is the basis of much current linguistic, anthropological, and even historical inquiry.[3] It also permeates, often unconsciously or implicitly, literary studies, in both the rhetorical use and analysis of tropes and ideology.

A structure of feeling, then, must possess a language, and that language in turn must, in some way, expressively fix feeling. In cultural and historical terms, it must situate feeling, positioning and locating the qualities and transformations of the affective life. To read this language of the affective life is to look for the signs, the series of cultural markings that effect the joining of text and referent. While it is accurate to say that the exact emotions, the precise understandings people had in the past cannot be read back, the traces, the resonances left behind, *can* be approached, with all due respect for historical distance and caution for subjective interpretation.

As intriguing and suggestive a notion as the structure of feeling is, it proves extremely difficult to pin down. Raymond Williams in *Marxism and Literature* defines structures of feeling "as social experiences *in solution*" (133–34), that is, not yet fixed or precipitated. Because Williams is especially interested in the forming and formative processes of societies, he concentrates on the role of structures of feeling as a kind of practical consciousness, "what is actually being lived" in contemporary life (131). He does not address the question of how structures of feeling may have functioned in the past or how one might recognize and approach them from the presumed point of view of completed history.

Similarly in this respect, cultural anthropologists, in studying the "anthropology of affect," have focused on contemporary cultures and on the relationship between individual and group in rituals, celebrations, and other expressive events, as human emotions are being transformed, creating in the process a structure of feeling that moves back and forth between and through group and individual. Such movement is, as James Fernandez observes, necessarily figurative, though grounded in the body, both socially and individually. These structures of feeling constitute a kind of narrative, which, as metaphorical truths, provide explanations for a particular culture. Clifford Geertz's classic study of the Balinese cockfight as "deep play" suggests that participating in such events is "a kind of sentimental education," enabling Balinese to see their own subjectivity and place within society (*The Interpretation of Cultures* 449–50).

In the one case, the Balinese story, it seems to me, is always the same, based as it is on ritual. Raymond Williams, on the other hand, in favoring as his object of study industrializing, modern societies, emphasizes the unstable, transitional nature of a culture in formation, and thus the changing character of its stories. He believes that by examining changes in structures of feeling, insight may be gained into the process and contradictions of historical change before it becomes petrified or institutionalized, before it is homogenized and molded into a consistent, rationalized form. In his attempt to overcome the theoretical opposition between base and superstructure, the Marxist critic also seems to draw closer to the material aims of those cultural anthropologists who examine the emotions of everyday practices (rather than the ritualistic alone), although it is not clear to me whether "structure" in Williams's case refers to a kind of abstraction made material, to a metacommentary, or to the actual structuring of feeling through social practices (my inclination is to accept all three possibilities).

Keeping in mind the differences, one can better appreciate what these approaches also have in common: the understanding and use of feeling as, simultaneously, a mode of cognition and as social practice. Williams insists that it is not a question of "feeling against thought, but thought as felt and feeling as thought" (132). Similarly, Geertz's "sentimental education" stresses the "use of emotion for cognitive ends" (*The Interpretation of Cultures* 449). Anthropologist Michelle Rosaldo writes with eloquent conviction, "that feeling is forever given shape through thought and that thought is laden with emotional meanings. . . . Emotions are thoughts somehow 'felt' in flushes, pulses, 'movements' of our livers, minds, hearts, stomachs, skin. They are *embodied* thoughts seeped with the apprehension that 'I am involved'" (143). While not rejecting the

36

psychobiological basis of human emotions, Rosaldo also implies that emotions are "involving," that is, they are social phenomena. As social practices, then, they have real consequences, producing effects as "simple" as marriage or as complex as the creation or destruction of nation-states. "Emotions," anthropologists Abu-Lughod and Lutz claim, "are sociocultural facts" (11).

How, though, can feeling be understood when it is expressed not in a living society or organism but in cultural artifacts that in some sense have died? If culture is to be taken "as an assemblage of texts" (Geertz, *The Interpretation of Cultures* 448), this does not mean that all texts are of the same kind and can therefore be approached in the same way.[4] The subject matter and aims of the disciplines dealing with these texts diverge. Such texts say and do different things. Artifacts like realist novels and period plays, salon reportage and albums, or the language of flowers and fans, all of which appear in my analysis, always come with a built-in metacommentary on the cultural construction of reality and the uses of emotion for cognitive, social ends. Arguably even contemporary societies do the same, thus providing the means to interpret or read the results. While it is certain (and useful) that art and literature "are often among the very first indications that . . . a new structure [of feeling] is forming" (Williams, *Marxism and Literature* 133), what critics deal with subsequently are the remains of cultural change and formation, the dissipated traces of social practices that have in this sense been displaced, become metaphorized as part and parcel of their narrative tropicity.

For example, Freud's accounts of hysteria do not point to "the emergence of history as narrative," a claim made by Steven Marcus (according to Deborah White [1036]), but rather to the functioning of a tropological structure as the principal determinant of Freud's case histories. In White's account, symptoms are generally founded (and found) in language and, hence, must be read as figurative. She concludes that what is created is "less a history than an allegory, for its referent is not a series of episodes . . . but the tropological structure of a discourse" (1036, 1044). The wider implications of this conclusion, however, make history impossible, or at least history making in the forms of historicization. Only allegory remains, very much along the lines of Paul de Man's thinking.[5] This, however, is to ignore the complex role of metaphor as imaginative, embodied thought, in other words, as a fundamental component in the construction of sociohistoric reality. We live—and die—by metaphors, to paraphrase and slightly modify linguists Lakoff and Johnson. Metaphorical thinking is always social, and hence historically inflected.

Nietzsche understood that the sense of movement conveyed and created by metaphor is inseparable from its context within time and space, that the movement itself expresses and makes possible a juncture of space, time, and thought, which is, in essence, historical. Stephen Greenblatt's metaphorical notion of an incessantly moving "social energy" (*Shakespearean Negotiations*), Michel de Certeau's "walking rhetorics," in which tropes perform and represent the movements of everyday life (*The Practice of Everyday Life*), and of course Hayden White's analysis of historiographical texts as forms of historical imagination (*Metahistory*), all re-elaborate this fundamental linkage between metaphor-movement-history.

To think in these terms, metaphorically that is, means to recognize the existence of structures of feeling in the world. In examining something as deceptively blurry as cursilería, the existence of a structure may not become evident. It is generally recognized when emotions are produced. Less apparent are the various cultural shapes the affective may assume, or how they come about. Shape implies structure, yet that which defines the affective is more mutable, more transformable, hence more unstable, than shape or structure seem to hold as concepts, which here threaten to rear up as abstract reifications. The distinction that Thomas McFarland makes between a shape of culture and a cultural form—"shape is what is left when form breaks down" (3)—provides some assistance in understanding the nature of cursilería. This notion of cultural breakdown, then, paradoxically has its own structure of feeling.

At work is a process in which a complex dialectic between the cognitive uses of feeling and social practices is allowed to come into transformative play. Metamorphosis as embodied change—in both the figurative and historical senses—provides a key to structures of feeling. In other words, to understand what is going on here means to look not only at what structures feeling but what feeling structures. In this regard, Marshall Sahlins's illuminating study, *Historical Metaphors and Mythical Realities,* the early history of the Sandwich Islands Kingdom suggests that, in the process of converting Hawaiian myth into history through the event of Captain Cook's death and his absorption into the mana of the powerful, fertile god Lono, metaphors called myths act in complex ways to produce the historical, just as history becomes "myth."

More broadly speaking, the metaphorical as embodied thought does what tropes in general do: it moves.[6] Descriptions of the term *metaphor* stress its movable character. Thus *metaphora* (Greek for "transference") is "the transference of properties of one thing, idea, image, or event to another in speech or writing" (Espy 108). Furetière and Littré define *metaphor* as a kind of "transport" that moves from the word itself to a figurative meaning. As Claire Lyu points out in her exhaustive analysis of Baudelaire's *Poème du hachisch*, "metaphor, therefore, is about places, about changing places, and about going from one place to another. The question of metaphor will necessarily entail, then, the question of space and of displacement" (729). Metaphor in this sense can be said to stand for the entire tropological structure of movement and transference.

It isn't necessary to go so far down the Derridean path of displacement as to lose sight of the rootedness of metaphor in experience and referentiality.[7] The transported and transferring nature of the metaphorical can only appear, as Paul Ricoeur points out, because metaphor, like all tropes, works on the level of "a second-order reference, of an indirect reference built on the ruins of the direct reference" (151). It is, he writes, "as though the tropes gave to discourse a quasi-bodily externalization" ("Metaphorical Process" 142).

Traditionally, metaphor is seen as a trope of resemblance. But that likeness cannot be understood without the presence of difference, or, as Ricoeur puts it, "To see the *like* is to see the same in spite of, and through, the different. This tension between sameness and difference characterizes the logical structure of likeness. Imagination . . . is this *ability* to produce new kinds by assimilation and to produce them not *above* the differences . . . but in spite of and through the differences" (146).

This notion of resemblance through difference, which constitutes the transferring of resemblance in space and time, suggests that the fundamental metaphoricity of thought cannot be separated from questions of identity. Ricoeur links the semantic and the psychological fields into a coherent theory proposing "a *structural analogy* between the cognitive, the imaginative, and the emotional components of the complete metaphorical act" (157). He, too, reiterates that feeling and thought are not simple contraries. Feeling "is thought made ours," he says (154), and, along with imagination, is essential to the metaphorical process. As a "second-order intentional structure," feelings are everyday, bodily emotions transformed.[8] Ricoeur's "poetic feelings" as interiorized thoughts point to the uncertain borderline between the verbal and the nonverbal, between nonbodily and bodily experience. Structures of feeling, I would add, operate in the equally fuzzy border between inside and outside, between an I and an Other.

We can thus extend Ricoeur's brilliant insights into the nature of the metaphorical process beyond the domains of psychology and semantics into the larger realm of culture itself. From within cultural anthropology, James Fernandez furthers understanding of the uses of metaphor and the tropological structures of feeling by focusing on what he calls the "mission of metaphor in expressive culture," explaining that "in the growth of human identity, the inchoate pronouns of social life—the 'I,' 'you,' 'it'—gain identity by predicating some sign-image, some metaphor upon themselves." In this process, subjects are first objects to themselves "by taking the point of view of 'the Other' " (35). Metaphor thus helps provide an identity, paradoxically, through difference. If identity is a product of "the will to differentiate" (Mitchell 41), then it must also be understood as a complex dialectic between likeness and difference, in which the Other is not only always within us, part of us, but intrinsic to notions of personal and cultural difference, that is, to identify itself.

How does metaphor "make" identity? Here, it is helpful to recall the Greek roots of metaphor as meaning "change in motion" (Fernandez 37). There is no way of understanding anything about identity without this notion of movement attached to it. The movement that metaphor both represents and performs is simultaneously literal and figurative. Its figurability is, first of all, based on a kind of split reference, the built-in ambiguity that metaphor exhibits in its relationship to the real and to reference in general. Second, metaphor is not simply directed inward; it is just as often acted out, performed in different scenes of cultural life, as Fernandez observes. This movement or "acting out of metaphoric predications" occurs in what he calls "quality spaces" of culture (39, 42).

The topographical metaphor applied to metaphoric acts provides a framework for situating the identity-making work of metaphor in specific cultural contexts. Like the notion of structure itself, however, and in particular structures of feeling which create these quality spaces, the topographical poses theoretical and methodological problems that need to be recognized as part of the limitations of cultural analysis (including this one) relying inevitably on metaphors as models. To what extent are space and structure empirical or material, in the case of contemporary societies; textual, in the case of cultural artifacts; to what extent are they metacommentaries offered as explanatory models? In most if not all instances, all three of the above questions come into play and tend to merge in the process of elucidating them. In this regard, Derrida's view that metaphoricity is inescapable may be apposite.[9]

Finally, the position of the observer or researcher is so imbricated with a subject as multiprismed and ultimately elusive as are feelings and their structure, that locating not simply the subject but even the observer is fraught with difficulties. As Andrew Delbanco notes how the salvationist doctrine of preparation felt to seventeenth-century New Englanders in his study of the affective life of Puritans: "The act of writing about even a small moment in the history of human feeling is rather like a game of catch carried on between players who are both in motion—a game with no clearly demarcated location" (2). In this regard, my own views of middle-class cursilería are as hybrid and "impure" as the phenomenon itself. What else is critical empathy if not the effort to make human once more what was imperfect desire?

The feelings of inadequacy and inauthenticity that lo cursi as a metaphor both embodied and projected are part of a larger story that I refer to as a ruptured middle-class narrative of identity, the fault lines of which can be traced from its presumed epicenter in Madrid to the southern periphery located in the commercial port city of Cádiz, where the word *cursi* appears to originate. This movement relocates the provinces within the mind and heart of the capital and repositions center-margin as a series of moveable cultural variants. Along the way, I stop at several moments in time. I begin with the 1830s and 1840s, moving on to the 1860s, where I linger at 1868, and take a break by the roadside in 1900. From there I come to an abrupt halt in the 1930s and, in a postmodern leap, land in the middle of the 1970s and 1980s.

These are, roughly sketched out, the geographical and chronological points along which one can situate the transformations of lo cursi. But this lineal tracking, which strikes me as necessary given the historical specificity and changing character of the phenomenon, buckles and then collapses when we attempt to uncover what lies beneath the outward surface manifestations of lo cursi because then the messy, tarry substance that we call the affective life reveals itself as infinitely spreadable and diffuse in nature. Before I return to the chronology of cursilería, I would like to explore more fully the nature of lo cursi's protean and amorphic capability of uncontainable shape shifting. Because the affective transformations of lo cursi unfold as a series of stories, they operate not only in time but in language, a language that takes the inchoate, nebulous forms of lo cursi and envelops them in the explaining powers of metaphor and metonymy, which in turn make even more problematic and layered the meanings and qualities of cursilería.

James Fernandez, speaking within the anthropological context of rituals and other expressive events, suggests that "metaphors and metonyms are being chosen to put forth three kinds of statements: statements of adequacy, inadequacy, and transformation or transcendence of state" (57). As a social phenomenon grounded in class differences, lo cursi functions as a cultural indicator of both inadequacy and transformation, registering profound social changes in the history of modern Spain. It is therefore a narrative not only of representation but of performance. The movements of this narrative performance include such things as substitutions, combinations, enlargements, miniaturizations, and fragmentation—forms of either metaphorization or of metonymy, the two being blood brothers and ultimately inseparable. This language of cursilería also expresses itself in forms of behavior and thinking, thus becoming, on a more literal and material level, another kind of performance. What, then, may seem simply linguistic or verbal—combinations or miniaturizations, for example—also reveals itself in the way people act, think, or feel. Socially and historically, lo cursi can be viewed as well as a kind of movement within middle-class culture, a movement reflecting contradiction, heterogeneity, and confusion, that is, an indication of how modern culture constitutes change and instability.

As performance and as representation, lo cursi is activated through the uneven relationship between an "I" and an "Other." It is founded on difference and a desired identity, or identification, with a hierarchically superior Other. The cursi text is both a sign and a countersign of the emerging middle-class culture that aspired to power and influence in the last century. Lo cursi is, in this sense, a form of rupture, middle-class in origin, that simultaneously constructs and deconstructs the cultural identity of this particular social group. The appearance of cursilería marks a social class by undoing it, operating here as a kind of destabilizing stigma. Rather than fix identity with a distinguishing if reductive brand as does stigma normally, however, lo cursi exposes the constructed nature of a particular social identity, and in this unsettling process it provokes yet another social construction.

When lo cursi is treated as an objectified entity—that is, perceived from a distance by someone (presumably) not cursi—such naming often becomes accusatory and, in the end, alienating, because the term is so emotionally charged. In Galdós's 1881 novel *La desheredada* [The disinherited lady], Isidora Rufete's socially privileged lover Joaquín Pez insults her honor and then delivers the coup de grâce by calling her *cursilona;* yet what really wounds her is not the attack on her honor, but the diminishing of her self-esteem. Verbally enunciated in these circumstances, the epithet of inadequacy and undesirable transformation creates a barrier between subject and other, a defensive screen that barely covers Pez's own cursilería. (The entire Pez family is one large melting pot of cursilería as subjected to Pérez Galdós's pitiless, satiric eye.) Lo cursi, when verbally expressed, exacerbates a particular libidinized economy in which a mix of feelings, difficult to pin down, circulates back and forth between subject and other. No one is immune to the charge. Metaphor is contagious.

As a result, some resolved to get rid of the metaphor itself, or at least its negative, contagious features. Over time, the image of cursilería undergoes radical transformation, especially as seen in early twentieth-century modernist texts by writers usually of middle-class background. Indeed, by suppressing explicit mention of lo cursi, such writers also tend to suppress their own middle-class origins. By the end of the nineteenth century, some members of the Spanish middle classes engage in a defensive counterattack, either by stressing the positive virtues and contributions of middle-class industry and self-discipline or by viewing such unfortunates as the señorita cursi as victims of economic and social hard times.[10] With the passage of time and sufficient distance, lo cursi is finally

43

viewed through the lens of nostalgia and sentimentally internalized. In 1906, for example, Pío Baroja evokes with tender irony, "the strange poetry of ordinary things," in the image of the accordion. He writes, "Oh, modest accordions, you truly represent our times: humble, sincere, sweetly plebeian, perhaps ridiculously plebeian; but you speak of life the way life perhaps really is: an ordinary, monotonous, common melody stretched out before the limitless horizon ("Elogio sentimental del acordeón" 55).[11] Baroja's accordion vibrates with an earlier image found in Galdós's *Fortunata y Jacinta* (1885–86), in which the novelist playfully links childhood and the *flin-flan*, cursi sounds of an accordion, while drawing a much more devastating portrait of the cursi infantilization of Spanish society and governance elsewhere in the text.

This same modernist tendency to convert lo cursi into the ordinary, or *lo vulgar*, is apparent in Azorín, as Ortega y Gasset pointed out long ago, noting that "in reverse order to tenderness, nostalgia is inwardly, pain, and outwardly, pleasure" ("Azorín" 159).[12] Lo cursi internalized is pure nostalgia, the absorption of quasi-maternal loss into the textual body of memory, the denial of historical time (and change), through dreamtime as in the early Valle-Inclán, or through repetition as in Azorín. Critics rightfully stress the difference between lo cursi and *lo vulgar* (see Rubert de Ventós 210–11), but, in doing so, ignore the slippery, polymorphous qualities of the former. Early twentieth-century modernists like Azorín, Valle-Inclán, and Baroja, and, slightly later, Ramón Gómez de la Serna, are less reactors to, than internalizers of, nineteenth-century realism. The intimate and social relationship between things and persons, which is characteristic of realism and often associated with cursilería, simply goes underground with many Spanish modernists; things become subjectivized as writers lean more and more heavily on the desired salvationist qualities of metaphor. "The human word," Walter Benjamin wrote, "is the name of things . . . language never gives *mere* signs" ("On Language as Such" 324).

The sign of lo cursi proves wonderfully elastic; it is even capable of being poeticized through verbal sleight of hand, as Gómez de la Serna cleverly does in distinguishing between what is bad and good cursilería (*lo cursi bueno* and *lo cursi malo*), or as Lorca shows in the delicately Chekhovian lyricism of his play *Doña Rosita la soltera, o, El lenguaje de las flores*. Yet from the perspective of the affective life, there is little difference between this aestheticizing nostalgia of Spanish modernism and the self-conscious sentimentality of actor Enrique Chicote in his memoirs, who says, "I adore dogs. I am a cursi. This ease I possess in being moved by things that leave many people indifferent, is a cursilería. I belong to that class of insignificant persons called cursis" (290–91).[13]

One can't help thinking here of the conclusion to Leopoldo Alas's 1889–90 story, "Superchería" [A hoax], when the much disillusioned main character, Nicolás Serrano, sees "a dog in a drab [*cursi*] cinnamon coat sauntered by. He was down-at-heels, quite ordinary and very pleased with life."[14] Serrano turns right as if, Alas says, to follow "the tracks of the cinnamon-colored dog, who took every *phenomenon* for what it was: a hoax" (49, 51).[15]

This image leads one straight to a later text, Unamuno's *Niebla* [Mist] (1914), which begins on a similar note with Augusto Pérez, "a chronic flaneur of life," wondering whether to go right or left: "I'll wait until a dog passes by, and then I'll take the initial direction he takes" (110). But he doesn't. Instead, a pretty young woman walks by, he follows her, and the story comes along. Unamuno's novel ends on a wonderfully tragi-comic cursi note, with the death of both Augusto and his faithful dog, Orfeo, who delivers—in the Cervantine tradition of "El coloquio de los perros"—a quasi-mock philosophical funeral eulogy of his master, dwelling hopefully on the possibility of a platonic hereafter filled with the idea of "pure men" and "pure dogs" (300). If all dogs go to heaven, it's because it's a dog's life in this world. Unamuno has taken a cliché, a verbal cursilería, and converted it into a philosophical-aesthetic commentary on the prospects for personal survival and transcendence.[16]

But let me backtrack from my digressions. The feelings that fill lo cursi—ranging from social ridicule to tenderly ironic nostalgia—do change over time (although they sometimes also revert back to an earlier affective content), but they also tend to spill over the edges of any attempt to limit this slippery and uncontainable phenomenon to a clear-cut sociohistorical one. This is partly because lo cursi can have many functions and can therefore lead one down many paths. Lo cursi is also an unstable entity, simultaneously constructing and deconstructing identity, oddly enough, much the same way Unamuno does with Augusto

Pérez in *Niebla*. This suggests that perhaps lo cursi as a social trait and the modernist project may very well have much more in common than critics usually suspect.

Niebla is about origins. The novel is a creation text. Unamuno creates a story out of nothing, out of a mist. He plays at playing God. He also suffers, like his characters, tremendous anxiety over his own immortality and is obsessed with the notion of transcendence over time. But his obsession with time, as *Niebla* demonstrates, is simply the reverse lining of his problem with being. Both Unamuno—in multiple textual versions of himself—and Augusto Pérez suffer from the neurosis of origins precisely because they don't seem to have any. What Don Miguel the character / author in *Niebla* does to his creation Augusto Pérez in revealing his fictional status is to expose his lack of real parentage and all the other linkages that go with it: a personal history, an identity, a relationship with one's neighborhood, town, country, a set of beliefs and values. When Don Miguel feels his own existence threatened by Augusto, he lashes out defensively, saying, "Well, yes. I am Spanish, Spanish by birth and education, in body and spirit, by my language and my very profession and work; Spanish above all and before all else, and being Spanish [Spanishness] is my religion, and the heaven I would like to believe in is a celestial, eternal Spain, and my God is a Spanish God, the God of our Dear Lord Señor Quixote; a God who thinks in Spanish and in Spanish said: let there be light! and his word was Spanish" (283).[17]

The stereotypical response to this passage might well be: how very Spanish! But what is missing here are all the details, the concrete particularities of Don Miguel as a character. Unamuno gives readers abstractions and clichés. Much earlier in the text he has Augusto Pérez enthuse lyrically over the poetry of everyday life: "This life of mine, placid, routine, humble, is a Pindaric ode woven with the thousand little things of the quotidian. The quotidian! Give us our daily bread now!"[18] This daily life is, he then adds, "an immense mist filled with small incidents. And this is life, this mist. Life is a nebula" (115).[19]

Of course one shouldn't expect to find in this modernist text the filled-in detail of a realist novel. But all that is known of Augusto Pérez is that he is "rich and alone" and that his mother died six months before. He has no employment, and he has nothing to do. In a word, he is a *señorito*, a well-to-do representative of the Spanish middle classes. Lacking purpose and direction in life, as the opening pages of *Niebla* effectively show, Augusto also lacks a history. He is born on the first page of Unamuno's novel. He begins literally by taking an attitude, a particular posture—extending his right arm, with his hand palm down, and his eyes directed upward—and choosing chance to set him off that day. Augusto's gestures and words are not so much acts as an acting out of consciousness; and his praise of daily life is a lyrical intrusion of the subjective self that leads straight back to his mind as expressed in the imagery of mist and nebulosity.

Unamuno's existential statements of overcoming time (the modernist utopia) also remain perfectly class-bound. The presence of social class in *Niebla* is barely noticed because the text glides over it, covering it up with the myth of creative autonomy. It is precisely this myth of art springing like Pallas Athena out of Unamuno's godlike forehead that exposes the desire and will to remove the imperfections of history from his narration. Just as Augusto Pérez, economically and socially well-off, has no reason to refer to the necessities of life, so, too, the novelist as sole originator of his text and characters has no need to connect his writing with a concrete, referential world. Unamuno simply refers to himself. He has no origins, needs no origins. Mind is its own fountainhead. In this way Unamuno establishes the uniqueness and originality of his name. And in this sense, *Niebla* is a quintessential middle-class text.

The middle classes have a history but no past to speak of. Conrado Solsona (1882) humorously put it this way: "In the middle classes talents are begot without fortunes, men without names, such *original* last names; last names that have to be invented, because their ancestors, who didn't read newspapers, didn't bother with such things" ("Mi clase" 145).[20] Unlike the aristocracy, the middle classes cannot look back to an illustrious parentage; they must create their own founding myths. Frequently, such founding myths are bound up with national as well as class identities. In *Niebla*, Unamuno attempts to solve the problem of a missing past by throwing it out and then essentializing identity, including one's class and one's nationality, as Don Miguel's claims of Spanishness illustrate.

There is, however, one significant element he either cannot or will not get rid of: the inchoate, nebulous quality of life that Augusto identifies with the ordinary forms of the everyday world, with domesticity and intimacy. Like Baroja, Azorín, Gómez de la Serna, and even Ortega y

Gasset on occasion, Unamuno takes the comfortable, quotidian middle-class world of the home, of small possessions and simple pleasures (Baroja's accordion) and elevates them to the level of poetry. But what a strange poetry this is! How do a material existence and material objects metamorphose into mist ("niebla") and a nebula ("una nebulosa")? In order to make acceptable what would otherwise be perceived as aesthetically cursi, modernists elide the cursi element by substituting and then poeticizing the category of the ordinary. The complex process of nostalgia allows them to retain an undesirable quality that is too close, too much a part of their identity, by calling it something else. Only Gómez de la Serna seems able to name the thing directly, but even so, he takes care to distinguish aesthetically between two kinds of cursilería.

By linking modernist texts to cursilería, my intention is not to see these texts as cursi, but rather, to underline how both modernist writings and cursilería arise out of middle-class longings and lack (or sometimes loss) of noble origins. These early twentieth-century modernist texts paradoxically encapsulate the historical fact of Spanish middle-classness through aesthetic denial. They also manifest the difficulties of grasping a notion as slippery as lo cursi, tissued as it is in layers of time and feeling.

Lo cursi is irredeemably middle-class and lacking in distinction both aesthetically and socially. It is a mark of inferiority that tears down the fragile edifice of constructed identities and thus unwittingly exposes the frayed edges of failed middle-class myth making. Lo cursi, as Ortega y Gasset perceptively noted, concentrates within its territory an entire social and economic history ("Intimidades" 655). It is impossible to separate the history of modern Spain from the history of that social class with which lo cursi is intimately linked. In this regard, Spanish history follows a path resembling at least in part that of most European nations. National identity, the sense of nationness, is a product of nineteenth-century liberal-romantic ideology, an ideology largely espoused by the middle classes and from which those same classes profited. Without forgetting eighteenth-century reforms, one looks, nevertheless, to the Cortes of Cádiz in 1810–12 as the real beginnings of a modern, liberal Spanish state. The Cortes de Cádiz had the makings of a powerful foundational myth for both the nation and the middle classes. While the

Cortes did eventually acquire a kind of myth status independent of the Spanish state, nineteenth-century Spanish nationalism was relatively weak on the whole. Adrian Shubert maintains that "[Spain's] liberal state failed to create a ritual or set of symbols which might have stimulated a strong national feeling. It failed to 'invent tradition' " (203). He claims that religious identity remained stronger than secular national identity, at least until the civil war (205).

Historians have argued that Spain, unlike England and France for example, had no "bourgeois revolution" and that the middle classes did not exercise any significant political control.[21] But in most of nineteenth-century Europe ruling alliances were forged among the middle classes and the old elite. Spain was no exception. Moreover, Spain's bourgeois or liberal revolution has too often been dismissed on the (arguably disputable) grounds that it resulted in political and economic failure. This view does not take into sufficient account the complexities of modern change. Rather than focus exclusively on a ruling class, one has to examine more closely the new ways society was being constituted and structured during the last century. Shubert and others suggest that the truly significant change for Spain was more legal than economic or political, with "the legal superstructure of the Old Regime . . . dismantled and a new type of society . . . created" (Shubert 5). Privilege did not disappear, but it was seriously undermined. Besides the disentailment of lands, other changes, such as economic and industrial expansion, the formation of a working class, growing urbanization and secularization, and political reforms of a constitutional, representative nature, indisputably did take place in nineteenth-century Spain. All of these factors made the cultural conditions of a Spanish middle-class society more than a theoretical possibility.

The phenomenon of lo cursi falls squarely within these newly constituted social conditions and changes. The cultural contradictions of lo cursi suggest a misalignment between modernity and modernization in which the economic organization has not yet caught up with the social changes produced by democratization within more urbanized and secularized circumstances. Moreover, awareness of what was modern did not always produce the modern. The middle classes prized newness, progress, and individual achievement, but in Spain, as elsewhere in Europe, many of them also looked to the aristocracy as social and cultural models. They looked, that is, to the past. Marriage alliances between the high bourgeoisie and the titled classes strengthened such cultural symbiosis. More frequently, however, social incongruity produced lo cursi, a hybrid class of indeterminate origins, a concentrate of the inescapably middle class, in effect, for what the lower middle classes in particular lacked were origins, the distinction that blood conferred on the nobility.

This exclusivity proved particularly strong in Spain and was exacerbated by a religious past in which "la limpieza de sangre" (purity of blood) had created mutual suspicion and fear and a caste system of Old and New Christians. While the nineteenth century mostly rendered this kind of blood purity a moot issue, the structure of exclusions and divisions that shaped it persisted for a long time.[22] The emphasis on lineage and the "quality of blood" transmitted through marriage had resulted in the strengthening of traditional social groups, especially the nobility (Contreras 130–31). One could, however, purchase, with some risk, letters patent of nobility and certificates of purity in the sixteenth and seventeenth centuries. In the nineteenth-century Isabeline and Amadean periods, and especially during the Restoration, besides allying oneself matrimonially, one could also have a title conferred for services rendered to the throne. The history and politics of nineteenth-century Spain are speckled with the names of industrialists, entrepreneurs, and generals sporting titles (see Tuñón de Lara 187–99).

More frequently, the notion of distinction that blood ties symbolized found a middle-class substitute in cultural distinction as sought in the artifacts, dress, and manners of the socially superior class.[23] Like the titles of the new nobility, however, this kind of distinctiveness rested on a rather shaky *faux marbre* pedestal of questionable authenticity. The quest for distinctiveness fuels innumerable narrations of the nineteenth century. In literature, *costumbrista* writings are filled with all kinds of socially pretentious character types of middle-class origin. Realist novels like Galdós's *La desheredada*, Palacio Valdés's *El señorito Octavio* [Master Octavio], Alas's *Su único hijo* [His only son], and Pardo Bazán's *El cisne de Vilamorta* [The swan of Vilamorta] come immediately to mind. Modernist writings generally smooth over or mask social inadequacy, converting it into a narrative of aesthetic (as opposed to social) distinction, and turning verbal adornment into a subjective, quasi-experiential necessity. Yet more important than the pervasiveness of the theme is how the quest for distinctiveness not only structures many fictions but can itself be considered a kind of story, a discursive space that, like narrative in general, helps make sense of things by lending a possible form or structure to something that appears to lack form.

In the case of lo cursi, there is not simply one, but many different stories of the desire for distinction. The plot lines and character shapes of lo cursi are so varied, so heterogeneous and overdetermined in meaning, that it would mean a distortion to try to limit lo cursi to a single ideological morphology. Indeed, the appearance of lo cursi not only denotes change, it also constitutes a response to change. The instability that lies behind lo cursi emerges out of a perceived absence: an absence of origins, which in turn fuels the need for narrative. This narrative necessity is, however, built on denial and unreal loss. In other words, it is, in a non-Freudian way, a peculiar family romance continually acknowledged and then denied, and which becomes a kind of necessary structuring supplement of subjectivity to lived experience.

Thus, on the one hand, lo cursi represents a narration that helps explain social and cultural change and can be retold through a roughly diachronic critical framework. On the other hand, the subjective heart of lo cursi is shaped out of the conflicting impulses of a false anachronicity and a missing genealogy. The feeling behind lo cursi is, in this sense, somewhat unreal, or illusory, precisely because it emerges out of misbegotten myth making, out of a fiction. Nonetheless, all sentiment, even when it is based on illusion, *feels* real inwardly. Indeed, the perception of social inadequacy, of being socially incongruous, can be and often is painfully real. The myth that lo cursi invents and promotes is foundational in nature, tailored to individual subjectivities certainly, but intimately bound to the collective body, to national, cultural, class, and gender identities. The simultaneous constructing and deconstructing of identity, which also depends on the position (and positioning) from which this process is being observed and experienced, for this reason lends itself to a more synchronic approach favoring the analysis of cultural variants over that of historical change. The multiple forms of lo cursi then become a series of cultural practices, as both representation and performance of a content that shifts according to the context. Lo cursi turns into a discursive "space of social transformation" (Lutz 20).[24]

Thus I am using the frame of a loosely diachronic and quasi-genealogical analysis, but the interior of the frame is a narrative that undercuts and dissolves those same framing impulses. This complex interplay between the lineal and the spatial is, I believe, appropriate: personal histories or stories of cursilería are often constructed along anecdotal lines held together by the connective tissue of familial origins and relationships, even as those same kernels of anecdote are being softened and loosened until the connecting tissues dissolve into amorphous masses of social indeterminacy. The social origin of the term *cursi*, as a verbal creation rooted in a specific context, as an invention or fiction necessary to explain something socially embedded in history, also points to a "founding" impulse in narrative.

Indeed, all the stories about lo cursi's origins are imaginative elaborations of a founding impulse repeatedly defeated by the very processes of history and culture. Why is this so? First, the same narrative drive to create foundations mythologizes them in the process, turns origins, beginnings, the building blocks of social phenomena, historical events, and individual life histories into mythographical forces. And second, lo cursi is a narrative of marginality desiring to occupy the center, to become the foundational heartland.

This book is not, however, simply an oppositional account of margins and center. Lo cursi is a small local narrative that exposes the instability and weakness of a master narrative, one based on centralization and oligarchy in nineteenth-century Spain. In other words, the inferiority complex of provincialism so visible in lo cursi is a moveable concept, thereby demonstrating the difficulty of locating center and periphery. This shifting of margins and center within Spain takes on even greater significance when considered in relation to the provincialized position of nineteenth-century Spain within Europe. Many of the attacks on lo cursi express nationalistic anxiety and defensiveness, and they see the phenomenon as an emblem of inauthenticity and inferiority, singling out one form of behavior especially—the imitation of foreign models (especially the French). The question of center versus margins, local versus master narratives, is not simply class- (and gender-) bound; it is also inscribed nationally and internationally. The all-pervasiveness of lo cursi exhibits the cultural contradictions of conflicting, changing realities within a social space in the process of being forged.

Despite certain historical anomalies, nineteenth-century Spanish society was indeed founding a modern European state and a modern middle class. But this consolidation of nation and class is based on a fiction of identity that the local narrative of cursilería both reveals and exemplifies. That fiction, moreover, discloses a profound uncertainty and anxiety over the specific makeup of such an identity. In other words, in contradistinction to the Latin American theoretical model of foundational fictions, which proposes that a symbiosis of history and fiction works toward community building (see Sommer), I would argue that the presence of lo cursi points to the weakness or absence of foundational fictions in nineteenth-century Spain. This failed foundational impulse is evident not only in the frustrated identity narratives of social classes and individual subjectivities, but in the weakness of liberal ideology in providing persuasive myths of national identity.

To see more clearly the complexities and contradictions of the practices wrapped up in this particular metaphor of cultural identity, one needs to examine more closely the presumed beginnings of the cursi phenomenon and the various narratives that have sprung up to explain it. The origins of the word *cursi* remain uncertain. Most accounts document usage in the 1860s and attribute its widespread currency to the social and political instability of the liberal revolution of 1868. The first official dictionary entry dates from 1869 (*DRAE*). In the 1870s and 1880s, references to lo cursi proliferate in newspaper articles, fiction, satirical poetry, essays, and pictorial representations. By the turn of the century the phenomenon has taken on new life in the depressed atmosphere of decline and uncertainty following the war of 1898. Usage of the term in literature and belles lettres picks up again in the 1930s during the Second Republic, becomes philological and sociological in the 1950s, and experiences a revival of sorts, in tandem with camp and kitsch, during the 1980s and 1990s.[25] Contrary to rumor, lo cursi, despite historical ups and downs, still hasn't died. One would expect that something inescapably tied to the historical conditions that produced it would eventually disappear. In this instance, however, lo cursi appears not only to shift as needs and expressive states change, but to accommodate itself to the continuing if modified presence of social and class anxiety in the face of unsettling cultural transformations.

The 1860s in Spain were a period of economic boom and bust in which overspeculation, a budgetary crisis, and commercial losses linked to the European market and the American Civil War sparked massive banking and credit failures and, ultimately, contributed to the overthrow of the Bourbon monarchy in 1868 (see Carr 299–300; and Sánchez-Albornoz, "El trasfondo económico"). The social and economic circumstances certainly proved ripe for rampant cursilería. Scattered references to the term are illustrative. In José de Castro y Serrano's popular *Cartas trascendentales* [Transcendental letters] from 1862, one reads "Agripina's boudoir . . . would surely be considered *cursi* today, compared with one belonging to the wife of any director of a *Crédit Mobilier*" (38).[26] The financial allusion reminds readers that, in just a few years, the Spanish subsidiary of the French bank *Crédit Mobilier* would crash, bringing down with it many other banking institutions.

A period of feverish speculation, the 1850s and 1860s also constituted a society of spectacle. In Pereda's 1861 play, *Tanto tienes, tanto vales* [Your worth in gold], a socially ambitious mother says that her daughter, if she marries up, will have a fine coach, a "gran berlina." Enriqueta disdainfully replies, "A calash, Mama: a berlin is cursi; / . . . A berlin with a mare!" (9).[27] In the same year, an anonymous reviewer critiqued *La cruz del matrimonio* [The cross of matrimony], a popular play by Luis de Eguilaz, noting that one of the female characters dances five times with the same gentleman: "This goes against the grain of good taste. A lady of quality is permitted to lavish all her favors upon a gentleman, but she will not dance with him five times in a row. That would seem to her sublimely ridiculous, or *cursi*."[28] Here, lo cursi is equivalent to making a spectacle of oneself in public.

The attack on lo cursi reached its first cultural apex in mid-1868 with Francisco Silvela and Santiago Liniers's *La filocalia o arte de distinguir a los cursis de los que no lo son* [The love of beauty, or art of distinguishing cursis from those who are not], a text to which I will return (see chapter 2; and fig. 5).[29] This satire targeted bourgeois Isabeline society, but not even revolution was immune. Of the revolution of 1868, the ultraconservative Aparisi y Guijarro wrote, "Although there are many bona fide

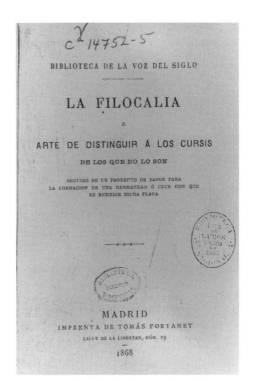

5. Cover page of *La filocalia o arte de distinguir a los cursis de los que no lo son,* by Francisco Silvela and Santiago de Liniers.

September revolutionaries, albeit deluded without any doubt whatsoever, it is impossible to deny that the revolution they serve is ungodly, and *CURSI* besides" (253).[30]

During the next few years, cursi allusions increase, in costumbrista sketches appearing in collections like *Las españolas pintadas por los españoles* [The women of Spain as seen by the men of Spain] (1871), *Los españoles de ogaño* [Spaniards of today] (1872), and *Madrid por dentro y por fuera* [Madrid inside and out] (1873),[31] and in social and literary satire like Ortega y Frías's *La gente cursi: Novela de costumbres ridículas* [Cursi people: A novel of ridiculous customs] (1872), Taboada's "Fragmentos de la vida de un cursi" [Fragments of the life of a cursi] (1874), and Moja y Bolívar's "Los cursis literarios" [Literary cursis] (1873). Above all, it was the postrevolutionary period of the Bourbon Restoration that supplied the richest material of cursilería for commentators and novelists all along the ideologically polarized political spectrum, ranging from the conservative Alarcón in *El escándalo* [The scandal] (1875) to moderate

Juan Valera with *Las ilusiones del Doctor Faustino* [Dr. Faustino's illusions] (1874–75), to liberals like Clarín (*La Regenta*, 1884–85; *Su único hijo*, 1891) and Galdós (*La familia de León Roch* [The family of Leon Roch], 1878; *La desheredada*, 1881; *La de Bringas*, 1884; *Fortunata y Jacinta* [Fortunata and Jacinta], 1885–86; *Miau* [Miau], 1888, etc.).[32] Publications such as *Madrid cómico*, *La risa*, *El mundo cómico*, and *La chispa* delighted in regularly taking aim with words and illustrations at all forms of cursilería. Luis Taboada made an entire career as a social satirist out of it.[33]

But let's retrace our steps. I too, like almost everyone else, was persuaded that lo cursi first surfaced as a phenomenon in the 1860s, with the understanding that people had no doubt used the term in conversation several years before it appeared in print in 1860. But this proved untrue. While searching for leads on the cursi trail, I ran across a 1962 article from *ABC* by the historian Ramón Solís (noted especially for his illuminating study of *El Cádiz de las Cortes*), in which he cites and partially reproduces an anonymously authored satirical piece called "Un cursi," published in a short-lived journal from Cádiz, *La estrella*, in 1842. This was a startling and fascinating discovery, with a series of implications I will deal with shortly. Perhaps because his article appeared in a daily newspaper, it was swallowed up in the flood of mass publishing and little noticed by other critics, even though he subsequently made use of the same material in publications easily available to scholars.[34] No one except for Solís, as far as I have been able to ascertain, has picked up on this early appearance of lo cursi and explored what possible significance its presence in Cádiz in 1842, with essentially the same meaning as we currently attribute to the term, might have.[35]

The next documented reference I have found to lo cursi appears in 1849, in a curious little volume—half travel experiences, half guidebook—by Francisco de Paula Madrazo, called *Dos meses en Andalucía* [Two months in Andalusia] (fig. 4).[36] Madrazo describes three social classes he sees strolling in the Plaza de Mina one evening in Cádiz:

Forman el primer grupo las personas de buen tono y de brillante posición . . . ; componen el segundo esas familias amigas de las sombras y víctimas de los cambios de la época; y por último, forman la tercera sección una clase de gente fina en la apariencia, y sin duda en el fondo, pero de condición menos noble y de ocupaciones más mecánicas, a quienes se distingue en Andalucía con el raro nombre de *cursis*. Esta calificación está universalmente extendida; y cuando allí se dice, elevando la palabra *cursi* a la categoría de adjetivo, que el paseo, el teatro o el baile han estado *cursis*, todo el mundo comprende que han estado malos; esto es, que no han concurrido a ellos personas notables y distinguidas.

[Forming the first group are persons of good taste and brilliant position . . . ; composing the second group are those families favoring the shadows who are victims of the changing times; and finally, forming the third section is a class of people genteel in appearance, and no doubt at heart, but of less noble condition and of more mechanical occupations, who are distinguished with the unusual name of *cursis* in Andalusia. This qualifier is universally widespread; and when it is said there, elevating the word *cursi* to the category of adjective, that the walk, the theater or the dance were *cursis*, everyone understands that they were bad; that is, noteworthy and distinguished persons did not go to them.] (41–42)[37]

He then goes on to paint a sympathetic and somewhat sentimental portrait of the young women who fit into this social category, daughters of artisans and shopkeepers, daughters who are the sole support of their mothers, daughters of retired army officers and the unemployed. They dress simply and decently despite their poverty: "they hide with their long cloaks the frayed condition of their dress, which embellished with a few ruffles seems like something other than it really is."[38] Madrazo sees them as genuine heroines, "the protagonists of those dramas of love which are played out amidst the shadowy foliage" (42).[39] Here, it seems already, are the vague outlines of Lorca's delicately wrought figure of Doña Rosita. In place of satire, the sentimental idealizing one associates with a much later period appears very early in the history of lo cursi. Madrazo brings out clearly the indeterminate class standing of the cursi group, situating it at the lower end of the middle classes, as likely petite bourgeoisie (Rivière 89), given the reference to "more mechanical occupations." He also points out the importance of appearance in this particular social class, in the two senses of appropriate public presence and one's public persona as role. Authenticity and pretense go side by side, uneasily jostling one another: "people genteel in appearance, and no doubt at heart."

Although Madrazo asserts that the cursi class and terminology are widely disseminated throughout Andalusia, his description contextualizes the phenomenon strictly within the city limits of Cádiz. Several years later, in 1857, Adolfo de Castro reaffirmed the Cádiz connection by including *cursi* in his *Diccionario de voces gaditanas* [Dictionary of terms used in Cádiz]. Claiming he is the first to put together such a compilation (i), de Castro lists three forms, "cursería," "cursi" (noun and adjective), and "cursilón, -a", and gives the following definition:

> CURSI, s. m y f. Persona que quiere ser elegante sin tener las condiciones necesarias para ello, bien por faltarle medios pecuniarios, bien por carecer de gusto.

> [a person who desires to be elegant without having the qualities needed for it, whether money or taste.] (viii)

This definition comes very close to the one later adopted by the Royal Spanish Academy.

I have found no mention of an anecdotal origin for *cursi* until 1873, when José María Sbarbi gave what appears to be the first such version in print. He talks about a family from "one of the most beautiful cities of Andalusia" (92), whose daughters dressed luxuriously but with very bad taste, and a group of upper-class young men who made fun of them by using a special, private language in which the trope of metathesis, the transposition of letters, sounds, or syllables, became the verbal weapon of choice. Sbarbi offers a vague and not especially convincing account, as he makes no attempt to connect *cursi* linguistically (or otherwise) to the Andalusian *señoritas* in question. Nevertheless, this particular narrative variant surfaces repeatedly in different forms and ends up becoming the prevailing explanation of *lo cursi*'s origins.

Sbarbi took up his cursi story once again in an 1882 exchange of opinions with Adolfo de Castro in the daily, *El imparcial*. Sbarbi writes that de Castro got it all wrong in his 12 June article and points out that in *El averiguador universal* of 1880, a judge from Oviedo, Manuel Sánchez Guerrero, says that the word *cursi* was coined in Cádiz by a Dr. Rafael Sarandeseo from Oviedo.[40]

Adolfo de Castro gives a somewhat garbled and confusing account in *El imparcial*. First he refers to a story about a doctor's daughters in Cádiz who dressed ridiculously and with pretensions to elegance. When they were away from public view, it was said that they were "de 'cursos'" (otherwise engaged), a phrase which was humorously changed to "cursis." But then he rejects this story—for which he gives credit, erroneously it seems, to Sbarbi—and goes on to propose yet another version of *lo cursi*'s origins, in which he brings up three disparate elements: a popular marionette theater in Cádiz, a conjuring trick (or *juego de manos*) called *manicurcias*, and a species of cloth that somehow he relates both to the marionette theater and to Quintus Curcius, author of an extremely difficult book on Alexander the Great. He only makes passing reference to manicurcias, a game played with hands, in which one pretends to do one thing while doing another. This entertainment, he says, is found only among uneducated, simple folk. His discussion of cloth centers on a social gathering of a Cádiz lady, Doña Gabriela Gamarra, in which a conversation about fabrics leads to the opinion that said cloths are cursi, the word having come from the phrase, "telas propias de Curcio" (cloth worthy of Curcio). And since for him "Curcio" referred to Quinto Curcio, the writer whose difficult style students of Latin considered ridiculous and detestable, de Castro concludes by making this extraordinarily tortuous and rambling linkage between *cursi*, cloth, and Latinity.

He reserves most of his apparently inexhaustible scholarly energies for what he considers the real story about *lo cursi*, which for him rings with indisputable authenticity precisely because it is located in the Cádiz of *his* childhood. This happened toward the end of 1836 when de Castro says, "I was thirteen at the time lo cursi was invented" (3). He describes a popular marionette entertainment, in which one of the characters is called Don Rete or Don Riti Curcio, a doctor whose affected behavior is a combined parody of the eighteenth-century fop or *petimetre* and the early nineteenth-century dandy of Cádiz, the *piri*. De Castro also relates Don Rete Curcio to the cursi cloths noted above. The same character, now a notary public though equally farcical, appears in José María León y Domínguez's memoirs (160; also Aladro 227–45).

Yet another story of *lo cursi* focuses on twin sisters—the *señoritas de Tessi Curt*—again from Cádiz, well-to-do but orphaned, who set the standard for good taste among their social class and merit a popular song filled with word plays on their name ("Tesicursi-si / tesicursi-cur," for example).[41] Here, the original connotation of *cursi* is positive, signifying distinction and refinement, with subsequent meanings pointing to social slippage and a fall from higher standards as well as to an implicit semantic instability. This particular narration obviously follows a certain gender-inscribed model, already apparent in embryonic fashion in Madrazo (1849), Sbarbi (1873), and de Castro (1882), and implicitly recognized in the innumerable señoritas cursis who populate sketches of social types, novels, satirical verse, and articles. The full-blown narrative model for this account of *lo cursi* does not appear, however, until the twentieth century, with a lightweight play by Javier de Burgos titled *La familia de Sicur* [The Sicur family] and produced in 1899 having partially prepared the way (fig. 6).[42]

Let us now return to Ramón Solís and his assertion that the cursi phenomenon begins in Cádiz during the 1830s and 1840s. Given the concrete documentation of the 1842 article, "Un cursi," published in Cádiz, the absence of any other references issuing out of other cities and regions of Spain until the 1860s, and the personal testimony of Madrazo, de Castro, and others, it seems fairly safe to conclude that lo cursi originated as a local narrative situated in the southern port city of Cádiz. I will have more to say about the political, economic, and cultural factors defining Cádiz's circumstances during the first forty years of the nineteenth century, circumstances that favored the eruption of cursilería in that particular city. For the moment, I want to set the stage for that discussion by examining here the merits of Solís's position on lo cursi.

Solís maintains that the word *cursi* arose from the presence of a French tailor's daughters in 1830s Cádiz. The Sicour(t) (or Sicur) sisters dressed French and, in so doing, called attention to themselves; but they also dressed badly, the ideal of simple elegance being beyond their means and tastes. Some medical students irreverently critiqued the "niñas de Sicur" by inventing a little song about them, which quickly became very popular in Cádiz; subsequently, the name "Sicour(t)" (or hispanized Sicur) was converted into "Cursi."

This story may seem no more reliable or valid than any other version of lo cursi, although in this case, Solís does have some justification to back him up. Two earlier accounts are based on the same narrative core, but offer some intriguing details to flesh out the story. In a 1946 article,

LA FAMILIA DE SICUR

SAINETE LÍRICO EN UN ACTO

DIVIDIDO EN TRES CUADROS, EN VERSO

original de

JAVIER DE BURGOS

música del maestro

DON GERÓNIMO GIMÉNEZ

Estrenado en el TEATRO APOLO, la noche del 16 de No-
viembre de 1899

❋

MADRID

R. Velasco, Imp., Marqués de Santa Ana, 20
Teléfono número 551

1899

1899

6. Cover page of *La familia de Sicur*, a one-act comic piece with music, by Javier de Burgos, based on his earlier work, *Las cursis burladas* (1881).

Millán Contreras believes the heart of the story to be true, but rejects the medical student feature. Since 1880 the name of one particular medical student, that appears variously as Sarandeseo, Sarandeses, and Zarandeses, kept surfacing as that of the real inventor of the word *cursi*. Millán Contreras researched the Cádiz guidebooks of the period, which at that time also listed the names of residents, but found no doctor or professor of medicine, he says, with the surname "Zarandeses."

Less than two months later, he received a reply from one Francisco Arias de Velasco y Sarandeses, who wrote back that the name was "Sarandeses" and not "Zarandeses" and that he should know, being the grandson of the person in question. Rafael Sarandeses, his grandfather, he claimed, was a medical student from Oviedo, who spent the years 1835 and 1836 in Cádiz at the Colegio de Cirugía.[43] He returned to Asturias in 1840. (What he did in between those years is not mentioned.) Witty and clever at social gatherings, Sarandeses also belonged to a clique of medical students who delighted in performing verbal surgery on the unsuspecting. This in itself was not unusual since medical students in the nineteenth century (and earlier periods) had a reputation for playing practical jokes and for being irreverent punsters. Sarandeses and his friends liked to speak metathetically, a kind of pig latin delivered in Spanish. When Sarandeses saw the pretentiously dressed Sicur sisters strolling by one day, he immediately went into syllabic reversal and created "Cursi." That, at least, is how the story went in the annals of Arias de Velasco's family history.

Given that Sarandeses was Asturian, lived in Cádiz for only two years, and probably boarded out, it is not surprising that his name—with or without a "Z"—may not have appeared in the local guidebooks. But what about the Sicur family itself? According to Ramón Solís, the family's existence is beyond dispute: "The story of lo cursi comes out of Cádiz circa 1835–1840, and the protagonists were the Sicour girls, daughters of a French tailor who lived near Mirandilla." He adds: "our grandparents could give us all the details about the goings-on of these señoritas, of their walks through Mina Square and their showy dress" ("La cursilería"). He also says that, from about 1870 on, the word *sicur* is used as a synonym for cursi in Cádiz. At this point in time, he argues, fear of wounding the susceptibilities of family members no longer existed—hence the open use of *sicur*.

From an etymologist's point of view, namely Corominas's, however, the connection remains suspect. "Is 'Sicur' a real name?", he asks skeptically. "If so, it is extremely rare" in Spain (2:301). But apparently it is not so rare in France.[44] Federico Rubio, renowned for his medical practice, remembers how *cursi* was pronounced when he was a child in Cádiz in the 1830s: "*Curr . . . sii!* (which was how it was pronounced originally and in my time, prolonging the 'r' of the first syllable and the 'i' of the second a great deal)" (55).[45] The initial pronunciation and accentuation of *cursi* still mimic the original French.[46] By 1861, the word has acquired its definitive sound and accent, to judge from the way Pereda reproduced it in *Tanto tienes, tanto vales*, by placing a written accent on the letter "u" of *cúrsi*. It is impossible to know, of course, precisely when and how the term changed orally, but the abbreviated sound, in combining the crisp tone of the initial hard "c" with the weak, somewhat indeterminate sibilance of the second syllable "si," phonetically encapsulates the connotations of social critique, on the one hand, and inferiority, on the other.[47]

All of these accounts of *cursi* offer an explanation that replicates, in one way or another, the problematic status of the middle classes, in particular the petite bourgeoisie. An origin proposed for a word as semantically and symbolically loaded as *cursi*, is, in truth, not an origin at all, but an invention. Lo cursi in this narrative is thought up on the spot, metathetically improvised, becoming in the process symptomatic of middle-class cleverness, for there is nothing more representative of the professional middle classes than the medical student. On one level, the word really comes out of nowhere. Or, at the very least, it originates in the insubstantial and the inauthentic. The Sicur sisters, after all, aren't even Spanish in origin. They lack substance. They have neither the means nor the proper qualities of taste and nationality to be more than poor imitations of the real thing—even though it is never clear just what the real thing is. On the other hand, they make do with very little. They, too, like the medical student Sarandeses, improvise, changing a ribbon here, adding a piece of lace there, to give the impression of new clothes. They create style out of the insubstantial bricolage of new combinations of old, often worn-out, démodé things, which tend to be interchangeable and reversible.

Indeed, the cursi style sartorially, architecturally, literarily, and otherwise, quickly became identified with this capacity for combining and synthesizing elements to form mixed, hybrid shapes of culture and accumulating the disparate and incongruous as statements of ornamental redundancy (see Roland 43; Ichaso 153).[48] In his memoirs, for example, diplomat Augusto Conte recounts an anecdote of three impoverished señoritas cursis who by virtue of "ingenious combinations made it seem that two dresses alone were really four. In those days fur boas were all the rage, so they placed a trap on the rooftop and with it caught a sufficient number of cats to make out of their skins three of those adornments, which looked like sable" (Conte 1:71–72; see also Fernández Almagro, "¿Qué es lo cursi . . . ?").[49] Roberto Robert observes that there is always one piece of clothing or adornment, among the variously dated styles pressed together and worn by a señorita cursi, that was never stylish but rather "the personal and exclusive creation of the person using it." And he continues, "That piece is a revelation; it is the individual stamp of each woman; no cursi would copy another's" ("La señorita cursi" 84–85).[50]

Not only combinations, but substitutions and transpositions form the troped substance and identity of the cursi figure. Going back to the Sicur sisters, it is clear that they are reversible images: they are both SICUR and CURSI. One side is French, the other is Spanish. One side knows what elegance is. (After all, they are French!) The other side doesn't. A walking metathesis, the Sicur sisters show inventiveness by inventing themselves, but as Solís perceptively remarks, they were, alas, misunderstood: their sense of daring and rebellion against social stratification were taken at face value for mere imitativeness. Had these daughters of a French tailor belonged to a more distinguished social class, their new style might conceivably have become the rage of the season (see Solís). Indeed, one of the cursi narratives I mentioned earlier—the Tessi Curts—suggests that lo cursi might have originally been regarded in a positive light. The instability of the cursi sign proves even more pronounced here within the social frame of class differences. Yet it is not simply a sign, as Benjamin reminds us; lo cursi figures as a particular naming of things. Its instability does not negate the significance of names (or the naming) of things. A trope, we recall, is "the transfer of the name of a thing to something else " (Bredin 46). What "occurs in a trope," Bredin observes, "is not a change in the meaning of a word, but a change in the object to which it normally refers" (46). In this regard, the Sicur sisters reveal the possibilities and conditions for cultural reversibility, but not, I would maintain, for the merely arbitrary. The very concreteness of their historical circumstance and social category situates them within certain limits both practically and semantically.

This concept of invention, rather than origin, is rooted, of course, in the romantic notion of originality, a notion itself profoundly tied to middle-class attitudes and perceptions.[51] It is this proposed invention of the word *cursi* to which the distinguished etymologist Joan Corominas strongly objects. He begins by citing Emilio Lafuente y Alcántara's 1865 *Cancionero popular* as the first to document *cursi*, although we now know that the word already showed up in 1842 (if not earlier) and made appearances in 1849 and 1857. Lafuente claims that *cursi* comes from gypsy slang and notes that the word is difficult to explain "because of the vagueness of the concept" (2: 88). As far as I know, no one else has ever accepted this explanation.[52]

Although Corominas doesn't mention Silvela and Liniers's *Filocalia* (1868), it is instructive to read that this contemporary text on cursilería makes fun of the search for the etymological origins of *cursi*. After suggesting a series of remote and largely unconvincing connections between *cursi*, *Coryce*, *corucayo*, *corosuna*, *Cursianum*, *Corsiae*, *Corsia*, and *Cursus*, Liniers, the author of this section of the book, concludes "Why shouldn't the word *cursi* come from any of these islands, peoples, or colonies? But at the same time, why these and no other? And why any of these? These are the practical results one gathers from all the etymologies" (25).[53] Similarly, Roberto Robert begins his 1871 costumbrista sketch of "La señorita cursi" by saying, "A bad year for etymologists! Go on and stir up roots and word endings, shuffle together all you like Coptic and Sanscrit, Greek and Hebrew, see if you can figure out where the word came from" (83).[54]

Corominas suggests two possible etymological explanations: a derivation from the English word, *coarse*, via Gibraltar; or from *cursiera*, *guarniciones cursieras*, a term applied to a horse's regalia, as noted by Leonardo Argensola in a description of a tournament of 1630. In a later edition of his dictionary, Corominas, agreeing with Leo Spitzer, admits that these etymologies are unpersuasive, as is Spitzer's own suggestion that *cursi* is an alteration of *cursado*, "versado en cosas de moda" (versed in current fashion) (Spitzer 282–83). Then Corominas proposes a new solution: that *cursi* is derived from the modern Moroccan Arabic word, *kursî*, pronounced *kúrsi*, meaning a "wooden chair," and, in classical Arabic, "science, knowledge" and "wise, knowing." The chair in question was often an imposing one, made for solemn occasions and personages such as a sovereign, a bride or a professor.[55]

I find all of these etymologies unsatisfactory. First, no documentation links any of these words with the development of *cursi*. Second, the connections between the original meanings of these words and *cursi* are remote and unconvincing. And third, if cursi really does come from *coarse*, *cursiera* (derived from Fr. *coursier*), or *kursî*, all words that existed long before the nineteenth century, why is it that *cursi* doesn't appear until the 1830s?

This last point leads to my final objection: Corominas holds an indisputable authority as an etymologist, but all the proposed explanations lack a historical base. He refuses to take into account any of the anecdotal material suggested because for him these are mere stories ("leyendas" and "mitos"). He fails to see the historical substance that lies behind these narratives. One cannot explain a social and historical phenomenon like lo cursi solely through linguistic or narrowly defined philological means. Similarly, if one takes a late twentieth-century, postmodern stance, mere word play won't do either since it, too, leaves things like lo cursi suspended in a historical vacuum, a free-floating signifier. *Cursi* doesn't exist in the Renaissance or in the seventeenth century because it is deeply rooted in the nineteenth-century development of the middle classes and in the emerging awareness of modernity.

The etymological view of historically modern phenomena like lo cursi is based implicitly on the authority of filiation, of origins: one finds the beginnings of words in earlier words. This approach constitutes a perfectly valid and extremely helpful endeavor and needs no justification from me. The diachronic pursuit of the etymologist indeed generally lends itself to a historically informed analysis grounded on philological principles. But the histories of linguistic and social change may not always coincide. Nor do all social changes reflect consistent, continual evolution. There may be breaks, the abrupt emergence of something new. We can usually find explanations for the rupture, but they do not do away with the sudden appearance of a phenomenon or the fractured character of such a manifestation. Some explanations may not conform or limit themselves to the expected model of analysis, whether it be evidentiary, philological, or other.

Corominas rejects the anecdotal as philological evidence in the case of *lo cursi*, because, I suspect, he sees as incompatible the anecdotal and the historical. He relegates the former to a "pseudoetymological" myth or legend. Yet the anecdote not only constitutes the underpinnings of early historiography but continues to determine its practice formally, as Joel Fineman persuasively argues (50). The anecdote, he observes, "is the literary form of genre that uniquely refers to the real." As such, it constitutes a "*historeme* . . . the smallest minimal unit of the historiographic fact" (Fineman 56).

For Corominas, the anecdotal origin of *lo cursi* lacks legitimacy, but I would also suggest that it lacks origins, the structure of filiation. As with

Unamuno's *Niebla*, the cursi story appears out of nothing, out of an anecdotal mist, emerging from time, as Enrique Anderson Imbert lyrically expressed it, like the Sicur sisters, "almost pretty, almost plain, sliding out of time like slow serpents" (120).[56] The anecdotal shape of lo cursi possesses an almost timeless quality in that it seems situated *out* of time, even though the element of historical conditioning immediately challenges this image.

Not all observers of lo cursi reject the anecdotal explanation. Francisco Ichaso, for one, urges an open mind in such instances, especially when dealing with "popular words, formed by the people from something verbally concrete, sometimes capricious, but almost always loaded with sly common sense" (158–59; also see Holguín 134–35).[57]

Paradoxically, what emerges from the various retellings of the cursi story—including my own—is precisely this: an attempt to account for its origins by reconstructing the narrative frame of something that noticeably lacks origins. There exists in the apprehension and in the formation of *lo cursi* an element of change, a quality of contingency, in that the very occurrence of the word—as improvisation through metathesis or as association through metonymy—suggests alternate possibilities. Why *cursi?* Another term quite possibly would have served in explaining the complex social and cultural changes surrounding it. The particularity of lo cursi, in other words, paradoxically stresses its contingency. The historical often "happens," as Joel Fineman observes, because "the anecdote is the literary form that uniquely *lets history happen* by virtue of the way it introduces an opening into the teleological, and therefore timeless, narration of beginning, middle, and end. The anecdote produces the effect of the real, the occurrence of contingency, by establishing an event as an event within and yet without the framing context of historical successivity" (61). The anecdote forms part of *la petite histoire* that master narratives (*les grands récits*) utilize to create the seamless whole characterizing the historiographical gesture.

The cursi narrative, in this regard, functions as a small rupturing, or perhaps better said, produces a rupturing effect, which opens up the text of history. But the reality effect produced is based on a fractured narrative of identity, part of an antifoundational / foundational dialectic, or the origins of nonorigins. Such a notion must necessarily prove profoundly unsettling to a mind more accustomed to the continuities and unfolding evolutions of the philological project. It may not be mere coincidence that in the entry for *español* Corominas omits the Swiss scholar Paul Aebischer's 1948 explanation that "the term *español* is of Provençal and not of Peninsular origin, and that it did not appear south of the Pyrenees until the thirteenth century" (Rodríguez-Puértolas 120). Aebischer calls into question the traditionalist view of Spain as a clearly articulated national identity with clearly ascribed autochthonous and ancient origins.

Similarly, the cursi narration upsets our conventional notions of beginning, middle, and end since it seems to happen in medias res, appears to lack a proper beginning and a definite closure. Yet this particular story really serves as a microtext of a larger narration, the history of Spanish history in the modern period. As an unwanted narrative signaling inadequacy and uncertain identity, however, lo cursi shadows the master narrative of Spanish history, revealing not only a flawed historiographical vision of modern Spain but the instability and inconsistencies of historical realities. Above all, within the frame of nation and national identity, lo cursi constitutes a marginal narration of the provinces that resituates the hinterlands as central and destabilizes the borders between center and margins.

From the beginning of the eighteenth century, with the accession of the French Bourbons to the Spanish throne, the ideal of a strong centralized state dominates the history of modern Spain. The creation of a modern, rationalized state apparatus, in which all roads led to Madrid, saw nineteenth-century constitutional, legal, and other reforms. The corollary functioning of caciquismo, in which local fiefdoms and spheres of influence were connected in a thickly woven web of political and familial relations and governance to the "big bosses" of the capital, reinforced the system, especially during the Restoration period from 1875 on. While dependence on Madrid created a kind of internal colonization on the periphery, provincial life did not simply languish, waiting passively to be jump-started into action by the capital, as David Ringrose, Peter Sahlins, and others have shown. The local histories of the provinces and provincial capitals, which need to be integrated into the larger narrative frame of Spanish history as a vital contribution to the making of modern Spain, demonstrate uneven, varied patterns of growth and stagnation, renewal and decline, that are affected not only by the influence of Madrid, but by international factors, rival provinces, and internal pressures promoting at different times change and retrenchment.

The history of Cádiz is illustrative of this uneven rhythm alternating between modernization and stagnation, a circumstance that undoubtedly fostered the incidence of cursilería. But as Ramón Solís has pointed out, there are also other reasons for examining more closely the connections between Cádiz and the cursi phenomenon. Middle-class insecurity and weak national identity pervaded Spain. Why would the cursi narrative first surface in this particular southern port city? Cádiz is remarkable for, among other things, having contributed three significant and interrelated concepts crucial to the understanding of modernity in Spain. These terms are: *liberal, romantic,* and *cursi* (see Solís, "La burguesía gaditana y el romanticismo" 102; 106). The site for the historic Cortes de Cádiz of 1810–12 and the first national constitution, Cádiz still resonates as a symbol of nation founding. Out of the heated debates and discussions of the Cortes emerged the word *liberal* as it is understood today, in the modern political, ideological sense and as a constituted political party.[58] Undoubtedly, the liberal mind-set of Cádiz's mercantile class, coupled with its long-standing openness to the foreign, provided receptive delegates of the Cortes a stimulating political and ideological forum.

The term *romántico* (and the related *romanesco*) surfaces in the lively literary dispute between the German consul of Cádiz, Juan Nicolás Böhl de Faber (father of novelist Fernán Caballero and husband of feminist and Catholic traditionalist Frasquita Larrea) and José Joaquín de Mora over the merits of Calderonian theater (see Pitollet). As Carnero, Solís (*Historia del periodismo gaditano*), and Flitter point out, this polemic— tied to German romanticism—set the stage for romanticism in Spain. The dispute also produced reverberations in the social sphere, a point to which I will return.

This interplay between the foreign and the indigenous is fundamental not only to understanding the appearance of words like *liberal, romantic,* and *cursi*, but to grasping the internal dynamic and development of Cádiz itself. The urban, commercial culture Cádiz produced beginning roughly in the mid-eighteenth century reflected a remarkable openness to, and assimilation of, foreign models. The years 1770 to 1820 mark the high point of the city's prosperity and vitality. Indeed, the periphery, especially Barcelona and Cádiz, proved far more dynamic demographically and economically than Madrid during this period (Reher, *Town and Country* 42; also Fernández Pérez). After the loss of the colonies, however, decline and periodic crises punctuated the rhythm of Cádiz's local history, although historians dispute the overall pattern of decline. And a good case can also be made for continuity and development (Cirici Narváez 42; Millán-Chivite, "Revolución política" 133). In this sense, historiographic interpretations of Cádiz's history with respect to its global historical patterns run parallel with those of modern Spain as a whole.

Cádiz in this period was both like and unlike the rest of Spain. A curious dyssynchronicity, much remarked by local historians in particular, placed Cádiz in the position of cultural and economic forerunner in the development of a middle-class ethos and way of life in Spain. Lively trade with the colonies, the influx of a considerable foreign population—Italians, French and English, especially—and a constant cultural-commercial interchange with other countries and foreign nationals had created in Cádiz a prosperous mercantile class that prided itself on being both utilitarian and cultivated. Indeed, the cultivation of good taste and the externals of wealth, good breeding, and refinement were considered inseparable from utilitarian goals. Well-off families sent their sons to England to receive education not only in another language but in another culture. This kind of education was thought of as a good investment for the future. As Solís observes, "A merchant's son doesn't inherit goods but credits and commercial possibilities" ("La burguesía gaditana y el romanticismo" 100).[59] A good education, the cultural and commercial knowledge wrapped up in English, contributed to the furthering of such credit.

Clear handwriting served as one indication of a young gentleman's social and business standing. For this, the English style of penmanship was recommended. In 1841, for example, photographer Jorge W. Halsey promoted the English method in his book *El pendolista universal* [The universal penman], in a local newspaper during a brief stay in Cádiz (Oslé 13–14).[60] The Colegio de San Felipe Neri, founded in 1838 largely by *indianos*, Spaniards who had returned home rich from the Americas, was intended to prepare middle- and upper middle-class young men for

70

practical careers, but especially for commerce (Rubio 249). Academician Eduardo Benot noted in 1886, "Do you know why that school [the Colegio de S. Felipe Neri] was the best? Because there they taught the English style of penmanship and fractions and decimals, besides" (qtd. in León y Domínguez 13).[61] The Colegio, whose first director was poet Alberto Lista, provides a good example of the impact that the local bourgeoisie and its values had on Cádiz and elsewhere, for it quickly became the school of choice for many families. Lista's *reglamento* for S. Felipe Neri served as the model for the establishment of many Spanish *colegios* well before national reform plans in education went into effect (León y Domínguez 12; also Rubio 266, 271).

Enrique Tierno Galván also connects the middle-class business practice of using the English cursive hand (*cursivo*) to the origins of cursilería. I will have more to say about this in the next chapter, but for now I want to emphasize how Cádiz was both provincial and urbane in the early nineteenth century. It was also both local and foreign. Indeed, what defined Cádiz was this cultural "mestizaje," as González Troyano calls it, an unstable and continually changing mix of local residents, other Spanish provincials, and foreign nationals, of tradesmen becoming ennobled and the nobility going into trade. Practically surrounded by water, Cádiz lacked a strong agrarian base and the subsequent deep-seated conflict (and dependence) between city and countryside that characterized other parts of Spain. A less complex social structure, coupled with a certain social fluidity, made class mobility more likely in Cádiz. Domínguez Ortiz has argued that such social movement did not, however, signify a greater democratization, but a larger desire to free up the opportunities for acquiring a noble title and then retiring from trade (13). The peculiar nature of the aristocracy in Cádiz was, as Comellas García-Llera remarks, a two-edged sword: "It permitted titled persons and gentlemen to engage in commerce without dishonoring their class, but it also encouraged those who were really bourgeois to crave the lifestyles of the aristocracy" (23).[62]

Something like three-fourths of foreign nationals in 1860s Cádiz became naturalized citizens or married into Spanish families (Ruiz Lagos, *Ensayos de la revolución* 44), thus facilitating commerce and trade. A significant amount of Cádiz's commerce was, in effect, in the hands of foreigners or consisted of commission work for other businesses, often

located abroad. Reinvestment in local industrial enterprises was noticeably lacking. People in trade preferred to retire and settle on country
estates or in opulent town houses once they felt financially secure.

Foreign influence permeated the culture of Cádiz. Genoese businessmen, English sherry dealers, French café owners, dressmakers, tailors,
and hairdressers were plentiful (see Enciso Recio). Cádiz had more
bookstores in this period—there were twenty in the eighteenth century—and was better provided for in foreign publications than the rest of
Spain (Domínguez Ortiz 24–25). Local merchants designed their offices
"in the British style" and possessed personal libraries stocked with
copies of the *London Directory, The Banker's Almanack,* and *Lloyd's Register* (Aramburu 143–53). The sons of the bourgeoisie, whether they
went into trade, the sea, the law, or medicine, all learned English. Alfonso de Aramburu claims that English "would be frequently spoken at
home, because our province is perhaps the one place in the peninsula
where English is most spoken" (151).

The mixture of other Spanish provincials and foreigners, of new-
comers and nouveaux riches, of old and new titled families, made for an
ebullient, cosmopolitan society in which commercial and social life were
deeply, and inevitably, intertwined and mutually interdependent. Cosmopolitan assimilation of foreign models did not mean, however, that
resistance to the foreign had disappeared. The story of the Sicur sisters
serves as a reminder that ambivalence toward foreign influence existed
side by side with assimilation.

Several years before the first print appearance of cursilería, another
social phenomenon, closely related to it, demonstrated a similarly conflicted attitude toward the foreign, which was more and more often
identified with the new and the modern. I refer to the figure of the piri, a
locally produced dandy who appears around 1817 in Cádiz. Unlike the
eighteenth-century petimetre, the piri, defined as an "hombre elegante"
(a man of elegance) in Adolfo de Castro's *Diccionario de voces gaditanas*
(xv), does not appear to be associated with the Court or the capital.[63] The
piri figure adopted the modern dress and manners soon to be associated
with the romantic movement in Spain, but he defended classical French
theater over the less rule-bound Spanish Golden Age dramas.

Eventually, the piris and the *antipiris* were drawn into the dispute over
Calderón. Oddly, it was the conservative German Böhl de Faber who

defended the Spanish theater of the Golden Age—sometimes under the pseudonym of the "Antipiri" (Solís, *Historia del periodismo gaditano* 93)—while the reformist-minded, liberal José Joaquín de Mora and the piris sided with the classical French model. The polemic itself, rather than the prevailing of either side of the argument, was instrumental in contributing toward the growing awareness and formation of romanticism in Spain. The participation of piris and antipiris discloses a wider social and political context than historians have usually attributed to the Böhl de Faber–Mora polemic, and it suggests how potentially disturbing the implications of coming modernity might have been to early nineteenth-century Spaniards. For what antipiris disliked especially in the piri was his affected, presumably effeminate appearance and behavior, as the beginning of this verse satire from 1819 reveals: "The Piris, with all their makeup, / are made up of the two sexes" (qtd. in Solís, *Historia del periodismo gaditano* 109).[64] And in an exchange between a piri and an antipiri also quoted by Solís, a piri is labeled an "anfibio," or amphibian, suggesting, again, ambiguous gendering (108).

Like the earlier eighteenth-century petimetre and the dandy, the piri was suspect.[65] He didn't wear traditional male dress; he overfocused on self and appearance; he was attuned to fashion and change. Printed attacks on the piri figure continued into the 1820s in Cádiz (Solís, *Historia del periodismo gaditano* 263). For the antipiris and traditionalists, the piri was neither sufficiently masculine nor sufficiently Spanish. Could the piri be considered an antecedent of the cursi figure? Probably not. There is no linguistic or etymological connection that I can see. The piri, moreover, is socially well-off, more akin to the señorito in this respect than to the often economically disadvantaged cursi figure. Yet the antipiri strategy of questioning gender and identity in the piri reappears, in much altered form, in the critique of cursilería. The attributes of weakness, inferiority, and inauthenticity perceived in lo cursi are consistently associated with the feminine and the foreign, as a projection of unwanted traits and undesirable change.

The 1842 article that Ramón Solís discovered describes a male cursi figure who stands out for his irritating, gauche social behavior in public places like the theater, the bullfight, and dances. "He is a pain in the neck at any gathering, a perfectly useless creature in good society," complains the presumably anonymous critic, who begins his article with these words: "It certainly isn't the most difficult or bothersome task finding a *cursi* in our streets; there is a veritable plague of them in my town" (see Appendix).[66] This early usage of the term coincides with the first modern instances of the *señorito*, a social category that appears as the disentailment of lands under Mendizábal and, later, Madoz, as well as other legal and economic reforms, contributed to the creation of a new middle class in 1840s Spain (see Marichal; Tierno Galván 90). A possible association with the piri may also have lingered.

But what had happened in Cádiz that produced such a proliferation of cursilería? By the 1830s, when the story about the Sicur sisters is circulating, Cádiz was in steep decline, having suffered heavy economic and subsequent demographic losses from the cutoff in colonial trade and repression and reprisal for an attempted liberal uprising, for which Fernando VII removed Cádiz's competitive *puerto franco* status as a free warehousing port. The wealthy mercantile class had fallen on hard times, into the discreet poverty of decaying gentility, and was soon to be replaced by a much less endowed, far more economically unstable, new middle class of functionaries and bureaucrats. The cultural halo of Cádiz began to dim, an indication perhaps of a weak cultural infrastructure, as one historian suggests (González Troyano 35).

This picture of decay becomes a leitmotiv in the impressions of foreign travelers to Cádiz, as a sampling of British commentary reveals. Richard Ford in his *Hand-Book for Travellers in Spain*, reflecting a visit in the 1830s, is pitiless: "Cádiz is soon seen; it is purely a commercial town. Mammon is now its Hercules; it has little fine art: *les lettres de change y sont les belles lettres* . . . poverty has damped the gaiety, and the society, being mercantile, has always been held low by the uncommercial aristocracy and good company of Spain; where men only think and talk of dollars, conversation smacks of the counting-house. Cádiz is now a shadow of the past" (318). It is helpful to remember that Ford's father was Sir Richard Ford and that his comments reflect aristocratic tastes and values. But George Borrow, protestant Bible seller extraordinaire, also accentuates the decline of Cádiz as seen in 1839:

It was once the wealthiest place in all Spain, but its prosperity has of late years sadly diminished, and its inhabitants are continually lamenting its ruined trade; on which account many are daily abandoning it for Seville, where living at least is cheaper. There is still, however, much life and bustle in the streets, which are adorned with many splendid shops, several of which are in the style of Paris and London. The present population is said to amount to eighty thousand souls. (695)

In 1850 William George Clark writes dismissively: "A man who cares for anything else, art or architecture, will find little to detain him at Cádiz" (253). Hugh James Rose in 1877 laments that "the trade of Cádiz is fast declining" (*Among the Spanish People* 1:210), undoubtedly a reflection of the hard times the port city had suffered after the financial crash of 1866. "Cádiz has fallen greatly from what she was of yore," he says (2:59). In 1884, Frances Elliot in her *Diary of an Idle Woman in Spain* writes: "who in the world cares to come to Cádiz?" (24). And, the coup de grâce: "Give me a week at Cádiz and I should die!" (25). The Italian writer de Amicis remarked: "But time has done something worse than take from Cádiz its ancient monuments. It robbed her of commerce and wealth, after Spain lost her possessions in America; and now Cádiz lies inert on her solitary rock" (344).

But not only foreigners saw the decay. Francisco de Paula Madrazo in 1849 wrote, "Cádiz was in happier times, when the fleet came in loaded with the gold of America into our harbor, the cradle of luxury. . . . Today no more. Times have changed; families have been transformed; fortunes have disappeared in some cases. . . . a modest, retiring life has substituted in many homes a previous existence of ostentation and pleasure" (*Dos meses en Andalucía* 40–41).[67] In a word, Cádiz was turning provincial. Conditions were ripe for the emergence of those shadowy young ladies of uncertain pedigree and of that ill-defined, third social class of "more mechanical occupations," who appear in the same Madrazo text.

Cádiz was still struggling to recover its former economic and cultural splendor on the eve of the September Revolution of 1868. Throughout Spain (and Europe), the financial crack of 1866 had hit banking and business in general very hard. In addition, a cholera epidemic struck in 1865; and in the surrounding province of Cádiz, a bad harvest coupled with depressed prices in the wine industry made things even worse. Money became scarce, credit bad. In 1866 the French consul of Cádiz (1862–80), P. Benedetti, wrote in his reports back home: "The most plausible explanation for this progressive ruin of Cádiz's commerce is found first of all in the weakening of its credit. . . . one cannot hide the fact that our standing is, even in Spain, the worst of the entire peninsula. Cádiz's paper is the most discredited at the Madrid Stock Exchange, and few persons nowadays would dare accept it" (qtd. in Sánchez Albornoz, "Cádiz, capital revolucionaria" 92).[68] A year later, he noted, "Credit is practically nil in Cádiz" (qtd. in Sánchez Albornoz, "Cádiz, capital revolucionaria" 108).

Corrupt speculation and other illegal business practices, meant to keep things afloat, were rife at the Banco de Cádiz and Crédito Comercial in particular, ending in bankruptcy and general panic. Families of all social categories in Cádiz were sorely affected. There was a run on the banks and violence in the streets, followed by military intervention. A state of siege was declared, and the press was muzzled on the subject (Sánchez Albornoz, "Cádiz, capital revolucionaria" 95–96). The situation had not much improved by the late 1870s. In a report from 1879, Benedetti deplores the alarming "commercial decadence" of Cádiz (Sánchez Albornoz, "Cádiz, capital revolucionaria" 107). Entire families were abandoning the city and moving to Madrid in hopes of bettering their prospects. By the early 1900s, there were fewer people in the city than there had been at the end of the eighteenth century.

The fin de siglo image of Cádiz was by then largely folkloric in literature and the arts, and, in that sense, dismissive of the city's historical significance, as Luis Fernández Cifuentes has remarked in his introduction to Palacio Valdés's representative 1896 novel *Los majos de Cádiz* (28). But the status of the provincial and the provinces in nineteenth-century Spain could not be so easily shrugged off. The tension between center (Madrid) and margins (the provinces) would become a national political issue by the early twentieth century. Regions like Catalonia and Galicia, and even less politically active provinces like Granada (see chapter 8), clamored for more recognition of what had been, arguably, the heartland of Spain all along.

Marginalized and provincial, Cádiz had passed into history. But the stage was set for another entrance: cursilería.

CHAPTER TWO

Adorning the Feminine, or the Language of Fans

IN A SEMINAL STUDY from 1952, Enrique Tierno Galván suggested that *cursi* derived from *cursivo,* or cursive, that is, handwriting. One particular style called the English hand, used predominantly in commerce and accounting, vied with earlier forms of handwriting in Spain for more generalized usage. The struggle for dominance between two systems of penmanship, on the surface seemingly of little importance, points to a deeper conflict between two sets of attitudes. The traditional Spanish script was associated with aristocratic values of prestige and class, while the English cursive hand, imported like other products through the channels of commerce, pointed to a freer, less class-bound value system based on exchange and movement. Popularized by Ramón Stirling's 1837 *Método para aprender a escribir en pocas lecciones, con rapidez y elegancia la letra mercantil o inglesa* [Method for learning how to write, in only a few lessons, the English or mercantile hand, with rapidity and elegance], and increasingly adopted by the nascent Spanish middle classes sometime during the 1840s (Cotarelo y Mori 1:68, 2:261–62), the English cursive style soon became metonymically identified with a social class criticized for its social and cultural pretensions, its lack of a centuries-old specific history and roots, and its consequent deep-seated insecurity. As the signature of the Spanish middle classes, the chiaroscuro flourishes and swirls of the cursive hand seemed to suggest to some an overall design of inconsequentiality, pretension, and weakness; to others it represented a sign of non-Spanishness. The provincial señorito became a prototype of this class: as recreated in Palacio Valdés's 1881 novel, *El señorito Octavio,* for example, he was an intellectual and social snob, somewhat effeminate, and his handwriting was a "magnificent English hand" (63). Another social type associated with the English hand was the lady writer, or *literata,* as Pedro María Barrera notes in a satiric sketch: "[The lady writer] learns to write in the English hand because it is a more distinguished form than the Iturzaeta style" (361).[1]

The initial adoption of *la letra inglesa* in Cádiz and throughout Spain (and the continent) was considered forward-looking and practical, especially for business. The eighteenth-century English running hand, further refined in the nineteenth, essentially followed English seaborne trade and exports (Fairbank 22–23). The mercantile style of writing—considered economical and speedy—has, since the Florentine period of the Renaissance, been seen as distinct from humanistic script. Florentine merchants wrote in the vernacular, using a hand that promoted privacy, the keeping of family secrets within the pages of account books and national documents. Humanists wrote in Latin, emphasizing legibility in their script (see Jed 13–14, 64, 74). While the linguistic distinction has since disappeared everywhere, the social one had not in the nineteenth century. Legibility, however, in this period became a commercial virtue, perhaps indicating a greater need for faster communication within a more public venue in an age of international trade.

The significance of this new handwriting, which first appears associated with Cádiz, has to be seen within a larger context than the port city itself. In Spain, the introduction of this more practical hand sometimes met with resistance from proponents of a script that would possess an intrinsically Spanish character. Handwriting became politicized, assuming nationalistic traits. Thus, for example, Vicente Naharro's *Arte de enseñar a escribir cursivo y liberal* [The art of learning how to write a cursive, liberal hand] (1820), written in 1818, was censured and did not see publication until the more liberal period of constitutional monarchy in 1820–23. Naharro dedicated the book to parliament (las Cortes Generales), judging his work to be under "the protection of the *Cortes,*" that is, the constitution. The association made between cursive and liberal is a slippery one. Naharro obviously referred to the running hand style with linked letters (not unique to the English hand) and to a freer, more open form of handwriting, hence the term *liberal.*[2] The expression *cursivo y liberal* is a stock phrase in penmanship manuals. But the author's politically liberal views, for which he was later persecuted (see Castañeda y Alcover 397–98), also clearly come into play here, as the dedicatory signed by "Citizen" Naharro attests (vi).

That cursivo and liberal were viewed as ideologically related is seen

in a curious, anonymously authored pamphlet called *Gerigonṣa liberalesca* [Liberal folly] from 1823, in which the writing of liberals is satirized as difficult to decipher intellectually and linguistically. In a section
of the pamphlet entitled "Ensayo de un diccionario neológico para inteligencia del lenguage revolucionario, formado de lo más selecto de los
periódicos y folletos publicados en la *luminosa* época de la *libertad*" (A
dictionary of neologisms essayed for understanding revolutionary language, taken from the most select of newspapers and pamphlets published in the *luminous* age of *liberty*), liberal jargon is placed in italics to
emphasize the point. Here, *cursivo* refers to the practice of italicizing,
not to handwriting, but the linkage between the two terms nonetheless
remains.

The ideological agenda behind handwriting goes back farther than
this. According to Tamar Herzog, in the eighteenth century Spaniards
identified foreigners not only through accent and surname but also
through the forms of their signatures (14). The calligrapher Santiago y
Palomares, whose own method of penmanship was often cited as exemplary by later practitioners, in his 1776 *Arte nueva de escribir* [New art of
handwriting] praised "the UNIFORMITY of a distinctive national Character, or Hand, as other nations have, and as we ourselves once had" (4).[3]
He attacks the bad taste of "a pseudo-round hand," which for him represents barbarity (5). One suspects his intended target is the English hand,
popularized by George Shelley, Charles Snell, George Bickham the El-
der, and others in the eighteenth century (Fairbank 22), although, as
Cotarelo y Mori points out, a form of the pseudo-round hand was used in
Spain prior to Palomares's *Arte* (2:139).

The debate over so-called national styles of handwriting spills over
into the nineteenth century. Like social manners and literary movements
and texts, handwriting became another sign of national identity. But
terms like *cursivo* and *liberal* show that the meanings attached to them
also tended to shift, proving as hard to pin down as the elusive national
Spanish character so vehemently sought by many. Thus Castellanos de
Losada in 1856 lambasted the prevalent English hand, claiming that it
quickly lost legibility, becoming so disfigured (*desfigurada*) that it wasn't
possible to read it: "For this reason it isn't used for deeds or protocols
that are necessarily kept in archives, merchants being those who most
utilize the hand, so much so that it can be safely said to be the official

handwriting in this particular social class" (199).[4] The "true national character" of Spain, he says, can only be found in the classic Spanish style of penmanship (*ell gallardo bastardo español*) still practiced by the Piarist Fathers and in officially adopted manuals like Iturzaeta's *Arte de escribir la letra bastarda española* (1827), where the English hand was much decried. Castellanos de Losada bases his argument on both national and class distinctions.

While some observers advocated adapting the Spanish hand to the English one, others would not compromise their position.[5] As late as 1896 attacks against the English hand continued to appear. Francisco Alcántara found English penmanship to be ordinary-looking and its adoption in Spain to represent a form of cultural betrayal of the nation:

Hemos abandonado la nuestra, gallarda y sobria . . . vibrante y alada en sus perfiles y ángulos, robusta y de sabrosa plasticidad en sus gruesos y curvas, firme y duradera como la huella de una garra poderosa y susceptible de reflejar por completo nuestro carácter, por la letra inglesa, redonda, fugaz, de pomposa elegancia, impropria de nuestros austeros gostos, hipócrita disfraz de las vaguedades del espíritu que quedan como congelados bajo el barniz de una distinción muy ajena a la vehemencia y libertad nuestras.

[We've abandoned our own style of handwriting, graceful and restrained . . . vibrant and wingéd in its angles and outlines, robust and delightfully plastic in its loops and curves, firm and lasting like the lines of a powerful claw, and completely capable of reflecting our character, for the English hand, round, fleeting, pompously elegant, inappropriate for our austere tastes, a hypocritical mask of the vagaries of spirit that lie congealed beneath the slick surface of a distinction that is very foreign to our passionate and independent character.][6]

Alcántara places the blame for this change on business practices and the legions of foreign governesses who had invaded middle-class and aristocratic Spanish families. One can scarcely find a sample of true Spanish penmanship, "picuda y enérgica" (sharp and energetic), he says; except here and there in the provinces is the rare woman whose carefully traced pen preserves the traditional flourishes.

Here, Alcántara equates *lo castizo* (traditional, authentic Spanishness) with the provinces. For him, it is city life—which he associates with commerce and the adoption of foreign customs and education—which is not only *not* Spanish, not genuine, but indeed, *cursi*, like the "cheap and tackily ornate furnishing [found] on the backstreets of our cities."[7] Worse to him, both the young girl of refinement and the lowliest of shop assistants or bookkeepers (*horteras* and *tenedores de libros*), their hands reddened by chilblains, use the English style of handwriting in the city, thus creating social confusion and contributing toward the breakdown of social hierarchies. He concludes his diatribe with these words: "Farewell, noble and true Spanish pen. Soon you will disappear even from the mailman's pouch, if the slow undoing of tradition [*descastamiento*] in this nation continues, as every day more and more of the things that most defined [Spain] in the world are allowed to fade away."[8]

This almost hysterical attack on the English running hand underscores how ideologically loaded both words and practices could become. The connection between English handwriting and cursilería is also evident, lending some credence to Tierno Galván's hypothesis that *cursi* comes from *cursivo*. It is enough to note that changes in middle-class life manifested themselves even in something as apparently unimportant as handwriting styles. Handwriting, as Tamara Plakins Thornton has pointed out, "is important . . . because it mattered to people in the past, in ways deeply embedded in their cultures. And it carried larger meanings and served broader functions; in particular, it embodied, regulated, and generated notions of the self" (x).

Significantly, the English hand was associated with foreignness in general and with the inauthentic and the hybrid. In Alas's 1891 novel, *Su único hijo*, Serafina, the English-born opera singer, uses the English cursive style but writes polyglot letters, mixing English, Spanish, and Italian together. Bonifacio Reyes, on the other hand, adheres to Iturzaeta (187, 283). Captain Bedoya in *La Regenta* (1884–85) plagiarizes, copying down other people's words in a beautiful English running hand: "As soon as he saw upon his own paper the paragraphs which he copied in the neat, graceful copperplate hand [*letra inglesa*] that God had given him, he considered them to be all his own work" (130).[9] Thus a particular form of handwriting associated with the foreign, the middle classes, and commerce, suggests not only shifts in meanings and nuances, but the adulterating of identities, national and individual. Alcántara linked la letra inglesa to lo cursi and the urban experience. Other observers, however, saw this writing practice as provincial, and therefore cursi.

Lo cursi, in this version of things, comes from a system of writing. As with the earlier explanation offered of cursi's origins, it is a kind of cultural text, or marker. In the case of the young ladies of Cádiz, we recall, an impoverished state had reduced the misses Sicur's gentility to a shabby appearance, which they vainly tried to disguise by switching and patching their old, out-of-style clothing (see chapter 1). This fooled nobody, and whenever they were spotted on the street, someone would cry out their name, meanwhile discreetly converting "Sicur" into "Cursi."

Whether this story, or Tierno Galván's version, is true or not holds little real importance. Indeed, I would argue for the legitimacy of *both* accounts of lo cursi—the metacritical and the anecdotal narrative— because both symbolically capture the fictive, fabricated nature of the phenomenon. What is suggestive is the narrative frame encapsulating these anecdotes about the word *cursi* (see Fernández Almagro; Anderson Imbert 120; Roland 47). Lo cursi tells us a series of stories about the shaping of one particular society. Studying such a phenomenon also illuminates the universal significance of these kinds of texts, namely, how ways of thinking are incorporated and composed as stories, especially those stories that point to human weakness and imperfection. The specific narrative context of lo cursi can be found not only in novels and other literary genres, but in anecdote, in objects, and in moments of significant cultural import.

By exploring the wider implications of Tierno's thesis, it is possible to see how writing and commerce make up a particular cultural sign, in which the external relationship between persons of the Spanish middle classes and objects of commerce increasingly overlaps and fuses with the internal relationship between these same persons and the identity of self (as in as handwriting). In this regard, handwriting, like other properties of the individual personality, becomes part of a larger system of "writing," which is the culture itself as it is represented and represents itself. It is to these texts of Spanish middle-class culture that I now turn.

From its very origins in anecdote, lo cursi clearly possesses a feminine identity (the Sicur ladies). Even the characters of cursive handwriting were considered by some delicate and coquettish, signs of their feminine nature (Tierno Galván 98, n. 14). The cursi quality of the middle classes would see translation into images of the feminine, thus underlining a perceived weakness. The feminization of middle-class society—in which women were important as domestic angels of comfort and powerless as political and economic forces—would find a symbolic corollary and enactment in certain genres such as the novel, in specific social behavior and settings such as the literary salon and the public outing, and in representative objects such as the album and the fan. These examples of cursilería, in turn, can be seen as spaces, cultural spaces in which Spanish middle-class society represented itself in a performance of images. This was especially the case in the last quarter of the nineteenth century.

Like all self-conscious, developing societies, Restoration Spain functioned in the display mode. The spectacle of Restoration life—while frequently the product of financial speculation—was more than mere exteriority; it was also specular, reflecting back the interior selves of a shifting social and historical order. What the spaces of lo cursi give as well is a narrative context generated out of middle-class desire. No one wanted to be cursi. To be found cursi was to be found wanting—that is, lacking and desiring at the same time. Lo cursi was the undesirable element in social and personal relations that, paradoxically, was based on desire. Call it a form of desired negativity, in that both the fear of being labeled cursi and the impulses behind cursi behavior moved Restoration life and culture forward—and backward—in complex, often ambiguous ways.

"The essence of *lo cursi*," wrote Leopoldo Alas (Clarín), echoing an earlier remark of Valera, "resided in the excessive fear of appearing to be so" ("Album-abanico" 257).[10] Lo cursi was a trap of unstable appearances, in which front and back, inside and outside, told different stories but came to the same conclusion, or accusation: cursilona! How could one avoid being cursi if the condition was to be found everywhere?

On the eve of the September Revolution of 1868, two young men, Francisco Silvela and Santiago de Liniers, decided enough was enough and, in mock outrage, together wrote *La filocalia o arte de distinguir a los cursis de los que no lo son, seguido de un proyecto de bases para la formación de una hermandad o club con que se remedie dicha plaga* [The love of beauty, or art of distinguishing cursis from those who are not, followed by a proposition for the formation of a society or club to remedy said plague] (fig. 5).[11] The *Filocalia* begins by squarely situating the phenomenon within public spaces like the Royal Academy, parliament, walkways, and social gatherings (7). But then metaphor takes over in this satire, generating a vast space of the imagination for lo cursi: "What is *cursería*? How far do the frontiers of this most powerful empire of *Corsia* extend, whose invading armies grow from one day to the next? . . . Where does the evil come from? How is it communicated and become contagious?" (8).[12] Significantly, the pathological metaphor becomes highly politicized in the conclusion of this derisive diatribe: "The empire of *cursería* is one of the dangers of revolution. It signifies the invasion of the masses into those terrains that are artistic, poetic, monumental, and sartorial" (26).[13] Liniers and Silvela attribute this ominous "invasion of the masses" to a growing democratization of culture, made possible by broader educational opportunities, large-scale mechanical production of art through photography, galvanoplasty, and lithography, and a book market flooded with cheap twopenny editions (22).[14] They stress that the word is modern and as a social disease, quite recent (22). While it is not clear precisely *who* constitutes the masses in the *Filocalia*, it is clear *where* they are. Not only are los cursis everywhere, they are also where they shouldn't be: outside their proper station or social sphere. The conservative stance of Liniers and Silvela is unequivocal here—lo cursi results from undesirable social displacements.

The authors of the *Filocalia* suggest two apparently diverging ways of perceiving lo cursi: as a specifically modern phenomenon, historically situated within a critical moment of Spanish history, and as an ill-defined, unbounded force of epidemic proportions. Historically, then, lo cursi is containable as a concept. But imaginatively, it remains uncontainable. Imaginatively, the empire of cursilería stretches out so far that the authors of the *Filocalia* feel constrained to offer a prize for the best "memoirs that contribute toward determining precisely the frontiers that separate *lo cursi* from the original, fashion from elegance and art" (57). What makes lo cursi contagious and spreadable is desire: "the fact is we think we know everything, see everything, desire everything, and there is this phantasmagoria of possessing everything: only, the gem is paste, the diamond fake, the gold a fool's, and the oak painted pine. . . . you catalogue artists, society chroniclers, gossiping gazeteers, secondhand dandies, you are all *cursi*" (23).[15]

The use of the term *phantasmagoria* is especially suggestive in this context. In English the word is first recorded in 1802, as probably deriving from the French *fantasmagorie* (1801) (*Oxford Dictionary of English Etymology*). In Spain, the first exhibition of these optical illusions made by a magic lantern, in which imaginary figures shift and multiply, diminish or grow in size through the projection of images on a screen, took place between 1805 and 1806. It was a popular entertainment for decades to come (Varey 29, 40–42). A mechanical contraption, the phantasmagoria projects fictions while giving the illusion of the real through movement and dimensionality. More accurately, it projects what the spectator desires to see: shades of romance, specters of horror, silhouettes of history. A product of the industrial revolution, the phantasmagoria disguises its material nature, uniting imagination with consumption, by providing a screen of emotionally satisfying substitutions. Eventually, as Terry Castle has pointed out, the word *phantasmagoria* shifted in meaning "from an initial connection with something external and public (an artificially produced 'spectral' illusion) . . . to something wholly internal or subjective: the phantasmic imagery of the mind" (29). Baudrillard would refer to this realm of bourgeois perception as a "phantasmatic logic" ("Ecstasy" 126). An object turns into a projection of desire. This transformation of things into representations of the inner needs of their owners or possessors intensifies in the latter half of the nineteenth century. As objects multiply and accessibility to them increases, the gap between the natural and the artificial widens, and lived experience takes refuge in private, controlled spaces such as the domestic interior, or what Walter Benjamin called "the phantasmagorias of the interior" ("Paris" 154; also see Ferguson 57–58). Objects become mediators of desire.

As Susan Stewart observes in her richly provocative study, *On Longing*, "the function of belongings within the economy of the bourgeois subject is one of supplementarity" (xi). It is a supplementarity that aims somehow to complete the owner of those objects. Nineteenth-century middle-class society throughout Europe and America found in the things and settings of culture something they had lost: themselves. Middle-class families had no long and illustrious genealogical history, and they no longer had immediate and direct contact with work as a bodily extension of themselves, nor security in the suspect scatology or occupation of making or exchanging money. I refer especially to the Spanish lower middle classes, or petite bourgeoisie, latecomers on the European scene and the inheritors of a traditional, historically grounded aversion to the forms of manual labor and usurious activity as a blood loss of prestige and status. This loss of identity is not, however, altogether a real one since the past of the Spanish middle classes is not only short but also unwanted. Over and over in texts of the last century members of the Spanish middle classes, like those of other national cultures, go about rejecting their class situation by imitating the more attractive models of the aristocracy and the French or other foreign cultures. They constructed their identities out of the artifacts of a specific culture, a culture belonging to the Other, to an otherness perceived as superior in prestige and status. While it is true that an appreciable number of Spanish families of the upper middle class or bourgeoisie had noble origins (see Cruz; Ringrose), even this group looked to the aristocracy and foreign manners as models of behavior and thinking. Madrazo's 1849 sketch of a shadowy third social class and innumerable references to the pretensions of a petite bourgeoisie in costumbrista articles and realist novels, however, point to less lofty origins and circumstances surrounding this particular social phenomenon. Thus social distinctions, arising out of what Baudrillard has called a "differential social logic," interact with those phantoms of subjectivity, those projections of the mind, in which everything is apprehended, everything is desired ("Ecstasy" 126).

This generalized desire—"todo se desea"—has to do in part with commodities, with the development of complex relations between persons and things, and with the way subjectivity transforms them. But what does one do when the object at hand is substandard, inappropriate, or inferior in relation to the feeling and imagination invested in it? A disproportion results, say Liniers and Silvela, between the ideal aesthetic effect wished for and the inadequate material means at one's disposal (12). In other words, lo cursi, or what Tierno Galván claimed was inherent to lo cursi: an "inner poverty of meaning" (99), but which, I would suggest, is not really empty. The insufficiency of lo cursi—its second hand, cheap materials (the signifier)—is impoverished, but, paradoxically, this same insufficiency carries with it a multitude of meanings (a host of signifieds). What lo cursi means, then, brims over with a superfluity of significance. Tierno Galván is right, of course, in one important sense. An object or a person or a form of behavior labeled cursi lacks depth, substance. Aesthetically, it offends. Yet judged from within, that is symbolically, lo cursi becomes a veritable treasure trove. As a symbolizing structure, lo cursi reveals a great deal in anthropological and sociological terms about the inner worlds of the nineteenth-century, middle-class mind.

Moreover, one cannot isolate lo cursi like a virus or a bacterium. As the *Filocalia* notes, it isn't an "absolute idea" or an "essential thing" but "a derived quality, an idea of relationship that varies according to the terms with which it is compared." (11; see also Tierno Galván 100).[16] In its relational configurations, lo cursi inescapably leads one to consider it not only as class-determined (i.e., superior / inferior), but as a cultural index of the fluctuations between public and private, inner and outer, visible and invisible, self and Other, self and world. Detection of lo cursi represents the public exposure of inner needs, insufficiencies, and weaknesses, at the same time as it suggests a rich dreamworld of frustrated aspirations projected onto an external screen of things and other forms of cultural capital. Such projections constitute a form of narrative, the narrative of desire.[17] It is in the story of lo cursi wherein we observe most clearly the gap between signified and signifier, between the means and the end results, between the dream of authenticity and the reality of imitativeness. The loss implicit in lo cursi thus refers paradoxically to an unexperienced one.

The variability of *lo cursi* that Silvela and Liniers already detected in 1868 makes this term semantically overcoded. Because *lo cursi* possesses many meanings and shapes, it is an overdetermined cultural referent. The word is untranslatable precisely because of the varied and changing nature of the image that *lo cursi* projects within a specific national and historic context (see also Holguín 131). Hence Valera calls it "so vague and indefinable that it depends almost always on one's personal criterion whether one finds it or not in others. What does commonly occur is that the accusations are mutual" (*Pasarse de listo, Obras completas* 1:485).[18]

The *Filocalia* speaks of the invasiveness and contagion of lo cursi, as though it were legion and porous. Not one virus, but many. The mutable and varied character of lo cursi suggests a shape of culture and not a cultural form, to use the distinctions Thomas McFarland has outlined in his *Shapes of Culture*. In other words, lo cursi does not present itself as a rectilinear, clear-cut form; it possesses an amorphous, shifting series of shapes, sometimes small and feminine, sometimes elaborate and profuse, marked by accumulation and bewildering heterogeneity. It is a trope for the uncertain, the partially formed, the nebulous, all traits expressing problematic identities, both individual and collective. Restoration Spain is on the verge of modernity, and the unity and stability of its earlier cultural profile are coming apart. "Shape is what is left," observes McFarland, "when form breaks down" (3). If form "suggests something definite and linear, Euclidean . . . shape, on the other hand, suggests something more amorphous and less privileged" (1). Fear of lo cursi is fear of loss of form.

Consider, for example, the shapes of the album and the fan. By shape I refer not only to their physical properties, but to their cultural configurations as well. Culturally and physically, these objects belong to the realm of the feminine. As the frequent object of satire, they are also lodged in the domain of cursilería. For its analogies to the book, the album, a heterogeneous collection of autographs, verses, drawings, and musical compositions, possesses an outer unreadable surface and an inner secret life that can be interpreted as the manifested signs of its owner's personality. Like the album, the fan also expresses a kind of intimacy, the intimacy of ownership and symbolic projection of the self. While both artifacts have high exchange and display values, their use value remains minimal. Both are symbolic extensions of the body, attached figuratively and otherwise to the hand by writing and movement. Notice what one expert says about the fan: it "had a personality which expressed the moods and customs of its owner as no other species of adornment could do. It was almost part of the costume, yet, not being attached to the dress, it could be closely examined and admired in a way that would have been impossible where part of an actual garment was concerned" (Percival 19). In allowing intimacy without risk, the fan euphemistically expressed sexuality, as the delicate wording of this quotation suggests. Association with the disempowered and undervalued feminine sphere also meant, however, that such objects carried ambivalent, even contradictory meanings: interiority on the one hand, and superficiality on the other.

To see how such conflictive interpretations could be attached to seemingly unimportant objects is to look at them as cultural texts scripted with a specific performative and representative syntax. One is cursi. But one also acts cursi. As symbolic constructs, objects like the fan and the album that have become "cursed" by cursilería present themselves through an "acting of images," to use anthropologist James Fernandez's phrase (216–17). They project desires through an insufficient narrative frame, so that what is told or created seems inauthentic. But the attention paid to the individual elements within the text—the details, the ornamentation—reveals a yearning for the firsthand experience, for the genuine article. The overloaded details of Francisco Bringas's hair picture in the form of a cenotaph, for example, create a ludicrous effect on the reader of *La de Bringas*. His *trabajo de pelo* is cursi art refined to its limits. The microscopically small dimensions of the mourning object, crammed with details made up of human hair, practically implode with the heaped-up desire for accuracy and realistic precision. Don Francisco literally splits hairs to achieve the desired effect. This verbal artifact embodies the trace of the real, a verbal hairline split, pasted and squeezed onto a text-object. Don Francisco confuses the real as material (the strands of hair) with the real as effect.[19] Nevertheless, in another sense, these details are not superfluous. As Susan Stewart puts it, "the ornament does not dress the object; it defines the object" (28).

Adornment marks the process of individuation and refinement characteristic of middle-class life (Stewart 28–29). Thus in realist narrative, description, for example, constitutes a kind of adornment meant to individualize characters and to establish differences by attending to meticulous detail and shading. But what happens when adornment is gendered within this system of values?[20] Traditionally, prestige, status, and authority have resided in the male sphere. Like children and other marginalized groups, women have had little authority (see Ortner and Whitehead 8). Until recently, the absence of female role categories has also signified the absence of individuation. The assimilation of lo cursi to the feminine produces curious results: adornment becomes an essential feature of nonindividuation, of a stereotypology of the feminine, in which women are defined—and text-contained—metonymically as cursi objects. Reduction of the feminine through the trope of the miniature conversely enlarges the significance of lo cursi. That significance is almost always negative, given the critical, ironic perspective from which it is most often judged and given the disproportion between means and results in the cursi object / text. One could say that lo cursi represents a kind of polarized desire: frivolous and inadequate on the one hand, yet intimate and sexualized on the other.

The question of its representational size in the text proves a key notion to understanding lo cursi. "Aesthetic size," writes Stewart, "cannot be divorced from social function and social values" (95). Smallness of size, coupled with feminine features, denotes intimacy, privacy, interiority. It suggests the world of the bourgeois domestic interior, a space largely viewed as a feminine achievement (see Lukacs 624; Rybczynski 75; Saisselin 67–68). When this cultural space comes under the gaze of male writers, however, intimacy is converted into a series of texts in which the resulting tension between euphemism and irony suggests an ambivalent posture toward the domestic and the feminine. But texts that are cursi in themselves—and they are legion—are written almost entirely in the language of euphemism, miming domesticity as feminine virtue. The feminine is flattered and yet made inconsequential by the writer's refusal to come to grips with temporality, history, and death. Language veils the real, placing a screen in front of anything unacceptable or unbearable in human existence.[21] Take, for example, these words of Juan Tomás Salvany, a minor poet of the Restoration period:

> El abanico . . . objeto como *ellas* delicado y frágil, prenda que a imitación de su señora, ya se pliega receloso, ya ostenta toda su gentileza a nuestra vista, inseparable compañero de la dama que con donaire le maneja, orea, agraviando al céfiro, las mejillas de su dueño; juega con la sedosa cabellera; evapora acaso una lágrima importuna; oculta discretamente una sonrisa fácil; ahoga al exhalarse un suspiro impertinente, y arrulla con el blando rumor de sus varetas delicadas, los oidos del amartelado amante que herido de amor suspira.
>
> [The fan . . . an object like the *ladies*, dainty and fragile, an article that, imitating its mistress, now demurely shies away, now reveals

all its charms to our view, inseparable companion of the lady who waves it with grace, wafts the air, brushing against the zephyr, the cheeks of its owner; it plays with her silken hair; practically evaporates an inopportune tear; discreetly conceals the too-ready smile; holds back the mere breath of an impertinent sigh, and soothes with the soft swish of its delicate membranes the ears of the anxious suitor who wounded by love swoons.] (57)

Here, vaporous language ends up dematerializing the object at hand. Language itself becomes a kind of verbal fan wafting away the unacceptable, shielding the reader from unpleasant questions. The lack of critical distance between the textual subject and the writer converts the object described into pure adornment, a superfluidity of signifiers. But the paradox of verbal ornament remains: without it, the fan as a text-object would not exist. Yet with it, the fan lacks "body." The trace of the real has evaporated. What held the piece together for contemporary readers was sentiment.

Texts that critique lo cursi maintain that distance through irony. Even here, though, irony is in continual play with euphemism, creating a setting of complicity between the narrator and the text. The narrating voice of Galdós's *La de Bringas* springs readily to mind as a superb example of such complicity (see chapter 4). Yet the writings of Mariano José de Larra already provide readers with this ironic immersion in the spaces of bourgeois interiority. At this point I would like to examine one of Larra's essays, "El álbum," published in 1835, as an initial frame of reference for understanding lo cursi in a later text of the Restoration period, Clarín's 1898 story, "Album-abanico." Two points to note: "El álbum" evidently predates the generalized usage of the word *cursi*, although the term is coming into existence in Cádiz precisely at this time. Larra's essays coincide with the early stages of nineteenth-century middle-class life in Spain. Incipient cursilería is gestating in Larra's satiric vision of a quasi-society, bursting at the seams of its badly fitted pretensions.[22] The 1830s also mark a high point in the polemic over cursive handwriting, spilling over into the commercial and private worlds of Spanish society (Tierno Galván 84).

Finally, as Susan Kirkpatrick argues, Larra and his costumbrista colleagues undoubtedly played an instrumental role in creating a middle-
class reading public for their writing and thus preparing the way for the
reception of the realist novel as the quintessential middle-class genre.
The essay on the album is no exception. Larra begins right away by
addressing the question of readership: "The writer on customs and manners does not write exclusively for any particular social class" (494).[23]
This is one more of Fígaro's tricky openings, since he writes this article
precisely for a middle-class female readership. His awareness of class
differences notwithstanding, Larra's claim that his article is meant to
instruct "the immense majority constituting this nation" (495), breaks
down fairly quickly in two ways. The initial explanation of the word
álbum assumes a highly developed linguistic competence and awareness
on the part of his largely invented readership. But more importantly, one
has to question whether a heavily illiterate society, without the means to
purchase luxury items like albums, could possibly work up an interest in
the subject of Larra's article. Moreover, on launching into the description
of his text-object, Fígaro's language rapidly turns prescriptive, as he
establishes the norms of the ideal album. "It should be, like men and
women themselves, on the outside bound in the latest luxury, and on the
inside, an utter blank . . . the most expensive, the most English, that
would be best."[24] As he recognizes the difficulties of acquiring a first-
class album in Spain, he advises the following: "I should point out that
one ought to be able to say: 'They just delivered the *album* I ordered
from London.' You can also say instead of London, Paris; but it's more
common, more ordinary. This is why we recommend to our ladies that
they say *London:* it comes out as easily as any other word" (496–97).[25]
    The advisory role Larra assumes toward women should not surprise
us in him. After all, he had already served as the director of a ladies'
weekly, *El correo de las damas,* for about six months in 1833 (Escobar
162). Like Mallarmé, who directed *La dernière mode* in 1874 and wrote
under a variety of pseudonyms in its pages (Bowlby 192), Fígaro instructs his female reader not so much in how to read or make sense of
fashion and fancies, but rather in how to read herself. More accurately,
first Larra reads woman as a text, as the album itself, so that she will
know what there is to read. But in reading this album-text, he turns
interpretation into script by writing out his instructions very clearly.

First, he physically connects the album to its feminine owner: "This would-be book is, like the fan, the parasol and the calling card box, an article entirely for the use of ladies. The well-dressed young woman without an album nowadays would be a body without a soul, a river without water, in a word, a kind of Manzanares" (497).[26] The album serves as feminine adornment, but as Larra's finely ironic language reveals, it is necessary adornment. Playing off the satiric tradition of the proverbially dry Manzanares river, he suggests to his female reader that she is lacking without such an item of refinement. In a more profound sense, the album provides a mirror of the owner's personality, thus supplementing externally some internal necessity or lack: "In its true capacity, it serves as a repertoire of vanity" (497).[27] Mutual vanity, of course, the owner's and the autograph signer's. Thus, Larra writes, the verses penned within the album's pages "are a series of springs where a single Narcissus stares and is reflected back" (498).[28]

The album as narcissistic text, as a phantasmagoria or white screen of projected wish fulfillment, also confers a mark of distinction on its possessor and signer. This distinction is a sign of status, plainly class-motivated, as Rémy Saisselin suggests: "In the old regime possession by nobility conferred cachet upon the work [of art]; in the bourgeois world it is the other way around" (xv). The "aesthetics of distinction" (Saisselin 6) converts luxury items into works of art and works of art into expensive bibelots. Why? Because it arises out of desire, the desire for the refinements of culture as a distinguishing sign of one's being. The real possibility of acquisition and possession fuels such desire. Larra clearly addresses a middle-class public with some buying power but relatively little family cachet—certainly not the aristocracy or the popular classes.[29] As an item of purchase—Larra even suggests where to buy it (Alegría's)—the album bestows distinction on the female owner. Significantly, Fígaro points out the economic value of the album: "the value . . . of an *album* can be considerable. A brush stroke of Goya, a caprice of David or Vernet, a fragment from Chateaubriand or Lord Byron, Napoleon's signature, all this can turn into a family inheritance in *album* form" (499–500).[30]

In the eighteenth century autographs of famous persons held no interest. The first sale of autographs did not occur until 1820 (Rheims 142; Thornton 86). Larra's remark demonstrates a new historical awareness of things as acquisitions, which can be bought and sold, even artistic things. He notes that the album craze, which had cropped up earlier around 1811 in Paris, is "a fad, recently arrived," a latecomer to Spain (499–500). The accent on the new is significant since market economies would increasingly renew themselves periodically by coming up with *nouveautés/novedades,* or new products. The album fad serves as an early example of such commodities exchange. Culturally, it even functioned by exchanging hands, by moving, in a literal sense, from one house to another. "The *album* isn't carried in the hand, but is transported by coach; the *album* and the coach are mutually dependent. . . . the *album* is also sent on ahead with the footman, from one place to another. And as it is always coming and going, there's always a footman to take it away. The footman and the *album* are as tutor and child" (497).[31]

The collecting of signatures and other marks of artistic prowess such as drawings, watercolors, poems, and musical compositions was the goal of this constant movement. The process of filling the white spaces of the album's leaves created a finished, personal product made up of other persons' thoughts and creative expressions about the album owner. The possessor of the album saw herself reflected in this composite of aesthetic otherness. A signature symbolically condenses in a small space the poet's originality; it is the mark of genuineness. Later, the collecting of such signatures would be considered a sign of cursilería in Spanish middle-class society (Liern 12; Taboada 7).[32] I would suggest that even at this early date Larra divined the problematic nature of the album enterprise. He recognized, first of all, the need for authenticity in such projects: "As the thing is to have an authentic keepsake, from that person alone, it is indispensable that what gets put down on paper be in the actual hand of its author."[33] But then he says, "an *album,* then, turns out to be a *pantheon* where a handful of notables come to be stashed away in the guise of loans given in advance to posterity" (498).[34]

A moment later he qualifies his remarks by substituting cemetery for pantheon, in which the interred signatures reflect a certain democratization of culture, the illustrious and the common having been buried together indiscriminately. Once again, Larra demonstrates an acute historical sense here, the sense of datedness. And he connects that datedness to the notion of economic worth and exchange, observing that album signatures are "loans given in advance" to posterity.

The mortuary metaphor also inscribes the album within a space of dead artifacts. Thus it serves as a reminder of the real nature of inanimate objects, that is, their material inertness. What gives life to the album is the accumulation of tiny bits of handwriting, remnants of personality and memories of second hand experience. These signatures are loans in this latter sense too, having been lent to the album owner, who invests in them a series of quasi-experiences—for the duration. Once the album is filled, it has served its purpose and tends to revert to its original inanimate or dead status. Larra's metaphor of the cemetery/pantheon has to be read in its relationship to size and time. We are witness to a miniaturized cemetery full of epitaphs without tombstones, that is, full of substitutions without substance. The time of the album is not historical time or even lived time, but the private, interior time zone of wish fulfillment, of an invented life destined for quasi-burial among quasi-epitaphs belonging to other names. In a word, the album presents us with its own narrative, a narrative written out literally in the form of prized signatures. But of course the plot line only makes sense to its owner.

Larra takes the dead album image to hallucinatory lengths. What are the pyramids, he says, but the Pharaohs' signatures writ large on the album of Egypt? What is history, if not an album where the peoples of the earth come to deposit their works (498)? He converts history into a grand text, but it is history petrified, fixed and buried forever. Larra sees humankind's irrepressible urge to leave its mark everywhere, as though handwriting were a form of immortality. We can detect a double message here. In comparing the pyramids and history itself to an album, the writer also ends up trivializing both. By the time he gets back to his advice for women, the reader is prepared for the final metaphor, woman herself as an album: "What is a beautiful woman but an *album,* at whose feet everyone who passes by deposits his tribute of admiration? What is her heart but an *album?* Forgive our presumption, but fortunate is he who finds in this kind of *album* all the pages blank! Fortunate is he who, though not the first (it's not always the early bird who rises) can at least be the last" (500).[35]

The ironic play between virginity, innocence, and the whiteness of the unfilled leaves of the album (from the Latin *albus,* white) further sexualizes the object under scrutiny. The poet—and Larra's narrating persona includes himself in this category—must summon up sufficient "fecundidad" (fertility) in order to leave something agreeable and flattering in the numerous "deposits" he is obliged to fill. Here is the female body converted into a writing surface, the blank page ready to be inscribed by the male poet (see Gubar). What is an album, Larra asks earlier in his essay. "*What is it all about?* It isn't about anything: just a book with blank pages" (497).[36]

The metaphor of woman as album arises out of a metonymic impulse. Larra first sees the album as a representative feminine object in contiguous relationship to its female owner. When he converts it into the female body, it retains a metonymic origin. The female owner is still viewed in her relation to the thing owned. This process in turn reduces the female body in size by equating it with a small object and, thus, with a part of an implied larger chain of metonymic signifiers, the system of cultural artifacts, of possessions, that define through the technique of adornment the middle-class female. In Larra's article, this adornment is a form of handwriting, a writing still attached to the body and to things. The album as object and as text is a form of narrative, a frustrated narrative in which the expression of self through handwriting never pays off. The album is called a woman's temple "hanging with all her trophies; it is her *royal purse,* her budget, or at least that of her *amour propre*" (500).[37]

Here, Larra reminds the reader of the classical origins of the album as a white tablet for inscribing registers, notices, and lists. The 1830s album, in contrast, recorded sentiments and at times even arranged secret amorous assignations (Lorenzo-Rivero 123–24). Fígaro, on the other hand, commercializes an object that is already a luxury item by associating it with remuneration. As the album exchanges hands, various "deposits" are made, a kind of investment in the lady's personal affects. The collected signatures are then saved, reflecting perhaps also a traditional savings economy in the guise of a collection. Once saved, however, the signatures are buried forever. Whatever they represented dies, hence Larra's metaphor of the cemetery / pantheon. The intimate connections between object and person, between object and meaning, are thus made doubly problematic as the natural and inevitable gap between them widens even more in the verbal graveyard Larra has dug for them.

Larra demonstrates the exaggerated inadequacy of language to be the thing it represents or to signify the original experience in his manipulation of size. The album image is first miniaturized as a pantheon of signatures, then magnified as the gigantic text of world history. The ensuing disproportion and incongruity of these images point to a consciousness of size and dimensions as a measure of culture. The attempt to squeeze culture into unseemly small proportions or outrageously large ones occurs as that culture becomes increasingly mediated, ever more distanced from its practitioners. The album as a cultural artifact lacks true experience. Its inner history or narrative is clearly manufactured. It isn't original, in either sense of the word. Indeed, as Larra humorously notes, composing fresh and appealing verses represents a real challenge for the poet, who contributes to several ladies' albums at the same time. For this reason album verses all sound alike, as Larra with finely tuned malice observes. "We have noticed that all the owners of *albums* are 'lovely,' 'gracious,' 'virtuous,' 'talented,' and 'ever so kind' " (498).[38] Every album poem is the same poem over and over again, with minor variations; and hence every album owner is the same lady praised and reproduced in an infinite series of repetitions known as clichés. At heart, the difficulties in being creative have to do above all with the writer—i.e., Larra's narrating persona—and not with the album owner. Fígaro obsessively returns to himself, here as elsewhere, in his concluding remarks concerning the demands made on a poet's time and talent.

I find especially apt the highly nuanced tone adopted by Fígaro, that intimately prescriptive yet frivolous, unserious voice of the fashion editor, a consummate ladies' man, who instructs women in the art of adornment while deconstructing the social and personal significance of that same adornment (the poet Bécquer will play a similar role). As fashion consultant, Larra's persona also binds his text-object even more closely to the world of commerce and the beginnings of modern advertising (remember his advice to buy at Algería's). Here, too, is the richly complicitous narrator of later realist fiction already emerging out of a specific cultural-economic "handwriting" intensely engaged with self and other, self and world. As handwriting, Larra's essay is tied inextricably to the body, figured through adornment and comportment. "Cum-portare," as Tierno Galván pointed out (81), is "llevarse con" (to carry with); comportment implies, thus, a special relationship between things and persons for defining behavior as well as a mode of being through the body's movements in space and time. In this sense, comportment is always "adorned" and always "moving."

This corporal movement constitutes the key symbolic figuration informing Leopoldo Alas's 1898 story, "Album-abanico" [The autograph fan]. Like Larra, Clarín capitalizes on a cultural practice devalued through the passage of time by repetition and inauthenticity. By the end of the century, the album and the autograph fan of this story had become risible objects of satire. Indeed, the notion of datedness incipient in Fígaro's essay is quite explicit from the very start of Clarín's story: "At the time when this true story of actual events begins, the album of verses and sketches was a pretty discredited thing, and the fan converted into an album, the height of lo cursi" (257).[39] An understanding of "Album-abanico" as figured through circulation hinges on a particular temporal framework that is suggested by a series of contextually dated cultural references. The intertextual substance of the story functions not simply as a sign of its literarity, but as a trope of cultural datedness in which things and persons become obsolete. Caducity, signifying the frailty of old age in humans and transitoriness in things and events, is stamped on this text in the form of writing as a narrative date of expiration.

Clarín packages his intentionally stale contents into a banal series of upper-class adulterous relationships and feminine inconsequence. The object of conquest, Julita Medero, alias la de Frondoso, practices the art of seduction with the same social skills that her lovers—nearly all artists, writers, politicians, and other ephemeral celebrities—demonstrate. The collected signatures on her autograph fan suggest at least two interconnected interpretations. The fan, as the guise for the more conventional album, registers Julita's social and sexual triumphs, thus taking on the literary function of the metaphor. As writing surface, however, the autograph fan assumes metonymical proportions by representing the female body and its inscription into a male-authored text. Julita's sexual adventures continue until she is too old to indulge in them. The experience is artificially and vicariously protracted when she passes on the practice of the autograph fan to her chaste daughter Luz. As the narrator comments, "What Julita Frondoso, a respectable old lady and very well preserved, was asking of the poet Ibáñez was, in effect, a few lines of poetry for Luz's fan. Luz also had an autograph fan, or more accurately, her mother had one in Luz's name" (266).[40]

By this time some twelve, possibly thirteen or fourteen, years have passed. Clarín, deliberately I suspect, makes fuzzy the chronological framework of the story, a narrative device intended to suggest the temporal in-betweenness of a lingering cultural usage fallen into social obsolescence. The attempt to date the piece internally through literary and other allusions is an unsettling experience for the reader, similar to the effect produced in *Su único hijo*, also a text profoundly influenced by cultural maladjustment—in this case, nostalgia for an anachronistic romantic sensibility. Romantic yearning, however, is completely absent in "Album-abanico." Its out-of-synch qualities arise, paradoxically, from a loss of nostalgia. Yet nostalgia, for Susan Stewart, is what narrative is all about: "By the narrative process of nostalgic reconstruction the present is denied and the past takes on an authenticity of being, an authenticity which, ironically, it can achieve only through narrative. Nostalgia is a sadness without an object." Nostalgia, she concludes, "is the desire for desire" (23).

Clarín, however, punctures nostalgic romance by privileging inauthenticity as pure textuality, intimating that behind the absence yearned for lies yet more absence, a fraudulent emptiness. The text ultimately becomes a screen for the writer's own impotence, his own inability to express more than the datedness of desire. The Asturian writer uses a particular narrative point of view, akin to Larra's fashion editor persona in "El álbum," to voice this sense of time and feeling being out of kilter with each other.

Before pursuing further voice and narrative persona, I would like to return to the notion of datedness as embodied in things. Material datedness is not simply crucial to the story line; it is built into the very nature of the object that fans into movement the fictions of "Album-abanico." As M. A. Flory's *A Book about Fans*, published in 1895 and thus contemporaneous with Clarín's story, makes clear, the scenes, events, and personages depicted on the fan reflect and record "the social and intellectual influences which . . . produced it; indeed, it almost defines what the artistic productions of a nation were at a given period" (36). There were calendar fans, fortune-telling fans, program fans, mourning fans,

7. Spanish fan adorned with female figure, circa 1890. Courtesy
of the Museo Municipal de Madrid collection.

wedding fans, fans with political and social caricatures, aide-mémoire
fans, commemoration fans, riddle and anagram fans, and so on (Flory
35; Percival 110–38, 179–83; James 218–19) (figs. 7–9). With the advent
of cheaper production methods in the late eighteenth and nineteenth
centuries, printed and lithographed fans, unlike the costlier hand-painted
artifact, became immensely popular, adopted by virtually all social
classes. These are above all popular objects, as another fanologist remarks, "made for a day, a week, or a season, or perhaps as souvenirs of a
special event; but they were essentially ephemeral. . . . [they] often reflect
the whims of a passing hour, and record fashions" (Percival 105). Un-
mounted fan leaves, deliberately overstocked, could easily be inserted on
demand so that the newest topical subject might provide an hour's worth
of conversation or amusement, bits and pieces of information functioning almost like an airborne circulating newspaper (Bennett 15).

Despite such popularity, the fan in the second half of the nineteenth
century was no longer seen by many as a necessary object of feminine
adornment ("The Fan" 254). In 1895, Mary Cadwalader Jones remarked
that the participation of women in politics, education, and other public
spheres and the growing emancipation movement had relegated the fan
to an obsolete status (qtd. in Flory 136). Nevertheless, she says, such
disuse is not universal. The fan continues to serve "as an aid or an

8. Postcard of actress María Palou, with fan, circa 1910. An example
of the "language of fans" in upper-right hand corner. Courtesy
of the Museo Municipal de Madrid collection.

9. Turn-of-the-century advertising cards, front and back, for fans and other ladies' objects. Courtesy of the Museo Municipal de Madrid collection.

accomplice . . . in countries like Spain, where women are still to some extent watched and secluded, and where the fan is still an ally as well as an ornament, with a language and etiquette of its own, and manuals in which they are fully set forth" (137). With all its built-in Anglo-American prejudices toward a Mediterranean culture, this particular commentary points to an essential cultural difference of perception in the relations between things and women. In Cadwalader Jones's view, the fan has become detached from the female body, having been converted into a museum object, autonomously situated within the space of private and public collections. Flory begins his book by alluding to the significance of the 1870 loan exhibition of fans at the South Kensington Museum (now the Victoria and Albert Museum). And Octave Uzanne already noted in 1882 how widespread the collecting impulse for artistic and historic fans had become (143). "Year after year," one reads, "every corner of Europe is searched by a little army of dealers' agents" (Cad-walader Jones, qtd. in Flory 140).

The same passion for fan collecting was also evident in Spain. Exhibitions of fans took place in Madrid and Barcelona.[41] Indeed, most cultural historians attribute the mid-century revival of the fan's popularity as a collectible and as an adornment to the Spanish-born Empress Eugénie, who is said to have possessed over six hundred specimens (Praz, *Illustrated History* 350; Flory 65). The instincts of acquisition and accumulation, characteristic of an age of bourgeois empowerment, pointed toward the object's separation and detachment from the body. But the notion that objects like the fan were emblematic of the feminine also suggested that things had an inner, secret life of their own made manifest by their relationship to persons. This gendering of objects meant an even closer attachment of the materially inert to the female body. To speak of the fan as feminine in nature was to effect a metonymic transference between part and whole.

The fan as a repository of signatures, or album, represents a richly articulated cluster of meanings that Clarín in his 1898 story self-consciously exploits. To judge from other sources, the autograph fan, sometimes thought of as a kind of memory or souvenir fan, was apparently considered hopelessly cursi by around 1885. Thus the comic writer Eduardo de Palacio thought the passion for converting fans into literary-artistic albums had largely passed: "This bad habit has not been eradicated yet, but the rage to collect the signatures of writers has finally dwindled" (3).[42] A few years later, Palacio Valdés in *La hermana San Sulpicio* [Sister Saint Sulpice] (1889) bemoaned the persistence of the custom in the provincial life of Seville. For the first-person narrator-author, the physical properties of the fan were not innocent, despite this apparently calm description: "I should point out that fans generally are made of paper, and this paper on one side is usually daubed with country scenes and, on the other side, is blank" (88).[43] That white verso eventually struck mock terror and sheer revulsion in the writer's heart, who probably felt much the same way the English poet Mrs. Hemans did earlier in the century regarding what she called the "album persecution" (qtd. in Sigourney 368).

If 1885 marks a turning point in the autograph fan's popularity in

Spain, then the loss of favor must have come about practically overnight. Only two years before, the third-rate society poet Juan Tomás Salvany could write, "While the album has become a *cursi* article, the fan is and will continue to be the most fortunate of objects."[44] He goes on to say, "floating album of the favored sex, a calling card that genius uses to introduce itself to the world, the fan offers the unknown bard perennial glory and pampered applause" (57).[45] Here, the link established between a feminine object and writing reveals two things. First, within certain settings, writers, usually society poets like the selfsame Juan Tomás Salvany or Antonio Grilo or José Selgas, used social gatherings such as tertulias and *saraos* as a way to self-promote their literary careers. And second, writing inevitably became gender-inflected, at least within some contexts.

This leads me back to Clarín's story and the internal dating that the narrator assigns to it. If, say, the action begins around 1885, when the álbum-abanico has become completely trivialized and discredited, then surely there are textual allusions to support such an assumption; and there are. Julita's fan is filled with the signatures of such contemporaries as Echegaray, López de Ayala, Campoamor, Núñez de Arce, and Manuel del Palacio, as well as a generous complement of fictitious lovers' names. With malicious aforethought, the narrator observes that all of Madrid calls Julita "la *Pródiga*", a marvellous dig at Pedro Antonio de Alarcón's 1882 novel *La Pródiga* [Lady Bountiful], whose main character is a woman of easy virtue named Julia. It also helps to remember that this novel, Alarcón's last, received especially harsh reviews, including one by Clarín himself (*"La Pródiga"* 44–46). Later, in feigned innocence, Alas would also ask rhetorically, "¿Por qué no escribe Alarcón?" [Why doesn't Alarcón write anymore?], a satirical piece he subtitled "Palique tal vez indiscreto" [Some (perhaps) indiscreet musings]. Alarcón, he knew, claimed a conspiracy of silence and a litany of bad press as sufficient provocation for his early retirement as a novelist. Clarín's sly poke years later furthers by ironic innuendo an air of scandalous narrative complicity that now has much less to do with Alarcón's reputation and a great deal more to do with his female protagonist's.

Other literary references abound in this text: "Julita got introduced to naturalism first through painting rather than literature. Precisely when the last embers of this lady's beauty were flaring, realism was beginning to be fashionable in Spain" (260).[46] The lucky fellow is a landscape painter who specializes in cows, a favorite subject of several northern local color artists, whose regionalist concerns were to culminate in the work of painters like Joaquín Mir. Pablito Fonseca's cows are "*slabs of reality* heaved onto canvas. It made you want to milk them."[47] This comment provokes yet another finely crafted bit of intertextual business when the narrator remarks that for several weeks la de Frondoso became "la de *Finojosa*." "You'll understand why," he says, knowing full well his readers' familiarity with classic texts like the Marqués de Santillana's fifteenth-century *serranilla*, or ballad, of "la vaquera de la Finojosa" (the milkmaid of la Finojosa).

Julita's literary tastes, however, run to popular novels, to melodrama and sentimentality à la Octave Feuillet. Her next lover, Angel Trabanco, a poet of the naturalist school and author of *El molino viejo* [The old mill], in an attempt at reeducation makes her read Balzac and the brothers Goncourt. Trabanco's naturalist poetics—Clarín elsewhere considered writers like Campoamor and at times even Núñez de Arce as *poetas naturalistas*—are reflected in the name of his composition, *El molino viejo*, which recalls by association Zola's "L'Attaque du moulin" [The mill attack] (in *Les Soirées de Médan*, 1880) or perhaps Daudet's earlier *Lettres de mon moulin* [Letters from my mill] (1869), as well as contemporary texts like Salvador Rueda's *El patio andaluz* [The Andalusian patio] and other regionalist titles. Significantly, the narrator converts this particular text into a thinly veiled sexual allusion to Julita's physical charms, just as he had earlier with Fonseca's bovine image à la Finojosa. Trabanco's verses depict "a mill tired of milling, in ruins inside and out; the old miller's wife, her clapper worn out."[48] These images of the ruined mill and the worn-out clapper are inscribed in tiny handwriting onto the leaf of the álbum-abanico. "I am that mill," thinks la de Frondoso (261). And she is right.

Only the passage of time puts a stop to la de Frondoso's sexual activities. As the narrator puts it, "that register of notables more or less ephemeral continued to be Julita's mania. Her lovers varied; her mania was always the same" (262).[49] Julita's lovers are like the serialized novels to which she is addicted. The names and details may vary, but the formula remains the same, and so does the ending. By the time Julita's daughter puts into circulation her own autograph fan, a new literary fashion has also replaced the reigning mode. The coveted signature is now the poet Ibáñez's: "Ibáñez was in fashion, he was half-mystical, half-diabolical, and with the ladies, he was much more popular than Trabanco in his best moments. Besides, he lived most of the time in Paris or London, and this kept his fame fresh and spicy" (266).[50]

In one sense, the chronology of "Album-abanico" is quite clear, as the unequivocal linear movement from realism to decadentism and modernism, from one literary generation to another, demonstrates. There is, however, another sense of time here, the material and cultural time attached to the autograph fan itself, which is out of synch with both the literary and familial generations presented in the story. Clock time moves inexorably forward. But the time of objects ages without, paradoxically, having acquired a sense of pastness. A significant part of this temporal ambiguity can be attributed to the difficulties of dating with exactness the birth and death, high and low points of a fashion, in a word, the social life of things, as cultural anthropologists put it (see Appadurai). While, for example, satirical and serious literature alike frequently poked fun at the fan as an object of cursilería, other writers continued to envision it as a sentimentalized miniature of the feminine and of romance. Thus one can still find at the turn of the century verses and sentiments like these: "such an article isn't / just an artistic object, / but a tiny parapet / or a Japanese screen, / where a blush is veiled, / emblem of the virgin, / where a smile is hidden, / like a flash of love" (Urbano 136).[51] Or this thought from a young *modernista:* "Every fan is beautiful, because it always preserves traces, the perfume or memory, of its owner. If art embellishes it, then the fan is the union of material and moral beauty" (Zozaya 45).[52]

Fan poetry proliferated in journals, albums, almanacs, and other publications during the second half of nineteenth-century Spain. In explaining why such trivial forms persisted so long, it helps to understand the practical purposes they also served. Literally thousands of occasional verses appear on pages often labeled "En varios abanicos" or "En un abanico" or some variant thereof.[53] Like the *charadas, logogrifos* (both word puzzles), and other small bits of information and amusements, these obviously served as fillers in most publications to satisfy the growing demand for print. Newspaper editors and magazine publishers had to scrounge for hard copy, often sketchily provided by wire or lifted from other papers, which explains in part the need for filler. Moreover, apprentice writers, eager to break into print, willingly offered for free their verbal wares to editors already on a shoestring budget. Many of these occasional verses are, I suspect, the product of such *grafómanos*, as Clarín unkindly dubbed them (*Nueva campaña*). The practice goes back, of course, to the album of the romantic period, which also gives an idea of the emotional hold such apparently trivial items possessed. Album and fan poetry obviously pleased the tastes of many people; they appealed to sentiment and vanity, and they provided amusing entertainments for an hour or two. The technologization of the word, to use Walter Ong's phrase, had democratized a romantic practice, putting it into popular circulation. It is also of interest to note that as newspapers and other publications became increasingly professionalized in Spain, this particular kind of filler—the unpaid work of amateurs—correspondingly diminished and finally disappeared. I would suggest that the overwhelming presence of filler items like album and fan poetry results in part from the transitional economic and cultural stage that Spanish newspapers, magazines, and other cultural repositories found themselves in. The traditional economy of scarcity and its savings mentality—beautifully illustrated in Galdosian characters like Torquemada and Francisco de Bringas—continued to shape a content that, having arisen out of the profound and personal attachment of the human hand to the thing made, was now turning into a product, an object of cultural consumption.

Fan poetry as it appears in newspapers, magazines, and almanacs reproduces commercially at one remove the same phenomenon handwritten on the object itself. This built-in—and yet very real—distance from the object converts such poetry into a kind of metatext in which the language of fans assumes a doubly symbolic function, referring simultaneously to a missing object (the fan) and to a missing body (a woman's). Something similar happens in Clarín's story. Like the fan poetry of the press, "Album-abanico" also circulates as a special cultural text with its own set of signs, movements, and gestures. The autograph fan represents a symbolic body language—without the body. Indeed, Spanish women of the eighteenth and nineteenth centuries were known especially for their skilled *manejo del abanico* (the art of the fan) (Uzanne 117). Blanco White, for example, wrote in 1798, "The Andalusian woman needs the fan as much as she needs her tongue. Besides, the fan has a great advantage over the natural organ of speech: that of transmitting thought over long distance" (72).[54]

This silent language of fans was not exclusively Spanish. Late eighteenth-century English fanmakers marketed novelty items like the "Fanology or Ladies Conversation Fan" and "The Telegraph of Cupid." The French apparently adapted the English style but filtered it through a Spanish system developed by Fenella, according to Anna Gray Bennett (176, n.1). In an 1878 manual intended for a female readership, *El lenguaje de las flores* [The language of flowers], its pseudonymous author, Florencio Jazmín, also includes a brief section on the language of fans (201–2). Here the position and movement of the fan in contact with the female body constituted a coded language of desire. Thus a closed fan carried in the right hand signified one's availability ("Deseo novio," I desire a friend); in the left hand, the contrary ("Estoy comprometida," I am engaged). A rapid fan movement meant passion ("Mucho te amo," I adore you), whereas a languid swish sent a message of indifference ("Me eres indiferente," I am indifferent to you) (see also fig. 8).

Like the language of flowers, fruits, handkerchiefs, gloves, and other small objects, the language of fans possessed a secret grammar, with special tropes meant only for the initiated. Both parties had to understand the code and agree to its rules for messages to pass from one person to another. By its very nature fan language is euphemistic. A double-layered screen of material and semiotic thickness papers the air. Nevertheless, messages do penetrate, actions are perpetrated. In Clarín's story, the autograph fan functions not only as a record of seduction but as a vehicle of exchange. For anything to be exchanged, however, it must also circulate. Yet the question is, what is being exchanged and circulated in "Album-abanico"? At first reading, readers might readily answer: sexual favors. Certainly no money passes hands. Yet Julita's physical and social persona finds satisfaction in both private and public domains; and her lovers evidently move up a notch or two on the social and artistic ladder. Each new affair bestows a curious sort of distinction on both parties, but the distinction is gained, ironically, by putting into circulation one's reputation.

Julita's autograph fan thus reveals a double-sided nature. As a repository of individualized signatures belonging to special categories of people (artists, writers, politicians), her fan possesses singularity and resides within the protected domain of the private. But when those same signatures become a matter of public record, they acquire a social life of their own. In other words, they become commodities, in the sense that *"any thing intended for exchange"* is a commodity (Appadurai 9). The autograph fan as a text writes out the story of a woman's reputation. In so doing, Clarín is playing off an old idea refabricated through a new economics of figuration: handwriting as a sign of character (Thornton 46–55, 99–101). The associations found in character and style led Unamuno to make fanciful impressions of men as metaphoric letters: "And being made by hand—in manuscript, or cursive—as well as with the pen, with steel, has given them their character, their style. Those that are typed, made by machine, like those printed, are already imitations, they lack style. The handwriting expert will have nothing to do with them. Aren't there also among men those who have a capital letter character, rectilinear and etched, and others who have a small letter character, curved and painted?" ("Estilo y carácter" 582).[55] At a farther remove, analogies of handwriting to a person's character are rooted in a centuries-old belief in the magical qualities of writing, as seen in Isidore of Seville's *Etymologiae* (Curtius 313).

In writing out their signatures and artistic prowess on Julita's fan, her lovers send a double message. Art is profoundly tied to a textual economy and an economic context. It is impossible to separate art from a social subtext closely woven into the very fabric of story and discourse. More specifically, what matters is how an object is put into circulation by desire, and how circulation of that object makes the story itself move. The particular discourse of desire—what one could call the language of fans in Clarín's narrative—is simultaneously privileged and advanced by being framed within the metascript of the fan text itself. As narrative movement, "Album-abanico" suggests remarkable parallels with the anthropological notion of *keda*, a term signifying road or journey in some Massim island communities off the eastern tip of New Guinea. Keda describes the path taken by objects of value as they move from one person to another, establishing the losses and gains of wealth, power, and reputation of individuals. In a larger sense, "keda is thus a polysemic concept, in which the circulation of objects, the making of memories and reputations, and the pursuit of social distinction through strategies of partnership all come together" (Appadurai 18). When we follow the passage of Clarín's autograph fan through the story, we read in anthropological terms the cultural biography of an object (Kopytoff). The process of understanding such histories is doubly complex in fictional narrative because of their embeddedness in a thick layer of textualization. Yet even the presumably direct study of objects and their specific biographies discloses sophisticated symbolic structures. Things, whether material or textual, can possess both a rhetorical and a social use; in that sense, they are "incarnated signs" with "semiotic virtuosity" (Appadurai 38). This is especially true of luxury goods that take on display value and souvenir items that become part of a collection.

Julita at once collects and displays the signatures she prizes.[56] Her own desires, sexually and socially motivated, thus circulate as a kind of text that produces yet another, her reputation (not to speak of the presumed fame and fortune awarded her lovers). Her reputation serves not only as a surface to be read, but as one that others can comment on and judge. The major vehicle for such socially inflected evaluations is gossip. As the narrator remarks of his protagonist, "nadie hablaba mal de ella . . . en detalle. Se reconocía, en general, que no había por dónde cogerla, porque eso era notorio; pero . . . *nada más*. . . . Tenía la gran *virtud* . . . mundana de no dar escándalo" [no one spoke badly of her . . . in detail. It was generally admitted there was no way to get at her; that was understood, but . . . *nothing more* . . . She had the great worldly . . . *virtue* of *causing no scandal*]. And a few lines later he says, "Secreto, siempre secreto. Nadie tenía pruebas, que pudieran valer en juicio, de lo que era una convicción común. 'Concretamente no se sabe nada,' se repetía por todas partes. En fin, aquello sí que era cursi y de clavo pasado: hablar de los adulterios de Julita. ¡Adulterios!: Jesús, qué palabrota tan poco oportuna y tan escandalosa . . . ¡tratándose de Julita Frondoso! Amigos, protegidos, así se debían llamar los amantes de aquella señora" [Secretive, always secretive. No one had proof, or any worth testing, of what was a commonly held conviction. "Specifically, no one knows anything," it was repeated everywhere. At any rate, all of this was truly cursi and passé: talking about Julita's affairs. Adultery! Good lord, what an unpleasant word, so inappropriate and scandalous . . . in Julita Frondoso's case! Friends, protegés, that's what her lovers should be called] (259–60).

The narrative device of reporting indirectly the anonymous voice of common knowledge cleverly brings out the sense of innuendo and hidden subtext that imbues all gossip. More importantly, the intonations and stylistic tics of the narrator himself are hallmarks of the gossip's voice. Gossip and storytelling have much in common. Both delight in partial revelations, the intricacies of relationships, and the naming of names as representations (and misrepresentations) of character.[57] Both are rooted in oral ways and voice as the bearer of life fictions. The voice of the narrator in "Album-abanico" takes on its peculiar coloration out of a specific gossip-ridden context: the refined, sugary accents of the society columnist, or *revistero de salones*, whose discreet tone of pervasive euphemism often masked, through veiled language or inexplicable gaps in reportage, premeditated malice.

The chronicler of high society came to the fore during Isabeline Spain with Ramón de Navarrete (1818–97), better known as "Asmodeo." Like Monte-Cristo (Eugenio Rodríguez Ruiz de la Escalera), whose heyday would be the fin de siglo Regency period of María Cristina, Asmodeo was closely identified with the conservative and tony newspaper *La época* (Martínez Olmedilla 170; Araujo-Costa 104–29). The reading public for *La época* was a select one, mostly aristocrats, financiers, statesmen, bankers, and other members of the privileged classes, reminiscent of Padre Coloma's fictional world in his 1890 novel, *Pequeñeces* [Trifles] (to which Alas refers in "Album-abanico" 258). *La época* rarely circulated publicly through kiosks or street vendors, but was sold by private subscription. It was also more expensive than most papers, four pesetas per month, rather than one peseta (Araujo-Costa 181, 187). Even its format suggested good taste and refinement, since it could be folded and made manageable more easily than larger, mass-circulation papers like *El imparcial* and *El liberal*.[58]

Subscribers, while numerically small, are said to have read the paper from front to back, dwelling with intense satisfaction on the society section pages as though they were "the descriptions of a novelist the likes of Flaubert or Zola jotting down to the last detail a lady's attire, coiffure, or embellishments" (Araujo-Costa 112).[59] Female readers, especially, scanned with great interest the habitually crowded lists of names that filled such chronicles.

Society columnists never, of course, reported social reality, but merely its adornments, translated linguistically into proper nouns and discre(e)te qualifiers, sprinkled like confectioner's sugar over the actual "proper names." Monte-Cristo's perfumed, candied words were spread across his text, as one cultural historian wrote, "not according to the qualities that the persons mentioned really possess but to those it is more fitting to attribute to them" (Almagro San Martín 257).[60] Most society reporters had a set number of preselected adjectives and adverbs applied according to a certain social hierarchy. Monte-Cristo, for example, used "hermosa" (lovely), "elegante" (elegant) and "bella" (beautiful) only for those at the top socially, financially or politically; words like "distinguida" (distinguished), "gentil" (charming), and "linda" (pretty) were meted out to the second echelon; and to the rank and file, "otras señoras que sentimos no recordar" (other ladies whose names regrettably we forget) (Almagro San Martín 257). Valdeiglesias ("Mascarilla"), however, often applied terms like "bella" and "distinguida" to those ladies he could not bring himself to call "virtuous." He reserved the epithet "aristocrat" only for those of his clientele descending from the twenty houses of grandees recognized by Carlos V in 1520 (Araujo-Costa 126–27). In this manner he carefully distinguished between the nobility and the aristocracy of late nineteenth-century Spanish society. None of these distinctions prevented members of the upper middle classes and the reigning literati and artists either from penetrating the inner circles of the privileged or from establishing their own rival coteries. As the century drew to a close, increased intermingling of different social classes and interests in social functions both private and public became the unsettling norm. In a highly refractory way, the institution of the society columnist often reflected this incipient breakdown and confusion of social differences. A cultural practice based on exclusiveness and exclusions, the *revistero de salones* would eventually fade away to irrelevance in the twentieth century as the trend toward democratization and modernization continued.

While later accounts sometimes mourned with exquisitely felt nostalgia the loss of the society chronicler and his world (Araujo-Costa; A. Escobar), the language of the *cronista de salones* is strictly one of *actualités*, designed to showcase through naming and qualifying a privileged, exclusive world. The relationship between the society reporter and his clientele was often symbiotic, each relying on the other to confer mutual status and distinction. Simply being named in the society section bestowed importance, established a reputation. For the reporter himself, whose social origins were usually inferior to those of his clientele, entrée into such a privileged world granted him by close association his own special distinction. Like many of his readers, the society columnist tended to live out a fantasy world, his experiences as a social sycophant mediated through the roseate vision of highly retouched accounts. In documenting the social activities of his clientele, he privileged the moment itself yet distanced any possible sense of immediacy by recourse to euphemistic language. The society section of newspapers also reported the various departures and arrivals of high society, particularly in the summer and early fall, occasional indispositions, a trip to the country, amateur theatricals and other privately held cultural amusements, and other bits of information and gossip. In other words, it tracked high society's movements, and in the process created a special verbal and cultural space in which to record those movements. Viewed this way, the physical and social circulation of an entire group can be seen as enclosed, metaphorically, within another kind of circulation, the commercial enterprise of the newspaper itself.

The print medium thus converted the movements and personages of high society into objects of reading consumption. As verbal bonbons or epideictic effusions of the ephemeral, society chronicles offered pleasures of serial sameness that were, however, nonaccumulating. A name appeared, emitted a quick glimpse of identity to the reader and bearer of the name, and disappeared into successiveness, a string of names—the lists of those who attended, those who dined, those who danced. This lack of singularity, otherwise possibly disturbing, is made unobjectionable and even attractive by its fictive qualities. I suspect that newspaper readers read these columns as fictions, narratives that made social relationships seem more significant through the enumerative device of contiguity and association, the setting of names side by side.[61] This special enclaving of people and events in a heightened, artificial account suggested their singular, distinctive qualities, even as the seriality and stereotypical interchangeability of style and person worked to undermine that perception of exclusiveness. It was the society chronicler's responsibility to keep reputations moving in the public memory, circulating as informational and rhetorical display. He stressed currentness, not pastness. Writing as product results, the subject of writing and writing itself becoming objects of exchange, used up and replaced by more writing.

This same sense of literature as product sustains the fictions behind Clarín's story. "Album-abanico" begins with the words, "O al revés, abanico-álbum *como gustéis*" (or in reverse, fan-autograph, *if you like*) (257), revealing from the start that lack of singularity and interchangeability will prevail here. The narrative gesture of benevolent accommodation toward the reader seems to point to the personal and individual, but it comes deceptively wrapped in a bow of fine irony. This narrator aims above all to please, even as the implied author undermines his position through an ironic shrug of the shoulders. This slightly cynical, slightly weary pose of the experienced narrative voice (narrator and authorial presence combined) is not at all unusual in Clarín. He uses it to devastating effect repeatedly in many of his fictions, but above all in his journalistic writings, especially those generally labeled festive or satirical, the *paliques* and other "conversational" pieces of pointed currency. Colloquially, conversation as style and substance becomes the code word in print for the ephemeral and the temporally marked, as this Clarinian comment, ostensibly directed toward a nonwriting Pedro de Alarcón, suggests, "What did you think, that we're going to like your writing less now than before, because of naturalism and idealism, because of the *human document* and photography, and art for art's sake, and all that talk?" ("¿Por qué no escribe Alarcón?" 51).[62] This acute sense of datedness is incorporated into the narrator's very tone and attitude in "Album-abanico."

The autograph fan as a sign of that temporal disjunction does not, however, evoke nostalgia in this story.[63] In dating desire, calling Julita's obsession with fan signatures "an outmoded mania," the writer makes it difficult to elicit a "desire for desire," or the presence of nostalgia. For that you need memories. Or at least the memory of memories. But the only time remembering occurs—near the end of "Album-abanico"—the narrator and the characters cut it short. When Julita and her old flame Trabanco meet up again after many years, writes Alas, "they looked at each other and smiled, like two old friends who remembered nothing of intimacies and tender caresses. . . . Trabanco, being a poet, still threw a certain mellow tint of philosophical *nostalgia* over their mutual reminiscences . . . but la de Frondoso, absolutely nothing, she appeared to remember nothing, that is, she remembered everything but said nothing" (266).[64]

Memories have been used up here, consumed semiotically by their overcirculation. The point of serialized lovers, serialized novels, and signatures is to forget them. As a cultural artifact, Julita's fan resides in a transitional space of meaning in which a personal object, intimately associated with the body and socially en-gendered, is saved, not as a private treasure house of remembered feeling, but as a public record of successive amnesia. Unwanted, excessive time drips off its edges. The fan as text-object has, paradoxically, too much time for its owner—and therefore, not enough for its readers. Its cultural insufficiencies are both affective and aesthetic, and as such, it functions as a perfect symbol of cursilería, the embodiment of exaggerated and immediate datedness.

Clarín has built into his story the property of datedness, by attaching the scene of writing to things as consumable products, in the same way the society reporter turns his clientele into objects of reading consumption. He makes his story the point of intersection between handwriting (signatures and fan literature) as character and reputation and the production of writing itself (as text). Culturally and economically, this juncture marks a moment of transition as the handheld, handmade object, figured as a kind of body/text with its own language, is mishandled and converted into a commodity, a product of exchange. The fan as a holdover from an earlier cultural economy is circulated as part of a newer economy, which now incorporates script into print, inextricably linking the private with the public. We cannot separate Julita's private understanding of her autograph fan from the public classification of that same object. Reputation—in the traditional sense of honor as tied to the female body—cannot circulate or be exchanged and still remain. Traditionally, a reputation is fixed and singular, enclaved within the body. This idea still persists in Clarín's story, but it is compromised by a complex intertwining with the social and cultural processes of a more modern consumer-oriented economic organization. Things and people move in interrelated ways, fueled by the same desires. As the fan moves metaphorically away from Julita's body, so too does her reputation. Rather than acquiring esteem as in the traditional keda, however, she loses it (even though she may gain a temporary social cachet—and another lover). Thus commodification makes the protagonist lose what is singular about her: her virtue. In being exchangeable, she becomes "common" in the double sense of the word (see Kopytoff 69).

Wrapped up in these traditional notions of the female as honor incarnate are more unsettling attitudes toward identity, in which authenticity and originality also play a significant role. For the autograph fan as an object of cursilería is seen as second-rate and full of clichés, in other words, as unoriginal. Since the fan is not unique, singular—especially as it circulates far too publicly—its value must lie elsewhere. When things lose their singularity, they sometimes acquire exclusiveness to make them desirable again. Even here, neither the fan nor Julita is terribly exclusive, that is, "hard to get." The fan, moreover, puts up a metaphoric screen of inauthenticity, since no emotional experience is truly felt or remembered. In sum, everything that is second-rate and secondhand, trite and unimaginative, becomes feminine in this story, or more properly expressed, socially and culturally gendered as feminine.[65] In this sense, there is nothing inert or impersonal about things, as Marcel Mauss wrote long ago (10), particularly when they lie at the heart of human relationships. Objects like the fan are as much culturally constructed as people; they possess their own biographies (Kopytoff 90).[66] They create other and more complex fictions out of their own life as cultural texts. The fictions circulating in "Album-abanico" are expressed through a specifically situated discourse that can be called the language of fans: a disembodied language of exchange and movement, ventilated by gossip and propelled by the fashions of time. In parodying the society chronicler of the press, Clarín's narrator makes the reader acutely conscious of the fictive qualities of social exclusiveness and of exclusiveness as a function of time itself. Above all, by showing how people, like things, can be consumed, used up, when desire is put into circulation, he turns "Album-abanico" into the perfect cursi text as an extended trope of cultural datedness.

Here, too, narrative complicity enters into intricate play with distance, the distance of irony and the more extended and elusive distance produced by the estrangement of experience. Larra's album-text reveals how much experience and authenticity are privileged over the secondhand and yet, at the same time, how much the secondhand, the symbolic object, event, or person, is sought out to find experience. Herein reside the beginnings of lo cursi. The phenomenon embodies a sense of exaggerated and immediate datedness in which experience is not allowed to ripen. Hence, in lo cursi, embodiment is never "full." In this sense, lo cursi tells us that texts such as the realist novel are based on a curious maladjustment between the satisfaction of the real (owning it, describing it) and the insufficiency of the real (as text, sex, objects). As later, twentieth-century treatments of lo cursi in Ramón Gómez de la Serna's "Lo cursi" and Lorca's *Doña Rosita la soltera* reveal, distance in time and space will not only exacerbate the double bind of cursilería's experiential and aesthetic inadequacy. It will also turn lo cursi into pure distance, the distance of nostalgia. But before I turn to this later period, I would like first to examine a related phenomenon, the impact of romanticism as both a trope of datedness and a sign of modernity, as, in a word, cursilería.

CHAPTER THREE

Salon Poets, the Bécquer Craze, and Romanticism

MANY YEARS AGO I came across this passage from a 1947 novel by Mary Westmacott: "St. Loo Castle has that bogus, that phony air of theatricality, of spurious romance which can only be given by something that is in fact genuine. It was built, you see, when human nature was unself-conscious enough to enjoy romanticism without feeling ashamed of it" (14). Mary Westmacott was the pen name Agatha Christie used to write romance novels. Her disingenuousness is wonderfully transparent. What most interests me, however, is reading beyond the irony in order to grasp her understanding—a special kind of empathy—of an earlier period, which, while perhaps more openly sentimental, was no less self-conscious than ours. It was an age that "was unself-conscious *enough* to enjoy romanticism without feeling ashamed of it" (emphasis added). Westmacott/Christie seems perfectly at home, moreover, in a cultural setting that, while unreal as romance, symbolically conveys the leisure, economic well-being, and power that, historically, the owners of St. Loo Castle probably would have enjoyed.

Westmacott/Christie's novel appeared, of course, well before the current age of cultural studies. In some versions of the latter, a largely uncontested tenet presumes that historical realities can be invariably organized into monolithic blocks of dominant and marginal groups. The "dominant elite" appears motivated purely by power and the desire to exclude the marginal, while the marginal seems uniquely characterized as the not-dominant, that is, as an essential (and often essentialized) lack, whose virtue derives from its nondominance. The result is a reductive impoverishment of our critical and historical understanding. As Stefan Collini remarks, absent from such studies is a sensitivity "to the rich texture of those cultural strands [regarded] as 'dominant.'" "It is the lack of imaginative sympathy," he goes on to say, "with those who lived and died before us (especially if they lived comfortably) that I find chilling and distancing. The past is 'interrogated' but not listened to" (457, 459).

The cultural experience I examine here has precisely to do with people who, for the most part, "lived comfortably." They belonged generally to the middle classes, some to the aristocracy, of the last century. And they all shared a common passion and ethos, a set of contradictory impulses that persisted throughout nearly the entire nineteenth century—I am referring to romanticism. Rather than review the literature on the nature of romanticism or rehash the literary histories attached to it, both of which are generally well known, I propose to look at something more modest: romanticism as a cultural practice, specifically the way it was lived and experienced by those "unself-conscious enough to enjoy romanticism without feeling ashamed of it."

Let me return once more to Westmacott/Christie to bring out two other elements in her text: the notion of authenticity and that of time. St. Loo Castle's theatricality is, paradoxically, genuine, partly because of its very qualities and partly because of its period. In other words, its character was built-in, not simply built, as a function of time and perception. If people were "unself-conscious enough" about romantic feeling in the nineteenth century, this did not mean that they lacked self-awareness. More significantly, romanticism itself was (and is) grounded in the modern notion of self-consciousness. Parodies of romantic attitudes and forms spring up almost at the same time as the movement itself, satirizing not only its excesses and infelicitous by-products but the problematic relationship between subjectivity and the authentic. Indeed, the quality of genuineness in romanticism derived legitimacy yet also provoked accusations of spuriousness from its subjective grounding. Equally important for my purposes here, authenticity, when subjectively based, became temporalized, that is, susceptible to time and, more specifically, to the sense of datedness.

Obsolescence as a uniquely modern phenomenon relies on two simultaneously held notions: that time operates as a kind of constant social and economic pressure to renovate and change; and that time runs out. Keeping up with time—with the times—suggests a certain paradox: the datedness of time itself. This awareness of time as an out-of-synch two-step, a fumbling, backward-forward movement, exists already in the last century, especially in industrially and technologically advanced countries like England, France, and the United States. One can also observe this sense of datedness in countries like Spain, where modernization lags behind an acutely held awareness of the modern. The uncomfortable fit between modernity, or the modern, and modernization has usually been labeled as Spanish backwardness. Thus, in this interpretation, Spain becomes a case of national exceptionality, in which modernity and modernization are positioned in opposition to backwardness. What has been poorly understood, however, is precisely how the maladjustment between modernity and modernization brings about a modern consciousness in nineteenth-century Spanish society. We can see reaction to different kinds of datedness as both modern and modernizing impulses, as, in other words, the way the modern gets worked out and through in Spain. (Think, for example, of the constant allusions to the influence of a presumably modern French culture over a more traditional Spanish lifestyle in both public and private spheres, with attendant invidious comparisons.) Thus it is not simply a question of lagging behind the modern or of preexisting the modern, but of conceiving it in the ragged edges, in the rough crosscutting of halting modernization and self-consciousness of the modern. This historical and cultural dyssynchronicity suggests that *both* resistance toward, and the embracing of, modernity exist as signs of the modern in Spain.

Time lags underline temporal and socioeconomic contradictions. Romantic self-consciousness did more than expose a split between self and society; it pointed as well to an internal, temporal split between past and present, between immobility and mobility, between the desire for stable identities based on traditional class values and the fearful attraction to destabilized, evolving identities that created and empowered new classes of individuals but were founded on anachronistic, aristocratic values and rooted in a dying culture.[1] In this sense, romanticism, when it finally came to Spain, was already outdated, but, and I must stress this, no less modern than other national forms of romanticism. Its persistence until the early twentieth century, in such forms as salon poetry and *becqueriana* verses, suggests both a literary variant of obsolescence and an enduring desire for heightened individual expression of the inner life.

Romanticism as a trope of datedness becomes, then, a form of cursilería, an admission of collective and individual inadequacy, as well as the expression of yearned-for new identities. Significantly, however, romantic fervor as a practice was often worked out through the production and love of culture and cultural refinement.[2] When we understand Spanish romanticism within this much broader context of cultural and socio-economic change, it becomes far less important to continue debating whether the poet Espronceda was as good as Byron or whether French and other outside influences compromised the authenticity and originality of Spanish romantic writing.

In this context of cultural production, Peter Gay points out that "while philistines and social climbers were, in the mobile and nervous nineteenth century, a palpable presence, there were many middle-class families that earnestly valued their cultivation. Few bourgeois households were complete without pictures on the wall, music in the parlor, classics in the glassed-in bookcase. Bourgeois, men and women, sang, sketched, faithfully attended concerts and literary readings, recited and even wrote poetry" (28). The bourgeoisie, despite all its material and cultural advances in the last century, nevertheless felt itself to be on the defensive. One of the ways in which it masked feelings of inadequacy and insecurity was to feed its insatiable cravings for culture. Artifacts of culture become comforting substitutions for the absence of a stable, hierarchical society.[3] They provide identities for members of a social group whose collective characteristics appear as variable, contradictory, even amorphous. This is particularly so in the provinces, which far more often than not were the bearers of culture. One also needs to keep in mind the complex relationship of dependency between metropolis and province in cultural development (see Gutiérrez Girardot 23–25). From the vantage point of the early twenty-first century, it is easy to misread the signs of culture in the nineteenth century and assign dubious categories of inferior / superior to them. Even contemporary authors like Emilia Pardo Bazán and Leopoldo Alas were prone to such distinctions. Rather than acknowledge that the culture itself was originating identities, many of doubtful parentage, they often chose to condemn the very class that had put into motion the idea of a culture feeding off and into creative personalities.

This latter idea is a romantic notion. We often think of the last century's bourgeoisie as chiefly materialistic and devoted to hard progress, but in truth, many of them were idealists, romantic in nature, or at least considered themselves romantics. They embraced the cause of creativity: it functioned as the dynamo behind both material progress and culture. Those pictures on the wall, those concerts and literary readings, confirmed what the bourgeoisie always suspected of itself: that they, too, were creative—or could be, with a little help.

Nowhere does this surface more apparently than in the salons, informal social gatherings (tertulias), albums, almanacs, poetic homages (*coronas poéticas*), and poetry competitions (*juegos florales*) that proliferated throughout nineteenth-century Spain and elsewhere. A closer look at the way romanticism was practiced by salon poets, Bécquer imitators, and others also reveals how socially embedded romantic attitudes and writings were, and how such practices simultaneously helped to define and question identities of various kinds. What emerges from these cultural events and reactions to them is, at the very least, twofold: the physical and material sense of culture as a matter of place and placement, and the en-gendering of poetry and poetic practices as a sign of changing, sometimes conflictive, gender roles within certain specific contexts.

Situating such phenomena as the salon poets and the Bécquer craze within a certain theater of action, discloses, first, how their texts and personas operated not only representatively but performatively as well, acting out a drama of identity in which private selves were validated in public settings. In the process they also created a poetic archive documenting the emergence of a new social class and, in some instances, a new national identity.[4] On other occasions, however, contemporaries of salon poets and Bécquer imitators viewed these phenomena as suspect, questioning their authenticity and originality and suggesting a blurring of gender lines. Many salon poets were accused of feminizing or effeminate qualities, which should not surprise us, given the close associations between them and women of high society. Moreover, the emplacement of such poetry in the homes and artifacts of the comfortably well-off, its continuing connection with court society, and the popularity of such poets in the provinces, are all elements perceived by some contemporaries as culturally dated, cursi (see also Holguín 133, 135).

Thus many observers of nineteenth-century Spain considered middle- and upper middle-class society at one and the same time modern and retrograde.

Take, for example, the popular practice of oral recitation and the reading of poetry as a form of creative self-identification. One of the most revealing instances is José Zorrilla's first public appearance and reading at Mariano José de Larra's funeral in February of 1837, which provided the practical and emotional mechanism whereby Spanish romanticism and a sense of national identity became fused at a certain moment in time through the agency of the human voice.[5] Nicomedes Pastor Díaz remembered the intense impression caused by Zorrilla's reading: "It was a composition right then and there, by that poet, in that moment, in that setting, for us, in our language, in our poetry, in poetry that stirred us passionately, that electrified us. . . . If he had been alone and read the poem individually to each one of his listeners, would he have produced the same effect? Would they have found it so ideal, so beautiful, so original and spontaneous? Surely not" (15).[6] Zorrilla himself was acutely aware of his effect on his listeners: "the silence was absolute; the public, most fitting and ready; the scene, solemn, and the occasion unequalled. I had a young, fresh, and silvery timbred voice then, and a way of reciting never heard before, and I began to read . . . but as I was reading . . . I was [also] reading in the absorbed faces surrounding me the astonishment that my appearance and my voice were causing them" (*Recuerdos del tiempo viejo* 35–36).[7]

The intense emotional bonding that occurred between Zorrilla the public reader and his audience marked a scene that was to be repeated over and over in the last century, not only by Zorrilla himself, but also by other poet-reciters like Antonio Grilo and Emilio Ferrari and by scores of middle-class readers. The popular practice of oral recitation and the reading of poetry in the nineteenth century suggests a curious merging of traditional, collective values (reciting aloud) and notions of individuality centered round the creative self. Moreover, Zorrilla's hybrid stance as a romantic poet, in which romantic subjectivity and self-consciousness promoted a collective national identity, points not only to a striking divergence from other European romanticisms but to a different agenda as well.

Zorrilla's act of homage to Larra was really a "text-event," a performance of historical significance in which the human voice becomes a vital "dimension of the poetic text" (Zumthor 67, 71). His voice acted on his listeners as pure revelation. No one today really knows exactly how Zorrilla sounded in his public readings, only that, as he said, he had "a way of reciting never heard before." One writer, Emilia Pardo Bazán, complained Zorrilla's voice sounded like monotonous singing, while Zorrilla himself claimed that he could read without taking audible breaths and that the public hung on his very words, following the movements of his mouth (Ramírez 159, 186).

Although the practice of public readings and recitations existed in the early nineteenth century, Zorrilla hugely popularized such events, starting in the 1850s when he went on periodic tours, earning as much as 36,000 reals for one of them (Palenque, *El poeta y el burgués* 242). Other poets, would-be poets, and men and women of cultural refinement everywhere in Spain much recited his poetry. From the 1870s until the 1920s, it was, however, above all Gustavo Adolfo Bécquer's *rimas* that were not only read and wept over but imitated by a veritable epidemic of aspirant writers of both sexes in Spain and in Latin America (see Arrieta; Cossío 1:416–74; Naval; and fig. 10).

Emilia Pardo Bazán, for example, satirized the Bécquer mania by creating the second-rate, provincial poet Segundo García in her realist novel, *El cisne de Vilamorta*, typecasting him as "the poet," "the reader of Bécquer," and "the Becquerian dreamer."[8] It helps to remember that Bécquer himself came from the provinces (Sevilla), became a bohemian of sorts (or *lipendi*, in the parlance of the day), and sought his fortunes in the capital (see Romero Tobar, "En los orígenes"; Lustonó; and Díez Taboada). But Segundo is above all a romantic because of the way he reads, which is, essentially, the way Bécquer himself reads. "Podrá no haber poetas, pero siempre / habrá poesía" (poets may disappear, but there will always be poetry), Bécquer writes in the poem, Rima IV. He goes on to enumerate those elements of nature, mysteries of the universe, and sentiments of the human heart that for him signify "poetry." It is possible to view Bécquer's concept of poetry as a curious textless— hence, poetless—manifestation of pure subjectivity. This interpretation,

10. Cover of the *La ilustración artística*, which is a special issue on poet Gustavo Adolfo Bécquer. An example of Bécquer's early canonization and popularity.

however, ignores a vital element in Bécquer's poetic universe: the presence of an implied reader (usually female). For who is to say that waves of light, human destiny, and a beautiful woman are objects of poetic concern if not a reader of these phenomena? The poet who does not write is the reader who experiences what Bécquer tries to communicate in words. Poetry only exists because of a thinking, feeling other, a subjective entity who reads nature and the signs of human activity as expressions of the poetic. When Bécquer asks in another well-known poem, "¿Qué es poesía?" [What is poetry?], only to answer "Poesía eres tú" (you are poetry), he is implying the presence of a listener who is perforce also a reader of the poet's words (see also López Estrada, Introduction 48). As he addresses himself to his female listener, he seems to be reciting to her at the same time—hence the identity of listener/reader (and the emphasis on the recitative element in his poetry, since it is clear that in Pardo Bazán's time Bécquer was meant to be recited). Without that listener/reader there would be no poetry. This is also true because the poet himself functions as the primary reader. And because being a reader is prerequisite to being a poet.

I would suggest that this is also what Pardo Bazán proposes in *El cisne de Vilamorta*. Wordlessly, the readers' feelings incarnate poetry. Subjectivity itself constitutes poetry. Hence, to be creative equals being romantic. Small wonder that Bécquer's work, once a short period of initial neglect had passed, would prove to be a durable parcel of the Spanish bourgeoisie's cultural baggage for decades to come. Perhaps this reception also explains in part why his poetry did not garner any serious critical attention until much later in the twentieth century. A public belonging to the same social and cultural class as the writer himself had thoroughly absorbed his popularity, the intrinsic appeal of a poet who flattered, probably unintentionally, his reader. There was no felt need to explain, to critique in an analytical or scholarly way, poetry that catered this well to the bourgeoisie's desire for creative expression. Bécquer was one of them.

In this imagined and imaginative movement between reading and writing, images and other allusions in Bécquer's poetry turn into a sort of script (in the dual sense) that the poet simultaneously reads and writes. Reading is directed inward, and the reader's exacerbated self-awareness reduces script to a closed, subjective state, in which the only communication occurs in the nebulous zones of inner voices speaking to each other and activated by print. "In the shadowy corners of my mind," writes Bécquer in the 1868 introduction to the *Rimas*, "curled up naked, sleep the extravagant children of my fantasy, waiting in silence for art to dress them in words."[9] And in the first rima: "I know a strange, vast hymn / announcing the dawn in the soul's darkness" (*Rimas* 79, 87).[10] The poet (always male in Bécquer) refers to the creative struggle to write, but I would contend it is implicitly as a reader that he does so since he perceives his feelings in the first instance as objects ("the extravagant children of my fantasy") that must be read into being. The inner voice constitutes a "hymn" not recognized as such until it is read (listened to) and then scripted into another, outer existence. A writer is first a reader of his own mind. Indeed, he is already writing in that act of inner reading because he is visualizing his print objects, something that an oral culture cannot conceive, as Walter Ong has pointed out (12).

This romantic form of reading that is writing and writing that is reading constitutes the unstated metatext of Pardo Bazán's novel. On the surface a "readerly" or classic representational text in the Barthian sense, *El cisne de Vilamorta* in reality textualizes another kind of writing (romanticism). In underlining the romantic mode, Pardo Bazán has made script of it. In this way, the text becomes writing twice over. A readerly text about writing, it may not be "writerly" as Barthes in *S/Z* would have it, but it is no less "scriptorial" for being so constructed. And this in the dual sense of the word: for it is script as writing and as manuscript, as programmed discourse. Romanticism provides the controlling key to both.

El cisne de Vilamorta's romantic script—as carried out by the protagonist, Segundo García, and satirized by the novelist—suggests that Bécquer mania can be viewed as an acting out or performance of representational significance. That is, the romantic writing of *becquerianas* becomes the script or vehicle for the representation of subjectivity. As seen with handwriting in the previous chapter, writing is "one of the places where the self happened" (Thornton xiii). Pardo Bazán's realist satire of this performance-text helps us see the connecting link between subjectivity and representational acts (including representational writing itself).

Did real, flesh and blood readers of Bécquer's time understand and use his poetry in similar ways? One historical reader, Valeriano Barrero Amador, has this to say in a series of articles appearing between 1892 and 1894: "I have spent many nights reading his poems, and in reading them my spirit felt itself transported to another atmosphere" (part I, 278).[11] Later he writes, "Reading the *Rimas* we identify with the poet . . . we are astonished to find in him feelings that we thought were purely and exclusively ours" (part III, 203).[12] His own criticism is "a merely subjective impression," although he also promises to be more objective (part x, 282). Barrero Amador's close identification with Bécquer, however, overrides all other considerations and ends up constructing a kind of verbal altar before the Bécquer icon. "We love the memory of the poet with fervent adoration; with a kind of idolatrous devotion, the way we love the memories of our loved ones" (part X, 284).[13] And finally, "This moving us and making us feel in such an intense way is the exclusive privilege of genius" (part XI, 290).[14]

Barrero Amador does not always remain in such ethereal, divine realms. Near the end of part XI, he gives a little sketch of his own frustrated poetic trajectory, which, like that of the "swan of Vilamorta" and so many other would-be writers, began in a small provincial town. He submits his verses to a local authority, Manuel Briones, who calls them "un engendro monstruoso" (a bungled monstrosity). Admittedly they were, he says, but "I who knew all this said absolutely nothing, convinced I would put my foot in my mouth, fearful of causing displeasure with my replies to someone on intimate terms with the nine muses . . . , and desiring not to incur the olympian wrath of a literary authority of such high esteem in the republic of letters."[15] He also points out that readers of *Revista de España* would not recognize Sr. Briones's name, "because he has neither written anything nor does he know how to write, reserving his pretensions to being a man of letters when he goes to my hometown, where he's contracted marriage with a local aristocrat" (part XI, 292–93).[16]

This outburst, which comes near the conclusion of his essay, is highly revealing, suggesting that Barrero Amador's reasons for writing the lengthy series, which was protracted over a three-year period (and apparently never collected in a volume), are deeply personal and ultimately self-justifying. He says that Bécquer's disciples (i.e., imitators) do not understand his poetry (part I, 280) and claims that, even more than twenty years after his death, many readers are either coldly indifferent to the *Rimas* or have no familiarity with them (part X, 275). Surely the critic is also thinking of his own ill-received poetry: had not Barrero Amador felt the sting of rejection? His judgment, however, contradicts, to some extent, the broadly held and generally accurate view of Bécquer's widespread popularity; evidently there were exceptions (see also fig. 10).[17] Barrero Amador asks, "In vain have I often searched for critical reviews of the Seville poet, but I have seen nothing of the kind . . . To what can we attribute this profound silence" (part X, 282)?[18] By implication one is given to understand that Barrero Amador's opinions of Bécquer are authoritative, because *he* understands the poet, he identifies with him, vicariously participating in this way with his poetic genius. His reading of Bécquer appears as a creative rewriting of the *Rimas* and the poetic persona in general.

Barrero Amador also lambasts the Bécquer imitators, those "detestable, romantic poetasters," launching into a vehement diatribe against them, while keeping secret until nearly the end that he, too, is one of them. He gloomily comments on the social and artistic decadence of the age, which he sees as filled with cynicism, vulgarity, and pornographic commercialism, notably in the theater, where audiences go only to see the semi-naked dancers and actresses: "In sum, this class of shows is nothing more than a pretext for a half-dozen immodest and lustful bacchantes to show off their calves and their jutting chins" (part X, 274).[19] A few pages later he describes Bécquer's poetic sensibility as feminine: "There is in Bécquer much melancholy, something of the hysteric, something feverish, and above all an exaggerated sensibility that turns him into the plaything of his emotions. He is an incurable hypochondriac. . . . along with a sweet voluptuousness, an extraordinary delicacy and a purely feminine sensibility, there is this beating, passionate heart" (part X, 278).[20] Here Bécquer has been transformed into a fin de siglo decadent spirit by Barrero Amador, who does not appear to be aware of the disjuncture and inconsistency between his aestheticizing (and femininizing) portrait of Bécquer and his critique of 1890s decadence. The disjuncture also suggests a temporal and affective split in Barrero Amador himself, in which we glimpse a vague understanding of himself as simultaneously cursi and creative, as dated as other Bécquer imitators (and Bécquer himself?) yet also modern. Hence perhaps, too, the need to update the image of Bécquer.

The association that Barrero Amador establishes between Bécquer and a feminine sensibility is neither surprising nor new. Bécquer himself insinuates a vaguely hermaphroditic quality in the figure of the poet ("Cartas literarias" 1, *OC* 656) and of course continually plays with the notion of woman as poetry, an image that both flatters and flattens women within the patriarchal scheme of things (see Mandrell). Bécquer's complex relationship with women, both real and imaginary, lies beyond the scope of these pages, but some of the social and cultural implications of that relationship bear re-examination, particularly with respect to the ways men and women seemed to understand and feel the cultural artifacts of romanticism.

Bécquer's early association with journalism, as many commentators have pointed out, proves crucial here. He contributed not only poetry but also prose pieces, including some that clearly demonstrate intimate knowledge of salon society and the key role women played in such circles.[21] From a list of unfinished projects, we know that he had intended to take full advantage of the increased numbers of comfortably well-off female readers, in itself a sign of a more visible and prosperous Spanish bourgeoisie. For example, he planned two series—the "Biblioteca del tocador" and the "Biblioteca del bello sexo"—around women readers. He described the "Biblioteca del tocador" series, meant for women of the aristocracy, as "very small volumes, with an unheard-of luxury. Bound in gold, with corner bands of silver, silk bookmarks, and a little box in which to put them, also in the form of a book. For aristocratic women— original little novels, gilt-edged—for forming a collection and placing it in elegant boudoirs on a small ebony table. Each one, with a steel engraving. Dedicated to different ladies noted for their beauty and position. To be published monthly or fortnightly. Expensive, very expensive. The point is to make them fashionable objects of luxury" (Gamallo Fierros 433–34).[22] The "Biblioteca del bello sexo" was clearly intended for middle- and upper middle-class women: "The idea is to put together a collection of works solely by women from every period and nation. An attractive series, neither expensive nor cheap, that will begin with Sappho. Flatter the vanity of women. Include the works of Arab and Indian poetesses; in sum, a lot of glitter. It should be successful if I write an elaborate prospectus flattering women and exciting readers' curiosity with a great many names" (Gamallo Fierros 434).[23]

He also conceived another publication to be called "El álbum," "a work of nothing but autographs in the form of an album, in which good, original poetry by the best contemporary Spanish poets would be included" (Gamallo Fierros 435).[24]

Bécquer's undisguised condescension and his manipulation of women as revealed in these notes not meant for publication (and therefore of special significance) should not blind the reader, however, to something far more interesting. For one, women counted, or, at the very least, they could not be discounted, for they represented nothing less than a new readership and market. Second, we glimpse an entire social world here, dominated by women (even down to the expensively furnished, elegant boudoirs!) that didn't simply provide material for Bécquer, but constituted the context and the agency for the production of romantic culture. The artifacts of that culture—the tertulias, albums, almanacs, journals, even Bécquer's poetry—are situated in specific spaces both material and gendered. In viewing that romantic culture as a matter of place and placement, we get a tantalizing view of how poetic cultural practices could be encoded and played out within gendered modes of perception and how en-gendered poetry and poets could act out and represent the drama of modernity as both datedness and a deepening individual subjectivity. Awareness of cultural obsolescence comes precisely from a more heightened self-consciousness, the consciousness that one is this but also that at the same time, that one's feelings and actions could be regarded as simultaneously authentic and inauthentic. In other words, the social world of salons, women, tertulias, the romantic reader seen in Barrero Amador, the "swan of Vilamorta," and Bécquer himself are not simply tightly imbricated but inextricably joined together as part and parcel of the same social and cultural reality.

At least some of this more visible, exacerbated—and modern—sense of self is encoded as feminine and feminizing, specifically in certain poets and poetry. Yet the reverse, I would suggest, also holds true: the increased if still very limited visibility of women manifests itself in the gender-encoding of salon poetry and poets, imitators of Bécquer, and others. The naming and perception of feminizing language, feelings, and behavior disclose an awareness of a more public role for women of the middle, upper-middle, and high-born classes—an awareness tempered by male unease, ambivalence, and sometimes outright dislike.

In one of Bécquer's contributions to the genre of society reporting, he observes how "some balls require not simply a *review*, but a meticulous, very detailed *chronicle*" ("Revista de salones," *OC* 1162), which he proceeds to produce with obvious enjoyment, dwelling on the ladies' garb, their adornments, the textures and colors of their dresses, all of this material culture inciting in him "a kind of poetic reminiscence" (1163). In the end, he begs forgiveness for having the temerity to "embark upon unknown regions, transforming myself into a dressmaker" (1172).

No doubt Bécquer writes with tongue-in-cheek irony, but the fascination he feels for this desirable and visually resplendent "ocean of lovely ladies"—many of them described and named as part of Madrid's high society in the 1860s, such as the condesa de Guaqui and the duquesa de Fernán-Núñez—is clear. More telling is the comparison he makes between the writer and the dressmaker. Here Bécquer clearly intimates not only a social (and by implication economic) relation between male writers and women, but a social role for male writers seen as feminized.

Significantly, as López Estrada has pointed out, in the same issue and "Variedades" section of *El contemporáneo* in which Bécquer's first install-ment of the "Cartas literarias a una mujer" [Literary letters to a lady] appears, one finds this anonymous commentary in a "Crónica de la Sociedad": "The social chronicler is a very special type, *sui generis:* he is neither man nor woman, he lives in both elements, and has therefore something of the amphibian. . . . Women see him as a man, men regard him as a woman" (qtd. in López Estrada, *Poética* 74).[25]

This sexually indeterminate or ambiguous state of the Becquerian poet figure / society reporter / dressmaker carries over into that of the salon poet as well. In a caustic 1888 satire, Moreno Godino describes the literary type in these terms: "He is born of poor parents . . . but generally in countries where men are more like women. He has ambition in his own way: the ambition of a woman who shows off her jewelry or silk shoes in the salons, and for this reason no sooner is he in the position of *salon poet,* he has reached his goal. Because it is said that all men have something of the poet in them, but the salon poet has very little of the man; he is no more a genuine poet than a gorilla is a man. The gorilla apes human nature; the poet, poetry itself" (5–6).[26] Worst of all for Moreno Godino, this facade of a poet even gets paid for his work! He weeps copious verbal tears over the dead child of a friend in his salon and then publishes the verses afterward. Every act, public or private, therefore is payback time of one sort or another: "At the heart of his poetry is a deceit, full of debts. He struggles to be gracious; in the salons he reads the verses of his fellow poets with the insidious complacency of the marriageable girl dressing a bride, but he reads them so well! He's so tender, so witty, so *local*! So local! I should think so, rather! This localness is revealed in his home life" (7).[27] The salon poet's home is meticulously run, with everything in its place, including "a *notebook for jotting down thoughts,* which is always at hand" (7).

Although it isn't altogether clear in my mind what Moreno Godino means precisely by the term *local,* it does seem to imply a kind of programmatic (and pragmatic) poet, a mail-order poetry catalogue filled with domestic detail. The salon poet even avoids salt in his meals! The attention to small, unimportant details and the housewifely sense of order found in the salon poet make him "local," that is, circumscribed to a limited, domestic setting that is above all feminine. Hence it is not surprising that women favor him, says Moreno Godino. The salon poet delights in his female adorers, like the master (or a eunuch?) in his harem (7). He concludes, "the salon poet in his role as male siren enchants the ladies" (10).[28]

The premier salon poet in the 1870s and 1880s especially was Antonio Fernández Grilo (1845–1906), a man whose work was as well known and as frequently recited as that of Bécquer, Zorrilla, and Espronceda, although it has been completely forgotten today (along with the poetry of José Selgas, Emilio Ferrari, Manuel del Palacio, Juan Tomás Salvany, and a host of other poets). Grilo was adored and detested in equal measure. Even those who appreciated and defended him tended to complain of how the constant social demands to produce and recite verses everywhere had ruined Grilo's poetic gifts (Sanz Cuadrado). Barrero Amador compares him favorably to Bécquer but hastens to add, "not the Grilo of today, not the flattering court poet who only writes trivial fluff" (199). Like Bécquer, Grilo possesses a "woman's soul" (Barrero Amador 199).

His detractors are legion, most notably among them Leopoldo Alas: "Grilo is such a bad poet that if there were no Velardes in the world, he would qualify as the worst poet of all," he declares in "Versicultura. Grilus Vastatrix" (93).[29] Acidly commenting on one of Grilo's poetic compositions, he says, "In sum, this [presumably] *unpublished* poem by Grilo is like one of those little wool doggies, with glass eyes, that quartermasters' widows who receive gentlemen in their rooms have; little doggies that are the remains of a badly understood, youthful romanticism."[30] In a word, Grilo is cursi. "That's not being a poet, Grilo," Clarín remarks, "that's being a dressmaker" (97).[31] His admirers ought to give him, the critic says, not a silver inkwell or a gold pen, but a *silent* Singer sewing machine (97). Once again, the image of poet as dressmaker, here wickedly funny, surfaces in the form of verbal transvestism.

Grilo, like other salon poets, also suffers attacks for his material success, for knowing how to put his business instincts to work in settings like private salons, court society, and poetry competitions. As late as 1901, readers could still come across comments like this one: "Verses by Grilo!

More verses by Grilo! Prices slashed by half!" (Carretero, "La vida
literaria" 250).[32] From the same critic, "When Grilo reads aloud, he
reads retreads" ("Mis vates" 465).[33] Antonio de Valbuena calls poetic
redundancy a "Griliada" (42).[34] Palacio Valdés reiterates Grilo's empty
verbosity ("Don Antonio F. Grilo" 1227, 1230). In a caricature, Angel
María Segovia says, playing off the similarity of sounds (Grilo-grillo):
"Rather than a Grilo, he's a *cricket*; he always sings to the same tune"
("Grilo" 135).[35] Finally, to put an arbitrary stop to the endless list of
Grilo detractors, Emilia Pardo Bazán writes, "Grilo, oh lord. . . . He
seems to enjoy the sympathies of the ladies of the court, and the queen
mother, who evidently is in funds, publishes his poetry . . . none of it
comes close to matching the best of Parnassus" (*El cisne de Vilamorta*
230).[36]

Pardo Bazán is referring to the royal patronage of Isabel II, María
Cristina, and Alfonso XII (as well as the support of many aristocrats)
that Grilo received. In a letter dated 26 February 1882, Isabel II writing
from Paris promised to pay for his next book of poetry: "Here, at my
side, you will publish your poetry." Publication of the book would be,
among other things, "an inheritance for your daughter."[37] More con-
cretely, it was meant to provide a marriage dowry for his daughter
Magdalena. Both Grilo and, perhaps more poignantly, his daughter,
however, had to wait until 1891 for *Ideales* [Ideals] to appear in a handsome, deluxe edition.

One may wonder how Grilo could possibly achieve the popularity he
did. The poet's attractive personality and his special talent for recitation
contributed significantly to his appeal. Like Zorrilla before him, with
whom he was on more than one occasion favorably compared (see
J. Navarrete), Grilo had a special flair for public readings, often with
piano accompaniment (Darío 203). His poetry was easily memorized,
having a certain singsong quality. His most often quoted piece, "Las
ermitas de Córdoba" [The hermitages of Córdoba], was so popular that
it was reproduced thousands of times in pamphlet form (*pliegos sueltos*)
and distributed along with postcards and other objects of interest to
tourists and pilgrims in Córdoba.[38] As late as 1928, in *Lecturas*, a publication aimed at a mass readership and specializing in *refritos* (recycled
literary material), the poem is reprinted next to photographs of the
religious retreats, a plaque commemorating Grilo, and another poem of

his, "A mi primer hijo, que nació muerto" [To my first son, born dead] ("Antonio Grilo. Poetas del siglo XIX" 775–77).

Carlos María Cortezo, a popular physician in his day, associated a sentimental cursilería with his fondness for poets like Grilo, Ruiz Aguilera, and Salvany. "There was a good reason I didn't want to become a doctor," he explained in his memoirs, "I am too sentimental, too romantic, too *cursi*, for the permanent exercise of consoling another person's pain, to resign myself to the role of being *impermeable*, of not letting the rain of other people's tears soak me through and through" (187).[39] Another Grilo admirer, Ramón Sarmiento, wrote with great enthusiasm that the poet's 1891 collection *Ideales* was selling like hotcakes (222), even four years after its first publication. For him, Grilo is the most popular and beloved of Spanish poets in the entire century. "And the poet," he says, "continues interpreting the sentiments of the Spanish people."[40] Popular reactions toward other poets, including Bécquer, echo the feeling that Grilo evoked in readers and listeners beyond the confines of court society. Barrero Amador recalled that he often heard Bécquer's poetry recited from the lips of an old peasant woman in his childhood: "Even then, without knowing why, I felt something strange inside myself hearing the poems" (188).[41]

How did Grilo recite and how did readers react? José Alcalá Galiano says in 1877, at the height of Grilo's popularity, that his admirers came from every social sphere, his friends "from every class, age, and type, whom he infallibly addresses on familiar terms, and they him, as the *tú* form seems to be the official style of address of this poet of poets" (395; also Criado Costa 203).[42] The increased use of the more intimate form of address ("tú") in an age of notable formality suggests that Grilo's persona and poetry reflected and promoted the already visible processes of democratization occurring in Restoration Spain.

Alcalá Galiano also calls Grilo a "Proteus" because of his many and sparkling talents for reciting, improvising, acting, and conversing with great wit and flair at salons and other social gatherings. He gives a long account of a typical evening spent with Grilo, part of which I reproduce here:

Dotado de portentosa fantasía, eléctrica viveza de comprensión, agudo ingenio, fácil y pintoresca palabra, tiene los elementos infalibles del éxito, los talismanes irresistibles de la seducción. Penetra en un salón, y apenas ha saludado a los hombres serios, piropeado a las bellas, adulado a las feas y alegrado a los tristes, óyese una voz que irremisiblemente exclama: "Grilo, diga V. versos." Como los rapsodas homéricos, los bardos, trovadores y minnesinger, él lleva, no la lira, el arpa o el laúd al hombro, pero sí la canción en el labio. El tomo vivo de sus versos, parlante, estereotipado indeleble en su memoria, espera sólo el manubrio de la voluntad para resonar en todos sus registros. No hay, pues, excusa posible, levántase el poeta, toma su actitud lírica, y de sus labios empieza a brotar un raudal de gorgeos rítmicos, modulaciones métricas, endecasílabas de oro, sáficos sonantes como el cristal, quintillas blandas como arrullos, seguidillas como mariposas juguetonas, estrofas épicas templadas como el acero toledano, lamentos enamorados, descripciones estereoscópicas, mosaicos de imágenes y arabescos de mil colores.

[Blessed with a marvelous sense of fantasy, an electric, lively intelligence, a sharp wit, and a quick, silvery tongue, [Grilo] possesses all the infallible elements for success, the irresistible talismans of seductiveness. He enters a room, and having scarcely greeted the solemn-faced men, paid compliments to the beautiful ladies, flattered the plain janes, and cheered up the melancholy, a voice is inevitably heard to exclaim: "Grilo, recite something for us." Like the Homeric rhapsodists, the bards, troubadours, and minnesingers of yore, he carries, not the lyre, the harp, or the lute over his shoulder, but a song on his lips. The living, speaking book of his poetry, indelibly impressed in his memory, he's just waiting to crank himself up and let all the registers resonate. There's no excuse possible then, the poet rises, takes a lyric pose, and from his lips begins to gush a torrent of rhythmic trills, metrical modulations, golden hendecasyllables, sapphic verses sounding like crystal, quintets as soft as turtle doves, *seguidillas* like playful butterflies, epic stanzas tempered like Toledan steel, passionate plaints, stereotypic descriptions, mosaics of imagery and arabesques of a thousand colors] (395).

In his poetic improvisations, Alcalá Galiano continues,

136

todo surge de allí rápido, vertiginoso, hirviente, volcánico, sin detenerse ni tropezar, como si de antemano estuviese presentido, profetizado, escrito en el entendimiento, y el poeta lo fuere leyendo en sí propio por medio de una pupila interna y sobrenatural. Las improvisaciones de este domador de consonantes son una especie de revista militar, donde las estrofas hacen evoluciones y se forman obedientes a la suprema voz de mando; parecen una evocación de sombras salidas al conjuro de un duende ebrio, un apocalipsis fantástico producido por el *hatchish* [*sic*].

[everything surges up like wildfire, vertiginous, boiling, volcanic, without stopping or stumbling, as if it were already intuited and prophesied, as if already written in his mind, as if the poet were reading it within himself through an internal, supernatural eye. The improvisations of this tamer of consonants are a kind of military review, where stanzas make turns and line up obediently to the supreme voice of command; they seem like an evocation of shadows conjured up by an intoxicated spirit, a fantastic apocalypse produced by the effects of *hashish*.] (395)

To read Grilo's poetry, he says, is to possess a mere trace or echo of his gifts, which were far more impressive as the spoken word than as the printed page.[43]

The art of recitation was considered a social grace in polite society throughout nineteenth-century Europe and the Americas. Sometime in the early twentieth century, it died out.[44] Mrs. Sigourney attached great importance "to distinct, deliberate utterance both in reading and conversation." "The recitation of select passages of poetry," she continued, "was found a salutary exercise in the regulation of tone and emphasis" (212–13). Recitation and reading aloud were also considered pedagogically sound as a form of learning, not only by good example but by bad ones as well. Thus one could not only improve one's speaking but writing by reading passages filled with *disparates gramaticales* (grammatical nonsense) and learning to spot the errors (Olózaga 238). Above all, correct, clear speech denoted the refinement of social class.

The formal recitation of verse, like the publication of salon poetry, was materially embedded in specific social and cultural settings and provided a mechanism for the social classes practicing such arts to transmit through public performance and in print a record of their own existence. The places of such poetry also constituted a matter of social (em)placement. As Marta Palenque has amply demonstrated, one can follow public events of a social nature and even private griefs by tracking the names to whom poems and books were dedicated, the albums and homages (to the dead and the living) in which poetry appears, and the subjects chosen for poetic compositions (the birth or death of a child, a wedding, or a celebration).[45] Salon poetry functioned, in this regard, somewhat like the society columns that flourished in newspapers during the same period (Palenque, *Gusto poético* 48). Salon poets like Antonio Grilo had much in common with the society chronicler, as both were culturally encoded as feminized, pointing, indirectly, to the more public role of middle- and upper-middle-class women.

To dismiss cultural phenomena like Antonio Grilo or the mania of *becquerianismo* as mere social fashions of the times is to seriously underestimate and misjudge the subjective intensity with which such poetry could be experienced. Grilo's improvisations seemed to one listener, we recall, "an evocation of shadows conjured up by an intoxicated spirit, a fantastic apocalypse produced by the effects of *hashish*." In his childhood, Barrero Amador internalized the poetry of Bécquer: "Even then, without knowing why, I felt something strange inside myself hearing the poems" (188). That sense of "something strange" was something new, a different way to represent and to act out the drama of the imagined self in a socially instituted forum, itself doomed to change.

CHAPTER FOUR

Textual Economies: The Embellishment of Credit

IT IS EASY to see how the stories of cursi inadequacy, datedness, and inauthenticity provoked laughter and satire in the past century—and how they still do. Indeed, the inability of present-day critics and cultural historians to take seriously the phenomenon of cursilería until recently reduced this rich cultural vein to a rather stale, one-note joke.[1] Of course, some of these stories really are funny. Whenever the social pretensions of people or of customs fall short and are then held up to ridicule, the cruel ironies of joking come out to play. The petite bourgeoisie's social climbing and its claims to culture made delectably easy targets for social and literary commentators everywhere in nineteenth-century Europe and the Americas. Precisely this desire to move ahead, however, suggests some of the deeper, underlying feelings incarnated in cursi behavior, feelings that not only took the shape of new expressive forms for individual personality but also assumed the ambitious desires of hoped-for prosperity and advancement. In other words, cursilería is not a uniquely negative phenomenon. There is a social and psychological drive behind cursilería that can only be understood as future-directed.

This sense of the self as projected forward, as therefore evolving and changeable, certainly isn't new, and takes especially striking forms in literature. Don Quijote hurled himself into an invented self and history to which only the imposition of death could put an end. Yet ironically, Cervantes' great character creation took on the anachronistic, dead forms of chivalry to forge a new self. He looked backward in order to go forward. Perhaps even more pertinent for my purposes here, Don Quijote worked through his illusions (in the double sense of the phrase) to acquire a form of self-knowledge. While self-interest arguably also plays a role in at least some of his actions (for example, in the *baciyelmo* episode), Don Quijote's espousal of chivalresque generosity and the virtue of disinterested behavior points away from self-interest as a primary motivating ethos in the novel. This is not to say self-interest can't be found in literary texts of the early modern period: the picaresque, socially and economically driven, suffices as an example.

The awareness of an illusionary self in Spanish fictions of the late nineteenth century is no less intense than it was in the baroque age. But something else has also emerged in the meantime: the ambiguous, difficult-to-define forms of the petite bourgeoisie, with a strongly developed instinct for commerce. By the 1860s, increased financial speculation in such things as railroads and government securities, abetted by proliferating credit societies and foreign capital, had created a climate of expectations, especially in Madrid, that did not disappear with the economic crisis of 1866 and the subsequent political revolution of 1868. Historians and others have examined this culture of credit in 1850s and 1860s Spain.[2] What is of particular interest here is the relationship between credit and social and personal behavior, between credit and the expression of personality. For it is in the interstices, or the interaction between the two where a different kind of capital is produced, one generally known as cultural capital (see Bourdieu). Cursi-behavior results from the interplay between personality and inadequate cultural capital. This kind of behavior—or persona—I would also suggest, emerges symptomatically as class-related forms of self-interest, not previously recognized, are redefined (and justified) as the interests of the public or collective body. In part, the insufficiencies of cursi behavior and personas expose the gap between the two forms of interests (private, class-related versus public or national).

In his brilliant discussion of the financial revolution of 1690s England, Pocock has observed that the expansion of public credit created a different kind of relationship between investors and government, a relationship of interdependency, which was itself a form of property. He goes on to say that this kind of speculation encouraged a mind-set that was both future-directed and imaginatively construed. By placing their faith and confidence in speculation and credit, investors gambled that the future would realize their fantasies, whatever those fantasies might be. As Pocock puts it, this "belief in such a future . . . [was rooted in] . . . imagination, fantasy or passion. . . . Men, it seemed, were governed by opinion, and by opinion as to whether certain governing fantasies would even become realized" (98–99). Indeed, the image of credit, like the goddess Fortuna, is seen as changeable, unreliable, and, above all, feminine. Unlike calculation, speculation is founded on fantasy, on the irrational (Pocock 69). It feeds desires, and illusions fuel it. In this sense, a culture in which credit runs rampant encourages self-interest and discourages the virtue of self-knowledge. Speculation and illusion go hand in hand, blinding private and public interest to the extent that both must stake their future in something intangible, something not yet existent, with the promise of actualizing itself in some desired form or another. This desire, situated as it is in the future, already constitutes a kind of property, personalized by the private motivations of the investor, motivations that, in the case of public credit, also become wrapped up, and identified with, larger, national concerns.

As commerce grew in the eighteenth and nineteenth centuries, and the advantages of engaging in commercial activities proved irresistible, the products of commerce, especially those considered unnecessary, or luxuries, came under attack. As had been the case for centuries, traditionalists used moral arguments to condemn "the commercial vice," while others, like Adam Smith in *The Wealth of Nations* (1776), whose ideas had been introduced into Spain during the reign of Carlos III, countered that "the economy *required* the free exercise of self-interest" (Sekora 104). David Hume allowed that "luxury is a word of uncertain signification, and may be taken in a good as well as in a bad sense" (299).

By the late nineteenth century, the critique of luxury had lost most of its ordering transcendence as both a general moral and ethical principle and as an explanation for individual and collective social decline.[3] Luxuries in the external form of things prevailed increasingly over the more inner-directed conception of the term, which once signified profound disorder, excess, and extravagance throughout Western society. The course of luxury was seen historically and morally as a form of entropic behavior, working from the inside out. Not only persons but entire nations were susceptible. It was no different in Spain. Fray Antonio Arbiol's 1725 *Estragos de la luxuria, y sus remedios, conforme a las Divinas Escrituras, y Santos Padres de la Iglesia* [The ravages of lust; and its remedies, according to the Holy Scriptures and Holy Fathers of the Church] (published in 1786) is a case in point. As Bridget Aldaraca has observed, writers like Fray Luis de León in *La perfecta casada* [The perfect wife] (1583) and Arbiol insisted heavily on the centuries-old association between *el lujo* and *lujuria,* between luxury and lust, symbolized and often incarnated in woman's frailty and vanity as the connecting link between the two (96). In moments of social and economic crisis, moreover, the charge of effeminacy was correlated with moral laxity and luxury, as Maravall has shown for seventeenth-century Spain (*Culture of the Baroque* 37–38). The same holds true for the eighteenth century, when the connection was made between luxury and the excessively fashion-conscious female figure called the *petimetra* (from the French *petit maître*) and between luxury and effeminacy in her male equivalent of the *petimetre* (see Haidt, *Embodying Enlightenment* 108–15). Examples abound in the theater of Ramón de la Cruz (as in *El petimetre*). Fernández de Moratín's *La Petimetra* (1762) readily comes to mind as symptomatic of such a connection (and as a precedent for a figure like Rosalía de Bringas).

As late as 1856, texts echoing a catastrophic causality between sin, desire, and history could be read in Spain as these words by Basilio Sebastián Castellanos de Losada reveal:

> El lujo, elevado a su mayor potencia, es el gusano roedor de la presente sociedad europea: es un cáncer devorador. . . . Ha llegado a imperar de tal modo el lujo en nuestra sociedad que la ha corrompido: ya nadie se contenta con una modesta fortuna; es preciso andar en carroza y vivir a lo príncipe, y para conseguirlo, no hay crimen que se economice ni bajeza que no se ponga en juego . . . Este cáncer devorador . . . tiene en el bello sexo su mayor fuerza . . . En el lujo vemos mucha parte de los males que aquejan a nuestra sociedad, cuyo origen es la falta de fe religiosa y la inmoralidad corruptora de las costumbres.

> [Luxury, elevated to its highest degree, is the gnawing worm of present-day European society: it is a devouring cancer. . . . Luxury has ended up ruling over our society to such an extent that it has corrupted it: no one is content anymore with a modest fortune. You have to go about in a coach and live like a prince, and to get that, there's no crime nor vileness impossible to conceive or do . . . This devouring cancer . . . has in the fair sex its strongest ally. . . . In luxury we see many of the ills which beset our society, which are

due to the lack of religious faith and the corrupting immorality of customs.]

He adds in a long footnote that the obsession with French fashion in everything, especially dress, has compounded the problem, creating an even more pernicious and extravagant luxury ("El siglo XIX" 671).

All the topoi related to riotous luxury are here: sickly depravity, social ambition, female corruption, irreligiosity, and enervating foreign influence—the whole enveloped in a literally vicious circle of material and moral excess. Luxury leads to more luxury, which is both symptomatic and causative of social, sexual, and religious disorder. The desire for luxury promotes, for example, class impertinence—"[luxury] has awakened in the lower classes plagued by these exaggerated ideas hostile to the rich, those whom socialism aims to dispossess"—but he does not say why luxury should be particularly harmful to the lower classes or women for that matter. Castellanos de Losada, a highborn archaeologist and scholar, was responding in part to the diminishing wave of post-1848 revolutionary fervor, relatively little of which had directly affected Spain.[4] More significant in this context and germane to his response were the effects of slow but steady commercial and industrial growth and expansion in 1850s and 1860s Spain. Clearly the traditional attack on luxury had acquired historical overtones that partially explain how luxury had become a displaced figure of social and economic change.

Several years later (and after the 1866 financial crash), another social commentator argued, albeit in an ironic vein, that luxury was not necessarily a bad thing. The passage is long, but exemplary, I believe, of a far more secularized if highly ambivalent view of luxury and commerce in the second half of the nineteenth century. What is luxury, the (once popular) poet-journalist José Selgas asks in 1871:

Siempre ha sido la señal evidente de la decadencia de las naciones, el síntoma grave de la corrupción de los pueblos, y el anuncio de su ruina . . . Pero eso era antes, cuando el hombre, envuelto en las tinieblas de la ignorancia, andaba a ciegas por el camino del progreso . . . Hoy el lujo . . . es eso que llamamos desarrollo de los intereses materiales, es eso que se llama economía por burla y ciencia por sarcasmo, es eso que con altanera satisfacción llamamos prosperidad pública. Pensadlo bien; el lujo es el fomento de esa vida del comercio, el alma de la Bolsa. Es el gran resorte que nos empuja por el camino del progreso moderno, es esa necesidad activa que a todos nos mueve.

[Luxury] has always been the clear sign of decadence in nations, a grave symptom of corruption in peoples, and the clarion of ruin. . . . But that was before, when man, enveloped in the shadows of ignorance, walked blindly on the road to progress. . . . Today luxury . . . is that which we call the development of material interests, or mockingly call economics and sarcastically label science; it is what we call, with high-handed complaisance, public prosperity. Think about it: luxury foments the life of commerce, the soul of the Stock Exchange. It is the great mechanism that pushes us along the road of modern progress, that active necessity which moves us all.] ("El lujo de las mujeres" 132)

Notice how luxury has now become a necessity whereas the two terms had stood in opposition to each other before (Sekora, *Luxury* xiii). Selgas then brings in the main subject of his piece: women and luxury. "The luxury of women!" he exclaims. "That is simply a captious way of presenting the question, because women have come to be regarded as nothing more than the luxury of men" (133).[5] Suppress luxury, he continues, and you bring on ruination (not the reverse). What (nonexistent) virtue can now replace luxury, which is the religion of materialism? How can we men, he asks, expect women to give up that which legitimately corresponds to them, "in the universal enjoyment of public ownership"? Why shouldn't women spend what they haven't got, when nations and governments do the same? By the end of his piece, Selgas has shifted his address from men ("vosotros") to women ("vosotras"), concluding: "If virtue condemns you, civilization absolves you" (134, 136).[6] Moral critique wrapped in sarcasm and irony should not blind readers to the essential ambivalence of Selgas's view here. Both men and women are complicit in the prevailing historical and socioeconomic process that makes questions of morality and virtue seem ultimately irrelevant.

Selgas was a moderate conservative who tended to go with the political flow of his times (Aranda 42–43, 51). He may also reflect more accurately middle-class aspirations and values than the rigid moralism of Counter-Reformation texts, no matter how many times they may have been redigested or reprinted in the past century (as in the case of Fray Luis de León's *La perfecta casada*). This isn't to say that traditional views on luxury (and women) went unheeded, simply that other perspectives on the subject also existed and that we don't know what kinds of correspondence existed between such thinking and actual behavior. Manuals and didactic texts in general are notoriously unreliable as indicators of real behavior, practices, and beliefs. Even the intertextual presence of manuals and tracts (particularly from an earlier period) in literary and other writings must be carefully interpreted since the literalness, the material impact of such didactic texts and messages, is no longer univocal once incorporated into other cultural and interpretive spaces such as novels and plays.

I note this difficulty in judging the role and impact of normative thinking—such as the attacks against luxury (and women)—for another reason. If one is to believe that such traditional ideology still dominated in nineteenth-century Spain, then how to explain social and other kinds of changes? There persists in critics an ahistoricist tendency toward cultural reification, especially when it comes to understanding the complex role and status of women in nineteenth-century Spanish society and literature. Investigators simply don't know enough about the historical, cultural situation of women in the past century to conclude that stereotypes like the proverbial frivolity of women (or the domestic angel, for that matter) define the condition of women or of texts (see Jagoe; Aldaraca). How does, for example, one read these words from Pilar Sinués de Marco's didactic work, *El ángel del hogar* (1859), "We do not absolutely condemn luxury, which encouraged the arts; and it is fitting that ladies of high rank dress with the elegance and expense that corresponds to them, thus passing on profits to the tradesmen, silversmiths, jewelers, and other artisans. . . . and because we who have cried out with all our strength against the detestable vice of avarice, desire that money circulate" (2:134).[7] While Sinués de Marco goes on to say that virtue is a woman's greatest luxury, she does not discount luxury, or commerce, for that matter, in her moral universe. By privileging normative representativeness, critics reduce the rich contradictions of the period to the one-dimensional, to prototypical sameness.

To illustrate my point, let's take a look at Selgas once more. Through irony and satire, he *seems* to condemn luxury, especially luxury in women, as a sign of modern times. But what does he reveal in the meantime? Whether Selgas is comfortable with modern commerce or materialist interests is, of course, germane to understanding his position. But in another sense, it is irrelevant because, irony aside, he also reveals that luxuries did indeed circulate in 1870s Spain. It helps to remember that much of Selgas's *Delicias del nuevo paraíso* [Delights of the new paradise], in which "El lujo de las mujeres" [The luxury of women] appears, was first published in *La ilustración española y americana,* a highly successful, commercial enterprise (1869–1921), which was marketed as a luxury item financed through subscriptions and advertising. The *Ilustración* was printed on high-quality paper and boasted excellent prints and lithographs as well as equally prestigious contributors.[8] Selgas got in on the ground floor with the *Ilustración.*

Luxuries and capitalist entrepreneurship didn't just spring up overnight in 1870s Spain.[9] Antonio Flores's social sketches of the 1850s give an indication of the adoption and absorption of modernizing attitudes in urban centers like Madrid and Barcelona. Flores is especially taken by the image of the window display. Nowadays, he says, everything and everyone are on display. "What else is the Stock Exchange of state finance but the showcase of national credit? And isn't journalism a windowpane, a kind of magnifying glass, into that exquisite armoir called public opinion" ("Los escaparates," *La sociedad de 1850* 192)?[10] He then takes readers window-shopping on a tour of luxury items—silks, fine porcelain and crystal, diamonds and other jewelry—that, he claims, are now attracting visitors to the capital, where before no one came to Madrid to purchase luxuries (199).

Not to belabor the point: there was, by the 1850s, some sort of market for such goods and, more significantly, a perceived need and acceptance of luxury items. This awareness of a new, developing relationship between persons and things, symbolized in the window display, suggests that by only looking at the attacks against luxury, critics miss the big picture: that something in Spanish middle-class life had changed. Moreover, the production and consumption of such things as luxuries pointed to a more intricate relationship between private and public spheres of the social body, or, as Flores comments, "Indeed to deny that the stomach has its glasspane in patriotic banquets, the conscience its own window in the casinos and clubs, the head its platform in the atheneums and public social gatherings, and that all of society doesn't live inside a crystal showcase, would be the same as denying our very existence and saying that publicity isn't the soul of this generation" (193).[11]

I take the word *publicity* here as symptomatic not only of commercial but of social enterprise, in the sense that persons of the middle and upper classes (however ill-defined these groups remain) were now moving in a theater of behavior that was an inextricable mixture of private and public life, a self-conscious creation and proclaiming of self *and* property. We can also detect a quasi-metaphoric sense here, in the commercial imagery of the display and publicity, of the material qualities of public behavior as though the latter were an object produced and utilized for a variety of purposes. Behavior thus becomes a kind of property of a particular class, in the dual meaning of character trait and possession.

Nowhere does Flores suggest an incipient commodification of persons, but he does indicate a complexification based on this relationship between persons and things (which does not, however, completely rule out commodification in some instances). This is also what the realist novel explores. It is not so much the purchase or possession of things in themselves but the complex and sometimes unpredictable relationship with things that paradoxically adds to the human dimensions of nineteenth-century texts and culture. Within an economic structure moving toward capitalistic practices, this relationship becomes linked to ambition and desire, to a future-directed dynamic which is increasingly, and alarmingly for traditionalists, secularized.

Luxuries, in the commentaries of both Selgas and Flores, are closely associated with a culture of credit, whether on an individual or collective level. Thus even the nation is not exempt: "What else is the Stock Exchange of state finance but the showcase of national credit?" asks Flores. Elsewhere he writes that "credit is the great fountain of public wealth" ("Las fuentes de la riqueza pública," *La sociedad de 1850* 183). Selgas equates public prosperity with luxury, with what he later calls "the universal enjoyment of public ownership," from which he does not exclude women (134). Such universal enjoyment comes with a price and, indeed, for both women and nations, the luxury of public prosperity seems to be increasingly purchased on credit. It is evident, moreover, that both Selgas and Flores (and they are not alone) equate middle-class culture with the national culture as a whole.

For Selgas especially, however, luxury and credit are still linked to the problem of virtue, as his conclusion to "El lujo de las mujeres," directed to women readers, attests: "If virtue condemns you, civilization absolves you" (136). Selgas himself sums up, however reductively, a dilemma that nearly all modernizing Western societies have had to face. This tension between virtue and commerce, as Pocock observes, never disappears. Indeed, he notes further that "the problem of personality persisted as the core of the matter" (122–23). Another way of understanding this relationship between commerce, luxury, and persons is to approach the question as an instance of what Terry Eagleton calls "a pervasive aestheticizing of social practices." Here, manners—the civilizing process— "[convert] morality to style, aestheticizing virtue and so deconstructing the opposition between the proper and the pleasurable" ("The Ideology of the Aesthetic" 20–21). Whether this change truly elides the tension between commerce and virtue or not is probably open to question, but certainly such social and economic transformations allow one to see a particularly complex structure of feeling expressed materially and psychologically through the exercise of personality.[12]

Once, however, the mobile instability of individual desire and personality come to play a major role in social and economic relationships, the question of virtue or morality, while still germane, loses its centrality, either as a social (or textual) practice or as a critical basis of understanding. Other considerations begin to occupy more space, especially in social classes increasingly future-directed and speculating in their own futures as individuals and as families. There is a close connection between financial speculation and the speculative imaginings of individual histories and familial narratives. In societies where such speculation not only clashes with traditional values and practices but must also contend with economic and cultural inadequacies—as is the case for nineteenth-century Spain—the stories emerging from these various speculations cannot be simply regarded either as morality tales or as capitalist recapitulations in miniature. Indeed, I would suggest that these stories centering on credit, commerce, and cultural capital (such as luxuries) are, more than anything else, interesting for their productive capabilities as fictions. They illustrate a particular kind of future-directed, social, and economic imagination that privileges and exploits the material world as the product, or child, of imagination. The driving force, characteristic of the middle classes in many national cultures of the past century, becomes especially problematic when material conditions are, for various reasons, inadequate.

In the pages that follow I will focus on two narratives constructed out of this intricate nexus of imagination and materiality. One is pure fiction: Benito Pérez Galdós's 1884 novel, *La de Bringas*. The other is historical: the story of the progressivist entrepreneur Pascual Madoz, and the part his young daughter Francisca played in her father's promotion of tourism in the coastal village of Zarauz. Both stories center, in the metaphorical and literal senses, on the child, not simply as a figure of the future, but as a kind of investment, or speculation on credit, capable of generating, or materializing, adult desires. Traditionally, of course, children *are* the future. Since at least the sixteenth and seventeenth centuries, family structures in Spain historically have played a crucial role in the complex ways specific families have tied their personal fortunes and future to that of the governing body.[13] The personal histories of many nineteenth-century state bureaucrats, high and middle levels alike, can be traced back to this earlier period of patrician court culture and governance. Jesús Cruz makes the point that, in both government and business circles, a large number of the Spanish upper middle classes in the last century were noble in origin (15). Equally significant were the interlocking relationships in kinship, commerce, and politics amongst these families.[14] This meant that placing one's children in the appropriate station of life in order to get ahead depended a great deal on patronage, endemic in Spanish culture until the present day. This network of family and friends, which generally had its roots in the provinces and from there spread to the capital, suggests a hybrid middle-class and upper middle-class culture in the second half of the nineteenth century, a culture in which slow modernization and timid capitalist ventures took place within largely traditional structures, such as kinship and patronage. It should be noted, however, that the historical continuity of hidalgo bloodlines and relations, while explaining one segment of Spanish society, begs the question of how a petite bourgeoisie of obscure origins emerged in Spain, and why many of those whose families could indeed be traced back to an elite class of early modern Spain felt insecure about their social status in the nineteenth century.

The figure of the child as future, imagined capital provides the metaphorical substance of Pérez Galdós's *La de Bringas,* a brilliant reenactment of the last days of Isabel II's reign in 1868 as seen through the family of a minor palace bureaucrat, Francisco Bringas. Most readers rightly regard the titular protagonist, wife Rosalía de Bringas, as the keystone to this text. Rosalía's out-of-control passion for expensive clothes, purchased on credit, and her subsequent indebtedness occur against the historical backdrop of the 1866 economic crash in Spain and the state's financial woes, which arose out of excessive speculation and insufficient credit (see Blanco and Blanco Aguinaga; and Rodríguez).[15] As many readers have observed, Galdós also draws parallels between the frivolous behavior of Rosalía and that of the queen Isabel II, and between the Bringas household situated within the Royal Palace and the larger national crisis (see Bly). But what fuels the frenzy for sartorial luxury constitutes, in my view, the heart of this novel, and that is the figure of the child as a metaphor for the domestication of credit and, hence, the legitimization of commerce and luxury in the middle-class Bringas family. Children make their appearance in this text not simply as characters of flesh and blood, but also as *hijos de la imaginación* (children of the imagination), in which the desire for things, for status, and for sensations conjures into existence those material conditions meant to ensure the success, well-being, and air of solidity for Rosalía and her family. That Rosalía's vision of the future is inadequate and, ultimately, cursi, underscores the degree to which this particular form of social and economic imagination propels forward the story, despite the narrator's critical, ironic slant. It also accentuates how thoroughly secularized the fictional world of *La de Bringas* is. Indeed, the devastating image of pervasive cursilería is transmitted through an economy of transactions based on credit. This association between credit and cursilería is fundamental: lo cursi represents insufficient cultural credit.

Precisely how Galdós establishes this linkage between lo cursi and credit (and, by extension, commerce) becomes clear in the remarkable verbal tour de force with which he begins *La de Bringas:*

Textual Economies

Era aquello ... ¿cómo lo diré yo? ... un gallardo artificio sepulcral de atrevidísima arquitectura, grandioso de traza, en ornamentos rico, por una parte severo y rectilíneo a la manera viñolesca, por otra movido, ondulante y quebradizo a la usanza gótica, con ciertos atisbos platerescos donde menos se pensaba; y, por fin, crestarías semejantes a las del estilo tirolés que prevalece en los quioscos. (53)

[It was ... how shall I put it? ... an elegant and highly ornate funeral artefact of great architectural daring and grandiose design. Some parts of it were done in the austere, straight lines of the Vignola school, while others were soaring, undulating and ethereal in the Gothic mode, with lurking touches of the Plateresque, topped off with intricate cresting reminiscent of the Tyrolean style so popular on those oriental pavilions you see in the parks these days.] (3)[16]

This incredibly detailed description occupies the entire first chapter, and it is only at the very end that we learn what the object in question is: a hair picture of miniscule size, parodically inflated out of proportion through such rhetorical devices as accumulation, zeugmatic enumeration, grotesque contrasts in miniaturization/gigantism, and other absurd stylistic disparities.[17]

What is the context for this wonderfully ridiculous exercise in classical ekphrasis, or verbal picture-making (see Bergmann)? The narrator immediately reveals, with finely turned malice, in the second chapter that the hair picture, or *trabajo de pelo,* was "[an] exquisite gift to pay off various debts of gratitude to [Bringas's] distinguished friend Manuel María José del Pez" (5).[18] The key phrase here is, of course, "debts of gratitude." Francisco's token of appreciation is not at all an example of the gift economy at work, but is in fact a modest payoff to don Manuel. Among the favors is a sinecure for eldest son Paquito within the state bureaucracy. For Rosalía, however, her son's new credentials are not a favor, but a "duty of the State" ("un deber del Estado"), in which *deber* (duty) also encapsulates the notion of a debt. In any event, debt (in its varied senses) and patronage are intimately intertwined, not only in the story line, but in the very fabric and design of the hair picture itself.

Hair pictures (and hair jewelry) were mementos of mourning, especially popular in the 1850s and 1860s. An entire industry in Europe and the Americas grew up around this fashion, but it was also common practice to make hair jewelry and pictures at home as both a diversion and a form of consolation, thus symbolically domesticating death, as Philippe Ariès has observed (ch.3; see also Douglas, ch.6).[19] The authenticity of the hair fashioned in this way mattered greatly, as don Manuel's wife Carolina makes clear in *La de Bringas:* "I will ask one thing of you. . . . Never to use hair that doesn't belong to us. The whole thing must be done in the family hair" (7).[20] Except for a bit of Carolina's white hair, Francisco's composition is made up of various strands of hair taken from the Pez children, both living and dead. The presumed memory-subject for the picture, however, is the eldest daughter of the Pez family, fifteen-year-old Juanita, who died the year before.

Sentimental fetishes, hair pictures were associated with both the feminine and commerce in the cultivation of memory. Obsessive sentimentality has been thought of as a particular form of the female fetish, in contradistinction to the male-inscribed fetishism of Freud and his followers (see Apter; and Schor, "Female Fetishism"). In *La de Bringas,* Francisco's hair picture seems to partake symbolically of both female and male fetishism, as maternal bereavement and as the sign of male impotence (along with Francisco's related, temporary blindness later). It should be remembered, however, that in practice men and women alike made hair jewelry and pictures, not only for profit but out of sentiment. Sentimentality was not the sole province of women in the last century. If hairwork implies on one level a certain feminization of the male imagination, it also suggests that men felt the same need to express loss, especially the loss of children, as women did.[21]

Galdós, however, does not dwell on loss in *La de Bringas,* but on the profitability of the dead in the service of the living. Francisco creates the hair picture not only in memory of Juanita but for the benefit of his son Paquito's future. Significantly, he uses the hairs of both the living and the dead, thus emphasizing symbolically the inseparability of the two realms and the sense of quid pro quo that circulates throughout the novel. The hair picture, with which Galdós's text begins, encapsulates the whole of the narration. It not only emblematizes in mock classical form the culture of inadequacy and of frustrated, myopic desire and ambition, but the

11. Examples of the typical tomb and willow tree scene of mourning pictures, taken from Mark Campbell's *Art of Hair Work* (1875).

very technique of presentation—a stylistic and thematic collage of fantastic and ludicrous proportions—underscores the question of size as a metaphor for culture (something already seen in Larra's "El álbum").[22] The dimensions of this object as object are diminutive, but so crammed with disparate styles and details to fill out the typical tomb and willow tree scene of mourning pictures that Francisco's hair work ironically implodes under the onslaught of the Galdosian narrator's expanding rhetoric (see fig. 11).[23] While the narrator luxuriates verbally in the profusion of incongruous detail, objects within the hair picture scene capriciously expand and contract, privileging the odd fragment over the whole, as this descriptive passage suggests:

> Tenía piramidal escalinata, zócalos grecorromanos, y luego machones y paramentos ojivales; con pináculos, gárgolas y doseletes. Por arriba y por abajo, a izquierda y derecha, cantidad de antorchas, urnas, murciélagos, ánforas, búhos, coronas de siemprevivas, aladas clepsidras, guadañas, palmas, anguilas enroscadas y otros emblemas del morir y del vivir eterno. Estos objetos se encaramaban unos sobre otros, cual si se disputasen, pulgada a pulgada, el sitio que habían de ocupar. En el centro del mausoleo, un angelón de buen talle y mejores carnes se inclinaba sobre una lápida, en actitud atribulada y luctuosa, tapándose los ojos con la mano como avergonzado de llorar; de cuya vergüenza se podía colegir que era varón. Tenía este caballerito ala y media de rizadas y finísimas plumas, que le caían por la trasera con desmayada

gentileza, y calzaba sus pies de mujer con botitos, coturnos o alpargatas; que de todo había un poco en aquella elegantísima interpretación de la zapatería angelical. (53–54)

[It boasted a pyramidal staircase, Greco-Roman plinths, buttresses, pointed arches, pinnacles, gargoyles and canopies. There was a profusion of torches, urns, bats, amphorae, owls, wreaths of ever-lastings, winged waterclocks, scythes, palm fronds, coiled serpents and other symbols of death and life eternal on all sides. These objects were clambering all over one another as if they were bat-tling amongst themselves for every available inch of space. In the middle of the mausoleum, a large and slightly tubby angel was leaning over a tombstone in a doleful and afflicted pose, covering his eyes with his hand as if embarrassed by his tears; which fact would seem to indicate that he was of the masculine variety. This young gentleman had a wing and a half full of tiny, curly feathers, which swept over his behind with swooning nobility, and his lady-like feet were shod with boots, buskins or espadrilles; for there was a little of everything in that supremely elegant rendition of angelic footwear.] (3)

A chain of metonymic, stereotypical associations of mourning is cha-otically heaped up and, instead of creating the desired unified effect, displays its individual parts as a kind of grotesque bricolage in which the sum is truly less than its parts. Meanwhile, the *angelón*, enlarged through the augmentative "-ón," suddenly shrinks to a *caballerito*, with his di-minutive appendage ("-ito") complementing a pair of daintily shod, pretty feet.

Galdós's brilliant deflation of any artistic pretensions to Francisco's hair picture has led some critics to dismiss the unworthy object as empty of any intrinsic content or significance, despite the emblematic, symbolic value usually attributed to it. Thus Hazel Gold, in a first-rate study of the hair picture, argues that "the [cenotaph] means virtually nothing; it is a monstrous, depersonalized cliché," "a purely decorative object" that "would thus seem to escape language" ("Francisco's Folly" 61). She also maintains that the cenotaph "moves further and further away from the representation of the realm of death [and] draws ever closer to other categories of perception and experience [such as] the financial, the esthetic and the sexual" (61). In one sense, of course, Gold is right: the story line of *La de Bringas* has little to do with real, material death. Juanita is immediately forgotten. And very little actual mourning takes place. Instead, as Gold points out, the hair picture is filled with other meanings. But does the cenotaph escape language? Does it move away from the realm of death?

On the contrary, as a visual and verbal cliché, the hair picture is literally and figuratively trapped in language, filled with dead meaning; clichéd language lives in the realm of death. Galdós understood this paradox particularly well. His narrator functions as an art critic here, ironically highlighting, in what has to be regarded as a spoof on critical practices (artistic and literary), the aesthetic, social, and cultural inadequacies of language use. Later, the narrator makes explicit this understanding, when he communicates Carolina's maternal wish for an appropriate homage in memory of her dead daughter Juanita. "What Mrs. Pez wanted was . . . like turning lyrical prose into poetry. . . . She wanted them to be pretty and to speak the same language as hackneyed verses, stucco, artificial flowers, gilt paint and easy Nocturnes for the piano" (6).[24]

Bringas is to serve as versifier of this poetic homage. Clearly, the hair picture is treated as, above all, a text here; language as an object; and culture itself as a form of language adornment. Here is culture at work, defining and demarcating the limits—and the limitations—of a particular period, social class, and family. The hair picture presents an image of monumentally bad taste—lo cursi to the nth degree—but is it also an "object of indifferentiation," as Gold says? The cenotaph is aesthetically and affectively unappealing (though quite wonderful as a Galdós text!) because it lacks a sense of proportion and unity while overflowing with heaped-up, heterogeneous details. This proliferation reflects nonselectivity but does not suggest indifferentiation. Indifferentiation indicates a move from the heterogeneous to the homogenous. Non-selectivity speaks for itself. Certainly Francisco's myopic vision of things refracts in miniaturized form an out-of-kilter and confused historical period. But this blurred, distorted vision, which Peter Bly has perceptively noted runs through the novel, should not lead readers to draw textually (or historically) unsustainable conclusions. It is one thing to say that *"La de Bringas* is a novel about the problematics and limits of vision" (Labanyi, "Problem of Framing" 25). It is another to argue that "the confusion of frame and centre creates a total collapse of forms" in the text (27).

Frames firmly rooted in social and historical realities always surround texts like *La de Bringas*. Moreover, the ideological underpinnings of this novel, centered on the continuation of a family, even in the midst of revolution, are never lost sight of. As Rosalía exits from the Palace and from our reading view, she reminds the narrator that the family fortunes now depend on her. Her husband and son made jobless, and her social position and virtue compromised through sexual indiscretion, Rosalía sets out, "serene and somewhat majestic . . . [and] her eyes shone with proud conviction, for she was conscious of her role as linchpin of the family in such dire circumstances" (185).[25] Readers may smirk like the ironic (and ethically questionable) narrator over her moral and economic fall, but her queenly departure—clearly reminiscent of Isabel II's fate—also evokes grudging admiration. Rosalía's eyes are on the future; she will hook up with the wealthy, newly aristocratic families of finance and banking in an exchange of favors that needs no spelling out.

For understanding this novel's social frame, it is also significant that Galdós chose the historical name "Bringas" for his protagonists. The real Bringas family history can be traced back to the first half of the eighteenth century, when Francisco de Bringas López arrived in Madrid. Apparently from Asturias and of noble origins, by 1780 he was "supplier of the Court and Royal Residences." His nephew, Francisco Antonio de Bringas y Presilla, would inherit his fortune, but also proved quite enterprising himself, well known as one of the largest lenders in Madrid and as a real estate speculator. By the 1830s, however, his descendants, according to Jesús Cruz, "lived off their inherited estates and their positions in the state bureaucracy" (40). Evidently, in Galdós's time, the Bringas family had disappeared from the first ranks of the business and social elite, although a saying had survived, "Si compras en casa Bringas o regateas o la pringas" (Shop at Bringas's, and it's either give and take or get taken) (Ortiz Armengol 248).[26] While Galdós's Francisco Bringas is unrelated to the historical Bringas family, the ironic parallels suggest otherwise. The fictional Bringas, a lowly state bureaucrat of a miserly nature, seems a much degraded version of the earlier, far more success-ful, real-life merchants of the same name. Perhaps the single most signifi-cant feature linking the fictional and the historical Bringas families to-gether is their common proclivity toward speculation.

For most readers of Galdós's novel, however, Francisco Bringas epit-omizes the economy of savings. He calculates his outlay of expenses for the hair picture down to the last strand (so to speak). Every penny in the household budget must be accounted for. He hoards money. In his tem-porary blindness brought on by fanatical devotion to completing the cenotaph, he obsessively touches and caresses the worn, greasy edges of the monies he's saved. His economic worldview is, apparently, the very opposite of the spendthrift Rosalía's. Critics have seen these two econo-mies as representing the tension between traditional values (Francisco's emphasis on saving) and a new, evolving capitalist mind-set in which money must be circulated and credit encouraged (Rosalía's extravagant shopping sprees).[27] Such tension undoubtedly exists in a transitional, hybrid economy and society. In this, the critics have also picked up on Galdós's flawless satire and exploitation of gendered stereotypes: the male miser and the female spendthrift.

But once again, we lose something by sticking to the obvious, to the representative, missing the one thing Francisco and Rosalía share: their enthusiasm for speculation (in the largest sense of the word), the particu-lar kind of social and economic imagination that not only motivates their actions, personalities, and the story itself, but also frames the novel within a specific cultural and historical context. Both husband and wife project their desires into existence by mentally constructing the material world as the children of their imagination. Whether it is clothes or the hair picture hardly matters since the same fetishizing impulse informs them equally. Francisco's down-to-the-penny, feverish calculations sim-ply represent the other side of his similarly obsessive speculations on the form his miniature masterpiece will assume: "[Francisco] was in the epileptic throes of artistic gestation. The work which had formed so recently in his mind was announcing, by the stirrings deep down inside him, that it was a living thing. . . . At the same time, he savoured the image of the work-to-be in his imagination, thinking of it delivered whole and quivering and complete, in the shape of the mould in which it was cast. And then again, he would see it being born bit by bit, first one part coming out, then another, until the whole thing emerged into the light" (8).[28]

Paradoxically, the cenotaph completely engulfs Bringas's imagination and thus grows progressively larger in his inner world, even as the narrator himself rhetorically magnifies the tiny object in each successive chapter. Enlargement and proliferation of details, however, occur within a miniscule, cramped space, the cultural-economic space of the miser. The cenotaph is a brilliant representation of the inner contradictions of late nineteenth-century middle-class values. Its fetishized nature, the obsessive insistence on its individual parts, become eroticized not simply as an extension of Francisco's own undisclosed desires, but for their own sake. The merits of the hair picture become less important than the all-consuming nature of the object, which assumes, as fetishes do, a life of its own. The cenotaph becomes a fiction within the fiction; it takes on an independence of existence that allows us not only to forget the origins of the object in real death and the bodies of dead children but in the living as well. The hair picture does what language does in the narrator's magnification of the same object: it creates the almost magical illusion of being unattached to its maker, projected as it is onto a future of completion (the cenotaph will never be finished), and at the same time it empowers — through contiguity — the maker himself.[29] Why should this be so? Because the hair picture itself makes for a kind of language, a language of the living and the dead literally and figuratively speaking. In seeing parts of the cenotaph arise prefigured in his overwrought imagination, Francisco gains empowerment as an image-maker.

It is important at this point to return to the object's material origins within this social-economic imagination at work. The hair picture represents partial payment of a debt of gratitude. Children as a figure of the future, as future capital, are literally woven into its fabric and composition. What finally emerges are Francisco's own children of the imagination, the bits and pieces of the cenotaph and, of course, the cenotaph itself. The individual parts of the object exemplify metonymy as the preferred "trope of fetishism" (Simpson 65), language and thing being inextricably linked together as magically endowed. The hair picture is, in this sense, a language-object. These children of Francisco's imagination also become a kind of narrative, which not only jump-starts the overall story of *La de Bringas,* but constitutes a mininarrative in itself.[30] Most suggestive is the close relationship between story (*cuento*) and account, or calculation (*cuenta*), with the bridge of credit connecting the two.

Galdós visibly links them through his structuring of chapters. At the end of chapter 2, Francisco goes from imagining and anticipating the completed hair picture to considering the budget available for it: "Certain notions about the budget of the work tended to come flickering into the artist's brain like will-o'-the-wisps. . . . Bringas turned them over in his mind, paying them the attention of a practical man who does not ignore the periodic itch of creative genius. He uttered the following words as he added things up in his head" (8).[31]

Chapter 3 begins, "Shellac varnish: two and a half reals. At most I might spend five reals on it . . . A pair of florists' tweezers, the ones I've got are too big: three reals . . . etc." (8).[32] "Contando" serves a dual purpose here: telling and counting (or accounting). Credit itself is the real glue holding them together. A token of appreciation, the hair picture is a response to a form of credit (patronage) extended to the Bringas family. In making the cenotaph, moreover, Francisco produces an object that in itself is an image of credit: the de-realized, symbolic bodies (hair) of children as an assumed guarantee of another child's future. Credit, as Pocock has shown and as Galdós puts into literary practice, is imaginatively construed.

Credit, then, becomes a form of fiction, predicated on future materializations. What does credit do? It empowers you, but it's not real. Fiction does the same thing. In *La de Bringas,* Galdós creates a rich dynamic that goes from cuento to cuenta and back again, thus suggesting the inseparability and interrelationship of both kinds of accounts. These accounts— the narratives of desire and money—incarnate fantasies, fantasies that Galdós eroticizes by presenting them in their most fetishistic forms, as individual parts and fragments endowed with quasi-magical properties.[33] By creating such an intense focus on these forms, the novelist also reminds readers of the fetishlike, illusory qualities of credit itself. The fetish-object, of course, substitutes for a lack, and in that sense Francisco's hair picture and Rosalía's clothes, appropriately, do not exist beyond their linguistic status. As David Simpson observes: "The more insubstantial the real, the more space there is for the imaginary" (36). The modus operandi of this social-economic imagination, this fascinating play between cuento and cuenta, is detectable in the behavior and thinking of Rosalía de Bringas. Like her husband Francisco, Rosalía visualizes the product of her desires in advance. As her friend Milagros suggests which combinations of colors and fabrics will be most striking, Rosalía prefigures the dress image in her head, "rapt in contemplation of what is still all in the imagination" (31).[34] And this: "ROSALIA —(*Embebecida.*) Sí . . . , entiendo . . . , lo veo . . . Será precioso . . ." (97). (ROSALIA [entranced]: Yes . . . yes, I do . . . I see what you mean. It must look lovely . . .) (32). Like the hair picture, the dress is a child of her imagination, the unrefined material image of Bécquer's more poetic "children of the imagination" in his *Rimas* ("Introducción sinfónica," *Rimas* 80). Although I have not found the precise expression in Pérez Galdós's novel, allusions to the workings and products of the imagination abound. Significantly, Rosalía's daughter Isabelita dreams into being a visceral symbolization of the phrase when she literally expels in a stream of vomit the images of her delirium (see chapters 8 and 34). In one nightmare, she envisions her mother so fantastically enlarged that she dwarfs the Royal Palace: "At this point, the poor child's delirium began to mount, and she felt all these foreign objects and bodies pressing on each other within her. They were all inside her, as if she had swallowed half the world" (124).[35]

In an ironic inversion, the child gives birth to the mother as a "daughter of the imagination." This expulsion of dream-objects is linked to a trait she shares with her father: hoarding instincts. Isabelita obsessively collects everything she can lay her hands on. These extremely heterogeneous and mostly useless objects are fetishized fragments of a material imagination in the process of being formed: "Scraps of embroidery thread, silk and material filled one box. Buttons, toiletry bottle labels, cigarette ribbons, postage stamps, used fountain pens, empty matchboxes; they formed an incalculable mass of nondescript things, meaningless fragments with no possible use" (146).[36]

Scatological imagery is closely bound not only to Isabelita's dreams and unsteady stomach but to money and transactions in general. The association between filth and commerce is of course traditional and, in this regard, needs no Freud to explain it. Thus the moneylender Torres's pasty smile sickens Rosalia, producing "a noxious vapour, permeating her whole being" (58).[37] The surface texture, or epidermis, of paper bills is greasy ("pringosa"). Rosalía's gorge rises in anticipatory reflux at the thought of having to beg money from her social inferior Refugio (277, 165). Without question, this sense of the cloacal and of the partially digested discloses the underbelly of fancy's conceits, as imaged in the euphemistic sentimentality of the hair picture or in the frivolous caprices of women's fashion.

From this, how easy would it be to condemn, like the narrator himself on different occasions, the unsettling moral confusion between the desire for things and proper conduct. After all, isn't it obvious that Francisco's blind miserliness and Rosalía's excesses are judged as symbolic extensions of generalized social disorder, culminating in the overthrow of an entire regime? Galdós deploys the same metaphoric (and metonymic) operations of gigantism and miniaturization used to characterize Francisco's hair picture, in a brilliant manipulation of changing perspectives, in the description of the Royal Palace, home to the queen and to the Bringas family. The fortunes of both are inextricably bound together.

Equally telling in this regard is the critical if ironic posture of the narrator towards Rosalía's fascination with clothes: "this female passion . . . does more damage in the world than revolutions" (31).[38] Several recent critics have skillfully punctured the narrator's moralizing tendency, only to replace conventional morality with another, more current variety that slips in through the backdoor of literary interpretation. Thus, Jo Labanyi sees "the newly established exchange economy [in *La de Bringas*] as a gain in freedom at the expense of commodification" ("Adultery and the Exchange Economy" 107). Silvia Tubert concludes that Rosalía's clothing ends up preempting her and transforming her into an object (386). Likewise, Paul Julian Smith stresses the thematic significance of commodity fetishism in Galdós's novel (see *Body Hispanic*). Akiko Tsuchiya sees Rosalía's textual image as an empty sign, "as alienated from her own soul and body, as literally dis-embodied" (42).[39] Despite a nod toward Rosalía's potential as a free agent (see especially Labanyi, Tsuchiya, and Tubert), all these critics, perceptive readers in their own right, ultimately fixate, in a curiously fetishizing critical impulse, on a single element: commodification.

For traditionalists and social conservatives, luxury becomes the great threat to social order and virtue; for Marxists and feminist-Marxists, it is the exchange relation in itself. The attack on luxury reifies women by essentializing them; recent critical theory, however unintentionally, also turns them into stone. But is either message what Galdós says? To claim either is to ignore as readers the complex and devious nature of Galdosian irony and an implied authorial presence that constantly undercuts the moral-ideological stance of an unreliable narrator. Above all, there is no room here for the workings of the imagination, that social-economic imagination that not only fuels the behavior of characters but the narrative itself.

This new kind of imagination can reveal a great deal about the intricate relationship between persons and things. I would suggest that in *La de Bringas* it is not so much that persons have undergone commodification as that things have become eroticized.[40] The significance of things in this text brings me back to the question of women and luxury. Catherine Jagoe argues that the thesis statement of *La de Bringas* "defines luxury as destructive, undermining the foundations of society" (93). She also maintains that, in the nineteenth century, "the spendthrift image [of women] dramatizes the fear that masculine capitalist society, which defined bourgeois women as consumers and displayers of wealth produced by men, felt at the power it had thus placed in feminine hands" (90). Noting the narrator's moralizing stance on this question, she gives as an example Galdós's variation on the Eden myth, which serves as a pseudo explanation of Rosalía's fall into the folly of fashion. Agustín Caballero's gifts (in *Tormento*), the narrator says,

> fueron la fruta cuya dulzura le quitó la inocencia y por culpa de ellos un ángel con espada de raso me la echó de aquel Paraíso en que su Bringas la tenía tan sujeta. Nada, nada . . . , cuesta trabajo creer que aquello de doña Eva sea tan remoto. Digan lo que quieran, debió de pasar ayer, según está de fresquito y palpitante el tal suceso. Parece que lo han traído los periódicos de anoche.

> [were the fruit whose sweet taste destroyed her innocence, and thanks to them an angel with a satin sword threw her out of Para-

dise, where Bringas had kept her well and truly under control. Really and truly . . . it is hard to believe that the story of Eve happened so long ago. For all the evidence to the contrary, one would think it only happened yesterday, it is such a burning contemporary issue. It seems as if it just came out in yesterday evening's news.] (30)[41]

While it is certainly quite conceivable to see in this passage the trivialization of women, as Jagoe does (91–92), what jumps out in the original Spanish is the wonderfully comic parody of the biblical story. How can the reader possibly take seriously the narrator's ideological viewpoint here?[42]

Indeed, an 1884 chronicle Galdós published in *La prensa* of Buenos Aires suggests that he neither condemned nor approved luxury in women (or society in general). Commenting on a fancy ball of the aristocracy, Galdós wrote,

All this needs to be considered in its economic aspects. . . . Many censure these entertainments because a great deal of money is uselessly spent on them, money that applied to more serious things could be productive. It's thought a million pesetas went into last night's expenditure; it may even have been more. But whatever the figure, it seems to me all this exaggerated fuss about it is inappropriate. . . . Beyond the fact that it is impossible and economically absurd to regulate the use that anyone might make of his pure strings, the sumptuary arts and industry, which give circulation and life to immense capital, would not exist without these constant demands of caprice and frivolity, a necessary, inexcusable element of all societies; far from being exclusive to ours, it appears as less dominant in the present generation than in previous ones. The English press complains all the time that the withdrawal and perpetual mourning in which the Court of Queen Victoria lives has paralyzed certain industries of great importance in the vast metropolis. ("Carta" 70–71)[43]

The view Galdós expresses here is commonsensical and economically laissez-faire. In the same piece, however, the novelist also makes clear that he will not, if he can help it, repeat this rare incursion of his into the

society chronicle (68). Galdós despised the subgenre of society reporting, calling it dishonest, pretentious, and sappily written, but he was not
above exploiting the world of gossip, fashion, and high society in both
this article and in a number of his novels.

There is no clear-cut statement of moral intention in this chronicle,
just as there is none in *La de Bringas*.[44] Maurice Hemingway comes
closest to capturing the essential ambiguity and ambivalence of Galdós's
novel. Noting Rosalía's "indeterminate moral status," he sees moral
relativism, ambiguity, and confusion as central to this text (17).[45] Remember when the narrator complains that the female passion for clothes
does more harm than revolutions? This remark comes at the beginning
of chapter 10, a narrative hybrid of dialogue (between Rosalía and her
aristocratic friend Milagros) and third-person narration (which shades
off into the first person on one occasion and slides into the voice and
feelings of Rosalía herself on another). Just before the narrator makes
the comment, he describes the heap of clothes and fabrics surrounding
Rosalía and Milagros. Right after the remark, he makes note of the two
ladies' excited whispers: "Los términos franceses que matizaban este
coloquio se despegaban del tejido de nuestra lengua; pero aunque sea
clavándolos con alfileres, los he de sujetar para que el exótico idioma de
los trapos no pierda su genialidad castiza" (94). [The French words that
gave their conversation such a special flavour strained at the fabric of our
language; but even if I have to stick them down with pins, I want to
capture them so as not to lose the peculiar quality of that exotic language
of materials] (31).[46] Then the dialogue:

ROSALIA (*mirando un figurín*): Si he de decir la verdad, yo no
entiendo esto. No sé cómo se han de unir atrás los faldones de la
casaca de guardia francesa.

MILAGROS (*con cierto aturdimiento, al cual se sobrepone poco a poco
su gran juicio*): Dejemos a un lado los figurines. Seguirlos ser-
vilmente lleva a lo afectado y *estrepitoso.* Empecemos por la
elección de tela. ¿Elige usted la muselina blanca con viso de
foulard? Pues entonces no puede adoptarse la casaca.

ROSALIA (*con decisión*): No; escojo resueltamente el *gros glasé,*
color *cenizas de rosa.* Sobrino me ha dicho que le devuelva el que
me sobre. El *gros glasé* me lo pone a veinticuatro reales.

MILAGROS (*meditando*): Bueno: pues si nos fijamos en el *gros glasé*, yo haría la falda adornada con cuatro volantes de unas cuatro pulgadas. ¿A ver? No; de cinco o seis, poniéndole al borde un *bies* estrecho de *glasé verde naciente* . . . ¿Eh? (95)

[ROSALIA [*looking at a fashion-plate*]: I must say, I just don't understand this. I've no idea how you're supposed to join the skirt-tails at the back of the French military *casaque*.

MILAGROS [*slightly at a loss, but relying on her infallible instinct*]: Forget the fashion-plate. If you follow them too closely you end up looking silly and overdone, anyway. Let's start by choosing the fabric. Do you want to use the white muslin faced with the silk foulard? Because if you do, you can't use the *casaque* pattern.

ROSALIA [*decisively*]: No; I'm definitely going to go for the *gros glacé* silk, in a rose-grey shade. Sobrino said I could bring back what I didn't use. He's charging me twenty-four reals a yard for the *gros glacé*.

MILAGROS [*thinking it over*]: All right then: supposing we go for the *gros glacé*, then I think I'd put four tiers of four-inch flounces on the bottom of the skirt. What do you think? No; make that five- or six-inch flounces, with a band of spring green *glacé* silk cut on the bias at the bottom. . . . How does that sound?] (31)

In the concluding paragraph to the chapter, we clearly hear Rosalía's voice through the third-person narrator:

Comprando los avíos en la subida de Santa Cruz, empalmando pedazos, disimulando remiendos, obtenía un resultado satisfactorio con mucho trabajo y poco dinero. ¿Pero cómo podían compararse las *pobreterías* hechas por ella con aquel brillante modelo venido de París? . . . Bringas no autorizaría aquel lujo que, sin duda, le había de parecer *asiático*, y para que la cosa pasara, era necesario engañarle . . . No, no, no se determinaba. El hecho era grave, y aquel despilfarro rompería de un modo harto brusco las tradiciones de la familia. ¡Mas era tan hermosa la manteleta . . . ! Los parisienses la habían hecho para ella . . . Se determinaba, ¿sí o no? (99)

[She would buy the stuff cheaply on Santa Cruz, stick various pieces together, cover up the mends, and come out with something satisfactory for a lot of work and very little money. But how could you compare her pathetic efforts to that exquisite thing from Paris? . . . Bringas would never authorise such a luxury, no doubt he'd think it utterly exorbitant, and she would have to deceive him if she were to get away with it. . . . No, no, she couldn't buy it. It was far too serious a step, and a waste of money that broke with all the family traditions. But the shawl was so beautiful! . . . The Parisians had made it just for her. . . . Should she get it, or not?] (34–35)

Only by contextualizing the narrator's more overt judgments can one understand the complexity of Pérez Galdós's narrative art and face the subsequent difficulty of making judgments about the novel. Narration is all here. The weave of voices in this chapter suggests anything but a thesis statement. Whose voice dominates over the rest? The deictic slippage from third to first person discloses not only a self-conscious instability of viewpoint but a narrative complicity in the ladies' passion. The narrator pins down the exotic lexicon ("clavándolos con alfileres"), but he does so both ironically and affectionately. Distance and intimacy are exquisitely calibrated here. The dialogue form and the focalized voicing of Rosalía's sentiments confirm this delicate dance of closeness and distance, subtly orchestrated through an implied author present in the ironic disparities of presentation.

Narrative complexity, moreover, is enriched through an almost tactile perception of the significance of things in this novel. Indeed I would suggest that precisely those frivolous luxuries like Rosalía's coveted shawl and Francisco's cursi hair picture, which some critics and the narrator in his more overt remarks appear to dismiss as either inconsequential or alienating in their effects—precisely these objects transmit an eroticized, intimate understanding of the real that one cannot reduce to the level of a morality tale. The proliferation of things in nineteenth-century society and texts is so closely attached, so fundamental to imagination and personality, that we risk limiting the interpretive and scholarly understanding of the period by prejudging material realities moralistically or shortchanging their importance. It is not simply that "mental categories are . . . metaphorically understood in material terms," as Alan Bewell observes in another context (213). It is the social and affective life of things themselves that circulates in a text like *La de Bringas,* much the way, for example, the language of fans did earlier (see chapter 2). Silvia Tubert has sensitively pointed out that "clothes become symbolic because they convey an inner dialogue" (382). Tubert then goes on to associate this "inner dialogue" with an unconscious psychological conflict and sense of loss within Rosalía, which the fetish of clothes emblematizes (see Freud, "Fetishism" 152). In the end, she says, Rosalía loses herself, her subjectivity becoming as fragmented and dispersed as the fetishistic profusion of laces, ribbons, and other adornments.

But could one also argue that, by the end of the novel, Rosalía *finds* herself, in the classic nineteenth-century sense of purpose? Her mission, to sustain the family fortunes, is, as the reader knows, self-serving and shot through with irony. Could it be otherwise? Neither Rosalía de Bringas nor any other character in this novel is given over to self-reflection. Self-interest motivates all of them, including the third-person narrator. In this sense, there is little growth of self and little inner illumination of spirit. On the other hand, Rosalía knows what she wants. How she goes about getting what she wants is illuminating.

Her mind filled with the thought of owning the wonderful shawl, Rosalía imagines the very weight and feel of the garment on her shoulders, resists no more, and buys the shawl on credit. She then tells her husband that the queen has given her the shawl as a gift. A month later, the bill comes ("¡zas!, la cuenta"). The connection between cuento and cuenta could not emerge more clearly. Rosalía fabricates a story of the Queen's generosity, thus putting into circulation a fiction based on disempowered desire. Indeed it is this disempowered desire—this cursi text of *querer y no poder,* of having the will but not the way—which produces fiction, the power of the text itself in *La de Bringas.* Rosalía lies so well on this occasion she practically wrings tears from her husband's eyes.

When the story about the queen's munificence begins to wear thin, Rosalía invents another fiction after Francisco unexpectedly pops in and sees the new purchases spilling out all over the room. This time she claims that her friend Milagros has overextended herself, exhausting her husband's purse and forbearance. Rosalía now is simply lending her home to the dressmaker to fashion the clothes for Milagros. Here, Rosalía's own lack of credit—and credibility—is spun out of another character's pecuniary insufficiencies. By this point, Rosalía believes she's found the perfect formula for explaining away the presence of so many new purchases, a formula that she first practices in her head, in the same way she tries on clothes:

> "Ya ves, hijito," decía para sí un mes antes que el hecho fuera real, "lo que ha pasado . . . No te lo quise decir para que no te disgustaras, porque, al fin, nuestra amiga es, y en casa se ha hecho este trabajo. Emilia le exigió el pago adelantado. . . . Pura terquedad. ¡De repente, cañonazo! . . . Sobrino le pasó la cuenta. Ni a una cosa ni a otra pudo atender la pobre Milagros . . . No tienes idea de las trapisondas. . . . Ya te contaré. En fin, que he tenido que quedarme con los vestidos por menos de la tercera parte de su valor y me los he arreglado yo misma para no gastar. . . . Es regalado, es una verdadera ganga. . . . Emilia se ha empeñado en ello, y dice que le pague cuando yo quiera . . . ya ves. . . ." (123)

> ["You see, my love," she would say to herself a month ahead of time, "something dreadful happened. I didn't want to tell you because I knew you'd get upset, after all, she is our friend and the work was done in our house. Emilia insisted on being paid in advance . . . wouldn't budge an inch. And then all of a sudden, boom! The bill from Sobrino's came. Poor Milagros couldn't manage to pay either of them. You'll never imagine the scrapes she's gone and got herself into. I'll tell you one day. Anyway, to make a long story short, I took the dresses for less than a third of their value and did the alterations myself so as to save money. They were a gift, a real bargain. Emilia insisted I take them, she says I can pay her whenever I want. So you see . . ."] (51–52)

Rosalía's fictions, in effect, propel the narration forward. If Francisco's hair picture forms the initial backdrop of the narrative, his wife's inventions foreground in a similar fashion the textual economy of narration itself. Galdós's third-person narrator works with a similar network of metaphors, referring to "the fabric of our language" (el tejido de nuestra lengua) and "the exotic language of materials" (el exótico idioma de los trapos) in one instance and to the "language" of the hair picture in another.

These are examples of a particular way of combining and appropriating individual materials—whether they are strands of hair and glue, pieces of fabric, or words themselves is irrelevant—so as to fashion an object, here, the object of narration. Like the near mythic cursi figures of the Sicur sisters, the Bringas family and the narrator himself practice a form of bricolage made up of bits and pieces of their social and material world. Bricolage is a combinatory activity of disparate, incongruous elements; and the *bricoleur* is "the handyman, the tinkerer, who gets surprisingly practical (and often aesthetic) results from the most unlikely material" (Caws 202).[47] Lévi-Strauss uses this largely untranslateable term as a characterizing metaphor for mythical thought, in the way it "expresses itself by means of a heterogeneous repertoire which, even if extensive, is nevertheless limited" (17). On a practical level, this making do with what one has at one's disposal privileges the material, handmade object. For Lévi-Strauss, the bricoleur "'speaks' not only *with* things . . . but also through the medium of things: giving an account of his personality and life by the choices he makes between the limited possibilities" (21).

The artist is something of a bricoleur too. Like Mr. Wemmick's suburban castle in Dickens' *Great Expectations*, the hair picture functions as a sign, in miniaturized form, of personalized workmanship, belonging not only to Francisco and the narrator but to Galdós himself.[48] "Signs," Lévi-Strauss reminds us, "resemble images in being concrete entities but they resemble concepts in their powers of reference" (18). While we may read nothing but signs in *La de Bringas*, these signs contain the traces of a form of intellectual-aesthetic bricolage, not only associated with cursi behavior and objects, but with the very compositional structure of Galdós's novel. I obviously do not mean to equate cursilería with Galdós's narrative art, but I do wish to point out the startling similarities in approach and thinking.

The Royal Palace in *La de Bringas*, for example, is described as a constantly evolving structure to and from which parts are added and subtracted ad hoc, almost, it would seem, improvisationally (67–68; 12–13). Later, Francisco promises to make his wife an armoire large enough and grand enough for her overflowing cache of clothes: "I'm going to make you a wardrobe for your clothes that will be so huge and so famous that people will need a ticket to see it, like in the Natural History Museum and the Royal Stables. The man who's got logging rights at Balsaín [forest belonging to the Crown] will give me all the pine I need. There is some mahogany stored down in the cellars of this building that is going rotten, and Her Majesty won't mind if I use a bit of it. The contractor who did the Royal Family's mausoleum at El Escorial has offered me all the marble I want." (90)[49] Appropriately (or ironically, if you prefer), Francisco imagines creating the armoire out of bits and pieces from the Royal Palace itself (or from entities associated with the crown). Even more ironic is the allusion to the Royal Pantheon, in which a large number of children are buried, suggesting an indirect connection to the hair picture imagery.

Similarly, Rosalía concocts her stories out of the same hodgepodge materials of palace life. All these examples—the descriptive set pieces such as the hair picture or the Royal Palace, the internal narrations—are the odds and ends, the materials Galdós had at his disposal to create his remarkable portrait of an era, a social class, and a culture. Chapter 10, in its compositional hybridity, is a perfect illustration of the bricolage approach to storytelling.

Through the intertwined stories of the Bringas family and the Spanish monarchy, bricolage also characterizes the patchwork nature of the economic system governing the narration at both the individual and national levels. But it is above all the literal and symbolic figure of the child that serves as a bridge connecting an economy based on credit and capital flow with another based on traditional patronage. Francisco's hair picture proves the perfect construct, aesthetically and ideologically, for expressing this hybrid reality. Like Rosalía's luxuries of dress, the hair picture is an imagined fantasy, or child, of the mind, which Francisco legitimizes through a process of domestication. As the object of his desire, the cenotaph is an investment not only in self, but in the future. Yet this investment is founded on insufficient cultural (and economic) capital, with an end product of cursi proportions. Of particular interest, however, is the two-sided nature of this cursilería. On the one hand, the hair picture sentimentalizes dead children, threatening to turn them into cursi objects as well. Yet this domestication of grief also works as a justification of material interests and transactions generated through patronage in a culture of credit and speculation. In this way a dead child could also be imagined as an investment in a future life.

This particular kind of economic and social imagination was also played out in real-life circumstances, circumstances in which a child became invested emotionally and economically as the symbol of adult desires. What makes this particular story stand out from other stories like it is a context that goes beyond the usual parental and familial boundaries initially defining it. Pascual Madoz (1805–70) today is remembered chiefly for two reasons (see fig. 12). First, as minister of finance for a brief period in 1855, the liberal-minded Madoz put into effect one of the more significant laws of disentailment (*ley de desamortización*) in nineteenth-century Spain, an initiative meant to encourage economic expansion and upward social mobility. Second, he produced a pathbreaking work that mapped out in sixteen volumes all the newly organized provinces of Spain, the *Diccionario geográfico-estadístico-histórico de España y sus posesiones de ultramar* [A geographical-statistical-historical dictionary of Spain and its overseas possessions] (1845–50).

Like Madoz's progressive politics, the dictionary project promoted the vision of a unified, single nation, administratively and politically rationalized into existence after a divisive period of civil war (1833–39). Thus he organized information not in separate volumes or sections on each province, but incorporated it in strict alphabetical order throughout the *Diccionario*. The dictionary was also a business enterprise from which Madoz profited considerably through private subscription and government subvention. These earnings enabled him to purchase land and build a large summer house with gardens in the Basque coastal village of Zarauz (now Zarautz). He gives an extraordinarily long description of this house in the dictionary entry for "Zarauz," including this telling detail: in the south garden, there is a gate topped with two spherical globes of cast iron. These globes, he says, "symbolize that this house, this garden have been built with some of the fortune that the author of the *Dictionary* acquired from publication of his work" (16:653).[50]

The Zarauz summer place took on added meaning for another reason. On 6 September 1850, Madoz's eight-year-old daughter Francisca drowned in the sea.[51] Ironically, the little girl had first been taken to

12. Portrait of Pascual
Madoz, by Antonio María
Esquivel (oil on canvas).
From Francisco Javier
Paredes Alonso's
Pascual Madoz.

Zarauz to improve the fragile state of her health. A few months later, the
family paid for the publication of a *Corona poética dedicada a la memoria
de la malograda señorita Francisca Madoz y Rojas* [A poetic homage dedicated to the memory of the ill-fated señorita Francisca Madoz y Rojas],
which appeared, appropriately, on All Saints' Day, 1 November 1850.
The core of contributors were poets (or would-be poets) who shared
Madoz's liberal ideology, such as Ventura Ruiz Aguilera, Carolina Coronado, Heriberto García de Quevedo, Gregorio Romero Larrañaga, Francisco de Paula Canalejas, and Francisco Zea.[52]

Such commemorations were not uncommon in the nineteenth century, beginning in the 1830s in Spain. This particular poetic homage is of
interest for what it says about the role that patronage and commercial
enterprise played in the memorialization of an eight-year-old girl. It also
tells a great deal about the kinds of emotional and symbolic investment
placed in the figure of the child as a conduit for adult desires and aspirations. Finally, as an object of cursilería, the corona poética reveals the
double-sidedness that Ramón Gómez de la Serna imagined as lo cursi

bueno and lo cursi malo. On the one hand, the coronas are inevitably dated objects and almost invariably examples of cultural inadequacy since most of the compositions were improvised for the occasion and relied on the commonplaces of the genre.[53] Indeed, many of the contributors never even knew personally the individual being memorialized, hence their verses' impersonal and superficial nature. On the other hand, there was real grief behind a publication like this one dedicated to Francisca Madoz, and behind that grief, the hidden, intimate recesses of family life. Most importantly, the cursilería attached to such an artifact cannot be separated from the future-directed, social and economic imagination producing it.

One of the specialties of the corona poética, which also celebrated living persons of distinction and memorable events, was the death of a gifted child. Thus, for example, we read that the señorita Alejandra Argüelles Toral y Hevía, who died at age fourteen, was remembered as a child prodigy, as Fernán Caballero writes in the introduction to the *Corona fúnebre a la memoria de la señorita doña Alejandra Argüelles Toral y Hevía* (1861). Faustina Sáez de Melgar, who says the same thing in her biography of Argüelles Toral published in the fourteen-year-old's *Ensayos poéticos* (1862), also uses the opportunity to defend the right of women to be writers.[54] In another, far more celebrated case, Jesús Rodríguez Cao, who died of meningitis at fifteen, was touted as a boy genius, a "bello monstruo" (beautiful monster).[55] Four volumes of his writings were posthumously published, along with a biography (in volume 1) and a *corona fúnebre* (funeral homage; in volume 4) in 1869–70. The family paid for the publication, as well as for a large mausoleum-monument and a literary prize in the boy's name. Cao even appeared as a fictional character in the first work to win the prize in 1875, Angela Grassi's *La gota de agua* [The drop of water], a rather sentimental tale of two orphans that nonetheless also meant to function as a social critique of the exploitation of children as beggars.

There is no way today to gauge the depth of loss or the emotional investment placed in children like Alejandra Argüelles or Jesús Rodríguez Cao. Clearly, no one then thought it appropriate to make value judgments on the literary worth of their writings. Manuel Gómez Marín said of Cao, for example, that "neither I nor anyone else ought to judge his work. There are things inaccessible to criticism" (vii). Rodríguez

Cao had been much taken with romantic poet Espronceda's *El diablo mundo*. "What seduced you in the poem," Gómez Marín said to him, "isn't the poem itself, but the prologue" (iii). This comment underlines something else as well: that Rodríguez Cao was nothing but a "prologue" himself.[56] What captivated admirers was not only his prolific output, but his ability to memorize, recite, and improvise in public. He was a model child prodigy. All of these children were mere promise, projections of future development.

Francisca Madoz's future, however, appeared to be wrapped up in that of Zarauz's, the tiny Basque village whose seas would also claim her life. To understand how and why the local villagers had intertwined the economic success of Zarauz with the health and well-being of a little girl, one needs to take a closer look at the situation of Zarauz in the 1840s. Both inland and along the coast existed a line of villages and towns then catering to the developing industry of tourism that had started prospering with the popularity of spas, hydrotherapy, and sea bathing. Sipping mineral waters and taking the requisite five-minute wade at the shore were becoming fashionable everywhere in Europe and the Americas, and Spain was no exception.

Zarauz in 1848 was just being noticed as a tourist spot, as Madrazo observed in his *Una espedición a Guipúzcoa, en el verano de 1848* [An expedition to Guipúzcoa, in the summer of 1848] (1849), a quasi-guidebook with a certain commercial and promotional aspect to it. The beaches of San Sebastián, Portugalete, and Deva were already well-known. To them, one could now add, he said, those of Zarauz, "which in a very short span of time has made known its aspirations to be chosen for the same honor" (29). Indeed, a friendly rivalry between Zarauz and the more developed town of Deva sprung up, some enthusiasts vowing that for seabathing Zarauz's "solitary and inconvenient beach" (Madrazo 57) was by far the better one. One *zaraucista* went so far as to publish in *La España* a poem praising the glories of Zarauz. A Deva proponent reciprocated.

Zarauz's prosperity partly derived from the fact that Francisca's father, Pascual Madoz, had decided to become its benefactor. Starting in 1846, he made many contributions in time, money, and energy to the town. He arranged for Zarauz to have a permanent doctor available; gave generously to the poor, donated a library to the local casino, or Sociedad

Zarauzana, established in 1849; and made street improvements. Three of the most important projects he promoted included the building of a usable road connecting Zarauz with Cestona-Zumaya and San Sebastián-Bilbao, the construction of a dock for fishermen, and the bringing of water to the town.[57] Madoz was a progressive and a humanitarian, but admitted openly that what benefited Zarauz also benefited him. He observed that although the gardens to his house were well situated for water, "we thought it a good idea to bring water to this property. Fortunately, our interests happened to coincide with those of the village in this way: the town hall lacked sufficient funds to provide this important improvement to the residents" (Madoz 16:653).[58] Madoz lent the money for two fountains to be built, with the understanding that both his property and the town would mutually benefit. Both self-interest and humanitarian aims motivated Madoz. The new road was particularly important for Zarauz to become "a town much visited in the bathing season, which would acquire a great deal of life and vitality and many benefits" (16:657).[59] Thus at the time when Madrazo in *Una espedición a Guipúzcoa* briefly noted Zarauz's emergence as a bathing and health resort, his commentary also reflected some of the improvements Pascual Madoz had made to the place.

When Madoz's daughter drowned, the townspeople reacted immediately. They were devastated. Francisca's uncle, Fernando Madoz, described it in these terms:

We do not doubt that Zarauz will weep for all eternity over the loss of a young girl who would have carried on the beneficent ideas of her parents and the special system of protection with which they have looked after the interests of a grateful town. . . . That day of such sad memory, in which an entire village anxiously awaited the sentence of either life or death, the sentence with their future contained in it, a commission had presented itself claiming possession of a *body*!

In their grief and desperation, the town of Zarauz was persuaded that this was the way to force its benefactors not to abandon their residence, forgetting, no doubt, that in the wounded hearts of their patrons these proofs of feeling, these manifestations of public gratitude, this painful, sad applause, spoke in the most eloquent of terms. *[Francisca's] body belongs to the pantheon of my family; my family will always belong to the disconsolate village of Zarauz.* (Introduction to *Corona poética* n. pag.)[60]

Much of what Fernando Madoz says is undoubtedly trite, or cursi, paying lip service to the clichéd expressions of sadness expected over the death of a child. Did the townspeople really care about Francisca? Who knows? But what a fascinating mixture of sentiment and economic interests emerges from this passage! Like Jesús Rodríguez Cao, Francisca Madoz was associated with charitable sentiments and behavior, partly, one suspects, because both were children who had now become "angels" in the stereotypical parlance of the times.[61] It does appear, however, that Francisca acted with particular zeal in dispensing charity, to the point of excess, according to her uncle: "The lovely child . . . could not be persuaded that other people should be unhappy when she herself was happy; and if there were black looks sometimes directed toward the authors of her existence, it was only when they resisted the whims and demands of their daughter to provide charity and beneficence."[62] To the local townspeople, Francisca Madoz's death threatened Zarauz's continuing prosperity, which depended on their patron Pascual Madoz, hence their request to have the little girl buried in Zarauz (she was taken to Madrid).

Patronage also played a role in at least one contribution to the *Corona poética*.[63] Ventura Ruiz Aguilera reprinted his poem in *Elegías y armonías*, with this appended note:

The inexhaustible charity of that angelic creature made her death doubly felt, which was wept over in tender compositions by poets in a corona, or poetic garland of mourning, a living expression of their pain and of the friendship that united them with the child's father, D. Pascual Madoz, that indefatigable champion of liberty. This corona was published in an elegant tome. I will never forget that he and the now deceased Count de las Navas were the first persons to encourage and favor me with their generous protection, when I had just arrived in Madrid, completely unknown and without a patron. (315)[64]

The grace with which Ruiz Aguilera intertwines charity and friendship with politics and patronage cannot disguise an underlying motive of self-interest, just as the townspeople of Zarauz were unable to hide their consternation over the possible loss of Madoz's patronage. They needn't have worried. Madoz did not abandon them, and the town eventually became a very fashionable summer resort, especially for the upper bourgeoisie and aristocracy. By the end of the nineteenth century, the society chronicler Monte-Cristo would write: "Zarauz is the beach of aristocrats. Many families of what we could call our *Faubourg* own country houses and magnificent palaces there, and others settle into the *Grand Hotel* and the *Terrasse*. Everybody knows everybody there, and almost everyone is on *familiar* terms with each other [using the *tú* form of address]" (192).[65]

Ironically, however, another observer saw it differently. In 1931, Antonio de Hoyos y Vinent, who really did belong to the aristocracy (he was the Marqués de Vinent) and had written novels about decadent aristos, felt that Zarauz circa 1900 was cursi, filled with "ugly, cursi, pretentious houses, the *want, want, want, but can't, can't* houses that were neither villas nor chalets nor mansions but an imitation and parody of the real thing. All because an invasion of the pain-in-the-neck, social-climbing cursis had descended upon Zarauz, which was once a summer refuge of peace for aristocrats" (*El primer estado* 130).[66] Both these views of Zarauz in 1900 were probably skewed. Monte-Cristo needed to flatter his upper-class clientele, and Hoyos y Vinent had moved far to the left by 1931. Nonetheless, Hoyos y Vinent is really talking about the loss of prestige and social authority that the Spanish aristocracy began to experience more and more from the 1890s on. While Monte-Cristo's avidly read columns provided a veneer of class affirmation, his chronicles couldn't disguise the social slippage perceptible in the confused mingling of different classes or in the increasing use of familiar forms of address noted above.[67]

Fifty years after Francisca Madoz's death, Zarauz had become emblematic of the embourgeoisement of Spanish society. Madoz himself, whose family was petit bourgeois anticipated the change when he built his large, handsome summer house in Zarauz, thus taking on in a very visible way the forms of a new and empowered aristocracy of money and enterprise.[68] The townspeople of Zarauz nervously read the "sentence with their future contained in it," finding at first only the inert weight of a dead child and dead hope. But Francisca Madoz's body and person also exhibit some of the same fetishistic qualities as Francisco Bringas's hair picture or Rosalía's clothes. Madoz's daughter symbolized her father's patronage and enterprise, an example of the mixed, transitional economic system that continued to function throughout the second half of the nineteenth century. The same kind of bricolage structure and mentality that produces cursi effects in objects like Francisco Bringas's hair picture also promotes change, such as the material improvements of Zarauz, because at work here is a peculiar form of economic and social imagination in both cases. This future-directed imagination, paradoxically, sometimes makes its emotional and economic investments in objects and figures already dated and, in that sense, dead in more ways than one.

CHAPTER FIVE

Fabricating History

THE CURSI SOCIETY brilliantly brought to life in *La de Bringas* spills over into the pages of many Galdós novels. One could easily dismiss the history presented therein as trivial, as quintessentially cursi, but I contend that what Galdós actually shows is how much the uses of history were made to legitimate middle-class aspirations. In this sense, the bricolage style of fabricating from bits and pieces a novel or a dress, as we've seen in *La de Bringas*, is also part of the very cloth of middle-class Spanish society. If the history of the period seems infused with cursilería, it is in part because history is seen as bricolage, as a fabrication like a performance or a fashion, intimately attached to one's person and carried about as costume or comportment.

This understanding of history permeates Galdós's novel, *Cánovas*. And yet, as the end piece to the unfinished fifth series of Galdós's *Episodios nacionales*, this final historical novel—published in 1912—brims over with irritating inconclusiveness, its symbolic talking head nodding off to sleep on the last page when Mariclío, Mother History, murmurs, "I, who already feel too classical, am getting bored . . . I'm so sleepy" (272).[1] Modern critics frequently find the fifth series, and especially *Cánovas*, unsatisfactory reading experiences. Historic events, covering the early Restoration period of 1874 to 1880, seem trivial, and are generally presented in an offhanded fashion. Fictional events remain equally inconsequential and seemingly unlinked to the larger historical picture. Thus Geoffrey Ribbans faults the novel for its "lack of an effective degree of interaction between the fictional plot and the historical events" (222). He also finds the work's allegorical structure inappropriate (221, 233). Diane Urey takes a completely different tack, deconstructing the fifth series into an endless chain of signifiers with no stable meanings in sight (149). These are not representational novels, she says, but rather, allegorizing, self-conscious, and self-enclosed texts. As such, they confirm de Man's contention that "allegorical narratives tell the story of the failure to read." "Allegories," he continues, "are always allegories of metaphor and, as such, they are always allegories of the impossibility of reading." (205). In a tightly constructed argument, Urey pursues de Man's point in all its ramifications, noting that "one cannot get out of these texts and into the world. There is no transcendence, no complete and stable sign, no origin, no end to discourse" (223).

I have been stopped flat, then, at the very point where history apparently ends and discourse begins. History doesn't mean anything in *Cánovas*. Or does it? The answer, however tentative its articulation, depends on what one thinks language does in a historical novel, what role language plays in organizing historical events, and what practices language initiates and incites within and without the text. If the verbal sign points only to other verbal signs, then it is clear that references in the text to Cánovas, the Bourbon Restoration, and Alfonso XII's young bride Mercedes cannot be taken for living history or documents as they once were. It is not clear, however, that they should be altogether dispensed with in our understanding of the text. Critics like Ricardo Gullón ("La Historia como materia novelable") and Urey are right to point out the metafictive qualities of *Cánovas*. But does metafiction rule out the historical? Galdós's last episodio nacional appears to be a contradiction in terms. As a metafictional historical novel, *Cánovas* implicitly poses a classic question: why spend time reading novels about history when, clearly, history is "out there"?

A historical novel, like historiography, organizes the out-thereness of historical events and people by bringing them "in here." It does so through language. In other words, the genre of the historical novel, no matter how unconventional the specific example, demands, through readerly expectations and knowledge, that attention be paid to the historical. Moreover, as Linda Hutcheon observes, genres "also enable readers to orient themselves and to understand the context in which they must situate the referent" (4). The linguistic context in which historical novels are immersed constitutes an index of a shifting, complex alliance of *langue* and *parole*, of language as an entire social world within and through which the writer sifts individual experience. Language, then, is inescapably social (Eagleton, *Literary Theory* 60). By being social, by being of the world that is always both out there and in here at the same time, language inevitably flows in time. It is a participant of history.

The language that constitutes *Cánovas* largely metafictionalizes history, but in so doing does not desert its historical function. Indeed, from the very start Galdosian language, as both early and later critics have seen (Azorín 54; Gullón 27), self-consciously plays off the language of the novelist's society, a language that can be characterized as *cursi*. Indeed, if we treat *Cánovas* as an ironic instance of a *cursi* text, we can better understand how figurative, metafictionalized language can also serve a historical function in literature. The Restoration period described in *Cánovas* is, above all, a world of political, social, and moral *cursilería*, of significant issues made trivial, of good taste made questionable, and feeling turned hollow. As one of the underlying obsessions of the age, the fear of being perceived as *cursi* fuels the behavior of the anxious middle classes, acutely conscious of their slippery hold on history and power. In many ways, both the revolution of 1868 and the Bourbon revival of the Restoration (1874–1902) appear as periods of middle-class legitimation. Even the aristocracy in Spain, despite its continuing hold on land and disdain for negotiability, was increasingly permeated with the values and power ethos of middle-class culture as matrimonial alliances between new money and old lines and growing commercialization prevailed (Bahamonde Magro and Toro Mérida 145; Bahamonde Magro; Otero Carvajal).[2]

This successful consolidation of a new power structure in politics and business, seen in the making with Segismundo García Fajardo and his mother's ambitious marriage plans for him in *Cánovas*, sometimes exhibited an inner tension arising out of a fundamental lack. For what the middle classes, particularly the petite bourgeoisie, lacked was a strongly marked sense of identity. Neither blood nor culture were sufficient in themselves to forge that collective and individual consciousness of self. What they needed was history. Galdós shows us in *Cánovas* how the discourse of history was used to legitimize the existence and power of a social class. In the process, of course, he also deconstructs, in a non-Derridian way, that very same discursive power base by putting into question the virtue of language to represent and to perform.

To see how Galdós writes out history as a cursi text of inadequacy and insufficiency, one first has to pay attention to Cánovas, the name behind the title and character of this work. Most critics dismiss the historical Cánovas, generally credited as the architect of a workable political system during the Restoration, because he remains largely absent as an agent in the novel. But Galdós's 1912 novel makes no sense without Cánovas. The ubiquitous Tito, narrator extraordinaire, is first of all a historian, a miniaturized burlesque version of the same symbolizing role that Antonio Cánovas del Castillo represents. The title is history writ large. Cánovas, as Galdós mockingly repeats throughout his novel, has come on the scene "to continue the History of Spain" (first noted in ch. 4, p. 45), a phrase coined by the Málaga-born politician himself (Quinn 21, 29 n.6). In his student days, Cánovas also ambitiously set for himself the task of continuing the *Historia de España* of the Jesuit historian Mariana.[3] (Hence, too, the doubly malicious Galdosian allusion to Mariclío as Doña Mariana, i.e., a Spanish Muse of History.) Thus Cánovas as Galdós's title character performs both an allegorizing and a literalizing role in his historical capacity. Cánovas is simultaneously real and unreal for the reader.

In some ways, Cánovas the historical persona fulfills the function of what Erich Auerbach called "figura," referring to the application of figural interpretation in biblical exegesis. "*Figura,*" he writes, "is something real and historical which announces something else that is also real and historical" (29). Thus Moses in the Old Testament prefigures or announces the appearance of Jesus Christ in the New Testament. In this context, he distinguishes figura from allegory. Like allegory, figura points to hidden meanings, but unlike the allegorical trope, it suggests form, substance, harking back to the earliest meanings of figura as "plastic form" (Auerbach 11). Figura, then, also takes on the appearance of the flesh. ("And not all are shadows, but there are bodies also," says Tertullian; qtd. in Auerbach 32.) "*Figura,*" Auerbach concludes, "differs from most of the allegorical forms known to us by the historicity both of the sign and what it signified. Most of the allegories we find in literature or art represent a virtue (e.g., wisdom), or a passion (jealousy), an institution (justice), or at most a very general synthesis of historical phenomena (peace, the fatherland)—never a definite event in its full historicity" (54).

This historical function of figural interpretation (Auerbach 56), aimed as it was toward convert nations, carries with it an understanding of historical events as revelation. Things to come, the futuricity of history, are grounded in a teleological vision of transcendental meaning. None of this particular aspect of this premodern view of history survives in Galdós, although, ironically, Cánovas as a historian adhered to a providentialist scheme of things (*Problemas contemporáneos* 48, 59; Quinn 20–21). Modern history is seen as a series of horizontally presented particulars, and events are always provisional because they are subject to interpretations that are incomplete (Auerbach 59). Does this mean, then, that Cánovas as a modern figura has no real historical function in Galdós's novel? Not at all. What complicates our understanding of the text and its relation to history is the self-conscious nature of writing in it, in which writing is metafictionalized while history seems to float disengaged from the activity of writing. Events occur within a fictional vacuum in *Cánovas*. History imparts a message (albeit mostly a negative one); writing undermines the message. Characters appear to exist somewhere in between the borders of history and textuality. Their vulgar insignificance, or cursilería, is converted into a kind of cursi(ve) script.

Metafiction makes readers acutely aware of the text as text, but, paradoxically, the process of reading itself also redirects readers back to the outside world because the ordering and decoding of the text in effect constitutes a reconstruction of it according to "a second ordered referential system" (Hutcheon 5). Readers make another world, a "heterocosm," as Linda Hutcheon has suggested. "This fictional universe is obviously not an object of perception," she writes, "but an effort to be experienced by the readers, in the sense that it is something created by them and in them. Yet here *is* a link to real life " (5). The referents created are not real, but fictive (3–5).

Because *Cánovas* is also a historical fiction, this fictive reference of the metafictional process becomes doubly complex. The nature of this particular genre draws readers back repeatedly to real persons and events— back to Cánovas, Alfonso XII, the Bourbon Restoration, and the Sandhurst Manifesto—because no one, then or now, has been able to dispute the authority of historical reality. Readers accept the fact of history, if not specific interpretations of it. In this sense, written history qua history retains its hold partly through the reader's authorization of it. This authorizing process is akin to what happens in reading realist narrative. As Sandy Petrey observes, "in realist fiction, the referent as classically defined is absent while the authority of the referent as classically extolled is omnipresent" (7).

In a metafictional historical novel like *Cánovas*, however, I would suggest turning the proposition on its head and stating it in these terms: the referent as classically defined is present in the metafictional historical novel, while the authority of the referent as classically extolled is absent, or deauthorized. Thus, on the one hand, Cánovas the politician-historian is present in the reading of Galdós's novel, made real in the mind's eye, even while on the other, he is being subjected to a deauthorization, a de-realizing through language itself.

Cánovas's historic function comes through clearly as a legitimizing one in Galdós's novel, just as, on the scene of politics and Spanish history, he functioned as the great legitimizer, "the holy word of the Restoration," to use a phrase of his ally, Alejandro Pidal (*Velada* 58). Today's readers can see the titular significance of Cánovas, still well remembered even in 1912 when Galdós wrote this last episodio nacional, if they examine some of the ways this historical figure was represented in his day. There were in truth many Cánovases. In 1912 Azorín referred to five of them when he reviewed Galdós's novel.[4] Whether hated or fawned on, Cánovas was recognized by his contemporaries as a formidable presence, possessing a strong symbolizing (and real) function in the survival of the compromise politics that would govern Spain for decades. The "Monster," as he was called by friends and enemies alike, loomed over Restoration society. He incarnated, said Pidal a few months after his assassination in 1897, "the living history of the Nation for twenty-three years" (58).

Contemporary rhetoric allegorized Cánovas, making him larger than life and turning him into a kind of monument. This monumentalizing of public figures, so dear to the nineteenth-century mind-set of bearing historical witness to itself, can be seen in the way Cánovas's "monstrosity" was constructed in print. Leopoldo Alas, no friend of the statesman, humorously alludes to this metaphorical enlargement in an apparently apocryphal story of a Frenchman whose mania was to measure cathedrals, statues, and castles by the length of his umbrella. He says, "Cánovas's admirers, then, are like the Frenchy of the story; like him, they measure their man with an umbrella, and the result is a monument of so many square umbrellas. But I measure him . . . the way Herodotus estimated the size of the Tower of Babel . . . by *estadios,* or furlongs [lit. stadiums]. And Cánovas, my friend, may have all the umbrellas . . . you want, but as far as stadiums go, he doesn't measure up to even one" (*Cánovas y su tiempo* 103–4).[5]

This lack of proportion between the man and his image, exploited to the hilt in Alas's 1887 satire, is built on exaggeration and malicious verbal puffery that for Clarín defined Cánovas in all his originality, originality being taken in the ancien régime ridiculing sense of the monstrous, that which departs from the conventional (Babbitt 187). Revealingly, an admirer of Cánovas—Alejandro Pidal—saw that same monstrosity or figural aggrandizement in completely different terms. During the Ateneo's *Velada en memoria de D. Antonio Cánovas del Castillo,* Pidal spoke at length with the traditional oratorical flourishes and anaphorical gravity on the public significance of Cánovas, as this excerpt illustrates: "and if a life were not only private but also public; if a history were to become as much the history of a nation as that of an individual . . . there is something like mourning in the air, something like the feeling of an orphan in society today; we are touching the empty space left by a great personality . . . we sense that a new era in the history of our times is beginning" (10, 12).[6] The future is somber, *tenebroso,* "as if Providence had joined the death of a man to the most terrifying problems of society and the nation, thus magnifying his funeral" (12).[7] The death of Cánovas is analogous to the death of the country at the hands of anarchists and *filibusteros* (proindependence colonials, in particular of Cuba) (13), thus alluding to two of the most serious social-political problems of the time. Near the end of his discourse, Pidal still can't believe Cánovas is gone. "It seemed like a kidnapping to me, carried out behind humanity's back by fantastic, evil spirits" (58).[8] It is curious how this last image seems to anticipate Galdós's fanciful-burlesque version of Restoration Spain and the man largely responsible for the Bourbon revival, Cánovas del Castillo. Pidal, steeped in the "great man of history" theory, intended such rhetoric to resonate with meaning; oratory was to clothe a man's death with the figures of praise. Galdós, fifteen years later, had no such agenda.

Indeed, he effectively buries Cánovas a second time by using rhetoric to kill rhetoric, a major strategy in his writing from practically the beginning.

Connecting Cánovas with rhetoric was inevitable in contemporary representations of the man. He was known as an orator, a historian, and a writer. The statesman's historical works made Leopoldo Alas feel quite unwell:

And if afterward, we close the book, lay down and dream, we see floating in our fancies, not the historical characters, not the places they have passed through, but Cánovas's archaizing, terribly correct linguistic strainings, his adverbial tics, the *these and thoses*, the *last but not leasts*, the *aforementioneds*, the *properly speakings*, etc., to which he clings; the dangling conjunctions, and, in sum, a *Walpurgis* of abstract words, a witches' sabbath of empty verbiage in prose. (*Cánovas y su tiempo* 72–73)[9]

Clarín tears into his poetry as well, reaching even larger conclusions by asserting that "Cánovas *fills life with rubbish* as though it were poetry. . . . *To fill life with rubbish* is to load the soul with debris in order to create a man of substance" (22–23).[10] A bit later he writes of those "great redundancies of the prose of his existence" (24).[11]

This insistence on Cánovas the man as an extended *ripio*, or verbal padding,[12] becomes a denunciation in the satire of Antonio de Valbuena (alias Venancio González and Miguel de la Escalada), who specialized in a series of books on the ripio. Valbuena wrote at least five volumes, from 1884 to 1905, on this corrosive element of bad taste in Restoration society. In *Ripios académicos* (1890), he devoted four articles to Cánovas. In *Ripios vulgares* (1891), he starts and ends with Cánovas as his principal target. Cánovas is the centerpiece of riprap; he is filled with verbal rubbish, or *cuerpos extraños*, in Clarín's diatribe (23), while in Valbuena, Cánovas fills in the front and back surfaces of the satirist's text. Cánovas himself turns into the textual filler or debris used in construction. Valbuena is acutely aware of his own framing device when he writes, "I began this book with Cánovas, with Cánovas I reached the halfway mark, and with Cánovas I want to finish it" (285).[13]

The last few pages of *Ripios vulgares* demolish the opening paragraph of Cánovas's historical novel, *La campana de Huesca* [The bell of Huesca]

(1852), which begins, "By the bank of the Isuela I found this chronicle; in one of those gardens of green dotted with fruit trees, whose thatched walls and hedges are supported by the stones robbed from the walls of Huesca" (Cánovas del Castillo 1).[14] In attacking the statesman's verbal and stylistic infelicities, Valbuena epitomizes the kind of myopic, scavenging polemics in which good numbers of journalists and critics delighted in late nineteenth-century Spain (see Zuleta 188–96). Such scurrilous diatribes generally masked a political agenda, as when Valbuena cuts apart the sentence, "whose thatched walls and hedges are supported by the stones robbed from the walls of Huesca." How can thatched walls (*bardas*) and hedges (*setos*), queries Valbuena, steal stones? He continues, "it is the moderates and conservatives, their successors, who have generally supported themselves on stolen stones, that is, the stones from churches and convents, but best not to confuse the issue," thus slyly alluding to conservatives' and moderates' tacit support of liberal disentailment of church property and lands.[15] Moreover, he says, thatched walls and hedges aren't built on stones, only *cercas* (fences) and *tapias* (garden or adobe walls) are (300–301). This trivial and detailed commentary—of which I've given only an excerpt—from a militant Carlist writer (see Botrel) hostile to the compromise politics of a temporizing conservative like Cánovas, is likewise built on riprap, fragments of an ongoing historical-political discourse, analogous to the broken stones used for foundations and sometimes thrown together irregularly to make a wall of stones.

Valbuena's oppositional text, like Clarín's, is subject to the same ferocious dissecting in Fray Juan de Miguel's (Fray Mortero) *Cascotes y machaqueos: pulveriʒaciones a Balbuena [sic] y Clarín* [Trashing rubbish: pulverizing Valbuena and Clarín] (1892). Dedicated to Cánovas, this first book by Fray Mortero directs the same ripio charge against Valbuena for whom "everything is converted into verbal padding" (121).[16] Indeed, he says, a title like *Ripios vulgares* is in itself excessive (125) since all ripios are *vulgares*, or common. He too—like Clarín and Valbuena—defends good taste (122) as a standard of verbal conduct, although it is evident that tastes are relative here. What carries across in all these ad hominem examples is the rhetorical construction (or deconstruction in some cases) of personality as a kind of verbal edifice either to be filled with substances (ripios) or pulverized into stony debris (*cascotes*).

This sense of the public persona as a rhetorical construction, as a linguistic fabrication of either good or bad taste, seems to hover somewhere between the literalizing and the allegorizing levels of representation. A substantive like *ripio* rests ambiguously between the physical and the verbal, as heavy as stone and as inconsequential as cliché. The ripio suggests that there are right ways and improper ways to adorn language and that good taste in language use is a reflection of the public persona's own cultural adornments and worth. Language use in a specific historic and social context has a heavy, weighted purpose that situates speakers and writers in lived time. The figural employment of language is never simply figural. The special significance of Cánovas, the historical personage, frames both oppositional and apologistic texts about him, even as he is being constructed into a particular public image. So Campoamor could say in 1884 that after Cánovas's own 1883 *El solitario y su tiempo* (the subject was his uncle, costumbrista writer Serafín Estévanez Calderón), someone would need to write a book called *Cánovas y su tiempo* (35). In 1887 Clarín did just that (though not the flattering recreation of Cánovas that Campoamor suggested).[17] In the 1897 Ateneo homage in memory of Cánovas, Gumersindo de Azcárate, a political foe of the statesman, paid tribute in pictorial terms by suggesting that the three speakers—Alejandro Pidal, Segismundo Moret, and himself—would together make a portrait of Cánovas. He ends with these words: "With what I have just said I have finished weaving the cord that will support the picture and the frame that you are now going to see fabricated. . . . The fabrication is rough-hewn because of the fabricator's qualities, but of great solidity" (*Velada* 7).[18] All of these earlier fabrications of Cánovas form a part of the socio-political weave, or fabric, that lies behind Galdós's episodio nacional of 1912.

In turning now to the opening pages of the Galdosian version of Cánovas, readers are struck first by the metafictional qualities of the text. Tito begins his narration by stressing not history, but story. As Ricardo Gullón observed over thirty years ago, Galdós's novel seems to be more about the act or *how* of storytelling than about the *what* of story ("La Historia como materia novelable" 26; see also Urey). Thus Tito directs himself self-consciously to his solid middle-class readers and steers them to "this still blank page" (7). By paragraphs two and three, however, he has moved away from story toward history with the insertion of Mariclío's missive in which she offers a seemingly incongruous mixture of historical portents and social manners (8–9). We are in a critical period of history—Victor Hugo's "hinge of history"—she tells Tito (and readers), in which events and characters have not yet declared themselves. Much is hidden, behind-the-scenes, gestating, all of which looks like a parody of revelatory, figural history. Here, Mariclío is talking less about history than the *making* of history, just as Galdós's text reveals how history is written rather than enacted. Both written history and story are organized discourses, narratives with similar organizing principles, as Hayden White has observed. This does not, however, make historical acts and narrative acts identical. To make sense of the world, the historian patterns events just as the storyteller does. But no historian, including Hayden White, equates history with language alone. Neither does Galdós. Rather, he shows how language is historically laden with meaning, how language wears certain historical labels. Language as intrinsic adornment—as a historical style, if you will—is also intimately related to Mariclío's advice about social manners.

After discussing Hugo's "hinge of history," she says to Tito,

> Don't you understand this, you naughty little historian? . . . Dress well, now that you have fresh pocket money, and don't go to some half-assed tailor. Pick up and cultivate your old friendships again and get ready to strike up new ones that happen to come along. Don't turn your nose up at rich men. . . . The rich man comes up to you with a firm step. . . . The poor scurry away on the heels of their shoes. . . . Farewell, son. . . . If you feel the need to read something, keep your friend Saavedra Fajardo at your side; entertain yourself with the *Manual of the Perfect Gentleman in Society*, devoting a few hours to the *Fashion Plate*. (9)[19]

Galdós does something quite brilliant in his use of language here: he turns writing, in the form of a letter, into a kind of comportment and, more specifically, the writing of history into a conduct manual. In both the literal and figurative senses, he is talking about how to "dress" history. On the level of story, he advises Tito—Mariclío's "little doll," i.e., the synecdoche of History—to adorn himself well. (Indeed, in chapter 2, without his new clothes, Tito becomes confused, disoriented. He does not know how to behave properly.) Similar advice is dispensed throughout the novel to other characters, as in the case of Tito's friend, Segismundo García Fajardo, who arrives on the scene in rags and eventually transforms into an *elegante* as he eases his way into Restoration society. A specific reference to sartorial improvements in his clothing marks each subsequent appearance of Segis. Dress and fashion serve as indexes of middle-class ascendancy into Restoration life, symbolizing entry into history.[20]

Mariclío's letter also functions on the level of discourse as a way of dressing history. The language of her letter—and of *Cánovas* as a whole—is infused with what one could call Peircean indexical qualities (see Brinkley and Deneen; also Sheriff), that is, signs of an ineluctable relatedness to history. Galdós binds verbal adornment to the social and historical cloth of his text, showing in the process how history—and, in the broadest sense, culture—is made, how it is fabricated. The language of adornment—the specific clothing references and imagery, the lexicon of good taste, the constant circulation of information as the inside track for social and historical behavior—all of these elements reveal culture as something worn in Restoration society. History is no exception. In adopting an ironic historical discourse dressed in the cursi language of the period, Galdós also shows how language is something one *does* (as speech act theorists like Austin and Searle have repeatedly demonstrated). Both public and private life in late nineteenth-century Spain were filled with things people did, ways of behaving that defined place and personage as a form of comportment. To comport oneself, *cum-portare*, implies carrying (*portare*) something with (*cum*) oneself. In fin de siglo Spain, one way to define the self was through fashion. Another was through good taste in speech, choice of cultural objects, and the right political knowledge. The consciousness that one's comportment was more often than not inadequate, incongruous, not up to the demands of presumed standards of the times, surrounds the shifting, ill-defined contours of cursilería. Lo cursi is, among other things, a form of comportment (Tierno Galván 81).

Cánovas is, like several other Galdós novels—*La de Bringas, Miau, Fortunata y Jacinta, El amigo Manso, La desheredada*—filled with cursilería (Ynduráin). In what sense is lo cursi bound to the figure of

Cánovas created in Galdós's novel? Another look at chapter 1 is in order here. After Tito reads Mariclío's letter, he proceeds to carry out her advice, renewing court acquaintances and his wardrobe (10). He runs into the penman Florestán de Calabria, whose calligraphic talents, in keeping with his new post at the Círculo Popular Alfonsino, are now sartorially supplemented "with the glittery appearance of cleanliness and elegance" (10). In line with this change of posture in Spanish society are the significant linguistic improvements of another friend, Leona la Brava. Her present protector is "very polished in his dress," in contradistinction to his predecessor, "an overblown figure with monumental-size hats" (10–11). Leona sprinkles "high-toned Gallicisms" (12) through her speech and has adopted an ambitious course of cultural refinement, which includes a box seat at the opera.

When Tito finally meets up with her once more at the Teatro Real, she tells him she is learning French and asks: "¿Tienes el cordón azul de la sobrina del hermano de mi jardinero?" (15), which is equivalent to phrases like "Avez-vous la plume rouge de ma tante?" Such absurd, decontextualized textbook phrases are, in truth, highly contextualized in the sense that a French grammar (of sorts) is, in this setting, an example of a conduct book. Hence, it is fitting that Leona use her newly learned French phrases to point out to Tito *le tout Madrid* present at the opera. "*Pardon, mon ami*," she says, "I know by heart all of Madrid's high society, what we call *gens du monde*" (16).[21] Significantly, she also gestures toward the historical figure, Ramón de Navarrete, "*le grand critique de société*, otherwise known as *Asmodeo*" (17).[22]

The entire theater scene is linguistically and narratively coded as gossip, something both Asmodeo, the Restoration's society columnist par excellence, and Leona la Brava understand implicitly as a form of social legitimation. Galdós subsequently hangs his narration on another hinge, as Leona turns to politics, or as Tito says, "the interesting, latest political news which, according to her, she knew better than anyone else in Madrid."[23] Here is the passage (somewhat abridged) that follows:

Recatando su rostro tras el abanico, me dijo con afectada reserva:
—Has de saber, querido Tito, que don Alfonso ha dado un Manifiesto a la nación, escrito en un colegio no sé si de Inglaterra o

de Alemania. Hasta ahora no se ha hecho público ese documento, que dice cosas muy bonitas.

—Lo has leído tú?

—*Pardon.* No lo he leído. Pero mi Alejandro, que recibió un fajo de ellos para repartirlos, me ha contado todo lo que trae. Cosa buena. Como que está escrito por Cánovas, *voilà*.

—[...]

—Dice . . . que seamos buenos. . . . *Pardon.* . . . no es eso. . . . Dice que viene a reinar por haber abdicado su mamá, que a todos abrirá de par en par las puertas de la legalidad, o, como si dijéramos, que todos entrarán al comedero para llenar el buche, *passez moi le mot* . . . Y pone más, Tito; escucha: que si al igual de sus antecesores será siempre buen católico, como hijo del siglo ha de ser verdaderamente liberal.

[Veiling her face behind a fan, she said to me with affected reserve:

—You need to know, dear Tito, that don Alfonso has declared a Manifesto to the nation, written at a private school somewhere in England or in Germany. Until now the document, which says some very pretty things, has not been made public.

—Have you read it?

—*Pardon.* I haven't read it. But my Alejandro, who received a packet of them for distribution, told me what's in it. It's a good thing. After all, it's written by Cánovas, *voilà*.

— [...]

—It says . . . we should be good. . . . *Pardon.* . . . that's not it. . . . It says that he's coming to be the king after his mother's abdication, that he is opening wide the doors of legality to everyone, that everyone will get his chance to drink at the trough, so to speak, *passez moi le mot.* . . . And he says more, Tito, listen: that while he will always be a good Catholic like those before him, as a child of the century he must also be a true liberal.] (17–18)

This deliciously satiric passage, which fittingly comes at the end of chapter 1, makes the first explicit mention of Cánovas. The lexical incongruities of the popular, pseudoinfantile, and tony French found in this mixed-style speech undermine the political seriousness of this allusion to the Sandhurst Manifesto, which served as symbolic prologue to the Restoration. Historians recognize the manifesto, written by Cánovas, as a significant document, a declaration of the political and religious principles behind the Bourbon Restoration, but Galdós's treatment of this historic piece of writing devastates its import.

Leona's frivolous characterization of the manifesto—"it says some very pretty things" and "and [that] we should be good"—nevertheless underscores a serious critical subtext. The manifesto is not so much a statement of principles as it is a condensed book of conduct. Like popular conduct manuals of the period, aimed largely at women (see Diego; Armstrong and Tennenhouse) but also on occasion at men, as Mariclío's epistolary allusion to a *Manual del perfecto caballero en sociedad* attests, this particular document possesses its own built-in authority. In this case, rather than social convention, the figure of Cánovas himself bestows authority on the Sandhurst Manifesto (even though the future Alfonso XII is the actual signer). "After all, it's written by Cánovas, voilà," says Leona. Of course Galdós is making fun of both the cursilería of a Spanish would-be demimondaine and the predicted hollowness of political gamesmanship. At the same time, he also encapsulates in this brief verbal exchange precisely how a combination of words and conduct legitimates a significant change in power. In short, Cánovas functions as a legitimizer of political and social power. *His* words, as they are reelaborated in the speech of Leona, take on the specificity of a particular social class and its desires.

In this first chapter, Galdós sets up two principle codes of language and behavior: the code of fashionability (elegance of dress, smatterings of French, Asmodeo's appearance) and the code of political expedience (Mariclío's letter, the Sandhurst Manifesto). Both these codes dominate the entire novel. By juxtaposing and then running them together in the speech and actions of characters like Leona, Tito, and Segismundo, the novelist appears to place fashion and politics on the same level and so to imply the insignificance of both. The emphasis on language in *Cánovas* is not, however, merely specular; it is also historically bound.

One way in which the language of *Cánovas* participates in history has to do with how language circulates. From the very beginning, both Tito and readers are caught up in a process of information gathering. Mariclío imparts, albeit confusingly, information in her initial letter about the coming historical change. Her female messengers, the *Efémeras,* convey more information. Casiana calls them "living newspapers" (46). Leona la Brava gives Tito the social picture on the level of gossip. Two journalists, Fabriciano and Mateo, give him news about political developments. Tito has his informants everywhere (and indeed calls one Efémera an "informadora," 252). On occasion, Tito himself is asked to give information, as when Cánovas suggests he spy on the escaped rebel cantonalists and report back to him (60).

Both Tito and Cánovas collect facts, data, rumor, gossip, opinions. Cánovas the historian cannot be separated from Cánovas the book collector. While his well-documented mania for rare books may not have helped Cánovas to govern (239), some of the titles of these prized objects noted in *Cánovas* indirectly further the thematic links between conduct and the contemporary historical situation: for example, *Memorial en detestación de los grandes abusos en los trajes y adornos nuevamente introducidos en España* [Memorandum in detestation of the great abuses in dress and adornments newly introduced into Spain] (1636), by Alfonso Carranza; *Geometría y traças pertenecientes al oficio de sastre* [Science and skills belonging to the tailor's art] (1640), by Martín de Andújar; *Tractados de la mesa, del vestir e calçar e de la mormuración* [Treatises on dining, dress, footwear, and gossip] (1499), by Hernando de Talavera.[24] At one point, Galdós has Cánovas say, "Things come to me, many interesting papers, pieces of living History that still drip blood having been torn from the body of Humanity. I read them avidly; I put them in order, I collect them" (56).[25] In analogous fashion, Tito collects and synthesizes his information: "I . . . sum up and synthesize the Efémeras' information, adding other notices and data that the wandering daughters of the wind give me" (253).[26]

Yet Cánovas and Tito do not function as the sole historians. Near the end of the episodio, a certain Padre Garrido introduces himself to Tito, saying, "I knew and admired him as an eminent historian. I too am keen on History, and in the new Colegio de Chamartín I shall be in charge of this important subject" (263).[27] Given the ferociously anticlerical position of this novel, it is not hard to see Padre Garrido's role of budding historian as a complete degeneration of the profession. Historians as a class don't really fare well at all in *Cánovas:* from Cánovas on down, all constitute bastardizations of one sort or another, that is, bastard sons of Mariclío herself, Mother History and Mother Country wrapped into one.

Significantly, the historian's function in this last *episodio* is more akin to that of the gossip, than to the elevated position normally assigned. Thus Tito becomes increasingly upset at his friend Segismundo, "for his zeal in bringing me notices that in my view weren't History but gossip" (131).[28] It should come as no surprise that Cánovas himself was frequently accused of being a gossip. Campoamor writes of him: "His close friends say that Sr. Cánovas is a gossip in the style of Tacitus. This is not true" (37).[29] Calumny, writes the poet, seems to surround Cánovas: "Despite his character not lending itself to slander, nevertheless, I've never known anyone so much the object of gossip" (7).[30]

The kind of information that floats around in *Cánovas* and that propels forward the narrative flow of the novel is—whether real or imagined, historical or fictional—gossip, something we also saw in Clarín's "Album-abanico" (see chapter 2). As Patricia Spacks comments in her richly observed study on the subject, gossip has much in common with fiction. While the two are not the same, gossip "embodies the fictional" (4). "Narrative, interpretation, judgment," she says later, "this sequence dominates gossip. . . . Together they generate a characteristic rhythm of investigation. And—more to the immediate point—they create story" (13).[31] Gossip also turns the private into the public, and vice versa, by disseminating information and misinformation through verbal and written exchange. Gossip flourishes in preeminently social settings, even when they appear most intimate. The feeling of being in the know, of mastering the inside track, fuels gossip. Its power can unite a community or divide it. Gossip as a social activity of narrative implications is closely connected with forms of social comportment and often is, in effect, a kind of behavior.

What makes gossip particularly fascinating in *Cánovas* is its linkage with history and the making of history. Whether written or oral, gossip constitutes a kind of conduit for history to be represented—and misrepresented. Ironically, much of the information conveyed in this manner is either useless or already known. No great state secrets are revealed in *Cánovas.* Documents like the Sandhurst Manifesto are made public record and are ready to be circulated in large quantities, as readers discover in chapter 1 (17). The novel itself is one extended hindsight; that is, the passage of time has laden the historical events and personages depicted therein with a doubled sense of pastness. Galdós's own awareness in 1912 of past history as something inert because finished, irremediable, came through in an interview: "Everything is dead here," he told journalist Javier Bueno. "We'll have to have a major catastrophe here or else this will simply disappear through decay. This is all dead, dead, dead" (qtd. in Blanquat 149; see also Dendle 182–83).[32]

Like gossip, *Cánovas* promises more than it delivers. For Galdós history itself proved to be no different. The deliberately superfluous nature of much of the gossipy texture of this novel could be likened to the ripio. It, too, is a form of verbal padding, often formulated through commonplaces, clichés, and, most often, euphemistic language. The overwrittenness or linguistic excess of gossip as history is analogous to a *metaripio*. Nowhere is this more ironically—and metafictively—suggested than in the episode of the "mágica péñola," the "magic pen" and the amorous liaison between Alfonso XII and singer Elena Sanz. An Efémera tells Tito he must write the real history of the period, "but, understand this, in the annals of the *internal being* of the nation. As you know too well, life in its external, superficial character isn't worth perpetuating in print" (203).[33] Only a page before this comes the praise society columnist Asmodeo metes out to the opera singer's performance: "Elena Sanz *reached great heights* in the *racconto* of the first act and in the toast of the third" (202).[34] The gossip columnist's arch style also infects the "calligraphic state" of Elena Sanz's life story (212) as told by the magic pen. You can only tell the truth with this pen, warns the Efémera. But truths come clothed in different verbal shapes, and this true history is soon fractured into a mishmash of historical periods and personages, fact and fiction, in ironic Cervantine fashion. Tito soon learns how to get around the incorrigible truth-telling of the magic pen.

The style of this history is set right away as overblown and mock euphemistic. It begins, "Elena Sanz was born in Castellón de la Plana in either 1852 or 53, and I'll give no more because one year or less doesn't take anything away from the documental value of this true history" (205).[35] This is burlesque history on the level of historiography proper.

On another level, it indeed constitutes true history since, linguistically, Galdós situates it within a specific context. The readers of Elena Sanz's life are referred to as "conspicuos" (distinguished) (210), a term especially favored by society columnists.[36] The euphemistic phrases of the magic pen, of Tito himself, and of fanciful historic sources parody both the style of the social columnist and that of the official reports and communiqués of the court and court etiquette. Thus the magic pen dictates the omission of certain things out of delicacy and reasons of state, putting it, however, this way: "In accordance with the inviolate custom of preterition, I reserve silence for those things of little import to my purposes" (207).[37] When Elena Sanz gives birth to a son by Alfonso, she learns of Isabel II's reaction through the mediation of a priest, who writes this "substantive little paragraph" to the singer: "I have been received and heard with inexplicable gratitude and graciousness, whose particular jubilation I *expressly* communicate to you, with all due spontaneity" (220).[38]

This verbal puffery, or *estilo ripioso,* is a perfect example of the affected style of good taste, visible in publications like *La ilustración española y americana* (see Palenque) and *La moda elegante* (mentioned in Mariclío's first epistle), the poetry of court favorites like Antonio Grilo, and the pages and pages of scribbled prose and poetry in albums and almanacs. The euphemistic style figuratively covers the raggedy Segismundo in chapter 9, as Tito alludes to "remedying his indecorous unclothed state" (107), i.e., dressing him in fashionable clothes. The language of elegance is one that simultaneously veils and discloses social and other realities. The rising middle and upper middle classes considered all such products of culture as signs of refinement, reflections of an aristocratic lifestyle to which the newest elite ardently aspired (Palenque 132). High society set the tone, the fashion. Galdós turns fashionability into a particular kind of history in *Cánovas:* the history of a class mentality and of the metaphors governing that mind-set.

Verbal adornments linguistically reflect other kinds of adornment. Thus the radicalism of Segismundo's uncle is no more than a "mental adornment" (119). And Bourbonism is "a politics of inertia, fictions and false formulas. . . . All this is *decorated* with the profuse handing out of honors, distinctions and noble titles" (124; emphasis added).[39] Political

pique is sartorially metonymized as "el sombrerazo" (the hat ploy) when
Cánovas grabs his hat and leaves the parliament in a huff (216). The
notion of adornment thoroughly permeates political thinking and behavior as well as social mores.

Writing itself is sometimes reduced to calligraphy, or adornment, in
Cánovas. Mariclío's letters, for example, are written "in the genuine style
of Iturzaeta" (10). This reference to José Francisco de Iturzaeta (1788–
1853), whose *Arte de escribir* [Art of handwriting] (1827) became an
official text for teaching handwriting, is one that also appears in Clarín's
Su único hijo. The writing of Elena Sanz's life history takes on a "calligraphic state" with Tito's magic pen. And the illiterate Casiana acquires a veneer of culture by learning how to read and write, this last
"with calligraphic neatness and the traditional Spanish handwriting"
(87).

Two paragraphs after this reference to Casiana's handwriting skills,
Galdós connects cultural adornment with the notion of cursilería. The
key passage (often cited) is this: "I still believe that the so-called *gente
cursi* [cursi social class] is the true third estate of modern times, for its
widespread visibility in the census and the bovine docility with which it
contributes to the taxes of the State" (88).[40] What follows immediately
afterward is, in my view, just as significant. Tito says, "Attention, gentlemen. My Casiana was her own dressmaker. Together we would go shopping for fabrics."[41] And then a paragraph later:

> Sepan también las edades futuras que mi compañera se arreglaba
> los corsés, echando piezas nuevas allí donde hacía falta, renovando
> ballenas, ojetes y cordelillos. En cuanto a los polisones, ¡ay!, yo,
> Prometeo Liviano, era el fabricante de aquellos absurdos adita-
> mentos. . . . Agradecía Casiana esta colaboración convirtiendo en
> lindas corbatas para mí los retazos sobrantes de sus vestidos. Sus
> hábiles manos *confeccionaron* igualmente un chaleco, que resultó
> tan bien cortado y *fashionable* como los de Orovio.

> [Let future ages know too that my companion mended her own
> corsets, putting in new pieces where it was necessary, replacing
> stays, eyelets, and laces. As far as her bustles went, oh my! I,
> Prometeo Liviano, fabricated those absurd additives. . . . Casiana
> showed her gratitude for this collaboration by converting into

pretty ties for me the leftover bits and pieces of her clothes. Her clever hands *concocted* just as well a waistcoat, that turned out to be as well cut and *fashionable* as those of Orovio.] (88–89)

Here, the material and the figural come together once again, as they do in the representation of Cánovas himself. Tito, our household historian, is also a maker of ladies' bustles. Is there anything more *ripioso* than the padded, superfluous extension of the feminine figure that is the bustle?[42] This additive or supplemental quality of the bustle ("absurdos aditamentos") as something worn may readily appear like unnecessary adornment, just as language in *Cánovas* may seem merely specular and ultimately nonrepresentational. Urey is right in speaking of the failure in the fifth series "to illuminate a transcendental truth about the historical epoch" (162). But she bases her conclusion that there is no historical meaning in novels like *Cánovas* on the assumption that only representational texts can give up meaning. Simply because one cannot find absolutes for truth, reality, or certainty does not signify the absence of all meaning (see Eagleton, *Literary Theory* 144). Urey notes that "Cánovas is unable to put into practice the theory he reads in books. His reading, then, is an activity without relation to his reality; it is not representational. In like fashion, perhaps, the fifth series has no representational value; it does not tell us the meaning of the epoch, nor what will become of Spain" (186). But this is to rely on representational arguments in order to defeat representational value; it is to use historical referents to attack the meaningfulness of history.

The figural and metafictive qualities of language in *Cánovas* are akin to the use of ripios, the circulation of gossip, and the wearing of bustles. They all have to do with the way reality (or texts) is constructed. Tito as much fabricates words as he does bustles. This sense of fabricating, of constructing, runs through *Cánovas*. Thus "las Cortes enredáronse en el arduo trajín de *fabricar* la nueva Constitución" (The Parliament embroiled itself in the arduous task of *fabricating* a new Constitution) (126). Consummate politician Romero Robledo is a master in the "fabricación de Parlamentos" (fabrication of Parliaments) (100). As a historian Cánovas attributed to divine providence the role of bringing into being, out of the diversity of cultures, a oneness of community, what he called "la fábrica universal" (the universal fabric) (*Problemas contemporáneos*

1:10).[43] Galdós's ironic critique of the "fábrica" created out of Restoration life and politics is apparent. Yet to what extent does Galdós participate in the very system he critiques? The authority embodied in Cánovas as figura is ironically deconstructed by an opposing authority, that of Galdós himself. The novelist's oppositional text and stance are situated within the very culture he questions.[44]

Galdós's ironic insistence on the fabrication of reality and of texts suggests that he, like his contemporaries, by implication saw language as intrinsic adornment, as historical style, in the sense that everything we are is worn, is carried with us as forms of comportment. The notion of wearing one's culture the way the hand wears or carries a pen suggests a "cursive" mode of literary and social representation, which in turn reflects the cursilería of which Restoration society was frequently accused. If, as Tierno Galván hypothesizes, *cursi* derives from *cursivo*, or cursive writing, then a cursive style seems to fall somewhere between the act of writing and the production of the writing performance, or between performance and production.

Even if Tierno Galván is mistaken about the origins of lo cursi, it hardly matters. The cursive mode represented in *Cánovas* arises out of the social nature of language itself. It suggests that what we do *with* language is what we do *with* ourselves and *to* ourselves, whether we make bustles or write histories. The performance value of language as something we do or wear takes on the particular historic coloration of the middle classes in *Cánovas*. As a class without a firm sense of its own history, as one with often uncertain origins—like the term cursi itself—the middle-class characters in Galdós's last episodio nacional show how, under such circumstances, one makes one's own history. History then becomes doubly significant, turning into something that one carries about with oneself. Thus, in a telling phrase, Cánovas says of the loyal opposition: "Si Sagasta no reniega de su historia" (If Sagasta does not forsake his own history) (Pérez Galdós, *Cánovas* 237).

Thus, too, Mariclío speaks for one last time in the final pages of the novel: "I recognize that in countries which are definitively constituted, my presence is almost an impediment." Then several lines later: "I cannot resign myself to the pathetic role of useless shadow" (270).[45] Here, Galdós seems to suggest that Spain is not yet "definitively constituted"[46] and therefore in great need of History, not History as pure allegory—"a useless shadow"—but rather as full presence. This historic insufficiency—reneging full responsibility toward history—is what falls between the cracks dividing performance and production. Galdós doesn't critique the failure to mean but the failure to act in historical terms. The significance of history is built into the very linguistic fabric of the novel. It is historical insufficiency, the cursilería of historical behavior, that drives Galdós's own "magic pen" and creates his own discourse of history in the pages of *Cánovas*.

CHAPTER SIX

The Dream of Negation

BY THE END of the nineteenth century, a deep sense of disillusionment and exhaustion had settled over Spain. A disastrous war with the United States in 1898 signaled the end of empire. The sense of having come undone nationally coexisted paradoxically with another feeling: the growing suspicion that the nation had never really coalesced ideologically or historically. Both regionalistic and political differences became more pronounced at the same time as increasing secularization pointed to a crisis of spiritual and moral values. Class distinctions grew more blurred. In this decaying, chaotic mess, the desire to evade unpleasant historical realities became paramount.

The feelings of confusion produced in reaction to the fin de siglo can also be understood as a kind of negation out of which emerges, in creative Nietzschean fashion, something positive. Or, at the very least, something different came about as a result of the old, existing structures and practices interacting and evolving, on individual and collective levels, to produce the work of culture.[1] From within another context (the psychoanalytic), Peter Homans remarks that "the creation of anything new and valuable . . . has its origins in the old and in the particular ways the old is abandoned and then altered" (4). Thus, historical discontinuity works in tandem with continuity. Negation does not simply state the opposite of affirmation, but stresses the inseparability of both, the dependence of one on the other as a principle of differentiation and thus of movement, change, and identity (see Kurrik ix, 1). In some instances, negation appears on the scene in the form of a cloud, that is, imaged as an amorphous, ill-defined nebulosity; things are in a muddle. No one knows which end is up.

What I want to look at here is a particular aesthetic expression of late nineteenth-century confusion that sometimes takes the emotionally laden shape of nostalgia and daydreaming and that is linked to the processes of negation. This phenomenon, which appears in artistic and literary forms of the day, can be termed "modernist cursilería," itself a form of negation in the way lo cursi is made to operate as a metaphor of marginality, one of whose functions is to subvert and critique through ironic negation, which sometimes becomes a form of negating negation itself.[2] The critical uses to which cursilería is submitted in the arts and literature (as opposed to the unwitting social practice of lo cursi) tend, however, to create a kind of bipolar condition in which the negative and positive applications of cursilería coexist simultaneously.

Cursilería as a social-historical phenomenon begins in the 1830s, is documented by the 1840s, reaches its first peak of excess in the late 1860s and early 1870s, and another high at the very turn of the century. Initially an expression of lower middle-class aspirations and pretensions, cur-silería—a form of disempowered social desire—shows up everywhere by 1900, in practically all social classes and forms of culture, yet nowhere can it be defined or identified as one particular thing or trait. The desire to differentiate—seen first in lower middle-class social aspirations and later in other spheres as well—has dissolved into a blurry field of indis-tinctness by the beginning of the twentieth century. Nationally, for some, Spain represents a cultural ruin fallen into misshapenness. For others, the question of Spain as a nation doesn't even arise. After the 1898 debacle in Cuba, Spain, in the international scheme of things, is relegated to a nonentity; the living past becomes irrelevant. In the eyes of Western Europe and the United States, Spain has turned into a cursi nation, a provincial backwater. Yet, ironically, Spain's turn-of-the-century crisis of identity also becomes a painful rite of passage into modernity.

In folding the more usual and limited meanings of cursilería into a larger national crisis of identity, I have deliberately moved what is habit-ually considered marginal into the center. The cursi phenomenon, which in its very origins in Cádiz, is at first peripheral—having developed in the provinces and being perceived as an extension of provincial weak-ness and inferiority—by the 1870s and 1880s now sees application by contemporaries not only to failed national political movements (the rev-olution of 1868) but, to judge from the Galdosian vision of Spain in *La desheredada, Fortunata y Jacinta, La de Bringas,* and other novels, to Madrid and to the country as a whole. It is against this backdrop of perceived inadequacy and inferiority that events and cultural movements at the end of the century take on their particular configuration.

Spain circa 1900 is both an old and a new country, moving into a largely undiscovered territory called modernity and reacting with ambivalence if not outright resistance to the changing shape of things. Small wonder that even enlightened writers like Unamuno, Ganivet, and Azorín would react in contradictory, conflicted ways, for what they saw was the passing of premodernity, the disappearance of traditional values, belief systems, and symbols. That urbane, middle-class writers would mourn the loss of largely agrarian values and peasant culture may seem ironic. It is important to note, however, that many members of the intellectual and professional classes in nineteenth-century Spain had roots in the provinces and in country life (see Cruz). Spanish writers and artists, in particular, were also reacting to modern life along lines common to their European and American counterparts: with a desire to return to simpler ways, as seen in the Arts and Crafts Movement, the revival of handicrafts, and the craze for medievalism (see Litvak).

Even those who most harshly critiqued Spanish backwardness and stagnation could not help but grieve over what seemed like the twilight of a dying culture. This kind of cultural mourning is sometimes referred to as the process of secularization. But as Peter Homans observes, the term *secularization* proves inadequate by itself as an explanation for what almost all societies, not simply Spain, have experienced in the modern period. In a Freudian turn, Homans sees secularization as "the process of mourning, understood as a complex response to object loss, in which the 'objects' that are 'lost' are social and cultural objects and not only familial and intrapsychic objects." He goes on to say that the social and cultural symbols of a community's life "organize psychic life. When such symbols become meaningless, when they 'die,' then the communities they represent undergo fragmentation, and persons in those communities undergo experiences of loss and are confronted by the need to mourn" (3). In response to this perceived loss there is the need "to replace what is lost with something new" (4).

To discuss this something new, as yet only partially formed at the close of the nineteenth century, my own approach to the subject must focus not only on what did happen historically and culturally but also on what didn't happen. It is one of the larger ironies and paradoxes of history that

Spain, the first recognizable modern nation-state created, had a fragile hold over its own national identity and resources, as civil wars, military coup d'états (*pronunciamientos*), and radical changes in governance in the nineteenth and twentieth centuries have borne out. David Ringrose, for example, questions the premise that Spain really was a nation-state and instead suggests that it was more "a collection of distinct, autonomous, and overlapping networks of regionally oriented activity" (10). This interpretation contrasts sharply with Jo Labanyi's assertion that writers like Unamuno (*En torno al casticismo*, 1895) and Ganivet (*Idearium español*, 1897) naturalized national history by writing out regional movements and identities in an attempt to create the illusion of a unified territorial space (the Castilian ideal), but in effect constructing or inventing the nation, as Hobsbawm and others have suggested with respect to specific national traditions (Labanyi, "Nation, Narration").[3]

These are two very different conceptions of nation. One, Ringrose's, is empirically rooted in the material and economic realities of a country; the other is ideologically grounded (Labanyi). A nation is both a physical reality and an idea, indeed usually a cluster of sometimes incompatible ideas. The Castilian version of a monolithic Spain, displayed in *Idearium español* [Spain, an interpretation], remains completely absent from another book by Ganivet, *Granada la bella* [Granada the beautiful] (1896), an exquisite, localist defense of the writer's hometown, in which he decries the physical destruction of the Granadine past, suggests urban planning and conservation, and makes very clear how much he identified with his *patria chica*.[4] Or take Azorín, known as the author of *El alma castellana* [The Castilian soul] (1900), *La ruta de Don Quijote* [Don Quixote's route] (1905), and *Castilla* [Castile] (1912). But he also wrote *Los pueblos* [Towns] (1905), *España* [Spain] (1909), *El paisaje de España visto por los españoles* [The landscape of Spain as seen by the Spanish] (1917), *De Granada a Castelar* [From Granada to Castelar] (1922), *Valencia* (1941), and many other books covering practically all the provinces of Spain. Azorín's essays and sketches not only provide a verbal map of Spain, but suggest a lifelong love affair with the country. Did he contribute, like Unamuno and Ganivet, to the mythologizing of Spain? Without a doubt. His map of Spain no less constitutes a cultural artifact than the "real" maps of classrooms and print sources (see Labanyi, "Nation, Narration . . ." 130) or the fabrication of Restoration Spain as masterminded by Cánovas del Castillo and reconstructed as artifice by Benito Pérez Galdós in his historical novel.

Labanyi rightfully stresses the invented nature of modern Spain at the turn of the century, but an exploration of the conditions and prospects, feelings and beliefs, poured into such historical constructions seems more interesting to me, especially since it allows us to see just how unstable these constructions are. The material and the figurative are less easy to separate when one considers the inchoate nature of cultural identity and remembers how often the figurative, the constructed, arises out of imperfectly understood and experienced material reality. Moreover, as Paul Cantor notes along the lines of Nietzsche's *Zarathustra*, "any distinctions we make between the literal and the figurative are the product of a particular moment in history, and always subject to change" (74).

Rather than concentrating exclusively on models of construction, which become reified set pieces in historiographical and cultural discursive writings, why not look at the structure before the structure, that is, the particular processes of negation, in this instance, that put into motion historical-cultural change, that disclose that something is happening even when it seems nothing is.

Such structures of feeling both indicate and promote profound social and historical changes. This, I believe, is the case for the texts I refer to as illustrative of fin de siglo cultural confusion: Antonio de Lara y Pedrajas's essay on Cánovas del Castillo (1901), Benito Pérez Galdós's Royal Academy acceptance speech (1897), José María Llanas Aguilaniedo's essay on aesthetics, *Alma contemporánea* (1899), his short piece "Los negadores en el arte" (1899), and Jacinto Benavente's play, *Lo cursi* (1901). What interests me here is the relationship between cultural negation and nostalgia and the space created by this linkage as a transitional zone indicating movement, change and, ultimately, the creation of something new.

Nostalgia makes for one particular instance of a structure of feeling. As an idea, nostalgia surfaces in 1688, when Johannes Hofer coined the neologism to refer to a medical condition often found in soldiers far from home.

and variously called *Heimweh, regret,* or *desiderium patriae.* "Nostalgia," he said, "is born from a disorder of the imagination" (qtd. in Starobinski 87). By 1835 the term has found its way into the *Dictionnaire de l'Académie.* Romantic thought made nostalgia incurable, that is, a permanent condition of loss and exile, childhood as a lost paradise serving as its central metaphor. As Jean Starobinski brilliantly points out, nostalgia issues out of the geographical sense of place and only later becomes interiorized as the place within the individual psyche. Nostalgia intensified when more and more people moved from their villages to the cities, losing that topographical, sense-oriented identification with the particular landscape of their lives. As he explains it, "the village environment, highly structured, constituted an important influence. The desire to return had a literal meaning; it was oriented toward a given geographical area, it concentrated on a given localized reality" (102; see also Nash 6–7).

As a side effect of historical processes, nostalgia is imbued with the historical. But since its inception as a medical condition, nostalgia has always been associated as well with absence and loss, that is, with what has already moved or been removed from the experiential present. Nostalgia means a form of deprivation, whether felt on the cultural or the psychological level. Taken to its limits, nostalgia becomes, in Susan Stewart's penetrating analysis, "a sadness without an object, a sadness which creates a longing that of necessity is inauthentic because it does not take part in lived experience." She continues, "this point of desire which the nostalgic seeks is in fact the absence that is the very generating mechanism of desire. Nostalgia is the desire for desire" (*On Longing* 23). One could say that nostalgia constitutes a trope for an unnamed desire. This seems odd, because its origins, if one can speak of origins in this case, are found in the notion of home and homeland, and, above all, in the maternal return, the matrix of wholeness. "Home" had a name. Thus the medical doctor Pedro Felipe Monlau spoke in 1853 of how the literal separation of infants from their mothers provoked terrible anxiety and sickness, which he called nostalgia or "memoria del corazón" (memory of the heart) (550), a phrase probably taken from Descuret's 1841 *Médecine des passions* (2:393; also Roth 27). Another doctor, Joaquim Salarich, gave the example of a child laborer who fell victim to homesickness

(282). The lack of open skies and countryside and the absence of a mother's love contributed to his death, he argued in a by then (1858) increasingly heard indictment of industrialization.

By the late nineteenth century, however, as Starobinski observes, psychoanalysis, and in particular Freud, transformed the return home into regression, a return to the individual's own history. Thus, "the village is interiorized." "What was at first defined in relation to the place of birth is thus redefined in relation to parental figures and to early stages of personal development" (Starobinski 103). But does mind have a name? Is it a place? At this point nostalgia takes on significant metaphorical properties, becoming a metaphor of a metaphor, to the extent that "metaphors speak of what remains absent. All metaphor that is more than an abbreviation for more proper speech gestures towards what transcends language. Thus metaphor implies lack" (Harries 82). So, too, does nostalgia.

This historical evolution of the nostalgic toward an interior world of nameless, sad desire provides an example of a structure of feeling at work (at least, here, in terms of intellectual history). For Kathleen Stewart, "nostalgia rises to importance as a cultural practice as culture becomes more and more diffuse, more and more a 'structure of feeling'" (227). Her take on the nostalgic, while justified within a postmodern context, does not, however, make clear the linkage between structures of feeling and historical or cultural change. Structures of feeling in this analysis threaten to dissolve into nothing or at best into a kind of psychocultural subjectivism projected onto a screen of unreality. What is lost is the element of change and the capacity to explain the transformative agency of human feeling through and in historical time.

Nostalgia as a particular secularized form of cultural mourning intersects, inevitably, with other manifestations of the social body, taking on the colorations of class and gender differences, local variations, and aesthetic / affective modes of expression. The perception of loss becomes the paradoxical ground for the space of nostalgia. More surprising is how nostalgic responses, often veiled as critique, can sometimes operate as a kind of cultural negation, signifying at one and the same time rejection of one thing and affirmation of another.

Listen a moment, for example, to what Antonio de Lara y Pedrajas, an apologist of political leader Cánovas del Castillo's conservative values, has to say in 1901 about class antagonisms, which he sees as an omen of social and political apocalypse:

Men of property, the capitalist class, are carrying on a ferocious fight amongst themselves over religious beliefs, philosophical doctrines, economic systems, political infighting, without anything to guide them, without shared aspirations to follow; it appears like an organism which is disintegrating and moving inexorably toward dissolution. In contrast, the proletariat, which has discarded anything that disunites and divides and is interested only in uniting and associating, has but one immediate goal, *the conquest of political power*. (68)[5]

Later, he links middle-class disarray to effeminacy of character (69). He attributes both the decay of the privileged classes and class conflict, which he labels a "duel to the death," to a desire for distinction: "The root of all this issues from the general aspiration of all beings and especially man, whether individually or collectively, to distinguish oneself, to stand out, to dominate, to lead, to command" (70).[6] Like most nineteenth-century conservatives and traditionalists, he feared the destruction of privilege—"privilege and . . . power which by a natural law and its very essence tends to stand out, to distinguish and to impose itself"—which he portrayed as being engulfed by lower-class advancement (67).[7] Thus, he links together distinction and power. Property and privilege are signs of a natural distinction in some members of society. Neither Lara y Pedrajas nor Cánovas see any contradiction in justifying, on the one hand, the acquisition of power through such distinctiveness and, on the other, the rejection of the same means and motivation in another social class. Nor do they pursue the question of how, inversely and by implication, power confers distinction. To do so would rock the ground of authority on which such a system had persisted for centuries.

Nothing even remotely nostalgic about Lara y Pedrajas's statements or beliefs becomes apparent at first. Whatever validity his values and assertions may or may not possess, they belonged to the here and now, to the concrete circumstances and lived reality that surrounded him. His partisan critique provides an insight into one of the most significant and, for many contemporaries, worrisome problems of the era: the blurring of class and social distinctions. This phenomenon, by no means unique to

late nineteenth-century Spain, is expressive of the period's cultural confusion. Threatened loss of privilege is linked to an acute sense of dissolution and the breaking up of the social fabric.

Even liberals like novelist Benito Pérez Galdós voiced similar concerns, albeit with respect to all social classes. A sense of muddied endings
and radical slippage fills his 1897 acceptance speech before the Royal
Academy. Vanishing social cohesion, dissolving political parties, a fractured society disbanding in full rout—these are the things he talks about.
Cracks are opening up, he says, in the heretofore solid rock of Spanish
society. All the social classes, but in particular the middle classes, are
losing their traditional character and physiognomy. In a poignant moment, he claims that even the faces of people are no longer what they
once were. This loss of distinctiveness in the human visage is duplicated
in the blurred contours of cities and towns, even the countryside, as they
submit to the ravaging effects of urbanization and leveling out (Galdós
refers to the "rodillo nivelador" and "nivelación"). According to the
writer, the same fuzzy lines of confusion appear in the arts. The collective body and soul are decomposing (*Discurso* 15–20, 23).

I would suggest that, like Lara y Pedrajas, Galdós is preparing for a
period of cultural mourning. Something is dying in the collective memory and experience and in the artistic forms that memory and experience
assume. Yet from within this rotting chaotic mass are fermenting new
social forms, for Galdós, forms that still defy comprehension and definition in the confusion and bewilderment engendered by modern life.

Something was happening that invited ideological critique and analysis—whether from the right or the left—but that could not be precisely
pinpointed or understood fully as experience. Dissolution, the spinning
apart and scattering of the social body: these are terms for suggesting
that, for some at least, things ultimately lacked cohesion, explanation,
and that a profound decentering of life was occurring. For how could one
explain the internal fracturing of one's own class? How does one continue to identify something in the process of losing identity? One could
point, somewhat simplistically, the accusing finger at the presumed cause
or scapegoat (the uppity working classes, for Lara y Pedrajas), but one
would still not come to grips with the sense of a structure falling apart, of
it becoming less and less differentiated. The desire for distinction leads,
in Lara y Pedrajas's analysis, to lack of distinction and, then, to becoming

indistinguishable. Galdós, however, draws another, more affirmative if hesitant conclusion: that out of this decomposition and confusion may arise new forms, at least in the novel. But the last words Galdós utters before that august institution of official culture, the Royal Academy, refer to ruin ("las tristes y desoladas ruinas") (28–29).

Anxiety over the state of national culture visibly surfaces in the realm of aesthetics. The modernist Llanas Aguilaniedo saw nothing but undistinguished mediocrity on the artistic and literary scene in 1899:

> At present, in Madrid, the negating word in fashion is *cursi*. Today everything is cursi here; very few paintings being exhibited are free of the epithet, and even fewer of this season's literary works, or those of the past, have not had applied to them the dishonor of that strange, half-English half-stupid word, notwithstanding its meaninglessness; it is the word which today in the capital city constitutes the inevitable, shorthand formula of any and all critical judgments in matters of art. ("Negadores" 275)[8]

Llanas Aguilaniedo's "negators in art" ("negadores en el arte") are clearly Nietzsche-inspired (with a probable dose of Hegel as well). In this brief piece written for *La vida literaria*, negation acts as a spur to produce the disequilibrium or rupture necessary for thought and creativity to develop: "Praise neutralizes and stultifies; negation is the only thing that can produce the disequilibrium necessary for ideas to spring forth."[9]

Negation incarnates the principle of differentiation: "without a difference in levels, without opposites, there can be no dynamism, no exteriorization of energy" (275).[10]

More suggestive is the way Llanas Aguilaniedo adapts the Nietzschean notion to the word *cursi*, which functions, on an immediate level, as a critical concept, an instrument of negation. As such, it is the verbal whip of fashion. With a sharp sense of self-conscious irony (evident in *Alma contemporánea* also), he simultaneously enlarges and deflates the significance of lo cursi: the negating principle behind lo cursi is creative yet ephemeral. This instability of the term arises, in part, out of the Nietzschean dynamic, which insists on restless dissatisfaction and movement as part and parcel of negation. But it also comes from the cursi side of things. Lo cursi is, first of all, an element within modern art and literature, and, as such, is something to be critiqued and condemned as aesthetically bad, similar but not identical to kitsch. Llanas Aguilaniedo also interprets the notion of cursilería as in some fundamental way an empty one, one ready to be filled with a content dependent on the cultural context, on the work of culture itself. Hence, he observes that cursi says "very little or nothing at all," that it is at best a shorthand formula of the day for bad art. On the other hand, he also sets himself up as the supreme negator and, in that sense, the embodiment of modernist cursilería.

To complicate matters even more, he concludes on an ambiguous note: "So, when I am unfortunate enough to witness how the *habitués* of some gathering or other of the usual crowd make mincemeat out of someone not there, I consider it my duty to inform the interested party and congratulate him to boot" (276).[11] Who then are the negators? Those who condemn the mediocre and worse in the arts (lo cursi), or those who reject the shock of the new (tainted by the threat of faddishness)? Or is it only those who stake out new directions in their field (276)? If, as Llanas Aguilaniedo seems to suggest, lo cursi as cultural negation appears conflicted from within, its very plurivalence may be an expression of cultural forces at war. I don't think it is coincidental that a renewed and heightened awareness of cursilería and a crisis of modernity should occur at the same time in Spain.

A year and a half later, playwright Jacinto Benavente, who won the Nobel Prize for Literature in 1922, took the negating principle of cursilería even further in his social satire *Lo cursi*, translating it into a pervasive uneasiness over confused moral and aesthetic values. Benavente, who belonged to an upper middle-class family and whose father was a well-known, highly respected pediatrician in his day, appears to have mixed socially with both the middle and the upper classes. His plays achieved popularity with both classes as well. Although *Lo cursi* centers on upper-class characters, Benavente's aristocrats also reflect, as my analysis hopes to make clear, either a possible bourgeois contagion or a projection of middle-class cultural anxiety on the upper classes (or, quite conceivably, both).

Critics have taken this play to be, above all, a finely honed skewering of literary modernismo, in which Benavente—a renegade modernista—

pokes holes in the feverish desire for the new. He calls it *actualismo:* "To despise everything that does not exist in the present moment. To eternalize the ephemeral, to fix the fugitive, to magnify the diminutive. That is what our art should be: actualismo—there is no other art possible" (131).[12] If it is not fashionable to be cursi in society, it appears that to be fashionable in the literary world is perfectly cursi. As a parody of modernismo, the play is clearly a period piece. But viewed within a larger context and from the distance that the passage of time has allowed, the play appears to say more about modernity than about modernismo; what it says about literary modernismo has much more to do with the fin de siglo confusion and crisis over modernity and modern identity.

The play, to sum it up briefly, intertwines the twin themes of social and literary fashionability within an upper-class setting, focusing on the fear and embarrassment of being labeled cursi. A classic drawing room comedy, *Lo cursi* opens with a married couple of privileged means and family background (Agustín and Rosario) fussing about style and manners. The real problem resides in the nature of their relationship, each one testing the other in an effort to probe their true feelings without appearing to do so. Benavente deftly works in the literary strand of his plot by using Carlos, the living model-as-collaborator for modernista writer Félix, to pursue the affections of Rosario. As Carlos remarks, "Felix and I are collaborators. I live [what] he writes. . . . The odd thing is, I've taken my role as the experimenter of life so seriously that now, in the simplest things I see the possibilities of a novel, and I no longer know whether it's him writing what I am living out or whether it's me living out what he's writing" (86).[13] This supreme self-consciousness of living an artifice, of creating art out of life, is shared by nearly all the characters. Artifice and the artificial, like fashion and fashionability, are closely linked to cursilería in Benavente's play. Unsurprisingly, the play ends by reaffirming the cornerstone of marriage and fidelity, but along the way it flirts with alternative values, which serves to destabilize the moral-aesthetic universe of the work.

The first scene begins with a discussion of clothing. "How do I look?" Rosario asks. Her husband replies: "You?" And she: "I? No, this dress." The dress comes before the person, style before substance. Rosario, the provincial out-of-towner, bows to her husband's metropolitan sophistication: "And as you say," she remarks, "the dressmakers don't know how to give one a style; style ought to be something unique to oneself, without style there is no distinction possible" (63–64).[14] A successful blend of style and personality produces distinction. The artificial thus becomes inseparable from the natural, from identity itself. Then Agustín confuses his wife by suggesting that the standard for distinction varies not only according to context but often to individual subjectivity and mood. Speaking of the palace of Rosario's grandmother, he says, "That really did have style; forget about electric lights and bells, or telephones; none of this new-fangled machinery which is so disagreeable and so tasteless."[15] Rosario replies, "You say that now, but before you wanted nothing to do with anything old-fashioned; you say that we are an incredibly backward country. . . . if what is distinguished keeps changing at every instant" (64–65).[16] Such, Agustín says, is the "modern spirit" and the *"modern style,"* which includes every style and form imaginable: "that's why they say that modern life has no character; as if not having one weren't a character like any other" (65).[17] This last statement goes to the heart of Benavente's understanding of the elusive, complex, and confusing modern world. Lack of style—shades of Broch's critique of eclecticism—is style. And style is identity.

This initial scene foregrounds issues of identity and modernity as played out on a highly urbanized and urbane stage, the privileged set of the capital. The necessary background to this scene are the provincial origins of Agustín's wife Rosario and her family, who represent older, premodern values, anchored in tradition and unswayed by the modern penchant for the new or the corresponding fear of the obsolescent. Rosario's grandmother, "a great lady" blessed with true distinction, says Agustín with reverence, stands in for this lost world. Like others before him, Benavente associates provincialism with the feminine (Rosario) and both with the threat of cursilería. Thus he takes a mixed attitude toward traditional Spain. On the one hand, genuine distinction and distinctiveness are attached to the traditional. On the other, the traditional is irremediably provincial, that is, backward and out of touch with modern life. It is here, within this unstable, ambivalent space between rejection of and desire for a return to older values and ways of being, that lo cursi flourishes. Something has been lost, something that possessed a localized sense of a place and time—the provinces (significantly, unnamed in

Benavente's play)—but that no longer has a style, a collective social identity by which and in which individuals may define themselves.

The juxtaposition between the traditional and the modern in this play is thus a deceptive one, stressing a loss not fully acknowledged as such. Indeed, significant remnants of the old order are still in place: class distinctions, family, social order. But in Benavente's text everyone is role-playing, not simply because these are characters on stage but because they are acutely self-aware of their own sense of role-playing. The play's metatheatricality reinforces this quality. The continual discussions and dialogues about social and individual behavior, about style and fashion, whether literary or sartorial, disclose an underlying insecurity over one's place in the modern world. Nothing seems to justify the existence of these characters except their all-consuming and self-conscious interest in talking about being upper-class, as though the audience needed to be convinced of their natural distinction. Speech really is behavior here, something already seen in Galdós's *Cánovas*.

Social insecurity translates into a fear of showing emotion here, a fear intimately associated with the dread of cursilería. To understand this linkage, one needs first to see how Benavente defines lo cursi:

> The invention of the word *cursi* complicated life horribly. Before, you had the good and the bad, the entertaining and the boring. . . . Now you have lo cursi, which is neither good nor bad, neither entertaining nor boring; it is . . . a negation: the opposite of distinguished; that is, plain old everydayness. Because the minute there are six people who think or do the same thing, it's time to think and do something else in order to be different; and to avoid what is cursi, sometimes foolish, outlandish, even bad things are done. (79–80)[18]

I think it quite likely that Benavente's understanding of lo cursi as negation comes from Llanas Aguilaniedo's *Vida literaria* article. (Benavente was the journal's first editor in chief in 1899.) The playwright modifies and downplays the Nietzschean creative cast to cursi's negating effects as seen in Llanas Aguilaniedo. Benavente converts cursilería into a liminal space of social habitus, in which daily life is neither good nor bad; it is merely undistinguished and, by implication, socially undistinguishable, given the underlying upper-class fear of the crowd here. Later, he makes clear that cursilería is a modern phenomenon of mass society: "The select few . . . flee from the masses; the masses pursue them everywhere. Some are cursi in their anxiety to imitate others; and others are even more cursi in their anxiety to distinguish themselves from everyone else" (133–34).[19]

This transitional, ill-defined space that lo cursi inhabits seems to require some sort of structure to deal with it. The amorphous, socially and culturally, creates dis-ease. If the feeling that produces self-awareness of being perceived as cursi is hard to encapsulate, to see as a feeling, it is equally difficult to conceptualize how and what feeling itself structures. In Benavente's play, insecurity about individual and class identity—in this instance, the privileged classes—does not translate into social angst, it becomes drawing room comedy. Feelings of inadequacy and uncertainty assume a recognizable, even brittle, shape that works to contain the messy edges and worrisome implications of blurred social distinctions. This association between insecurity and form is articulated as a stylized fear of sentiment in the Benavente text. Thus, not only are patriotic, mawkish plays regarded as cursi, but so is anything in art that emotionally moves the spectator. In the social sphere, notes the Marquis de Villa-Torres, "it's a bad thing to disguise one's feelings, but to avoid seeming cursi we often disguise them, and we oblige others to do the same" (79–80).[20]

This fear of expressing sentiment lies at the heart of the play, providing the motive and modus operandi of characterization and action. Carlos's scheming to seduce Rosario is predicated on this knowledge. "Rosario has heard it said" he remarks, "that showing jealousy is simply not done; it's really common to be jealous over one's husband. Oh! Fear of lo cursi will be my accomplice." A little later he says, "For Agustín there's neither good nor bad. Everything is either cursi or distinguished. It's cursi to be jealous; cursi to be alarmed because his wife is so friendly to me; cursi to mistrust me, his best friend" (93–94).[21]

Fear of cursilería points to a tension or disjunction between sentiment and class identity. The dissolving of a clear class, or socially inflected, identity puts into question exactly how sentiments are to be expressed. The burden of sentiment gets placed more and more on the individual interior or subjectivity, and less on the defining boundaries of class. To avoid being perceived as less than aristocratic, the privileged character builds an even higher wall or class self-consciousness around that specific social identity, but the wall serves more to spotlight, ultimately, the inadequacy of such social categories in the late nineteenth century. The wall between privilege and populace confirms how class is based not simply on differentiation or distinction, but on incorporating the Other into oneself as well. The wall is, in other words, permeable. It can be breached.

Benavente's play is about the dislocation of feeling, not about its denial. The genre of drawing room comedy embodies a particular class form and constitutes a reaction to a more complex, more amorphous cultural shape that now inhabits this form and receives the name of cursilería. Because lo cursi already resides within the formal boundaries of this well-made, highly artificial dramatic structure, it becomes impossible, finally, to escape being cursi. If in the end Rosario and Agustín clarify their true feelings, Rosario establishes her fidelity, and the tradition-minded Aunt Flora asserts as well that "the good is never cursi," the reader / spectator may be tempted to believe that Benavente has in this way affirmed the value of a solid bourgeois marriage, even for an aristocratic couple. On the other hand, it is clear from certain discreet allusions that Agustín has been dallying with someone else ("ésa"), but he never really gets caught at the affair—it is simply glossed over. This reliance on appearances and order, moreover, receives reinforcement with the last two lines of the play: "And now that morality has been upheld, as in the most common of comedies," says the Marquis, to which Flora replies, "The only thing missing is the applause [Curtain]" (151). Clearly, Benavente's fine-edged sense of irony is at work here, but, I would suggest, so is his essential conformity with the prevailing social order, an order that, appearances to the contrary, is eroding as new forms of being and behavior begin to emerge.

Benavente's flirtation with a structure of feeling that supports class differences, defining to some extent both class and nation (relying on the traditional / modern divide), is not exceptional in this period. The all-pervasive preoccupation with cursilería, which becomes a defining mark of identity, or loss of identity, of late nineteenth-century Spanish society, also suggests that the expression of one's feelings and the significance of that particular feeling were genuine concerns of the period.

My final example of such concerns within modernist cursilería is taken from Llanas Aguilaniedo's *Alma contemporánea* [Contemporary character], in which he develops an aesthetic theory of *emotivismo*. Llanas Aguilaniedo (1875–1921), until recently a somewhat sketchy figure, was by vocation a pharmacist, but he was also a journalist, theoretician of the arts, sociologist, an expert in such areas as criminal anthropology, urban studies, and alcoholism, and, of course, a novelist and essayist.[22] Like many other reform-minded fin de siglo writers and thinkers, he wanted to "hygienize the social body and the human spirit." His 1899 essay, subtitled "Estudio de estética" [A study in aesthetics], is a "recipe of spiritual pharmacopoeia" (Broto Salanova 17, 72).

But paradoxically (and following Nietzsche), the regenerative goal that informs *Alma contemporánea* is based on what was generally perceived as degenerative art. Signs of degeneration, physical and moral, fascinated Llanas. In the comparative pathology of such conditions as hysteria, epilepsy, alcoholism, and madness he found clues, through metaphoric analogy, to the behavior of supposedly superior decadents, those special people, for example, who populate the novels of Huysmans, Rachilde, and Llanas Aguilaniedo himself. *Alma contemporánea* was meant as a harsh attack on what he perceived as the artistic and cultural degeneration of his times (echoing Max Nordau, Pompeyo Gener, and others): "A generation of decrepit, exhausted souls," he writes, "of psychathenics, of impotents and tormented self-analyzers, parades through the theater, the novel, and all the varieties of today's art" (*Alma* 7).[23] These represent worn-out organisms who bear the stigmata of chronic fatigue and moral corruption turned inward, as though to die, in rejection of the outer world.

Yet it is this very same refined spirit that he exalts as an ideal in his essay and fiction. Llanas enthrones an art for the happy few, an exquisite, cosmopolitan writing in which inner sensations and moods are morbidly dwelt on as the spiritual-aesthetic gateway to both cultural and personal redemption.[24] Thus, in the introductory pages to *Alma contemporánea*, he develops a Seville landscape description that evokes, for him, a dream of nostalgia:

The peaceful beauty, tranquillity, and delicate enchantment of re-signed Nature as the sun went down, contrasting with the hubbub of coaches and the murmuring of those going by, awakened in the soul a complicated harmony of feelings, individual states of vibra-tion, akin to those that certain compositions of Chopin provoke in us, that seem to speak of the extinction of a race, in which the great composer weeps over the misfortunes of his compatriots, the po-etic sadness of a defeated Poland. . . . An exquisite picture this, that symbolized so well the spirit of our time.[25]

This word picture, he also says, "like everything incomplete, made one dream of completion" (5–6).[26]

I could not help thinking of how Ortega y Gasset's *Meditaciones del Quijote* [Meditations on the Quixote] (1914) begins, with a description of the natural wooded landscape surrounding the monastery of El Escorial. Like Llanas Aguilaniedo's opening, Ortega's set piece stresses imperma-nence and incompletion. The passage is adamic, situated in a kind of garden that stands for an Orteguian firstness. Thinking functions as a recreation of the world—and at the same time as a means of salvation. The silence of the place makes us aware of our own mortality, "we hear the beating of our own heart." "Every beat . . . seems like it is going to be the last one," Ortega writes. Underneath each "new redemptive beat" lies emotion (98). Temporality. The fear of emptiness. In Ortega, what lies behind thinking is feeling. This subjective foundation for Llanas Aguilaniedo constitutes precisely the heart of writing. He calls it emo-tivismo: "The work of art has always been a reflection of the emotion experienced by the artist; but if we amplify this concept of emotions so as to form the basis of all artistic production, we arrive at a literature of *emotivos*" (*Alma* 157).[27]

"Emotion constituted as a principle" is, above all, troped as feminine in *Alma contemporánea*. Woman, for Llanas, is "art in action," "who makes us feel and moves us as no other" (*Alma* 230), a notion he elevates to the ennobling aesthetic principle of "Feminidad" (taken from Cham-brun). It is curious, however, that elsewhere he relates the feminine to the atavistic and the unfinished: "The female is an incomplete being" (*Alma* 151). Yet he began by stressing the suggestiveness of *lo incompleto*. Contradictions abound.[28] This same "disordered desire for emotion" seems to complete itself—to find the "complement"—by attaching itself to a typically fin de siglo inexorable chain of progressive disaster. Out of this "yearning for emotions" come hysteria, madness, and finally suicide or early death (*Alma* 238). One could argue that writings like those of Llanas Aguilaniedo enact a form of male hysteria.[29] As a split subject, the hysterical text never heals itself. The contradictions and ambiguities are inherent to these "twilight souls of our time," as Llanas called them and of which he is a fascinating representative.

Going back, then, to Llanas Aguilaniedo's introductory description, it becomes clear that this twilight moment in Seville is symbolic of something dying—and something beginning to take shape. If Benavente, Lara y Pedrajas, and Galdós all in their own way perceive the dissolution and indistinctiveness of particular social classes, Llanas Aguilaniedo relates the same phenomenon to a very special class of people, the artists and writers who deliberately exploit their own uniqueness—the romantic myth incarnate—as the distinguishing mark of identity. The Seville landscape description is quintessential modernism, suggesting what can only be intuited, leaving blank and unfinished what cannot be said. This fertile space of the imagination evokes the world of dream, of images half-formed that stand in for the creative process itself. Llanas sees this word picture as "symbolizing the spirit of [his] time" and refers to "the progressive adaptation of the unadaptable, the return to simplicity by those disenchanted with too much complication and analysis; the gathering together of these twilight souls of our time in search of utter forgetfulness, absolute repose of spirit."[30] He concludes with this sentence: "It is the sign of the night of intellect which will be reborn into a new day" (6).[31] He also relies on a kind of parallel cultural and biological determinism, heavily promoted in the fin de siglo, to explain this "extinction of a race."

Llanas Aguilaniedo's *emotivismo* presents readers with a contradictory and confusing blueprint for a structure of feeling that supports class difference, in this case, the fin de siglo need for differentiation as embodied in the privileged artistic elite, or, as he observes, "that special aristocracy of souls who have attained the maximum degree of differentiation from their time" (*Alma* 147).[32] We cannot divorce this obsession with artists and artistic creativity in Llanas from the national context. The only vitality he sees in Spanish literature comes, revealingly, from the provinces, notably Catalonian modernism (67–70). Significantly, the Seville landscape that appears in the beginning of his text reflects the local literary circle to which he belonged during this period and to which he attributed the genesis of his book. In order to write *Alma contemporánea*, he says, he needed a stimulus, a shock, and he found that initial impetus in a Seville sunset (*Alma* 4).

Like Benavente's play, this description of a sunset falls within the category of modernist cursilería, first, because there is something irremediably dated and clichéd about the image, making it in that sense, modern. But in line with my understanding of lo cursi as a bipolar critical concept in the arts and literature, that is, containing negative and positive poles of meaning and significance at the same time, Llanas Aguilaniedo's description also operates through a kind of ironic negation. The vision of twilight is obviously related to the image of twilight souls, a race threatened by extinction. Twilight, as Verlaine and other symbolists well knew, evokes a vague melancholy, a sense of endings. Llanas modernistically links the visual space with the strains of Chopin's music. The composer's misfortunes and poetic sadness are specifically connected to Polish history and his Polish compatriots, but it is evident that the real sadness behind this image has nothing at all to do with Chopin or Poland. The melancholy that Llanas feels has no apparent object. In this sense, the passage is filled with the aura of deprivation that the nostalgic represents. Later it becomes clear that mourning *is* taking place, mourning for those very twilight souls to whom he is so attached and with whom he identified. Llanas loves the half-formed, the incomplete, the in-process. The cultural—and personal—mourning found in *Alma contemporánea* is full of confusion and, as such, is a fascinating manifestation of what Raymond Williams in *Marxism and Literature* called the unfixed practical consciousness of a culture in formation.

The structure of feeling that nostalgia and daydreaming put into practice in this passage is only apparently rooted in a specific topography. For even though Llanas begins with this Seville landscape and acknowledges his debt to his Seville literary friends, "place" here has evidently undergone internalization. It is, moreover, a space doomed to disappear, "in utter forgetfulness" and in the "extinction of a race," even if a "new day" is prophesied. Significantly, too, this space is meant for dreaming; it is a dream of the incomplete ("soñar con el complemento"). *Lo incompleto* in Llanas is of course always missing. It is the split in his subjectivity, the desired return home or need for centered rootedness and wholeness that will never take place.

For home is permanently displaced in this text. (So too, then, is feeling.) Home has become a diffuse twilight, a dream of completion, the unending desire for emotion in the form of art, the troped feminine. Ultimately, home within Llanas Aguilaniedo's text psyche is something that no one can ever really fathom, a half-formed identity image that dissolves, metamorphosing out of the eclipse of intellect into an untold new day.[33] This cyclical use of time in nature suggests a possible return, perhaps even a return that is in some way new or different. The pivotal moment of negation may thus point to "a return to what may have been excluded, lost, dominated, or suppressed . . . or a return to what was as yet undifferentiated, nonelaborated, whole, or unified before the act of negation" (Kurrik ix). The image of twilight, with its impressionist and symbolist associations, seems at first more likely as a return to a scene of undifferentiation.

The will and need to differentiate—on which identity of all kinds is based—drives this text powerfully. It is this very act of differentiating—of making its own claims for literalness—that privileges, paradoxically, the figure of lo incompleto. The incomplete is intimately tied to the feminine, as is the atavistic, making this a figure of unresolved ambivalence in Llanas's text, impossible "to complete," in other words, impossible to return to. Freudian negation may also help here, the notion that "the content of a repressed image or idea can make its way into consciousness, on condition that it is *negated*. Negation is a way of taking cognizance of what is repressed; indeed it is already a lifting of the repression, though not, of course, an acceptance of what is repressed" (Freud, "Negation" 235–36).

Whatever it is, finally, that drives Llanas Aguilaniedo, feeling structures the image of twilight in this passage, making it symptomatic of a "con-fusion" of values and meanings, of the simultaneous blending/breakdown of forms and the search for a different meaning. The craving for emotion—the desire for desire, or nostalgia as a trope for unnamed desire—that Benavente identifies as the thirst for the new, resulting in both obsolescence and a desire for distinction, provides a kind of structure to what seems not to have one, the passage into modernity. If loss structures feeling, then feeling—Llanas Aguilaniedo's transformed emotions—seems to structure the modern here. Indeed, feeling, its force a driving structure for the times—here, specifically modernist cursilería—appears to be a sign of modernity itself.[34] Llanas's twilight souls ("almas crepusculares"), like the confusion found in Lara y Pedrajas, Galdós, and Benavente, in recording the cultural change and loss that have occurred, also seem to signal, at the same time, something new that has yet to be.

CHAPTER SEVEN

The Margins of Home: Modernist Cursilería

THE DREAM of negation is about forms of loss and, in particular, the loss of centeredness, of home, or what passes for home symbolically and affectively. This notion is itself tied to questions of origins, whether individual or collective. Modernist cursilería operates, however, from a position of marginality, in that a peripheral phenomenon, lo cursi, becomes the fulcrum of critique. One of the key proponents of this slyly subversive practice was Ramón Gómez de la Serna. His 1934 essay, "Lo cursi," has become a modern classic of vanguard writing. To my knowledge, the text has not, however, received serious critical attention.

Turning his gaze on the age of the belle epoque, Gómez de la Serna assumed an ironically retrograde stance by shifting his attention to something that most observers in the 1930s probably wanted to forget: cursilería. In so doing, he suggests ways in which to rethink the location of center and margin in establishing major and minor categories not only in literature but in other areas as well. In practice, writers themselves often overstep the lines between core and periphery. In the case of the cursi phenomenon, the margins of a culture have evidently invaded the very center, whether of texts or of social groups. Gómez de la Serna's essay also furthers the notion that the margins can function subversively as ironic negation, the beginnings of which we have seen in such turn-of-the-century texts as Llanas Aguilaniedo's *Alma contemporánea* and Benavente's play, *Lo cursi* (see chapter 6).[1] The supplementary nature of lo cursi then becomes a critical concept or instrument that operates on the textual body of cursilería itself. In following Gómez de la Serna's tack, I am thus employing the notion against itself to suggest the power of the marginal and the supplementary to negate and subvert. To see more clearly how this works and to draw out more of the implications of modernist cursilería and the centrality of the "margins of home," I will be looking, through the prism of Gómez de la Serna's essay "Lo cursi," at one of the canonical texts of Spanish literature, the *Sonatas* (1902–5) of Ramón del Valle-Inclán.

In Gómez de la Serna's essay, lo cursi emerges as a feminized, domestic object of desire, one perceived as doubly marginalized for its cultural inadequacies that are both socially built-in and sexually en-gendered. This text also functions as a narrative of origins and of loss, in which the feminine—and in particular the maternal—while identified with the marginal (lo cursi), paradoxically takes center stage as the sought-for object of writing. The feminine, maternal or otherwise, takes on the aesthetic and material shapes of real objects metaphorized within a series of metonymical associations. These examples of cursilería are things represented as images of domesticity and enclosure; and they are remembered with intense longing as both out-of-date and timeless. Gómez de la Serna's simultaneous looking backward and forward imbues his text with an ironic awareness of the marginal, insufficient qualities of lo cursi as anachronism, even as he attempts through writing to salvage—and thus make central—that transcendent moment of self when self counted. The essayist thinks he is saving things; in truth, as with Llanas Aguilaniedo in *Alma contemporánea,* he is saving the feminine as an early, lost part of himself. "Lo cursi" is a narrative of home.

In many ways, Valle-Inclán's initial modernista writings are also narratives of origins and of interiority, in which he views the past as loss and incites memory to recover—over and over in works like *Femeninas* (1895) and the *Sonatas* (1902–5)—that one irretrievable, central loss of the feminine. Modernista writing arose at an awkward transitional time in Spanish history when old forms of life were disappearing and new ways were still incipient, ill-defined. The settings of the *Sonatas* in particular emphasize, as Maravall ("La imagen de la sociedad"), Vilanova, and Predmore have observed, the contradictions clinging to an aristocratic, quasi-feudal, traditional social structure (here, Galicia) placed in the midst of a developing bourgeois, individualistic, and embryonic capitalist system. The *Sonatas* also underline how deeply and persistently familial the narrative and social framework surrounding both kinds of social organizations in Spain is. Here, as in Gómez de la Serna, are texts that look backward and forward at the same time. Socially, back toward an earlier society—a rural, archaic world that is dying—and, in literary terms back to an anachronistic romanticism. Forward to sensation and the individual's perception of sensation as a kind of timeless presentness, explored through dream and illusion, fragmented pieces of reality, and the fetishistic glorification of language as language. This incipient fragmentation of the novel form into moments of sensation leads ultimately to the complete loss of transcendence in Valle's later work. In the *Sonatas*, however, such loss is temporarily staved off by clinging to the sense of time as pure memory.

In one sense, these works reflect ideologically the tenet of individualism prized in advanced middle-class Western cultures. But at another, deeper level, the *Sonatas* suggest a crisis of individualism, to the extent that Bradomín's narcissistic pose puts into question the cult of personality. Valle-Inclán's use of irony, his parody of stereotypes, the smooth specularity of his modernist prose, and of the sense of persona enveloped glasslike in the Marqués de Bradomín, all deconstruct in subtle ways the wholeness of self and writing.

Socially and historically, these cracks in the mirror surface of writing and self-containedness of the individual may reflect Spain's rough jump start and gap in development between the traditional ancien régime social structure and the change to a more modern middle-class system. Spain's middle-class strength developed late, at a time when Western nations like France and England were far more advanced economically and politically. This historic dyssynchronicity sometimes results in a resistance to modernity, which in itself is a sign of the modern in Spain. The *Sonatas* are imbued with this same feeling of the dyssynchronic. Temporal maladjustment makes these works move uneasily within an unsettled, shifting frame of time and space. Readers become acutely aware of the sense of time as being partly defined through its own contradictions. The notion of time as rooted in a dying culture ironically brings about the production of anachronistic values. In a word, it produces lo cursi and situations and characters impregnated with romantic cursilería.

Valle-Inclán also creates a chain of relationships linking the feminine, objects (or objectified parts of the female body), and what can be called the cursi effect. This effect, in which the feminine is devalued through such ironic distancing techniques as stereotyping and association with objects lacking depth or substance, works, in essence, as a process of marginalizing the feminine in the *Sonatas*. Yet the feminine constitutes their central quest motif. As does Gómez de la Serna, Valle-Inclán, in the guise of Bradomín, really seeks himself, or that lost part of himself called the feminine. Bradomín defines himself in large part through his relationship with women. The feminine performs the symbolizing role of speculum, the mirror of man, in the *Sonatas*. Indeed, gender structures these narratives to a remarkable degree. In such a highly sexualized fictional world, language itself becomes a weapon of seduction, and the images fashioned out of this verbal seductiveness are fetishes. In 1904, Ortega y Gasset commented that Valle was an "original stylist, who at the same time adored his native tongue, to the point of fetishism" ("Sentido del preciosismo" 56).[2] In this extraordinary display of verbal fetishism objects and parts of the female body are treated as modernist cursilería. Yet they also stand for the desired feminine, now broken into fragments, having lost the wholeness of home, the space of enclosure and origins.

Valle lodges his narrative in this discourse of home, from which the feminine has been marginalized by being reproduced as a kind of adornment, or domestic supplement. The relation between persons and things thus becomes significant because things have cultural meanings attached to them and because things function as metaphors, as adornments worn in time, hence dated.

As a narrative of origins, the *Sonatas*—and Gómez de la Serna's essay on "Lo cursi"—function like the souvenir. They trigger memory, which begets desire for the original experience. The object or souvenir becomes through narrative the focus of attention, but never the heart of the matter. As Susan Stewart says in her illuminating analysis of the souvenir, the narrative of origins "is a narrative of interiority and authenticity. It is not a narrative of the object; it is a narrative of the possessor" (*On Longing* 136). Things as secondhand experience are laden with time: their own time, remembered time, and the original moment of firstness often associated with infancy and childhood. That final image of a sled burning in Orson Welles's *Citizen Kane* shows only the banality of Kane's childhood memory, the memory of a sled he called "Rosebud." Yet it provides the key to his life. Writing itself marginalizes such immediacy of experience. Modernist writing in particular suggests—as in

Rubén Darío's line, "Yo persigo una forma que no encuentra mi estilo" (I seek a form that my style cannot find) (177)—that displacement of desire is the price for modern self-consciousness. By the turn of the century, a sharp awareness of the transitoriness of things, of the capacity of things to be used up, consumed, has also exacerbated the charge of time hanging over the material world. Objects once considered simply trivial or banal now become doubly cursi as the swiftness of time makes them dated, unfashionable and, finally, unwanted.

By 1899, lo cursi seemed to have acquired new life as a cultural index of late nineteenth-century Spanish society and its often bewildering complexities and contradictions. I have already noted how Llanas Aguilaniedo treats lo cursi as a critical concept and relates it to aesthetic preoccupations. Behind the notion, he says, lies "the negating imperative," a relentless dissatisfaction with the conventional and the habitual in art. Negation fuels the use—and abuse—of trite terms like cursi, which in themselves remain relatively inexpressive or amorphous in shape and content.

Other signs of a newly perceived fin de siglo cursilería appear. Also in 1899, popular playwright Javier de Burgos refashioned an earlier play called *Las cursis burladas* [The cursi ladies mocked] (1882), titling his new work *La familia de Sicur* [The Sicur family] (see fig. 6). The title (and setting in the Cádiz of 1862) harks back to the possible anecdotal origins of the word *cursi*. Eusebio Blasco satirized the desperate quest for fashionability in a utopian city called "Cursinópolis," where everybody, oddly enough, speaks Spanish. Magazine stories and light verse continued to exploit the theme. In a story by Luis González Gil called "La niña cursi" [The cursi girl] (1902), the protagonist's name is Filo, which I suspect is an ironic allusion to the 1868 Silvela-Liniers satire, *La filocalia, o arte de distinguir a los cursis de los que no lo son*. A few years later would appear a story by Antonio Roldán, "Cómo caen las niñas cursis" [How the cursi girls fall] (see fig. 13). A poem titled "Cursilería" (1900), by J. Tolosa Hernández, begins: "Loving you the way I do / my dear, / pinning all my hopes / on you, / they tell me is perfectly cursi, / for loving this way / is no longer in style" (487).[3]

And, as noted before, this link between lo cursi and fashionability reached a high point in Jacinto Benavente's play, *Lo cursi*, which premiered on 19 January 1901 at the Teatro de la Comedia in Madrid.

El Cuento Semanal

Cómo caen las niñas
cursis POR ANTONIO ROLDÁN
Ilustraciones de Víctor Miguel

30 céntimos

13. Víctor Miguel's
cover for the short story
"Cómo caen las niñas cursis,"
by Antonio Roldán, pub-
lished in the popular series,
El cuento semanal (25
August 1911).

Significantly, both cursilería and fashion (*la moda*) are now strongly
connected to a critique of modernismo. For one contemporary reviewer,
this work represented a complete turnabout in Benavente, erstwhile
modernista. The play is "a violent diatribe, a sharp and cruel satire
against all manner of *modernisms*, social, political, literary, even religious" (Laserna, *"Lo cursi"* 3).[4] Fittingly, Benavente had prepared his
public the night before by presenting a one-act piece called *Modas* [Fash-
ions] at the Teatro Lara, where he proved himself to be a "Worth of irony
and satire" (referring to the celebrated haute couturier Worth) (Laserna,
"Modas" 1).

The implied similarities between art and fashion in Benavente's play
are made explicit in an anonymous 1898 satire called "Manual del perfecto modernista" [Manual of the perfect modernist] or in Manuel del
Palacio's "El modernismo (fábula)," in which a frustrated inventor—
Silvestre Boberías—proclaims his originality by wearing his clothes inside out. By claiming that modernismo and fashion were part of the same

ephemeral, changing circumstances, critics in effect meant that both were subject to the devastating consequences of cursilería. By 1900 lo cursi had become, on the one hand, emptied of content, assuming a multiplicity of forms. On the other hand, as a cultural marker, lo cursi was now intimately and irretrievably tied to the outdated. Everything in a consuming culture was vulnerable to losing its relevance. Modernismo, in this sense, became burdened with time.

It may seem strange to discuss modernismo as a kind of cursilería. Critics generally think of the literature of this period as an "edad de plata," or silver age, to use Mainer's phrase. Many of the writings identified with this period—Valle-Inclán's *Sonatas*, for example—are now considered canonical works. Yet some of the later hostile reaction to modernismo originated precisely with its perceived excesses, with what one critic has called a " 'kitchification' of feeling" (Barnstone 291). So Machado would write disdainfully of "old cursilerías" in the poem, "Tocados de otros días" [Toilettes of days gone by]. Here, objects of a dead romanticism—faded lace and silk, yellowing daguerrotypes and letters, pressed flowers—in reality have their referent in his generation's own fin de siglo form of romanticism, modernismo (Machado 123). These are objects doubly dead, smothered in time.

By the 1920s and 1930s, literary modernismo scarcely received serious attention. The architectural splendors of the modern style had fared even worse. Buildings were torn down, facades remodeled or allowed to decay. In 1929, at the time of Barcelona's second Universal Exposition, a small guidebook appeared—*L'art d'ensenyar Barcelona* [The art of showing off Barcelona]—in which the author, Carles Soldevila, explained to tourists that Barcelona "had had the misfortune to build a good deal of the city's expansion following the so-called modernist style" (qtd. in Mendoza 158).[5] As late as 1932 the municipal government received strong encouragement to force Barcelona store owners to eliminate "all the ornamental crests and reliefs and to strip the artistic facades from their *modern style* houses, getting rid of all the excess and ornamentation ruining and overwhelming the architecture of the building" (qtd. in Mendoza 158).[6] Only by exception—as in the case of Salvador Dalí—was modernismo defended.

230

In the midst of a volatile and politicized Spain, and amid violent attacks against fin de siglo art and other manifestations of the decried petit bourgeois spirit (see Brihuega 14–15; Arconada), appeared Ramón Gómez de la Serna's 1934 sui generis essay "Lo cursi" (revised in 1943).[7] This marvelous essay seems like a pocket of time inexplicably filled with the remembered objects of an earlier period and preserved against time itself. By design regressive, this essay returns to the fin de siglo by focusing on the disdained—or marginal—elements of the period. Like much of the writer's work, this piece takes a lateral view of things, approaching the subject obliquely.

As an index of insufficiency and inadequacy, lo cursi points to what Tierno Galván called "an inner poverty of meaning" (99), transmitted through images of secondhandedness, imitation, and inauthenticity. Viewing certain moments of modern Spain's cultural history through representations of cursilería may appear paradoxical and even eccentric. Yet the presumably minor or inferior angle of vision obtained in such an interpretation is, on closer examination, not so minor as one might think. Fear of cursilería remains one of the most consistently held manias of the middle classes in modern Spain. Taken in a larger sense, this feeling of being inadequate to the circumstances, whether social, aesthetic, political or economic, appears to drive the thinking and writing of many nineteenth-century and early twentieth-century Spanish intellectuals. I am thinking of writers like Unamuno, Maeztu, and Ganivet, generally categorized as members of the Generation of 1898 (see also chapter 6). Feeling marginal and marginalized paradoxically lies at the center of Spain's modern culture, from mid-nineteenth century on.

Ironic negation seems especially appropriate as a way of approaching something so slippery and moveable as the notion of lo cursi, already conceived by 1900 as a kind of "negation" (Llanas Aguilaniedo). Gómez de la Serna's own iconoclastic lateralizing focus is also, I would suggest, an example of such negation, subverting conventional ideas about the relative importance of lo cursi in modern Spanish life and letters. The first thing he does is to upset the usual academic methodology of defining one's intellectual horizon. One expects an essay on lo cursi to define the subject and delimit the contours of the field. But the opening sentence reads, "Just as the baroque has its final explanation in lo cursi, lo cursi has its first explanation and antecedent in the baroque" (7).[8] This is clearly a circular argument with a vengeance. The writer refuses to define his subject since for him the baroque does not make for a measurable field, its shape or morphology appealing only to "the errant street dwellers, without a home anchor, without any academic credentials whatsoever" (7).[9] Right away, Gómez de la Serna sets *his* margins on the margins of his culture: the streets as a nondomestic, nonacademic space or discourse.

This marginal discourse, however, will focus on a peripheral topic, lo cursi, by placing it in the center of Spanish culture: the home. Gómez de la Serna starts with the baroque to show how profuse ornamentation, common to both the baroque and lo cursi, signals in architecture the beginnings of more intimate spaces, the sense of a structure as "furniture." The development of privacy and domestic intimacy—the sense of a house as reflecting the soul of its owner—emerges as an invention of the bourgeoisie. Comfort is not simply a physical construct, it is also a cultural one, and it required centuries to develop, facilitated by mass production and industrialization (Rybczyinski 220, 230). Before that could happen, a certain way of looking at exterior space and living in that space had to coexist with a richness or adornment of the interior spirit. John Lukacs put it this way: "The interior furniture of houses appeared together with the interior furniture of minds" (623). This kind of interiority, or deepening human consciousness, constitutes a part of "our bourgeois heritage" (Lukács 630). Gómez de la Serna makes the same connection in a more poetic vein when he says that baroque architecture "folds inward toward the inner consciousness of a body living inside it as if the attempt to be its own sinuous shell were the reverse side of the conch's mask as a whole" (10).[10]

This sense of home as a shell winding, sinuous, and spiraling inwardly runs through Gómez de la Serna's essay about interiorities. It is only a matter of moving from one serpentine, flowing image to another for him to reach the fin de siglo and "vermicelli art alive on the street" (14).[11] Composing in fragments and fragments of images, he gives us a series of cultural set pieces that visualize but do not define the period, a period he divides into "cursi" and "modern style." It soon becomes clear, however, that for him the initial distinction made between the two styles cannot be maintained; and that what is cursi and what is modern style tend to merge into one large and endless picture of the fin de siglo.

Thus he writes, "The head goes dizzy in thinking about things in the Nouveau Style, or in the Atelier d'Artiste or demi-mondaine style, in Lalique pendants, Maxim's or the Aeolian Room of Paris" (14–15).[12] Then in the very next paragraph he says, "What sex appeal all these things and those electric bulbs had! A veil of gallantry fell over objects, such devotion to screens and shades" (15).[13] This miniature tourist guide to Paris has a mixed effect: aesthetic values are nestled inside the buying values of consumption. Art and voyeurism jostle one another so intimately that it is difficult to know whether Gómez de la Serna is talking purely about modern style or whether modern style really represents a heightened form of cursilería. I suspect that the writer doesn't care. The instability of his references—the fact that art can turn into the sex appeal of an electric light bulb—is precisely what charms him.

For Gómez de la Serna both fin de siglo art and lo cursi flow out of the same source: the feminine. "The women seemed like screens," he writes, "and the screens like women. Because the cult of woman presided over everything" (15).[14] Later he observes, "In the Modern Style the triumph of woman and her long hair reached an apotheosis. Everything in her that was curvy and undulating, soft and sinuous, became the wave lengths of the new forms" (23).[15] Gómez de la Serna is not the first, of course, to see feminine forms recreated in the flowing shapes of art nouveau. But then he connects these forms with the domestic graces emerging out of the private space of women and home. Modern style, he says, is lo cursi elevated to art (23). Modern artists have simply modified what was "appliqué, a domestic invention of young ladies" (23).[16]

By seeing the fin de siglo aesthetic movement as a kind of domestic art, Gómez de la Serna merges the margins into the center. At this point, as he enters more deeply into cursi territory, home and the feminine arts of domesticity begin to occupy more and more space in his essay. Lo cursi is, above all, domestic: "it's something private, simply a kind of homey and personal charm" (21).[17] It is a particular way of life, he continues, "another way to adorn the domestic sanctuary of the home, family harmony" (21).[18] Gómez de la Serna is talking about hominess, but a special kind of hominess in which the focus lies on the peculiar quality of objects adorning the home. He gives the example of "a lamp that wants to be a flower, something other than a lamp, the unbending will to be. Nor had this lamp given up on the desire to be a jewel, nor had it stopped thinking about the feminine fashions of its time or about the design of adornments on dresses and hats."[19] He concludes this fragment by saying, "This lamp wanted to think and breathe adorned conversations, frilled thoughts, passions dressed in lyrical fervor" (22).[20]

Lo cursi, then, is a form of domestic adornment, some of it valid and some of it invalid.[21] Redundancy—an excess of sentiment or design or materials—vexes Gómez de la Serna. In his spectacular conference shows, he would pull the offending object out of a suitcase and smash it to bits, converting the antiaesthetic into a sideshow of vanguard parody. "I took revenge in the destruction of an absurd canephora or a Japanese maiden made into a lamp or a plaster ragamuffin badly painted," he wrote gleefully (31).[22]

As image after image of cultural artifacts drawn from the 1900 period takes shape in Gómez de la Serna's essay, it becomes clear that no definition of lo cursi will ever emerge, and that even the division between lo cursi bueno and lo cursi malo is a relatively unstable one, based as it is on the vagaries of taste. It becomes apparent, too, that Gómez de la Serna gets enormous verbal pleasure out of describing even the most banal and ridiculous of cursi objects. The undefinable and untranslatable nature of cursilería, its mixed, incongruous qualities, stimulate the writer's high-intensity linguistic inventiveness, as he gives free rein to neologisms and strange compounds, which I can only approximate in English, like "musmé lampadarizada" (Japanese maiden made into a lamp), "cursicional" (cursitional), "folicularon" (folliculed), "consolas funambúlicas" (funereally balanced consoles), "bomboneras de presagios" (candy-box portents), and "chineros de corazonadas" (secreting china cupboards). Gómez de la Serna's *greguería* style at least partly derives from the objects and settings of his fin de siglo childhood. His prose constitutes a series of images, or adornments, which emulate verbally the cursi mode itself. Thus he writes that lo cursi "prepares honeycombed caresses for the flutterings of time as it nests, desiring little niches, rufflings, and tiny traceries" (38).[23] Then the next paragraph: "secreting china cupboards, candy-box portents, jars marbling with dead eyes, mirrors framed in dancing dresses, funereally balanced consoles" (38).[24]

In keeping with the supremacy of metaphor in the vanguard period (Generation of 1927, Ortega y Gasset, Gómez de la Serna himself), the essay metaphorizes lo cursi. But it has a metonymic base to the extent that things stand for domesticity, in a stream of contiguous relationships and associations.[25] Gómez de la Serna's essay is a collection of remembered objects, in which he safeguards them against the ravages of time. "People in the era of cursilería pantheonized their things, they shielded them from the pneumonia of time and for that reason they invented bell glasses in which the cascade of time solidified as it fell from conch to conch" (38).[26]

In this exquisite passage, the essayist actually addresses the subject of death, and how to ward it off. Memory is an attempt to recover something dead, pantheonized, and solidified.[27] The phrase "se solidificó" recalls an earlier one taken from Dalí, where he refers to modern style as the "realización de los deseos solidificados" (the realization of solidified desires) (16). This material firmness of fin de siglo things provokes a play of opposites—between the solid and the liquid and elsewhere between the crystalline geometric and the smoky curve (24)—characteristic vanguard imagery that Pérez Firmat has labeled a "pneumatic aesthetics" (see esp. his ch. 2). Images of cursilería tend to break down into softer, more sinuous parts, held together only by Gómez de la Serna's imaginative memory. Lo cursi turns into a series of shapes, amorphous and porous.

Most significantly, lo cursi begins to mold itself to the human body and to the biological: "we are smoke, deliquescent, soft, slow, languishing, dying away, so then we lean toward the curve of buttocks and hips, toward the sinuous" (24).[28] Later, he talks of body organs as shapes of cursilería: "Seen in isolation, aren't the trachea and the lungs one of those cursi objects?" (35).[29] Emphasizing the decorative qualities of turn-of-the-century cursilería (references to "filigree" and "frippery"), he says, "What is styled without recourse to filigree and frippery doesn't have the veininess pulsing in our insides. Everything ought to have handfuls of viscera, curving, gnarled roots, tendencies toward hydrography and the complexity of the nervous system" (36).[30]

The domestic and the biological come together: "The intimacy of affection, the body's own intimacy within, have something of what is clustered around lo cursi" (37).[31] Both "the intimacy of affection" and "the body's own intimacy" are images of interiority. What holds them together in the text is the notion of home as a domestic space of refuge and comfort. "*Lo cursi* is created," he writes, "out of the desire to bundle up life warmly and sanctify its swaggering about" (38).[32] What Gómez de la Serna finds most salvageable in the nineteenth century is precisely this cursi element as a "vital ingredient" (32). He admits openly that his essay poses the possibility of return, return to one's origins, to one's childhood, to what is lost: "Rest is only possible within lo cursi, and we all feel the desire for that return, which is a return toward the past and toward the future, because what is most gratifying about the future is its new forms of cursilería" (37).[33]

The protective warmth of lo cursi, that "spontaneous, ingenuous adorning wanting to cuddle us against emptiness" (35), is a room—"that desired cursi chamber" (34)—possessing the intimacy of a family museum filled with tiny objects (35).[34] With its folds and spirals, roots and veins, such a space of enclosure is above all maternal, uterine. The very form of Gómez de la Serna's text lends itself to this conchlike, inward-bound structure repeated over and over in his imagery. He says of the essay form: "It is difficult to make distinctions using a spontaneous exclamation, but that's what the *essay* form serves, with its crystalline, multiple tube lines for different cultures" (32).[35] As a genre, the essay, with its personal touch and informality, with its built-in tendency to digress, seems most appropriate when speaking of the amorphous and inchoate forms of lo cursi. The generic tentativeness of the essay provides a perfect medium for gestating, as the image of "crystalline, multiple tube lines for different cultures" suggests. Gómez de la Serna's essay appears like a uterine construct, or a conduit leading to the matrix of things, to the mother-space. From the very first sentence, the writer's argument has proven circular, revolving and spiraling deeper and deeper into the imagery of interiorities. The biological and the cultural coalesce in a powerful image against time and death. This fin de siglo maternal space has its referent, of course, in Gómez de la Serna's own childhood years (he was born in 1888). His relationship with writer Carmen de Burgos (Colombine) also possessed a strong maternal character (Cardona 25). These biographical references aside, the text works on its own as a regressive construct of memory.

The closing sentence reinforces the essay's circularity: "But let's end this essay on lo cursi here, which could keep on referring to so many reasons and things that it would be interminable" (54) (see fig. 14).[36] The writer simply stops his essay at an arbitrary point because he knows the

RAMÓN GÓMEZ DE LA SERNA

(Dibujo de Bores.)

14. The last page of Ramón
Gómez de la Serna's essay, "Lo
cursi" (originally published in
Cruz y raya, July 1934).

number of cursi objects constituting his textual universe is limitless.
What is this essay after all? It is a collection of objects, whose inner
meanings are brought out through the imaginative use of figurative
language. One can read "Lo cursi" in conjunction with another Gómez
de la Serna essay published in the same period, "Las cosas y 'el ello'"
[Things and whatness] where he insists that "things are our salvation."
He continues, "things are like ourselves. . . . What, we're not a thing?
But we are, we are a soft thing, with a circulation to kill us and a digestion
to make us ill" (203).[37] All of this is also present in "Lo cursi." Both
essays point to what he later called "a lateral reality" ("Prólogo a las
novelas de la nebulosa" 7).

Things in Gómez de la Serna's world are adornments. In that sense,
they function like the adornment attached to the merged world of cursi
objects and fin de siglo art. Adornment in this context is not supplemental or superfluous, but necessary. As Severo Sarduy observes, in the
modern style one finds "the rhetoric of the accessory becoming the
essential, the proliferation of adjectivals as substantives." (14–15). For
the Cuban novelist, such "things added to the body are its signs; false

237

elements, its condition" (30). Disguise and display revealed through such adorning body metaphors in Sarduy's text are analogous to the functioning of the collection image in "Lo cursi." In showing off his collection of fin de siglo cursilería, Gómez de la Serna also displays his self through the verbal act of possession.

Both the space of home described in his essay and the space of his essay have much in common with the idea of the example found in the collection. As Stewart remarks, "in contrast to the souvenir, the collection offers example rather than sample, metaphor rather than metonymy" (*On Longing* 151). The collection is made up of a theoretically unending number of examples, taken out of context and time, as Gómez de la Serna's arbitrary conclusion to his essay implies. Unending, because one can never acquire enough objects to fill the private museum that functions as the fin de siglo bourgeois home in his text. By implication, this is a world of consumption and not one of production.

As I have noted before, "Lo cursi" also functions as a kind of souvenir, an inner space of memory intimately attached to the body (see Stewart, *On Longing* 156–57): here the maternal body functions as interiority, as home. The souvenir is a narrative of origins in which the possessor of those memories and things seeks to recuperate what is lost through the imaginary relocation of that loss in words or images. Gómez de la Serna's insistence on the importance of things in "Lo cursi" also opens up a way of providing continuity with tradition—the tradition of the real and of realism, its love of detail—while critiquing and renovating it at the same time.

Gómez de la Serna's infrarealism, to use Ortega y Gasset's term (*Deshumanización del arte* 48–49), focuses on the marginal and in the process makes it central to his writing project. Viewed historically, his essay also allows one to look at the phenomenon of modernist cursilería in canonical texts like Valle-Inclán's *Sonatas*. By treating lo cursi and fin de siglo aesthetics together, Gómez de la Serna suggests a hybrid, "impure" mode through which to approach this period of instability and transition. One critic goes so far as to propose a cursi style, which is precisely "that moment of transition from the romantic to modernity." The cursi style, he observes, is marked by accumulation and profuse adornment, hybridism and amalgamation (Roland 48, 50). One can only speculate where to draw the lines of classification in such a potentially expanding grab bag of a category.

Discussions of lo cursi emphasize the significance of things and the relationship between things and persons as key elements to understanding the nature of the phenomenon. By the turn of the century, mass production and industrialization were making considerable gains in Spain, as they had elsewhere. One reaction to growing mechanization was the revival of handcrafts, in which "there was a desire to singularize the object, to distinguish it from mass production, a desire to impress upon the object the owner's and the maker's personalities" (Litvak, *Dream of Arcadia* 27).

Fin de siglo writing, too, evidences an analogous desire to singularize the image. In Valle-Inclán, the image often takes on the near material qualities of a fetish. This veneration for the image, as handcrafted in its own way as the most refined objects of material culture, fittingly, is set within a preindustrial, traditional society in the *Sonatas*. Very little of Gómez de la Serna's middle-class, cursi world, it would seem, seeps into this unreal, yet strangely decaying universe. But consider more closely how Valle-Inclán favors the fin de siglo device of converting his female figures into objets d'art. In *Sonata de otoño* (1902), for example, "Concha's neck flowered from her shoulders like an ailing lily, her breasts were two white roses scenting an altar, and her arms, their slenderness delicate and fragile, were like the handles of an amphora surrounding her head" (26).[38] In another passage, Bradomín says that he dressed her "with the same loving, religious care that devout ladies use in dressing the images for which they are maids of honor" (17).[39]

In the first example, Valle-Inclán characteristically focuses on parts of the female body in a fetishizing gesture of possession. Elsewhere, he dwells on Concha's feet and her hair. Here, Concha's altar / amphora image at first suggests that singularized object I mentioned, dear to the tradition of the handcraftsman. But the breaking into parts or fragments of the female body has the effect of reducing Concha's dimensions. In emphasizing, fetishistically, parts of her anatomy, Valle-Inclán miniaturizes her presence through metonymical segmenting. Rather than an example of the aristocratic rare arts tradition, Concha is really more like a bibelot.

The bibelot, as Rémy Saisselin remarks, is characteristic of the bourgeois style of nineteenth-century interior decoration (63), in which small objects accumulate, filling up space. The bibelot had nothing to do with the aristocratic rare arts tradition, but it was nevertheless considered a luxury. Above all, it was thought of as feminine luxury. Ramón Gómez de la Serna, for example, in *La viuda blanca y negra* (1917/1918) describes a woman's legs as "the miniature, the bibelot sketch of a naked woman" (91–92).[40] The bibelot lacked grandeur, depth; it could be acquired like any other commodity. The bibelot's relative inferiority as a sign of distinction and of art was even linked to modernismo. Criticizing the current "artistic disorientation," a doctor from Cádiz—Ramón Ventín—says in 1900, "Prettiness rules over beauty; today, the *bibelot* lords over sculpture, and the Venus of Milo backs off in the face of a modern dancing figurine" (qtd. in "El modernismo" 108).[41]

The second example from *Sonata de otoño* diminishes Concha's status even more. In being compared to the holy images dressed by devout ladies, Concha may at first seem spiritualized in this sentence. But these sacred figures have traditionally been fashioned in the most deplorable *cursi* taste. Moreover, converting Bradomín into a figurative (and at times literal) lady's maid—"Let me be your maid!" (16)—firmly sets much of this *Sonata* in the intimate, feminine space of the bourgeois boudoir. Descriptive details like the styling of Concha's black silk stockings and garters—"stockings of black silk, with lightly embroidered mauve-colored arrows" (17)—link literary modernismo with fashion and the feminine figure.

Erotic scenes like this one were meant to tease the reader (see Litvak, *Erotismo*). They are not at all unusual in the iconography and writings of fin de siglo publications like *La vida galante, Instantáneas, Láminas sueltas, París alegre,* and *Sicalíptico* (this last recalling the theatrical trend of erotic *zarzuelas,* revues, and other spectacles); in series such as "Colección sicalíptica" and "Las mujeres en la intimidad"; and in novel collections such as "Regente" and "Galante" (Ezama Gil; Vega). The audience for these publications was in large part comfortably middle-class. Language used to seduce also usually sold well, according to most accounts (Ezama Gil 74). This context of early erotica places Valle-Inclán's *Sonatas* within a certain kind of readership and social class. "Epater le bourgeois" did not emerge out of the aristocracy (and certainly not the working classes): it is a middle-class phenomenon. Aristocratic disinterest in middle-class morality precluded such attitudes.

The same holds true of Bradomín's dandy pose. It, too, is meant to shock and, likewise, is an effect of the middle-class writer reflecting inner tensions arising out of problematical identities (see Seigel 58). By stressing these middle-class qualities in Valle-Inclán's early work, I am not trying to lessen the evident effect of the aristocratic settings imagined in the *Sonatas*. Rather, these works mirror an "impure" world, in which the aristocratic and the bourgeois blend and sometimes clash. The effect is unsettling, creating dyssynchronicity. Presumably aristocratic values come up against an implied commercialized world of consumption and display, in which the ideology of ownership and possession of artifacts produce scenes of refined voyeurism and fetishism which are strangely coated with a decaying romanticism.

Art did not define or give distinction to the ancien régime aristocrat; rather, the aristocrat bestowed distinction on the object (Saisselin xv). The reverse holds true in the bourgeois world. Yet I would suggest that the purely aristocratic vision is no longer possible in the world of the *Sonatas*. The dreamlike, archetypal, and seemingly atemporal settings of these works are shot through with contradictions of a historical, ideological nature. Thus, for example, the middle-class notion of home is inserted into an anachronistic aristocratic background. Homey details like this one abound: "The two girls applied themselves to unraveling the sheet, darting furtive glances to see who was making more progress in the task. Concha and Isabel were whispering together. A clock marked the hour of ten, and in their childish laps, within the luminous circle of the lamp, the lint was slowly forming a snow-white ball" (60).[42] Compare this with one of Gómez de la Serna's examples of cursilería: "The little girl made of porcelain who threads a needle beneath the shade of the lamp" ("Lo cursi" 16).[43]

Scenes of domestic intimacy and interiority stress the significance of family in the *Sonatas*. Yet the obvious patriarchal structure rests on a wobbly base. The wonderfully silly and fabulous explanation of the Bradomín family line, in particular the title Señorío de Padín, in *Sonata de otoño* ironizes through the parodic use of myth the entire patriarchal enterprise. More significantly, Bradomín himself throughout the *Sonatas* threatens the legitimacy of aristocratic patriarchy by reducing much of his behavior to a pose. His deliberate inauthenticity is largely founded on earlier literary and cultural stereotypes, thus further complicating the temporal discontinuities of the *Sonatas*. Moreover, by defining himself through a web of intertexts and creating his identity out of earlier models, Bradomín points once more to insecure middle-class origins. In this way, Valle-Inclán transforms Bradomín into a composite literary artifact, just as the marqués performs a similar operation with Concha in *Sonata de otoño* or with María Rosario in *Sonata de primavera*.

What partly salvages patriarchy is the framework of memory. As *memorias*, the *Sonatas* privilege the first-person point of view of the Marqués de Bradomín. This remembering also tinges Bradomín's narrative with regret and nostalgia, giving it yet another temporal overlay and indirectly lending the narrative authenticity. The memoir form also proves ideal for a narrative of interiority. Repeated imagery of distances and depths—"in the mirrors' depths" (*Sonata de otoño*)—furthers the notion of pastness and of looking inward, but much of this imagery shatters against the smooth facade of specularity reflected in the writing and in the characterization of Bradomín. The language of longing in the *Sonatas* never manages to get past Bradomín himself.

Produced in a transitional, conflictive period of social and economic change, the *Sonatas* retain the outer walls of a traditional society but reveal the center, the inside of that structure, as hollow, like its most representative member, the Marqués de Bradomín. His constant posing converts him into pure surface, to be filled with other literary surfaces, or intertexts. His wandering exposes desire without an object, an essentially homeless state of being. His quest for the feminine is in truth conquest, which ultimately means marginalization of the feminine Other. Marginalization occurs when Bradomín reduces the feminine, turning her into a fragment of the whole.

And yet without the feminine Other, Bradomín simply would not exist. His existence, like that of the four *Sonatas*, is predicated on the necessary supplementarity of the feminine. This means the feminine, while essential to Bradomín, finds its primary use in *his* adornment. He never really experiences the feminine; he merely appropriates it. Authenticity of experience is turned into literature, into art, into fashion. It is this erasure of the feminine through the literary artifact itself, through the language of anachronistic styles and attitudes, that produces modernist cursilería, converting the feminine as well into a dated piece of art and experience into the plaything of time. The inability to grasp the nature of his desire produces a protagonist who has to reinvent himself as somebody else's desire (through earlier stereotypes and literary models). In marginalizing the feminine, he never finds himself and even loses the notion of home.

When viewed as a metaphorical home wrecker, Bradomín assumes a figurative function in the *Sonatas,* in which we see the inner tensions generated out of antithetical discourses represented, out of the oppositions between the bourgeois and the aristocratic, between the feminine and the masculine. Home and homelessness tangle endlessly with each other in these works. By refracting the *Sonatas* through Gómez de la Serna's essay on lo cursi and his notion of home as feminized, dated space, one sees how the feminine as adornment may seem cursi, trivialized through language, in Valle-Inclán. Paradoxically, however, the feminine is central to this modernist discourse of home and interiority, since it enables writing in the texts of both authors.

The use of Gómez de la Serna's cursi figure as ironic negation makes clear the centrality of the supplemental, the necessity of the marginal, to a dominant tradition or text. Ironically, it also reveals that through time itself, the marginal can be made more marginalized as a trope of anachronism. The term *modernist cursilería* does not imply an aesthetic judgment; it constitutes a statement of supreme ambivalence about texts that are modern yet dated, about texts that are, finally, datedly modern.

CHAPTER EIGHT

The Culture of Nostalgia, or the Language of Flowers

THE FIGURING OF home as feminized, dated space is intimately and irresistibly linked to the phenomenon of nostalgia. In the 1920s and 1930s of pre–civil war Spain, a period habitually associated with the fast-forward of vanguard experimentation and radical sociopolitical change, the nostalgic may seem out of place.[1] In a more profound sense, nostalgia is, metaphorically and affectively, truly something out of place, operating as a narrative of loss and memory and centered on a phantom topography of desire. Yet it is not surprising that the nostalgic should appear in highly experimental, self-conscious writers of the period like Ramón Gómez de la Serna and Federico García Lorca. Unstable, rapidly changing times stimulate different kinds of responses, particularly within a context of uneven development and belated modernity. The subject or content of the nostalgic may appear wrapped in a timeless, idealized mist, but its cultural manifestation is a function of historical change and movement.

Nostalgia as a text of marginality, ironically, takes center stage in Ramón Gómez de la Serna's essay, "Lo cursi." Gómez de la Serna locates the nostalgic in the maternal space of bourgeois domesticity, recreating it through richly profuse detail that describes things of symbolic-affective value to him. Cursilería, understood as a trope for cultural inadequacy and converted into a form of self-conscious nostalgia, becomes a local, miniaturized narrative of home reconstructed and duplicated metonymically in forms of feminine and feminized adornments that are both rhetorical and substantive. The heart of Federico García Lorca's text, *Doña Rosita*, on which I will focus in this chapter, is also maternal, at once physically and psychically.

Gómez de la Serna's essay appeared in 1934. In December of 1935, Lorca's play, *Doña Rosita la soltera, o El lenguaje de las flores* [Doña Rosita the spinster, or the language of flowers], opened in Barcelona (see

fig. 15). With its delicate Chekhovian resonances, this beautifully constructed drama of frustrated aspirations and spinsterhood evokes the
passage of time in a young woman's middle-class, Granadine life, focusing on three different chronological moments—1885, 1900, and 1910—in
three acts. The aging process, from young woman to middle-aged spinster, is reflected metaphorically through the image of the *rosa mutabile*,
which is "red in the morning [and] in the evening turns white. At night
the petals fall" (102).[2] The story is simple: a young woman waits years
and years for her intended to make good his promise of marriage while
he emigrates to the New World to make his fortune; she is jilted, and in
the end, the family is ruined and must pack up and leave their home.
Until that point, neither the audience nor the characters ever leave the
house. This enclosure, symbolic of the condition of women in much of
Lorca's drama, also underlines what Christopher Soufas calls "a deeper
unwillingness [in Doña Rosita] to engage the world" (124; see also
Fernández Cifuentes, "*Doña Rosita*" 326–27).

Sentimentalized nostalgia rarely appears in Lorca's text in unadulter-
ated form.[3] Indeed, the play is not about nostalgia or sentimentality.
Lorca himself made clear in interviews and elsewhere the matrix of *Doña
Rosita:* it dealt with cursilería. "It's a family drama," he said, "what I call
the great poetic drama of cursilería" (*Alocuciones argentinas* 14).[4] On
another occasion the writer insisted: "It could best be called the drama of
Spanish cursilería, of Spanish prudery, of the desire to live a full life that
women are forced to repress in the deepest, most passionate part of
themselves" (Massa 668).[5] *Matrix* has two uses here: first, as an unstated
keyword, or "the structure of the given," in Riffaterre's terminology
(12–13); and second, as the maternal center or heart of the matter in
Lorca's play.

Let me make clear from the start what I am not saying: *Doña Rosita la
soltera* is not a cursi text, that is, artistically or otherwise lacking the
fullness of aesthetic and affective experience. How does Lorca avoid
being cursi—overly sentimental, tacky, aesthetically shallow or facile—
while writing a play full of cursi characters and objects and at the same
time infused with a nostalgic feeling for a flawed earlier period?[6] As
realist novelists, Galdós and Clarín created ironic narrating voices, distancing themselves in this way from their own critique of the era's
cultural inadequacies. In Lorca's text, too, cursi objects and secondary

15. Grau Sala's 1935 poster for the Barcelona production of Lorca's play, *Doña Rosita la soltera, o El lenguaje de las flores,* with Margarita Xirgu playing the title role. Courtesy of Fundación Federico García Lorca.

character types bear the weight of the playwright's satire. Significantly, members of the solid middle and upper middle classes are by now perceived as having acquired some of the less desirable traits earlier attributed, in the 1840s and later during the Restoration period, to the socially more marginal lower middle classes. Like Gómez de la Serna, Lorca also embraces cursilería by stylizing it and turning the phenomenon into a series of metaphors, beginning with the very title of the play. Significantly, his main character, Doña Rosita, is never intrinsically cursi or presented as such. Only the three *solteronas,* or old maids, bear the explicit label of "cursilonas" in the second act; by the last act, in a brief reappearance, solterona number three is dressed in mourning, and the label has been dropped.

By then, too, the elegiacal prevails. A deep sense of loss, of the "unlived life," to use Edward Engelberg's phrase, seeps into the play. If Lorca's character Doña Rosita was not cursi before, the very passage of time has converted her into a living trope of radical insufficiency and a figure of anachronism. The explicit examples of lo cursi found in the satire of provincial, middle-class Granadine life have little to do with the intense emotional charge with which Lorca has infused *Doña Rosita*. This charge lies elsewhere and issues out of a culture of nostalgia, turning cultural inadequacy—*cursilería*—into something else, an unstated aura of loss and desire.

In 1935 Lorca's play already constituted a period piece—a literary-cultural artifact—and at the same time a living text (see Fernández Cifuentes 322–25; and Martínez Cuitiño 19). Like Chekhov's *Uncle Vanya* and *The Cherry Orchard, Doña Rosita* is an extraordinarily layered text; the layers of emotion and the layers of social-historical culture form a complex, delicate weave of mutual containment in which what is *not* said, what does *not* happen in the play, build powerfully through the protracted passage of time (see A. Anderson, "Las relaciones familiares" 215). The play still speaks to us, perhaps then as now, precisely for the poignancy with which it presents the plight of human beings as unwanted, alone and aging, as, in a word, artifacts.

Lorca took great pains (and delight) in recreating the nineteenth- and early twentieth-century settings, costumes and objects for this work, which he labeled a "poem of 1900 Granada, divided into various gardens, with scenes of song and dance" (see J. Walsh 287; and Morris 123–27).[7] *Doña Rosita*, above all, flaunts the local, reveling in the provincial, the outdated, and the comic grotesque. Yet the play was a big hit well beyond the confines of Lorca's hometown Granada (see Fernández Cifuentes 319–22).

We must situate the impact and resonance of Lorca's play in the context of a much larger issue than dramatic conventions: namely, the problematic relationship between modernity and historical-cultural identity as an individual and collective matter of place and placement. In dwelling on the aging and unmarried female figure of Doña Rosita, Lorca does two things: he puts the marginal—the feminine as doubly provincial (obsolete *and* Granadine)—squarely at the center of his play; and, in the process, he subtly conflates gender identity with cultural identity (local and national). Tellingly, Lorca's brother Francisco drew the same parallel: "Doña Rosita becomes a symbol of Granada, a city Federico identified with collective frustration. It is a city lyrically forgotten, in the backwaters of time," and he added that "the poet was quite sensitive to changes in historical reality" (226–27; also Loughran 291).[8]

If we read *Doña Rosita la soltera* alongside and through the city-text of Granada, other Lorca texts, and the social-cultural frame of the period in general (from the 1880s to the 1930s), it becomes clear that *Doña Rosita* is both allegorical and historical—private (literary) and public (historical)—developing out of an implied political-cultural debate over core/periphery that critics are only beginning to address in Hispanic cultural studies.[9] I don't believe one can fully appreciate a late-modernist play like *Doña Rosita* without bearing in mind the historical-cultural context of the period. Conversely, so as not to create an impoverished understanding of the cultural life of a provincial capital like Granada, or the historical and political reverberations of center/margins in the midst of significant changes (and continuities), it is important to read at the same time such profoundly affecting literary texts like *Doña Rosita*, which register personal and collective experience through the cognitive use of feeling.

The intricate relationship between the writings of a specific author like Lorca with a public persona and a social body like Granada (or Andalusia for that matter) does not, however, lead me to conclude their necessary homology. In other words, I do not suggest that one can map Lorca's complex and ultimately elusive individual psyche onto Granadine culture. The Granadine character of Lorca's writings represents a strand of the culture in question, not the entire culture. To the extent that Lorca echoes, reflects, or refracts other *granadinos*, Granadine history, or attitudes, to that extent is he representative of a larger cultural whole. But he evidently also remains uniquely nonrepresentative. The question is, what kind of significance does Lorca's interpretation of Granadine (and Andalusian) culture acquire when set against a larger context of historical change and modernization? What follows is an attempt to explore, if not ultimately to answer, the implications of that question.

As I hope to show, Lorca's play exploits, although with considerable ambivalence, the identification of the feminine with the local. Because local culture, in this instance turn-of-the-century Granadine society, is viewed largely through the idealizing lens of nostalgia, it appears that Lorca simply carries out, in effect, a form of cultural mourning similar to Llanas Aguilaniedo and Lara y Pedrajas. In Lorca, this mourning, I

248

would suggest, is filled with unresolved, conflictive feeling. In Freudian terms, the work of mourning in *Doña Rosita* remains incomplete, perhaps in part because Lorca can neither relinquish nor fully embody an object of loss whose partial articulation is disseminated in the details, in the attention to the local as cursi objects (and persons), as objects of inadequacy and insufficiency.

If on one level Lorca criticizes the provincial backwardness and immobility of Granadine culture, he is also drawn to that same space when recreated as poetic interiority and maternal refuge. Doña Rosita's simultaneous dread and desire to remain in the period of her youth, not to experience the passage of time, can be read as an allegory of Granada's (and Spain's?) reluctance to enter into modernity and resistance toward the modernizing impulses of the early twentieth century.

But if this is so, the other side of Lorca's critique of a timeless, static, nonmodern Granada reveals a desire precisely for that being critiqued: the domestic, the feminine, the interior, and, above all, the diminutive, which in Lorca's eyes represents the most exquisite and authentic expression of Granadine culture (see Lorca, "Granada"; and Seco de Lucena Vázquez de Gardner). It is also the diminutive that is so closely linked in this play to obsolescence, anachronism, and sentimentality, to provincial cursilería, as in the example of the saint's day gift to Rosita, a pendant, described as "a mother-of-pearl Eiffel Tower over two doves bearing in their beaks the wheel of industry" (116).[10] The play brims with these small, dated objects used as stage props and verbal artifacts: Rosita's parasol, the housekeeper's Louis the Fifteenth thermometer case decorated with a fountain, rose arbor, and nightingale, a saint's day card with "a little girl dressed in pink who's also a barometer" (125), and, above all, the names of things—muslin and Marseilles lace, poplinette blouses and buckles with serpents and dragonflies—and, of course, flowers—hellebore, musk, fuchsia, heliotrope, Louis Passy violet, damask, and jasmine.

The playwright's ambivalence toward modernity (and modernization), embodied and experienced in traditional Granadine middle-class culture, suggests that Lorca does not simply enthrone the local. One of his comments from 1936 illustrates my point: "Lost forever were an admirable civilization, a poetry, an astronomy, an architecture, and a delicacy unique in the world, to give way to a poor, dejected city [Granada]; to a land of the cent where the worst bourgeoisie in Spain presently holds sway" (qtd. in Morris 68). As C. B. Morris observes, Lorca's lament about a vanished Hispano-Arabic civilization "is doubly nostalgic: it mourns the loss of a Granada he could only have read or dreamed about, and it does so in terms that echo closely those of Angel Ganivet at the beginning of *Granada la bella:* My Granada is not the one of today: it is the one it could and should be, the one that I do not know will ever be" (83).

The personal sense of suffocation and stifling frustration that Lorca felt living in provincial Granada has been well documented (Gibson, *Lorca's Granada* xi). Nostalgic mourning for a lost cultural past clashes sharply with the poet's own experiences of the city. Lorca may have feared his creative juices would dry up in his provincial backwater hometown, but he also could not do without the stimulus and memory (whether real or imagined) of Granada (McInnis 42). Morris rightly insists that "nostalgia was for Lorca both elegiac and creative" (83).

I would also suggest that his feminization of Granadine culture in *Doña Rosita la soltera* may have been a way of representing and preserving, however tentatively, an ideal, wished-for model of the city he loved *and* detested, that "delicacy unique in the world." Something dies in Lorca's play—illusions, love—but something else persists like a ghost, haunting readers and spectators alike: the image of Doña Rosita herself. And even more faintly: the trace of a Granada at once historical and phantasmatic, the memory of Granada.

Lorca's conflicted views of Granada call for critical reserve in dealing with the problematic question of local culture and its representation in texts. Distinctions between context and culture, between texts and culture, suggest that the critical cloth we construct resembles a patchwork quilt more than a seamless tapestry. Representing the real obviously does not equal the real.[11] As Alan Liu points out, "context throws over the surface of culture an articulated grid, a way of speaking and thinking culture, that allows us to model the scenes of human experience with more felt significance than appears anywhere [else]" (99).

We should resist the temptation to "idealize the local as the real" (Probyn 187). With ethnicity and other kinds of identity studies proliferating, it becomes even more imperative not to fall into the romanticism of authenticity, romanticizing local culture as somehow more genuine and superior to something else. Nothing exists in a pure state, as Elspeth Probyn observes (187). Nor is it possible to find, recreate, or recover the origins of a local culture as though it could retroactively spring up, full-fledged and pristine, untouched by outside influences.

Another variant to this approach sees marginalized local cultures as heroically pitted against the center, forgetting how difficult it is to pinpoint the exact locations of either margins or center. The truth is, all local cultures possess something of the Other, whatever that otherness may be (Bhabha 4). Vincent Pecora takes an example analyzed by Clifford Geertz—Sukarno's rule in Indonesia, the 1965 aborted palace coup, power struggle, and subsequent massacres—in order to critique the anthropologist's view of the event as purely local, or internal to the country, thus ignoring the external, global context of "cold-war, East-West political conflict" in Indonesia (256). Geertz's privileging of local knowledge over other kinds of knowledge—bolstered by distinctions between inside(r) and outside(r)—collapses in the face of vanishing borders, intercultural permeability and interference, and the invention of tradition.[12] As Pecora, writing in 1989, puts it, "What is inside and what is outside in El Salvador? In Nicaragua? in Afghanistan?" (259).

The presence of nostalgia complicates even more an understanding of local culture. Nostalgia nearly always issues out of something that once possessed detail, a specific shape, time, and place—out of localness, in other words—but the effects of nostalgia tend to deterritorialize and dematerialize the original object or event, mythicizing it and enveloping it in an aura. This nostalgic aura or feeling appeals to universal longings for permanence, centeredness, and embodied meaning in our lives. In this context, William Carlos Williams's remark that "the local is the universal" (233) takes on added significance, as does the notion that "there is community embedded in the details of our lives" (P. Walsh 26). But whose community is it when that space and time are later disseminated as nostalgic artifacts to a much broader spectrum of participants? Lorca himself sought the universal within the local ("the truth [which is] Andalusian and universal") ("*Romancero gitano*" 340). Nostalgia as an aesthetic strategy allowed him to reach beyond the parochial confines of Granada, appealing to a larger audience and to a greater, collectively shared imagination. By the same token, the nostalgic mode put him on a less secure local footing, threatening to turn historical memory into the memory of memory. In the writing and enacting of *Doña Rosita* we see the early effects of that accelerated, increasingly fragmented and ruptured notion of history that characterizes much of twentieth-century thought and life and that prompts cultural historian Pierre Nora to ask: "What is being remembered? In a sense, it is memory itself" (16).

Historically, however, the details of Granadine culture in *Doña Rosita*, of which the Lorquian emphasis on the diminutive and cursilería is a prime example, form part of a larger (yet concrete) community than Granada itself. That broader context takes in both Spain and the views of non-Spaniards on Spanish, Andalusian, and Granadine culture. Lorca did not conceive of his Granada in a social or cultural vacuum. All of Spain was struggling with the contradictions of a belated modernity in the 1920s and 1930s (the period of *Doña Rosita*'s genesis and composition).[13] The saturated atmosphere of provincial behavior, expectations, and things in *Doña Rosita* takes on special significance within two contexts, with which it appears at odds. One is internal, the deliberate out-of-synch pacing in the play itself, the sense that time in the provinces is small and static but also caught up in larger, more vertiginous temporal changes. We detect some of this in the impatience and rapid movements of Doña Rosita's first appearance in act 1. She rushes in, searching frantically for her hat, grabs it, and rushes out. "She wants everything at top speed," complains the housekeeper, "It's today and she already wants it to be the day after tomorrow. She flies off and . . . she's slipped through our fingers" (101).[14] But of course Doña Rosita's "day after tomorrow" will stretch out interminably, to day after day of waiting. The day after tomorrow never comes.

The other context is external. The ironic, terribly sad inner tension that Doña Rosita's unstated but understood dilemma creates in the play—her refusal to admit openly that she has been jilted—would, I think, have been richly appreciated in December 1935 by the sophisticated audience of Barcelona theatergoers. After nearly two years of a right-wing government, stalled or repealed socioeconomic reforms, the bloody repression of an Asturian working-class revolt in October 1934, and increasing political militancy and violence, the Second Republic was in very bad shape. There was a sense of stagnation, of running in place, even while changes occurred that seemed to go nowhere, or to lack meaningful design in relation to the aspirations and desires of ordinary people. The nostalgic aura of a bygone era enveloping Lorca's play, along with his implicit critique of inaction and evasiveness, appear as evocative of a corresponding resonance with the Second Republic's social and political crisis. It is worth remembering, too, that Lorca started thinking seriously about this play of social frustration and repressed emotions during the dictatorship of Primo de Rivera.

The play can also be seen as an oblique response to the conventional image of Spain and Andalusia in particular—often conflated into one Andalusianized Spain since the romantic period—as "ornamental" cultures, that is, as exoticized, marginal societies of little consequence to the modern world. The key to this ornamental view lies in the coded application of the detail to national or regional characteristics, in reducing Spanish or Andalusian culture to its surface features.

How Lorca turns this argument on its head and uses detail—in the form of the diminutive and lo cursi—to suggest the unspoken depth and originality of Granadine (and, by implication, Spanish) culture is, I think, crucial to understanding the significance of the language of flowers in *Doña Rosita la soltera*. In turn, this language of flowers is linked, by social convention and by authorial design, to the feminine; and both are commonly associated with cursilería, that is, with dated sentimentality and insufficiency, whether aesthetic or experiential. In a remarkable upset of conventional values, Lorca manages to enlarge to an extraordinary degree the significance of cursilería by giving it symbolic weight as the sign of women's sexual and emotional frustration and lack of freedom. Lorca himself made the connection between the historical realities of Spanish women and his character Doña Rosita: "So here is my Doña Rosita. Gentle, childless, and aimless in life, cursi. . . . How long will all the Doña Rositas of Spain continue to be this way?" (Massa, "Estreno" 668).[15]

The nostalgic aura Lorca casts over Doña Rosita, however, at once poeticizes and diminishes her, suggesting a precious, shining object whose light has gone dim. Her dependency on family structure and the promise of marriage—like that of Granada itself, tied to paternalistic policies of centralization—in the end condemns Doña Rosita to immobility, to a living death (see Frigolé 84–85). Her last appearance is ghostly: "She is pale, dressed in white, with a coat to the hem of her dress" (154).[16] Her voice falters, and, nearly collapsing, she utters her last words (which are now in a third-person verse reference to herself as a rose image) before her final exit: "And when the darkness surrounds her, / Her petals begin to fall" (154).[17] Before our very eyes, Lorca has turned her into a spectral presence, as she slips quietly into the aura that preserves the figure of Doña Rosita but also converts her into a phantom trope of nostalgia.

Before delving more deeply into Lorca's play, I would like to examine further nostalgia as a frame within which to consider it. Nostalgia as a modern phenomenon, especially in the late twentieth and early twenty-first century, often seems culturally degraded or at best historically inconsequential, subjected as it is increasingly to prefabricated molds of economic design and substituting for an ever more unsatisfactory present. But the nostalgic does not and has not always functioned in the same way in different historical periods and contexts, as I think the example of Lorca's play demonstrates both as an individual expression of a poet's soul and as a representative manifestation of a local elite.

George Orwell, for example, explained the post–World War I nostalgic appeal of A. E. Housman's *Shropshire Lad* to educated middle-class readers and writers by noting that "the *rentier*-professional class was ceasing once and for all to have any real relationship with the soil" (227). By 1900 England was no longer primarily an agricultural country. Another example, of more recent vintage: the yearning of former East Germans for their preunification status, as expressed through the neologism *Ostalgie* (*Ost* + *Nostalgie*), or nostalgia for the East, which they now see to embody a sense of order and stability. "It's our way of dealing with the past, with a touch of irony as well as nostalgia," said one former Easterner, "life was a lot calmer and in some ways more pleasant. That's why Ostalgie is so popular. Easterners want to assert their own identity by recalling our common experiences" (Drozdiak A29). This in a period when the East appears in a state of arrested development. Significantly, the coining of a new word is needed to express a new feeling, or perhaps better said, a new structure of feeling in the making.

Kathleen Stewart argues that, in the postmodern era, nostalgia is a "cultural practice, not a given content; its forms, meanings, and effects shift with the context" (227). Along the lines of Baudrillard and Jameson, she sees nostalgia taking over when the present is experienced as loss or as an unreality. In this sense, historical circumstances can perhaps be construed as having produced an ahistorical effect.[18]

Nostalgia did not necessarily operate this way in earlier periods. While I agree that nostalgia as a cultural practice varies contextually — and this is true for all periods, not simply the late twentieth century — I would also argue that the nostalgic possesses an intrinsically historical character emanating paradoxically out of its metaphorical properties. Nostalgia metaphorically and emotionally conveys historical change by signaling the passing or absence of something or someone. It registers the past as past through a special form — a kind of second order or level — of remembrance.

Still, how can one even begin to find the roots of a structure of feeling as wispy and amorphous as nostalgia? How does one picture "the desire for desire," as Susan Stewart calls it in her book *On Longing?* One doesn't, of course. Something else takes its place, something that can be visualized as, or at least conceived of as, something that translates well from and into this unrepresentable affective phenomenon: in Lorca's case, the language of flowers as a doubly coded image of desire (see figs. 16 and 17).[19] This double-codedness is present from the start, in the very title of the play. As Riffaterre observes, titles of works in general "function as dual signs. They . . . introduce the [texts] they crown, and at the same time refer to a text outside of it" (99). A dual title like Lorca's underlines the additional presence of a code, or conventional discourse (Riffaterre 105).

The language of flowers alludes, on one level, to a strictly conventionalized floral code of love in vogue since the early nineteenth century; and on another level, to the long tradition of flower imagery as symbols not only of love but of the transitory nature of life (Fernández Cifuentes 326; Martínez Cuitiño 13). The worn-out topos equating women with flowers is part of this code of meanings.[20] First then, the language of flowers is a dated (indeed antiquated) verbal construction of artifice, which is limited and highly typified, as these sample verses from "What the flowers say" illustrate: " 'Only on you do I set my eyes,' / The heliotrope would sigh. / 'And I can never love you,' / Is the basil-

EL LENGUAJE

DE LAS

FLORES

Y

EL DE LAS FRUTAS

CON ALGUNOS EMBLEMAS

DE LAS PIEDRAS Y LOS COLORES

Edicion aumentada con varias poesías alusivas á las flores

EL LENGUAJE DEL PAÑUELO Y EL DEL ABANICO

adornado con diez magníficos cromos

POR

FLORENCIO JAZMIN.

3.ª EDICION.

BARCELONA.

MANUEL SAURÍ, EDITOR.

1882.

16. Cover page of the popular *El lenguaje de las flores*, by the pseudonymous Florencio Jazmín.

flower's cry. / The violet says, 'I'm timid.' / The white rose says, 'I'm cold.' / The jasmine says, 'I'm faithful.' / The carnation boasts, 'I'm bold' " (131).[21]

Nevertheless, the notion of language points to a more universal desire for communication (and, of course, love) that the restrictive floral code simply cannot express. Near the end of the play Rosita says, "What can I tell you? There are things that can't be told because there aren't the words to tell them. And even if there were, who would understand their meaning?" (150).[22] These lines point to a hidden subtext in Lorca's play that the deployment of the language of flowers allegorizes. Indeed, the floral code itself is based on the assumption of enigmatic meanings that requires decoding from within its peculiar grammar.

Freud, in his *Interpretation of Dreams* (1900), partly founds on the language of flowers one of his most acute observations in trying to make sense of the hidden linkages and causal relationships in dreamwork (315).

17. Examples of the coded "language of flowers," taken from Florencio Jazmín's *El lenguaje de las flores.*

For my purposes, two features of Freud's seminal text are of particular interest: first, his belief that one must employ interpretation *"en détail* and not *en 'masse'"* (104); and second, his "idea of *psychical locality"* (536). Freud insists that even with his interpretive mode one can never fully decipher the meanings of dreams. The composite, thickly clustered and tangled detail of these dream-texts precludes definitive solutions to the questions dreams pose. On the other hand, it is clear that Freud delights in doing just that—finding the answers to other people's dreams. With his own dreams, however, he resists such closure, as in the case of the botanical monograph, when he says: "For reasons with which we are not concerned, I shall not pursue the interpretation of this dream any further" (173). This tension between overcoming patient resistance to interpretation and his stubborn refusal to divulge his own secrets of course continues both to captivate and annoy readers of Freud.

By also suggesting that dreams possess a psychical locality, Freud

257

seems to imply the quasi-presence of literalized metaphor in dream language and a way of locating inner thought processes if only we possessed the key to the dream-door. Interpretation *en détail* greases the keyhole, while literalized metaphors provide, or perhaps are, the details waiting to be interpreted.

It is this discourse of hidden desire in the language of flowers that prompts Francie Cate-Arries in a suggestive article to apply Freud's symbolic dream-content as a kind of speech to Lorca's play, asserting that "the basic tension" of *Doña Rosita* is found in "the socially condoned world of acceptable appearances . . . versus the repressed realm of unfulfilled wishes and passions. . . . The first is represented in polite conversation or lively exchanges about mundane, often banal topics; the second— the discourse of desire—is released in the 'language of flowers' " (60).

These well-observed comments ignore, however, the extremely conventionalized meanings of the language of flowers, which constitutes a perfectly trivial, indeed cursi grammar of sentiment. Similarly, Catherine Nickel says that the flower ballad ("Lo que dicen las flores") in act 2 is "part of the folklore popular in Spain in the early 1900's" (523), but the language of flowers is not folklore, as Jack Goody and Beverly Seaton have made clear.[23] It was an invention of the French bourgeoisie, which began with publication of Charlotte de Latour's (pseudonym for Louise Cortambert) *Le langage des fleurs* in 1819 and was commercially disseminated throughout Europe and the Americas. These vocabulary lists of flowers with their corresponding symbolic meanings represent an "expert system," or specialist knowledge, as Jack Goody notes (xii). By using the coded language of flowers either in writing or in bouquet offerings, one could paradoxically suggest something secret and individual contained in a presumably universal system of symbolic meanings (Goody 238).[24] This is a deliberately constructed, written language that requires memorizing (or the consultation of a book), a flagrant example of the "invention of tradition," as Goody observes (254). Thus in a popular Spanish version of the publishing phenomenon, *El lenguaje de las flores,* Florencio Jazmín points out that "what is difficult to retain in one's memory is the symbolic meaning appropriate to each flower" (32) (see figs. 16 and 17).[25]

Nickel's reading of "Lo que dicen las flores" [What the flowers say] as traditional and folkloric constitutes part of her argument that the play works contrastively by alternating "between free creative expression and restricted standardized speech" (527), although she also notes that, like *The Cherry Orchard*, *Doña Rosita* masks an "intense interior reality" beneath daily routines and banalities (530). Both Cate-Arries and Nickel see the underlying tensions and dualities of the text, as expressed in its linguistic and symbolic-affective levels, but do not fully pursue the implications of Lorca's poetic strategy: namely, that the trivialized nature of the language of flowers is inseparable from, and fused with, the deeper, less sayable meanings of the play.[26] In this context—as in Freud's assertion that there is no "either-or" in dreams, no yes or no, but both possibilities (*Interpretation* 316)—Lorca seems to suggest that cursilería is also *not* cursilería, that what appears conventionalized and transparent is also individual and concealed. Herein lies a significant part of the double-codedness of the language of flowers.

Lo cursi—the language of flowers being a prime example—acquires hidden depths in *Doña Rosita* precisely as an expression of Granadine detail, which at the same time functions in some ways like Freudian detail buried deep in a psychical locality. Lorca's wonderful essay on lo diminutivo as especially Granadine (and Andalusian in general) provides a key to understanding this association between smallness and depth, as well as between culture and psyche.[27] "The genuinely Granadine aesthetic," he wrote in his 1926 essay, "Granada (Paraíso cerrado para muchos)," "is the aesthetic of the diminutive, the aesthetic of diminutive things" (133).[28] "The Granadine diminutive is like a startled bird that opens secret chambers of feeling and reveals the richest nuances of the city. The mission of small things," he says, "is to de-limit, to bring inside and place in our hand objects or ideas of large perspective" (132).[29]

This provides an exquisite instance of the "locality rule," as Elaine Scarry applies it to floral imaging. Flowers, she says, are "the perfect size for imaging"; with their curved and cuplike shape, they incarnate "intense localization" and interiority (93, 97). The relationship between smallness and closeness of vision ("the ratio of extension to intensity") shows up in the way "the localization of intensely filled-in surfaces" on a smaller surface is imagined (98). Thus Lorca believes in the need to domesticate immense things and terms (6) by creating appropriate interior spaces for them. "We need to incite and explore our own inner life and secret being," he says (136).[30] Throughout the essay, Lorca interweaves this lyrical mission of personal identity with the expression of local identity; Granada becomes "an inner soul, a small garden" (136). Granadine culture and identity are turned inward, converted into a myth of transcendent immanence, as Lorca's somewhat enigmatic comment suggests: "Everything has, of necessity, a sweet domestic feeling about it; but who truly penetrates this space of intimacy?" (9)[31]

Lorca's revalorization of the diminutive is all the more remarkable when we recall how Andalusian culture in general suffered repeated stereotyping and was even scoffed at precisely for what Ortega y Gasset dismissively called in 1927 "this southern bric-a-brac" ("Teoría de Andalucía" 175).[32] Spain and Andalusia in particular had long been seen as the European Other. Mario Praz mercilessly skewered this cultural stereotype in *Unromantic Spain* (1929).[33] Spain, he declared, is not picturesque or romantic. In fact, it's downright boring and monotonous, provincial. A prime example, he says, is the proliferation of repetitive detail found in the Alhambra. Detail, for Praz, is "a provincial art which confuses redundancy with richness, and overdoes it." "The detail is not an organic one," he observes. "It does not answer to a special function, neither is it part of a whole" (107). He ascribes this ornamental, formulaic mode to the Arabs, noting that "as for the structural part, it is well known that the Arabs did not invent anything" (106). European art means development, whereas Arabic art, and, by extension, Spanish art, is characterized by repetitiveness (104–7). In this way, after demolishing the romantic myth of Spain, Praz ends up not only reinforcing yet another cultural preconception and bias, but also reinstituting Spain as a European Other in his engaging if occasionally infuriating book.

We can see the persistence of this notion of Spanish art and culture as Andalusian provincial in art historian Oskar Hagen's categorizing as "essentially Spanish" "the allover pattern" of ornamentation (33). The unchanging and unassimilated national character of Spain, he claims, can be adduced from the way "every one of the ornaments on the pilasters and the walls 'knows its place'; for they are kept there by the stern enframing borderlines" (37). This example of dominant "Moorish principles" is taken from the Sacristy of La Cartuja in Granada. Hagen's 1943 study typifies an unstated ideological argument in which sculpture and art in general become ethnic principles and art criticism a form of national ethnography.

Within Spain similar views prevailed, despite protests and dissenting opinions. The use of Andalusian provincial stereotypes to characterize the entire country reached propagandistic levels of *españolismo* during the Franco regime, which attempted to create the image of a unified, homogeneous nationalistic culture (García Montero 102). The provincial in general has provoked at best a mixed reaction from most Spaniards, who did not appreciate the label "provincials" within Europe, but who were often ambivalent in the nineteenth and early twentieth centuries about the place of the provinces in the national scheme of things.[34] To be provincial was to be cursi and backward for the educated and not so educated middle classes in the nineteenth century. But was it Spanish? Or was it simply an expression of provincial life? These concerns were symptomatic of an emerging awareness of change and incipient modernity, which seemed to threaten local values and which were often formulated as an updated version of the old struggle between Madrid and the provinces. Still, while commenting on Lorca's trip to Madrid in 1919, his brother Francisco wrote that "in the provinces, Madrid enjoyed considerable prestige as a center of cultural activity, and that idea was well-founded . . . intellectual life in the provinces did not have much to offer" (131). Writings from the middling classes, such as conservative romantic Gustavo Adolfo Bécquer's complaint in the late 1860s that modern life was homogenizing unique cultures like Sevilla's ("La feria de Sevilla" 1231–33), suggest, nevertheless, that provincial experience was still valued, even if being perceived as provincial was not. Indeed, in Bécquer's 1869 sketch, what adulterates the Seville Fair and the purity of its traditional customs is the "element that some call elegant, and that others, with regard to this kind of festivity, would go so far as to label cursi" (1233).[35]

The provincial image of Granada in particular reflected a very real historical problem of socioeconomic stagnation. By the late nineteenth century, one observer wrote in *O'Shea's Guide to Spain and Portugal* that "Granada, like Toledo, Burgos, Oviedo, and most Spanish towns, is now but a dull, unsocial, depopulated and inert provincial capital. There is about it, notwithstanding its sun and sky, an air of stillness and decay, a mournful silence. . . . Indeed, the whole of Spain is now but a vast cemetery, wherein the 'disjecta membra' of the dead past lie buried in cities which are like so many tombs. Granada is thus truly a living ruin" (Lomas 171).[36] "Dirt and decay reign in its older portions," and beggars abound, says Baedeker in 1908 (332). And even though several large beetroot-sugar manufactories had opened since 1898, residents complained that the industry had "practically left the city unbenefited" (Baedeker 332). While artisanal goods such as hats, leather, furniture, ceramics, and embroidery took an upward swing in 1900, heavy industry did not develop. In sum, the Granadine economy in the early twentieth century could best be described as "casera," or homegrown, as local historians Gay Armenteros and Viñes Millet have observed (266).[37]

It was only after 1910 that the city experienced radical, large-scale changes in its urban habitat (Gay Armenteros and Viñes Millet 349). But some change occurred even before, much to the dismay of certain local elites who also represented a nascent intellectual and artistic *andalucismo,* a regionalistic nationalism coming into play at the turn of the century. Ortega y Gasset has rightly pointed out that socioeconomic and political life, like the population of Spain itself, was largely centered in the provinces during the nineteenth and early twentieth centuries. National policy and politics may have issued out of Madrid, he wrote in 1927, but the nation itself was and is elsewhere (*Redención* 199).

It is one of the great ironies of Spanish constitutional practice that a parliament created to serve the needs of a centralized state ended up encouraging decentralizing, local movements, precisely because election results were arranged beforehand through local agents, or *caciques.* Under such a system of limited democracy controlled from above, the local notables found it much more advantageous to serve local interests rather than Madrid's.[38] The result was, as Ortega points out, the provincialization of Madrid, in which local politics from 1876 to 1900 came to act more and more independently of the central government. As Ortega observes of this imposition of *provincianismo:* "Madrid had forgotten the provinces, and as Spain was *nothing but* an immense province, what inevitably happened was not a national policy, but a provincial one that was localist and rural in the worst sense of the word" (*Redención* 217).[39]

Yet from this experience of inbred, political localism, one could argue, sprang the more ambitious and more independent-minded national regionalist movements, to which Federico García Lorca and local elites lent their support in the 1920s and 1930s. While I believe Ortega y Gasset is essentially correct in stressing the impact of the provinces on the central government, it is also important to bear in mind that Granada, like the rest of Andalusia, was heavily dependent not only on Madrid but on the economic directives and trends of the more industrialized north of Spain. Some historians have gone so far as to suggest a colonized relationship, considering the quasi-feudalistic structure of Andalusia's largely agrarian economy.[40] The relationship, which I cannot treat exhaustively here for reasons of space, is far more complex, given the significant political role of Andalusians in the central government and the tangled web of alliances and deals made between the government and the southern oligarchy in the nineteenth and twentieth centuries. Nevertheless, this dependency, along with the southern landowners' centralist politics, served to prolong economic and social backwardness and to proletarianize the rural and urban working classes. This pattern of uneven development and imbalance among different national regions constitutes a long-standing feature of southern European countries like Greece, Italy, Spain, and Portugal, but it is the "particular historical conjuncture rather than an originating process in itself," which has resulted in the more specific forms of unequal modernization (and modernity) and regional poles of development (Hadjimichalis 86).[41]

Attempts to create an independent Andalusian region in the modern era date back to the 1860s and 1870s, with the rise and fall of the federalist movement or cantonalism. In the teens and twenties, Blas Infante's political andalucismo movement grew steadily, although it never gained the popularity and strength of Catalan nationalism. The Floral Games (Juegos Florales) of Sevilla were resuscitated in 1907; the magazine *Bética* appeared in 1913; the first anthology of Andalusian poetry in 1914; Blas Infante's *Ideal andaluz* in 1915. In 1919 the first Andalusian Constitution of Antequera, dating from 1883, was reprinted. Local associations like the Centro Andaluz spread across southern cities. The Primo de Rivera dictatorship dismantled regionalist movements, but under the Republic projects like the Statutes of Andalusian Autonomy (1933) were proposed.[42]

In Granada, the movement had a more cultural nature, but it is impossible to separate political purpose and ideology from cultural aims since local cultural identity was (and is) already a statement of political naming and thus wrapped up in independent political expression. Journals like *Idearium* and *Renovación* (1918–19) emerged. In 1921, after a long lawsuit, the Generalife and the Casa de los Tiros passed from private hands to state property. There was renewed interest in the artistic monuments and history of the city, with the proper restoration of the Alhambra a matter of lively dispute. Intellectuals, artists, and writers like Lorca enthusiastically embraced cultural organizations like the Centro Artístico de Granada and celebrations like the flamenco Cante Jondo festival in 1922. Timothy Mitchell argues that this promotion of a noncommercial, nonbastardized musical form of flamenco and "the Falla group's [including Lorca] search for purity in the utterly local, with emphases on the unshared and the exclusive" represented the desire "to shun history, to escape urban society . . . and modernity" (169). While this may very well be true, particularly as a manifestation of a local elite's developing group identity, it is also relevant that Lorca and Manuel de Falla promoted *Granadine* culture, that is, the concrete expression of lived, local culture.

This localist fervor for lo granadino already existed at the turn of the century, with the writer Angel Ganivet and his circle of friends. The quest for local authenticity—noticeable in the Falla group as well—meant rejecting a large portion of modern history and times, specifically the industrializing process (see Lavaur; Isac). By using authenticity as the standard for local (and national) identity, Ganivet leaned heavily toward tradition and the past, and away from presumably inauthentic foreign influences; that is, he tended, to use Elspeth Probyn's words once more, to "idealize the local as the real" (187).

Ganivet sought to define the "natural constitution" ("constitución natural") of Spain as well as Granada. He constructed that ideal, or natural, essence that encapsulates both *patria* (Spain) and *patria chica* (Granada) by selecting those elements of Spanish (and Granadine) history that he thought authentic. But as Maravall points out, one can't "choose" what a country or city's history has been by declaring some of it not Spanish or not Granadine ("Ganivet" 399). Ironically, Ganivet—the quintessential restless modern in search of a past—has, since his suicide in 1898, become a symbol of Granadine culture and tradition. In a return of symbolic appeal, his remains were brought home from Riga and reburied in 1925.

Two interrelated elements of the Ganivetian vision of Granada as city and culture interest me here: his passionate dislike of the city's modernization and his espousal of Granadine culture as richly hybrid, in which the Moorish presence becomes once more highly visible as an answer to Castilianization. Lorca embraced his views on both these issues (see Handley; Morris). His brother Francisco remarked that *Granada la bella* "was the only work of Ganivet Federico ever paid any attention to" (104).

Ganivet loathed what was happening to his city in the 1890s.[43] Under pressure of the newly enriched classes of sugar beet producers, who foresaw profits in real estate speculation, Granada experienced a brutal makeover: the Darro river was rechanneled and covered up and Gran Vía Street was greatly widened. As a result, the old center of the city, with its narrow, twisting streets, small, intimate dwellings, and out-of-the-way corners, disappeared. The straight line—or the Haussmann effect, which had already demolished much of the past elsewhere in Europe—triumphed over the centuries-old accretions of Granadine culture. Tradition-minded *granadino* Manuel Gómez-Moreno complained in 1892 that the Paseo de la Bomba's view of the sierra had been totally obscured "with a sugar factory, the building of which the Municipal government did not oppose" (230).

Ganivet was even more blunt:

This architectural vulgarity came after being booted out of Europe, and was to the liking of men of business, the hucksters of land deals and real estate, and the builders of cheap housing. The passion for the straight line grew, and the moment arrived when men could no longer sit still if their street wasn't being torn up. Where the conditions of a city necessitated these urban expansions, they made a sacrifice of aesthetic values, and where the expansion wasn't justified, they ended up creating ugly and uninhabitable neighborhoods. (92)[44]

Significantly, Lorca's father had made his fortune in sugar beet production during the 1890s (Gibson, *Lorca* 6). The industry, however, had fallen into crisis during the 1920s and 1930s when Lorca conceived and wrote *Doña Rosita* (Gay Armenteros and Viñes Millet 269–71). It is ironic that a landowner's son created a character (Doña Rosita) who lives a life made possible through such business endeavors yet who appears to symbolize everything that the very processes of industrialization and modernization would destroy. This inherent contradiction may explain part of Lorca's ambivalent stance toward his character and his reluctance to disclose some of the more enigmatic qualities of the play.

We should also see the passion that Lorca and Ganivet felt for their city, the desire to preserve what was unique about Granada, against the larger backdrop of similar predicaments experienced elsewhere. City life as the quintessential—and disturbing—modern had been a preoccupation with intellectuals, writers, and artists certainly at least since Baudelaire (Clementa Millán 253–63). More to the point, Granada was not the only city to bury a river and demolish entire neighborhoods. The Senne in Brussels, for example, was also covered over, and more than 5,000 structures were pulled down. In response to such wholesale Haussmania, projects to create (as well as preserve) national or local models of architecture and city spaces that would also fit modern times had started to surface in many national cultures by the late nineteenth century (Isac 31, 40). One need only recall culturalist models incorporating the preindustrial city, such as those of William Morris, John Ruskin, Camillo Sitte, Charles Buls (the Grande Place restoration in Brussels), and the Garden City utopia of Ebenezer Howard. Above all, these urban models embody a late nineteenth-century form of historicist nostalgia, ruled by a particular "vision of a cultural community," hence the term *culturalist,* which I've taken from Françoise Choay's work. To her, such reform-minded projects are nevertheless, in psychoanalytic terms, "regressive," that is, "associated with the comforting image of the maternal breast," because they reject the effects of modern industrialization (31, 102–8).

Ganivet's romantic, urban historicism, his aestheticizing nostalgia for the old Granada, is distinguishable from other national (and local) romanticisms for his conception of Granadine culture as hybrid. He admired the physical sinuosity, the detailed surfaces, and intimate smallness of the old Cathedral quarter as Moorish in character. In a letter to his friend Sebastián Gasch (April 1927), Lorca revealed, albeit somewhat cryptically, how much he understood this yearning for an ideal past that would also explain the present as something other than the conventional stereotype of the South: "Undoubtedly there exists here a *form of nostalgia* that is anti-European, but is not oriental. Andalusia" (qtd. in Martínez López 316).[45] Mario Praz and Oskar Hagen misunderstood and condemned the Arabic presence. Both Lorca and Ganivet struggled against erasure of the Arabic past as an unmentionable and glossed-over alter identity, whose repression began in the sixteenth century (Martínez Montávez).

That this culture was also associated with homosexuality made it doubly vulnerable to censure. Certainly the complex symbolism of the South itself as "an archetypal space for the interchange, intersection and evasion of cultures" (Perriam 48) is apparent not only in places and literatures like those of the American South (both hemispheres) and the Mezzogiorno of Italy, but in the transgressive attraction such sites offer, imaginative and real, to marginalized groups. More pertinent to my purposes, Daniel Eisenberg observes that "in the early twentieth century Granada had the most important homosexual subculture in Spain." As a case in point, he maintains that "one of the first gay guide-books in any language [was] Martínez Sierra's *Granada: Guía emocional,* with photos by 'Garzón' ('an ephebe')" ("Granada" 490; and "Guía *gay*"). If this is so, then Martínez Sierra's 1911 text not only signals Granada as a special code-site of homosexuality, but suggests a veiled language of sexualized ambiguity that served as a significant precedent and context to Lorca's play.

Unfortunately, the evidence that Eisenberg gathers with respect to Martínez Sierra's book is largely circumstantial and, in at least one case, erroneous.[46] The "dear reader" in *Granada* is pointedly female, which Eisenberg interprets as coded for homosexual, doubting that a guide-book for Spanish women would have been a commercial possibility in 1911. He ignores, however, the spate of publications (conduct manuals, guides of all sorts, magazines, novels, etc.) from at least mid-nineteenth century on directed primarily at women (see Simón Palmer). Spanish women did travel by then; simply because they rarely went alone does not mean that a guidebook for women was out of the question. Eisenberg also reads the photographer's name "Garzón" as code for homosexual. Alas, Garzón was the name of a real Granadine photographer of the period (Fontanella 276, 282 n.18).[47]

The rest of Eisenberg's textual evidence is also pretty thin. Martínez Sierra refers to "the involuntary artifice of my tangled text," which will no doubt, he says, put off or confuse male writers who read it (*Granada* xii).[48] He also appears to advocate a third sex, "neither male nor female—given that men and women have destroyed each other's lives—but a spiritual being, cool and consoling, maternal and childlike" (74).[49] Eisenberg points out as well that Martínez Sierra's book explicitly invites leisure, the glorious wasting of time, which the critic associates with a hidden homosexual lifestyle. Along these lines, Martínez Sierra's coy allusions to the roses of Granada would also qualify as encoded. "Talk about flowers is dangerous, since from flowers it's an easy leap to the stars" (19).[50]

All such interpretation risks forgetting that Martínez Sierra's book is above all a modernista text, stylistically and thematically loaded with lyrical self-consciousness and teasing playfulness, and that the association made between Granada and leisure, was, on the one hand, a cultural stereotype of Andalusia, which, while harshly criticized as inertia by some granadinos and other Andalusians, was also defended as an aesthetic ideal elsewhere, such as in the late-romantic Gustavo Adolfo Bécquer's "La Pereza" (Idleness). On the other hand, quietude as an inner wellspring of creativity is a modernist credo (the classic example is Valle-Inclán's *Lámpara maravillosa*, 1916). Martínez Sierra's book on Granada combines both strands of thinking.

We can read the equation of leisure or idleness to an Andalusian or, more specifically, Granadine ethos, under a harsher light, however. Ortega y Gasset's well-known image of "the vegetative ideal" immediately springs to mind. In his 1927 essay, "Teoría de Andalucía" [Theory of Andalusia], Ortega envisioned the South as an edenic garden (182). Like the writings of Lorca and other poets of the 1920s and 1930s vanguard period, his interpretation is essentially a romantic one (García Montero 111). But Ortega is also ambivalent toward, if not at times downright hostile, to Andalusian culture in this essay, condemning past political influence of Andalusians in government and sniping at the superficial tourist image of the South. Ortega's Andalusian paradise is, moreover, a quasi-modernist well of collective narcissism (175). In Ortega's scheme of things, the vegetative image was also feminine, as he suggested in his 1923 characterization of Anna de Noailles' poetry: "the soul that this poetry expresses isn't spiritual; rather, it is the soul of a body conceived as vegetal" ("La poesía de Ana de Noailles" 32).[51] The "vegetative genius" that Ortega ascribed to de Noailles reproduces the traditional image of women (and women writers) as irrational, passive creatures subject to the vagaries of sensations and absent a true sense of the individualized self. If the botanical metaphor ultimately dismisses women, what does its application mean for an entire culture?

The philosopher's metaphorical recreation of Andalusia never comes down squarely either on the side of philosophy/aesthetics or on that of social critique, hovering uneasily between poetic praise (mythos) and political ambush (ethos). It is difficult, today, to reconcile the ideal of idleness—which, from a more realistic perspective, the parasitical señorito type of the upper classes embodies—with the chronic underemployment and poverty of the South's agrarian working classes. During the Franco regime, this kind of idealization readily lent itself to the political airbrushing found in statements like this one from a 1954 guidebook: "Granada is a tranquil city, almost static, the spirit of contemplation." The essence of Granadine character, Prieto-Moreno continues, "lies in domestic life. . . . The Grenadine is unable to adapt himself to the bustle of modern life" (9–10). This sort of banal comment typifies what Barthes years ago critiqued as myth, the dehistoricizing for ideological and other reasons of historical and material realities (*Mythologies* 74–77).

Martínez Sierra's guidebook, for the most part, uses Granada as a modernist pretext in praise of an ideal topography of dream and contemplation. (Only in the last few pages does he descend to such mundane details as housing and transportation.) Certainly the androgynous element in *Granada: Guía emocional* mildly sexualizes the text, but, once again, these kinds of allusions also partake of the modernist mythology. Critics have still not sufficiently decoded the multiple ideological masks these texts wear. For example, Eisenberg thinks Martínez Sierra published the book in Paris precisely because it contained a prohibited language of desire ("Guía *gay*" 113). More likely the political attack Martínez Sierra made against the government had more to do with the book's place of publication.[52] At any rate, it was not unusual then for books by Spaniards or Latin Americans, whether they were considered dissidents or not, to be published in Paris.

Eisenberg's well-meaning attempt to find the key to Martínez Sierra's *Granada* does not take into account something else: modernista writers were sometimes accused, in thinly veiled language, of being homosexual

(Moreno Hernández 134). Refined, sensual writing was often characterized as feminine; for some, it was a small leap to effeminate. Language in
this sense seemed to possess a gendered identity. The apparently permeable border between real behavior and identity and fictional inventiveness suggests the seductiveness of language to some readers. It also
means that we must read these texts very carefully because all of the
examples—Lorca's *Doña Rosita*, Martínez Sierra's *Granada: Guía emocional*, and even Ortega's "Teoría de Andalucía"—beckon appealingly
across the border to what looks real. Lorca's loving attention to detail
unfolds within a genre (the theater) that creates illusion out of real things
used as props. Martínez Sierra hybridizes the empirical genre of the
guidebook, which locates and describes material objects of cultural and
historical interest, by practicing a form of personal contemplation from
which emerges a subjective poetics of things and places. His book is,
above all, narcissistic in nature, precisely what Ortega y Gasset accused
Andalusian culture of being. Ortega's Andalusian object of analysis is in
his essay part history and part myth, turning that most amorphous and
labile of genres into something as metaphorical yet real as the vast
garden he envisions the South to be.

How slippery these writings are! And how frustrating a process it is to
tease out flashes of the real from the representation of the real. Engaging
in these kinds of texts also pinpoints some of the difficulties encountered
in trying to deal with the relationship between theory, the notion of
object as object, and the problematic, unresolved status and understanding of representation as a *part* of material reality.[53]

Let me return once more to the significance of the language of flowers. I
have been arguing that Lorca's complex use of this nineteenth-century
expert system is layered and encoded in ways that do not easily lend
themselves to such neat distinctions as conventional versus poetic or
conscious versus unconscious discourse. My detour into the southern
paradise of Martínez Sierra (and Ortega y Gasset) marks a pause (a
transition, if you will) to allow us to reflect more on the nature not simply
of linguistic and psychological but of cultural-historical meanings attached to such object-images as flowers and gardens. Here my argument
lends support, for the moment, to Eisenberg's hypothesis, for these mar-

ginalized subtexts of a hidden, homosexual Granada may also be part of a secret language of flowers. Recalling the figure of Oscar Wilde, Lorca, who sometimes wore a rose, scandalized conservative bourgeois circles of Granada (Sahuquillo 252).[54] The language of flowers itself may have begun in a Turkish harem, among women only, either to amuse themselves or to express through a code lesbian attachments (Goody 234).

Flowers have wide-ranging symbolic-cultural meanings, and Lorca's use of such imagery created multiple layers in his poetry and plays. It would be unwise and terribly limiting to restrict the Lorquian language of flowers to a single frame of reference. Flower imagery in *Doña Rosita* is associated first with germination, then with sterility and, by implication, death, in the opening scene when Rosita's uncle inquires: "¿Y mis semillas?" (69) (Where are my seeds?) (99). These are the first words of the play, deceptive words suggesting something incipient, something about to grow. But a few lines of dialogue later, we learn that at least some of the flower seeds have been scattered and stepped on: "Yesterday I found the dahlia seeds trampled into the ground" (99). Shortly after this, the housekeeper explicitly links the odor of flowers with death, barrenness, and sacrifice (71, 99–100).[55]

The sense of decay that lies beneath the sweet delights of flowers anticipates Doña Rosita's wasted life and years but, more immediately, suggests a strong link with sexuality when the housekeeper—after commenting on the smell of flowers—slyly refers to a woman's sexual organs as an appetizing (and fruitful) thing (71, 100). One cannot help thinking of some of the traditional associations made between flowers and female sexuality, namely the "flores de muerto" (literally, "flowers of the dead") or "monthly flowers," an allusion to menstruation (Monlau 312; Enright 10).[56] In 1875, Hugh James Rose, an English chaplain of Jerez and Cádiz, came on a glass case of flowers made of wool at a girl's school in Spain. He thought at first they were of wax. But the interpreter said they "'are made of what you English call old rags.'" "This was quite enough," wrote Rose, "I apologized to the señora, and hurriedly beat a retreat" (*Untrodden Spain* 1:211). This rather grotesque Victorian reaction serves as a reminder of cruder material realities that the language of flowers covered over, creating a garland of rhetoric similar to the roses that festooned Spanish paintings (like Murillo's) of the Immaculate Conception (Haig 283–84).

Should we conclude, then, that flowers "speak" simply as substitutions for something else, that their very multiplicity of meanings, some of which I've mentioned here, makes it either impossible to determine definitively their meaning or to say they even mean anything, at least in relation to some outside referent? Both Jean Genet and Jacques Derrida hold this position. For Derrida in particular, the continual process of metamorphosis that flowers undergo and represent precludes symbolization (*Glas* 31, 40, 47). Flowers and writing in Derrida's view are intimately linked in the same work of dissemination, of the squandering of seeds (or semes). Drawing on Derrida's perceptions in *Glas* (as well as on Freud and feminist studies), Claudette Sartiliot has fashioned an exquisite garland out of this *herbarium-verbarium* association. Instead of asking "what do flowers express?" she suggests that "we should ask rather what motivates their appearance in texts, and what their appearance obscures. . . . we should recognize the kinds of substitutions and translations they provoke" (17–18).

While Sartiliot does not say that one cannot find any meaning at all in the discourse of flowers, she does discard the classical, linear conception of the language of flowers in favor of a language of the unconscious, in which flowers, "rather than referring to a reality outside themselves (like real flowers) . . . reveal the work of repression" (28). But the clear-cut distinctions she makes between the conventional language of flowers with its straightforward symbolism and the language of the unconscious (or, in similar fashion, the feminine, the irrational, the sexual) are not, in my view, quite as diaphanous or as opposed to one another as she suggests. In this transference between the garden of flowers and the flowers of rhetoric there is a continual flow, a scent of permeability, that does more than simply destabilize the meanings of flowers, real or otherwise. The exchange of meanings and forms between herbarium and verbarium, first of all, performs symbolic and symbolizing operations, despite all protestations to the contrary. Flowers may "appear only to disappear" (Sartiliot 17), but along the way, at different points in this disseminating process, they stop; here they are fixed in some sort of meaning—historically, culturally, affectively—before moving on. More importantly, the very analogy made between verbarium and herbarium reveals just how profoundly thought—even in advocating the most adamantly nonteleological, nonlinear arguments—is metaphorical, and, in that sense, ultimately symbolic. The "substitutions and translations" flowers incite *are* indeed symbolic, if only in pointing to the process of symbolization itself.

I find puzzling the assumption that the work of repression or the unconscious is somehow unattached to, or separate from, the real or an outside reality, whatever that might be. What is real? Doesn't the language of flowers tell us that what the mind fabricates is as much a kind of "object" as the object we call a flower? And that the power of representing objectness, whether in a play or on the stage of life, resides significantly in its capacity to partake in material reality? This, I would argue, is precisely what Lorca understands and achieves in *Doña Rosita la soltera*.

One would like to say that the language of flowers in *Doña Rosita* may very well represent a coded discourse for homosexual desire and frustration, but as the example of Martínez Sierra's *Granada* illustrates, such an interpretation is fraught with difficulties. It is far more probable that Lorca really was thinking, first of all (though not solely), about the plight of the unmarried woman in Granada when he wrote *Doña Rosita la soltera*. The problem of the soltera granadina appears in print well before Lorca in texts by Pedro de Alarcón and Ganivet.[57] In the collectively authored *El libro de Granada* [The book of Granada] (1899), Ganivet proposed a "flower fair as a weekly philanthropic go-between" for women to find husbands (qtd. in Martínez López 50).[58] Martínez López remarks that "in some ways the *Book of Granada* is a kind of map of Granadine spinsterhood" (51).[59]

Lorca's play actually has much in common thematically and technically with Gregorio and María Martínez Sierra's immensely popular stage hit, *Canción de cuna* [Cradle song], which was produced the same year—1911—as *Granada: Guía emocional*. This sentimental paean to domesticity and motherhood, which, amazingly, was adapted to the screen as recently as 1994, is infused with the faded fragrance of modernist cursilería.[60] The play is now rather dated, but in 1911 would have been innovative in favoring intimacy and feeling over action, in portraying female religious as maternal and human (though still idealized) rather than mystical romantics, and in eschewing the entrenched star system for a collective protagonist embodied in the choruslike speech of the nuns (O'Connor 30; M. Martínez Sierra 273, 275).[61]

The story line of *Canción de cuna* is pure minimalist symmetry, constructed as an arrival-departure movement. In act 1 a foundling (Teresa) is left at the door of a convent. Eighteen years later, in act 2 the foundling departs, in a blur of teary-eyed joy, for marriage and life in America. Almost nothing else happens. Like *Doña Rosita*, the Martínez Sierra play focuses intensely on embodied feeling as expressed in the space and time of home (here, a convent). A lyrical *Intermedio* provides the temporal transition between acts and the poetic justification of this hymn to everyday life: "The poet would like / to know how to tell you the day-to-day story / with all its emotion, but in vain. / Can anyone express the drama of daily living! / The weave of life is made of rhythms so regular, / that time itself has fallen asleep in the fragrant stillness; / who knows if a century or an instant passed!" (67).[62]

Canción de cuna—like *Doña Rosita*—really deals with the frustrations and repressed desires of unmarried women. Maternity as fulfillment, as a woman's mission in life, is sacralized—ironically—in a setting where women are denied a natural maternal experience. The Martínez Sierras never openly question either the mission of motherhood or the rightness of religious vocation, but the play abounds in gentle ironies and contradictions. Thus, for example, Sor Juana says, "Whenever I take communion, I imagine that I am receiving God in the form of a child, pressing him tightly against my breast" (39–40).[63] Another sister overcomes depression and the urge to escape the convent with this remedy: "she catches the sun's rays in a mirror and passes the reflections through the branches and on the ceiling and walls of the cell. In this way, she takes comfort, imagining herself as a butterfly or a bird, going wherever her thoughts take her" (79).[64]

Canción de cuna encases motherhood and home as sacred relics, akin to the actual relics offered as gifts to the departing orphan Teresa. In the tradition of nineteenth-century melodrama, the play reframes and reprises in miniature the action and accumulation of experience in the final scene: "The coach bells are heard off-stage. The sisters begin to exit. The curtain slowly falls as the sisters file off. Sor Juana de la Cruz remains alone on stage, collapses onto a chair, weeping unconsolably" (126).[65] The similarity of dramatic technique in Lorca and Martínez Sierra is unmistakable. Here is the ending to *Doña Rosita*, also delicately stylized: "[Doña Rosita, her Aunt and the Housekeeper] leave and the stage is left empty. The door is heard banging. Suddenly a french door at the back blows open and the white curtains flutter in the wind" (154).[66] Lorca learned how to milk emotion skillfully not just from Chekhov but from the use of set tableaux and props symbolically impregnated with feeling in nineteenth- and early twentieth-century sentimental melodramas.[67]

Valle-Inclán and Gómez de la Serna, Martínez Sierra, and Lorca—all these writers obsess in their texts over recovering home, mourning a maternal loss in the only way they can, through metaphors of absence. Like Doña Rosita, they are orphans, regressive spaces of the mind in which the details of that psychical locality are nonetheless deeply rooted not only in the familial but in the historical as well.[68]

Still, Lorca's play displays an essential ambiguity, even an ambivalence, in the way his character Doña Rosita is presented, as though she were in effect merely the materialized trope of the language of flowers, made visible not only through speech but through the stage effects of dress, objects, and music. In this sense, she is the ultimate "artificial flower." We never learn *who* Doña Rosita is, or why ultimately she clings so long to the worn-out illusion of her engagement. By so doing, she refuses to engage in the outside world of time and change.

What is the secret life of Doña Rosita? Is it simply a void that talk occupies, as C. B. Morris sharply observes (121), where language is wasted like the uncle's spilled flower seeds at the beginning of the play? In the last act, Doña Rosita speaks of her dead hopes, and of how she would rather not remember them: "I want to run away, not to be able to see, to be calm, empty" (149).[69] Here, desire becomes unwanted, and the only desire that remains is the wanting not to desire. Shortly after this, Rosita says, "I am as I am. And I can't change myself. Now the only thing left to me is my dignity. What's here inside me, I keep to myself" (149).[70] Lorca's talent in seeing that the strengths and limitations of his character are one and the same is remarkable. Remember, too, Lorca's other words: "But who truly penetrates this space of intimacy?" This secret Granadine garden. . . . This "wanting and not finding the body," as the housekeeper describes Rosita's living death (140).[71] Or, as Doña Rosita herself says, "Each year that passed was like an intimate piece of clothing torn from my body" (148).[72]

As the last piece of furniture is being carted off from the house Rosita and her aunt no longer own, everything lies in ruins, stripped of its "body," of life. Ironically, the uncle's lack of business sense, his inability to adapt to modern business practices, to modernize, has led to the family's financial downfall. (He relied too heavily on fixed income from property.) Lorca seems to intimate two things at once here: the modern—the straight line that doesn't love the detail, the hybrid curve, or the secret language of flowers—has made Rosita and her world obsolete, a fading memory. (Here, Lorca's own modernity, one could also argue, paradoxically lies *in* the language of flowers.) Yet an understanding of what changing historical realities call for—"Well, you have to keep abreast of things!" (144), says Don Martin—might have preserved the illusion of hope, the annulment of time, for Doña Rosita. Instead, Lorca ends with an empty stage, a banging door, the wind blowing through the balcony and the white curtains.[73] The spectators and readers of this play have witnessed a symbolic funeral, in which Doña Rosita's house and garden—the traditional Granadine *carmen*—turn into a kind of cemetery.[74] The housekeeper sees it as a burial without a corpse. It is not simply Doña Rosita who has vanished, but a piece of the past, a small section of the Granadine heart torn away. With the details stripped away, there is no more local. There is no more home. Everything central to this play, to Lorca, the supreme *vanguardista*, the modernist artist, was contained in these cursi provincial artifacts, in the feminine, in the marginalized, whatever name or identity it possessed. There is only loss, historical memory turned into the culture of nostalgia.[75]

CHAPTER NINE

Coda: The Metaphor of Culture in Post-Franco Spain

In the cursi stories presented here, the middle classes found a language to deal with the sociohistorical change the cursi phenomenon embodied. These stories, told in literary and nonliterary texts alike, reflect middle-class anxieties, desires, and fears over the group's own changing and uncertain status in society. With Lorca's play *Doña Rosita la soltera* one reaches a historical turning point. Less than a year later civil war plunged the nation into devastating turmoil and swept away the traces of Doña Rosita's gentle little world. The repressive Franco regime that followed brought stifling and often hypocritical social conformism as well as a rigid insistence on national political unity, while the hungry postwar years made a virtue out of economic and material scarcity and poverty. Inevitably, as a sign of the times, a new cursilería crept back into middle-class life.

Spokesmen for the regime, meanwhile, busily turned Spanish backwardness and isolationism into a myth of exceptionality. Proclaiming that "Spain is different" may have increased tourism and set the country apart from its neighbors, but it couldn't eliminate the contradictions between official ideology and everyday life. Women, for example, were told that marriage and family constituted the highest ideal to which they could aspire, but postwar reality forced a surplus of unmarriageable women to work out of economic necessity. Given these circumstances, the infantilization to which the regime subjected women at the same time must have seemed terribly anachronistic. Women received advice like the following in 1943: "A woman cannot feel pleasantly content if she isn't under the protection of a stronger shadow. Stronger in everything: in what is felt and what is imagined. Our femininity needs to feel fragile and protected."[1] As Martín Gaite points out in *Usos amorosos de la post-guerra española*, the working single woman became an object of derision, an example of mid-twentieth-century cursilería (47, 51). Only this time lo cursi wasn't associated symbolically with home: it circulated in the streets and in the workplace. Doña Rosita had been thrown out of the garden. The war and its aftermath had displaced home, in both the literal and symbolic senses. Entire families, split ideologically during the war, had been torn up; others had disappeared. It comes as no surprise, then, that the Franco regime invested so heavily in family values, values woven into the very fabric of a belief system incarnated in "National Catholicism" and founded on a repressively paternalistic order.

That order was already an anachronism in the mid-twentieth century, which may in part explain why a nineteenth-century phenomenon like cursilería still existed in middle-class Spanish society. The continuing presence of lo cursi signified inner contradictions, social and material disparities, between economic shortages and the need to keep up appearances, or between the ideal image of family life and the harsh reality of unrewarding labor. While I have concentrated in this book on nineteenth- and early twentieth-century examples of cursilería, I cannot leave the subject without at least a brief look at the post-Franco period as both a reaction to, and continuation of, Francoism.

Space does not permit me to explore more fully the presence of cursilería during the Franco regime, but its anachronistic persistence has been remarked on in many memoirs and essays reflecting back on the period (e.g., Martín Gaite, Vázquez Montalbán, Sopeña Monsalve) as well as from within the period itself ("Frida" 21). The Franco era seems steeped in cursilería, especially from the perspective of Spaniards looking backward, but not simply because things from the past often don't age well. Remembrances of Francoism dredge up images of an official culture, an ideology that self-consciously modeled itself on a glorified, dead past: a mythic Spain of imperial grandeur and Catholic tradition, reincarnated under a fascist regime. As one commentator recalls, "that ridiculous, antiquated fascism which was imposed on our childhood with memorization, textbooks, and a good measure of slaps on the hands while our thin diet was supplemented with powdered milk and American processed cheese, has a lot to do with the mentality and attitudes that today constitute the physical micro- and macromosaic of the diverse powers and forms of Spanish life" (Cámara Villar 15).[2]

Francoism was both grim and cursi, marking an entire generation with unwanted memories it could not shed. After the death of Franco in November 1975, a strong move emerged toward willed amnesia of the immediate past, accompanied by a newly found sense of liberation. The period of the Transition—moving from dictatorship to democracy, starting in the mid-1970s until the early 1990s—was experienced in many different ways. One of the more local forms, which began in Madrid and spread to other cities, was the *movida* (lit., "the action"), a somewhat frenetic, cultural underground movement, largely centered on Spanish youth and an anarchically inclined artistic world, which flourished from the late 1970s until the mid-1980s. Spaniards and non-Spaniards alike paradoxically saw this local narrative of Madrid, the movida, as a postmodern phenomenon, thus suggesting simultaneously a nonlocal or unrooted quality about it. I see la movida as the latest example of a displaced narrative of home, in which localness—symbolized by Madrid, in this case—substitutes for home, for a sense of place, even for the provincial, something already observed, for example, in Lorca's conception of the Granadine local.

But the rootedness sought expresses at bottom a perceived loss. Some critics, such as Teresa Vilarós, have maintained that resurfacing as the repressed is the symbolic figure of Franco, for whom many Spaniards have mixed feelings (*El mono del desencanto* 16). Francoism represented a sense of order and a strong patriarchal structure, within the home and the state. The anarchic movida may seem a million miles from this authoritarian image. Yet the immediate post-Franco period in some ways constituted a continuation of Francoism and remained deeply tied to it familially and socially. Indeed, the new professional middle class that the Franco regime in the 1960s and 1970s promoted within the state apparatus, technology, and industry (in part through Opus Dei and the technocrats in office) both anticipated and laid the groundwork for the emergence of another professionalized middle class closely tied to the state and to the burgeoning culture industry in 1980s Spain. The movida itself is an example of that 1980s middle-class phenomenon. If the movement seemed unstructured on the surface, its cultural expression in the arts, literature, and even the fashion industry resulted, nonetheless, from a concerted effort.

More to my point, the movida can be seen as a local narrative of Madrid in which rupture and continuity both play a role. The sense of anachronism, of obsolescence, which persists in this period, is sometimes translated into forms of kitsch and camp, both closely related to the phenomenon of cursilería. Kitsch, which derives from the German *kitschen*—"to slap (a work of art) together, fr. G. dial., to scrape up mud from the street"—is, according to *Webster's,* "artistic or literary material held to be of low quality, often produced to appeal to popular taste, and marked esp. by sentimentalism, sensationalism, and slickness." Like lo cursi, kitsch is often associated with the domestic or familial, but unlike the former, kitsch originates in a mass-produced, industrialized society. The high self-consciousness of camp places both cursilería and kitsch in quotation marks, in a kind of mock nostalgia for things past or for more punctuated forms of identity (see Sontag). All three categories tend to break down the divisions between high-, low-, and middle-brow culture.[3] The movida is a kind of kitsch narrative and experience, which turns such minor forms of culture as cursilería, kitsch, and camp into a central metaphor for modern Spanish culture itself. The use of these forms may be postmodern, but it is also deeply rooted in the specific context of Spanish history.

The movida at first seems like the perfect postmodern narrative. For Lyotard postmodern means "incredulity toward metanarratives." Such legitimizing metadiscourses would include, he writes, "the dialectics of Spirit, the hermeneutics of meaning, the emancipation of the rational or working subject, or the creation of wealth" (xxiii, xxiv). People have lost faith in the grand narratives told and legitimized in the shape of nation-states, parties, professions, and historical traditions (Lyotard 14). This holds particularly true since 1968, when political developments in the West have undoubtedly profoundly affected what some have called the "discourse of the end of utopia" (Huyssen 87). The universalizing and rationalist principles of Enlightenment have come under particular attack (see especially Foucault's "What is Enlightenment?").

Fredric Jameson suggests, however, that the great master-narratives may not really have disappeared, but gone "underground as it were, their continuing but now *unconscious* effectivity as a way of thinking about and acting in our current situation" (Foreword xii). Jameson's "buried master-narratives," as he calls them, underline not only the persistence of such stories, but perhaps even their inevitability. It is difficult to see otherwise how Lyotard's appealing notion of little narratives (*petit récits*) can inventively work themselves out in local contexts (xi, 60). Big or small, narrative establishes the conditions for understanding and explaining, provides a sense of form or structure, and offers possible modes of identity. Narratives, above all, are relational. They make us conceive things in ever increasing complex relationships to each other. A small story doesn't exist in a vacuum, any more than a person does.

The relationship connecting small and large narratives is even more complicated than this. One imagines the perceived breakup of master-narratives, like pieces of a heavy mass shooting off in different directions. But where did that heavy mass come from? How does a grand narrative come to weigh so much? Why do the smaller narrative units—the marginal, the forgotten, the local—even exist then? How are they produced out of this supposedly undifferentiated, monolithic mass of dominance? Or did they exist before the appearance of mass?

Either we explain these pieces of varying size as part of the whole, in functionalist terms, so that everything fits the picture and coheres, narratively and otherwise, or, contrary to this organicist model that narrative tends to favor, we declare the existence of contradiction, disjunction, and randomness.[4] One recognizes ruptures within the presumed uniformity and homogeneous strength of a culture and the role human agency plays in catalyzing the process of rupture. Significantly, as Baudrillard has remarked, the more closed and seemingly impervious a system or culture is, the more vulnerable it becomes to internal fissuring and ultimately to its own collapse ("Symbolic Exchange" 123). The breakup of the former Soviet Union and the crumbling of the Berlin Wall are recent examples. Collective historical amnesia also inflicts symbolic death on repressive systems. It can, of course, also signify the failure to take responsibility or to account for the past.

The Franco period is a case in point. Francisco Umbral in *Guía de la posmodernidad* [The postmodernity guide] lends a note of finely honed malice when he tells how one of Salvador Pániker's sons reacted to seeing Franco in one of his last televised appearances with these words: "Qué viejecito tan camp" (What a campy little old man). "In that moment the postmodern was born," writes Umbral, "There is a generation that knows that dictatorship is a question of waiting, that there's no longer a need to struggle against it, that the campy little old man is going to die by himself or we will end up killing him by natural death" (38).[5] Ironic hindsight aside, Umbral's cynical commentary suggests a symbolic death through metaphorical miniaturization that had in fact occurred even before Franco began to die body part by body part (see also Vázquez Montalbán, *Crónica sentimental de la transición* 72). The Generalíssimo had become a kitschified dwarf, shrinking before the viewing public's very eyes.

Umbral's little story, within a book subtitled "Crónicas, personajes e itinerarios madrileños" [Madrid chronicles, characters, and itineraries], seems to illustrate the oppositional model as a frame for the acting out of cultures. Yet to impose this particular theoretical model on all historical-cultural contexts is ultimately reductionist. Umbral's commentary arises out of the changing, unstable character of social realities. In contextualizing it, one detects a tone of combined opposition and complicity: opposition to the Franco regime and, at the same time, a winking proleptic complicity that discloses how an authoritarian, closed system had already undergone modification from within by dissent, the passage of time, and the development of a new perception of cultural realities ("what a campy little old man"). Umbral's remarks, which we could multiply by those of countless other witnesses and agents of historical change in Spain, can be read as both a sign and countersign of the culture in which he lives. His petit récit is part of a larger story predicated on an inverted—or, perhaps better, perverted—metanarrative of Enlightenment. The anecdotal is also history, which is registered as kitsch, a form of degraded utopia, as I will argue.

The death of Franco marked the loss of oppositionality. His demise produced a deep fissure in the Spanish social imaginary, as Teresa Vilarós has observed ("Revuelo de plumas" 21; *El mono del desencanto*, ch. 1). This sense of rupture strikes me as fundamental to any understanding of post-Franco society, particularly in light of the postmodern label frequently attached to it. Most associated with this postmodern turn is the movida. Vilarós incisively dissects the movement's relentless insistence on the present as a refusal and inability to come to terms with the past, above all with that dreaded yet familiar father figure, Franco, who belonged to the collective family history of all Spaniards. The rupture also of course produced the well-known *desencanto,* or disenchantment, which has very real roots in the sellout of the Partido Socialista Obrero Español (PSOE) following the 1977 Moncloa Pacts and the party's subsequent opportunism and corruption (see Lewis 173–74, 180).

Tom Lewis sees the emergence of the *movida madrileña* and Spanish postmodernism in the late 1970s and 1980s as at least partly brought about by a decade of PSOE policy making (181). Here, presumably the PSOE's betrayal of Marxist-socialist principles represents in its own way abandonment of the grand narrative of emancipation. From this truncated story emerges the process of rupture itself, which appears as a rapidly multiplying series of individualized proclamations of manumission expressed in various tonalities of hedonism, anarchy, aestheticism, consumerism, and so on. The postmodern movida can be viewed alternatively as capitulation to the breakdown of coherence and explanatory models or as a critique of that same phenomenon. In other words, the movida, too, functions as both sign and countersign of the culture producing it. The actors immersed in the movida in its headiest, most vibrant moments during the early 1980s not only came from socioeconomic and cultural backgrounds and ideologies similar to those of the PSOE ruling elite. They also duplicated the ideals of emancipation and plenitude in a fracturing process of multiplying individual fault lines. Bent on the utopia of self-realization, these fault lines open up an abyss in the Kantian thought that "Enlightenment is man's release from his self-incurred tutelage" (90).

In this sense, postmodernism is less a rupture produced by and out of modernism than it is a continuation of the rupture that modernism itself represents and produces.[6] Under modernism, the grand narratives of the Enlightenment turned inward, reincarnated as individual quests of self. Postmodernism, I would suggest, still exhibits some of these traits, albeit often through the distorting lens of parody and pastiche. Despite claims to the contrary, the sense of self has not disappeared from contemporary life. Baudrillard has argued, for example, that "what was projected psychologically and mentally, what used to be lived out on earth as metaphor, as mental or metaphorical scene, is henceforth projected into reality, without any metaphor at all, into an absolute space which is also that of simulation" ("Ecstasy of Communication" 128). In other words, the loss of boundaries between public and private, the saturation of surface and screen, the continuous and invasive sense of the present, signal for Baudrillard "the end of interiority and intimacy" in an age of constant communication (133). A peculiar form of schizophrenia is instituted, in which there is "too great a proximity of everything . . . with no halo of private protection" (132). In another postmodern take, Jameson proposes the close relation between schizophrenic language and the postmodern experience of time as a perpetual present of discontinuities and fragmentation ("Postmodernism and Consumer Society" 118–20).

Despite their differences, both these analyses hinge on two possibly incompatible notions: indifferentiation and fragmentation. On the one hand, the self appears to have merged with the world; and on the other, the self appears as ruptured particles. The unstated context here is a presumed earlier self that could know its inner life and the world through exercise of the rational faculties. By implication, both Baudrillard and Jameson express a perceived loss, the loss of this earlier self. In the process, they demonstrate an admirable application of reasoning that in itself argues the very opposite of their position. More significantly, to assert the "death of the subject" or "the end of individualism as such" (Jameson, "Postmodernism and Consumer Society" 114) is to invent and then reify another subject—the autonomous self—that is a fiction. It never existed. The autonomous self would be a wild child, one unexposed to the world of otherness, one therefore not fully human. The construction of an autonomous self, a monad self, serves a theory that ultimately privileges language as the inventor of an alienated self.

Self-awareness is predicated on others, on our separateness as well as our connectedness with others. Human beings are literally torn into the world, coming into life as fragmented existence. *We* are the rupture. The individualized self *is* the fractured self, each fracturing following its own fault lines. Fragmentation and instability of the subject or self do not negate the subject at all. It is what constitutes us as humans, complexifies our being, and grounds our fictions.

What does this mean for postmodernism? In a provocative assessment of the phenomenon, Celeste Olalquiaga sensibly maintains that "postmodernism is a state of things, not a structured and coherent ideology" (xiv). As a state of things, "it is primarily determined by an extremely rapid and freewheeling exchange to which most responses are faltering, impulsive, and contradictory. What is at stake is the very constitution of being—the ways we perceive ourselves and others, the modes of experience that are available to us, the women and men whose sensibilities are shaped by urban exposure" (xi). She subtitles her book *Megalopolis*, "Contemporary Cultural Sensibilities." By emphasizing sensibilities over ideologies, Olalquiaga returns us to the sphere of sentiment as an expression of identity.

What if we look at the postmodern experience in post-Franco Spain as a displaced, ruptured narrative of identity diffusely structured through complexly ambivalent feelings expressed as metaphorized movements? In this narrative, big and small narrative units tend to get both confused and fused together; and it becomes increasingly unclear what the larger picture is. This kind of narrative works, consciously or unconsciously, with a usually invisible metanarrative as the wished-for driving force behind it, a force simultaneously denied and acknowledged through figures of displacement. Such metanarratives are, to use Jameson's suggestive phrase in a different context, "buried," displaced by smaller narrative units that constitute projections of self onto cultural screens of deceptive unimportance. What is buried can also be conceived of as what is lost and must, by implication, be retrieved if possible. Until it is found again, no substitute will last or permanently fill the void, itself a kind of deeply repressed (and displaced) anguish or sadness.

The postmodern may indeed constitute a form of mourning for the modern. As Dean MacCannell remarks, "much of our current critical and political project appears to me as a kind of unrealized mourning in which all of life has become reorganized around something that 'died,' bestowing upon the purportedly dead subject, dead epoch, dead values, etc.— honors, privilege, and prestige denied them in life" (xi–xii). He goes on to say that "current criticism is a self-conflicted exercise," in mourning precisely what it seeks to critique and deconstruct (xii). He also questions (as do I) the privileging of the postmodern sense of epochal exhaustion, lack of interiority, and denial of history over other forms of contemporary experience (x).

The self-referential, inward turn of postmodernity relies on heightened self-consciousness, an intense subjectivity. But that intense subjectivity is used to neutralize feeling through mechanisms of displacement. Because we cannot adequately identify the source of dis-ease and rupture, we cannot properly deal with the feeling arising from it and must move it somewhere else or onto something else. This is, however, a temporary strategy, since the metaphorical placement of a feeling onto an object or a person merely highlights the substitutional nature of the process. So images circulate, incessantly move on. The metaphorical movement of feeling imposes a loose structuring on texts and narratives, which constitutes, in essence, the very process of rupture itself. At heart lies a deeply seated inability to handle feeling in a complex, often frightening universe.

By focusing on the metaphorical, I am suggesting a closer examination of certain "structures of the imagination," or feeling, which is to say, the emotional expression of narrative as it is sifted and shaped through deeply felt or pervasive cultural forms and imagery.[7] I am borrowing here, in part, from a certain trend in cultural anthropology, the "anthropology of affect," which asserts the primacy of human feelings—and thereby the fundamental role of the body—in understanding cultures through the study of the relationships between individual feelings and group structure (see Fernandez; Gilmore; Brandes). This approach suggests that feeling possesses a structure evidenced through a series of transformations; and that what is transformed are human emotions (Gilmore, ch. 9). Feeling as expressed in metaphor is represented through figurative movement between different domains in an effort "to find identity in domains other than those we actually occupy," as anthropologist James W. Fernandez persuasively argues (xiii).

This movement is not, however, merely figurative since metaphorical language also carries the burden of meaning in the realm of the social, incarnating acts of persuasion and performance (see Fernandez). Or as linguists Lakoff and Johnson with simple eloquence say in their book, *Metaphors We Live By:* "metaphors are not merely things to be seen beyond. In fact, one can see beyond them only by using other metaphors.

It is as though the ability to comprehend experience through metaphor were a sense, like seeing or touching or hearing, with metaphors providing the only ways to perceive and experience much of the world. Metaphor is as much a part of our functioning as our sense of touch, and as precious" (239). I take their experientialist description of metaphor as fundamental to my analysis of a postmodern displaced narrative of identity in post-Franco Spain: "metaphor . . . unites reason and imagination. Reason, at the very least, involves categorization, entailment, and inference. Imagination, in one of its many aspects, involves seeing one kind of thing in terms of another kind of thing—what we have called metaphorical thought. Metaphor is thus *imaginative rationality*" (193). Baudrillard's contention that the metaphorical scene, at least as "projected psychologically and mentally," has disappeared—along with referentiality—into the space of simulation cannot be sustained ("Ecstasy" 128). The very notion of hyperreality as a "world of self-referential signs" sets in motion a clearly metaphorical beyondness (Poster 6; and Baudrillard, "Simulacra and Simulations").

Nevertheless, we cannot simply dismiss Baudrillard's relentlessly postmodern world of screen and surface. Indeed, I would suggest that certain cultural metaphors in post-Franco Spain—or, more provocatively, the metaphor of culture itself—have served as a kind of screening surface for at least some of the participants in the 1980s movida phenomenon. In the delightful and outrageous book called *El kitsch español,* Antonio Sánchez Casado insightfully remarks: "Culture is the sign of the 1980s. You have to recycle yourself in order to be in step with things. Everything is done in the name of culture and, as the standard of living has increased, everyone wants to appear as sophisticated as possible, rushing to devour the culture that institutions are continually hurling at us. . . . Whatever bears the cultural seal is unquestioned, the same way what came from outside Spain was before" (17).[8]

Culture—as an institution and a profession, as a symbol of artistic status and identity, as contested national identity (or identities)—dominates the scene and language of 1980s Spain. The relationship between culture and power, between culture and the state, becomes a crucial question. "To what degree are power and culture in bed together?" asks

Leopoldo Alas Mínguez somewhat rhetorically (*La orgía de los cultos* 21).[9] As if in response, Rafael Sánchez Ferlosio calls culture "that invention of the Government" and caustically remarks that the reigning party might as well be saying, "As soon as I hear the word *culture* I write out a blank check to whomever" (11).[10] Governments, central and regional, banks and saving institutions, municipalities, anyone with a culture budget, has gotten into the act. And act it is, according to Sánchez Ferlosio, who says the *acto cultural,* or cultural act, has turned into *actomanía,* a peculiar kind of mania (12). This institutionalization of culture seems to have gone hand in hand with an increasing professionalization of artists, intellectuals, commentators, and others linked to the culture industry (Gallero 98). Significantly, Leopoldo Alas Mínguez refers to them as "authentic professionals of culture" (*La orgía de los cultos* 21).

As status symbol, culture is everywhere, particularly in the new, upwardly mobile professional class—usually connected to the party in power—that rose to the top in this period (Lewis 176–77; Vázquez Montalbán, *Panfleto* 26). But among artists and intellectuals—some of whom can be considered in this group of professionals—the proliferation of cultural acts and the constant visibility and presentation of culture in the much hyped Spanish fashion industry, in film, literature, and the plastic arts have also provoked criticism, an ill-defined discomfort, and dissatisfaction. Some picture contemporary Spanish culture and society as lightweight and pallid, using such labels as *cultura light* (light culture) and *cultura descafeínada* (decaffeinated culture), or even *designer culture* (see Subirats, *Después de la lluvia* 79). For Leopoldo Alas Mínguez, the 1980s signify banalization and consensualism, in which differences are dissimulated, and risk and passion provoke disdain (*La orgía de los cultos* 20, 47). For Enric Benavent, "*Light* means not getting mixed up in anything, not getting involved, remaining on the sidelines" (qtd. in Alas Mínguez, *La orgía de los cultos* 72).[11] For José Antonio Fortes, it represents a contemporary *trahison des clercs,* in which the writer's function in society has been "decaffed" and reality imaged as unproblematic: "Problems, what problems. . . . No tensions. . . . Please, everything's fine. Just fine. And light" (20).[12]

Critiques of perceived cultural inadequacies also disclose thinly veiled anxiety over Spain's position with the rest of the world, which accelerated modernization and the desire to eliminate differences with

Europe have exacerbated. Thus for many culture in Spain is more apparent than real (Javier Sádaba, qtd. in Gallero 284; Subirats, *Después de la lluvia*). "The cultural level of this country is very low," says another commentator (José Manuel Costa, qtd. in Gallero 76). Comparisons with what is European translate into "the [latest] imported model" for Enric Benavent and underline "a great inferiority complex" (qtd. in Alas Mínguez, *La orgía de los cultos* 75). National dis-ease quickly slides into the personal, as when Borja Casani speaks of "a personal awareness of cultural instability that I share permanently" (qtd. in Gallero 76).

National prestige and position revolve significantly around the same question that appears to haunt personally many of the movida's participants: originality. In a satiric series of "Normas de Vida *Light*" (Norms for a light life), Alas Mínguez declares that "the first norm . . . consists of annulling oneself as an individual under the unraveling mask of an overwhelming personality" (*La orgía de los cultos* 33).[13] Umbral writes in a similar vein, "The most disheartening thing about any project of rampant individuality at any cost is that it is constructed with the remains of multiple identities. Being different isn't a sin, as the philosopher said, it is impossible" (*Y Tierno Galván* 44).[14] We seem to have gone from "Spain is different"—propaganda disseminated, ironically, during an era of stifling internal conformism—to something like, "Spain, alas, is no different," in a period when, globally, difference is fraught with pitfalls of all sorts (see Labanyi, "Postmodernism" 397; Hooper 445). Neither of these reductionist clichés can be taken very far in an analysis of national and individual identities.

Originality is closely linked to authenticity. Postmodernism in general and Spanish culture of the late 1970s and 1980s have been characterized as addicted to the apocryphal, the simulated, and the falsified. Almodóvar speaks of the early 1980s as a period when "we had no memory; we imitated everything we liked and had a great time doing it. . . . the more we plagiarized, the more authentic we were" (ix). Umbral comments that "the passion for the apocryphal leads the postmodern to madly admire transvestites, even if he isn't one himself. . . . The transvestite is postmodern without knowing it" (*Guía de la posmodernidad* 55).[15]

This simulation of identity incarnated in the postmodern *travestí* can be read as culture-positive and / or -negative. On the one hand, it privileges the creative invention of self. (Think of any number of Almodóvar characters in his films.) On the other, simulation of identity also suggests inadequacy and inauthenticity, as the comments of Alas Mínguez and Umbral seem to imply. It can, however, be viewed as both: as a potentially enriching split screen of self-projection that, nevertheless, oscillates alarmingly between kitsch and utopia and probably falls somewhere in between.

The postmodern screen of self is now doubly figured as an object. In the displacement of feeling onto cultural objects or onto object-persons of symbolic import, metaphor becomes narrativized, attaching itself to the myths, large and small, that fuel stories. In the postmodern version of 1980s Spain, two cultural metaphor-myths dominate the scene: kitsch and utopia. Kitsch is a form of degraded utopia, or debased myth, deriving ultimately from romanticism and historically nonexistent until the advent of industrialization and consumerism.[16] Like schlock, camp, or cursi, kitsch does not constitute a fixed category. As Andrew Ross notes, "these categories are constantly shifting ground, their contents are constantly changing" (145).[17] Nevertheless, both late nineteenth-century kitsch and twentieth-century neo-kitsch share the condition of "aesthetic lies" (see Moles; Calinescu). The element of self-deception basic to kitsch, aesthetically and ethically, reveals itself especially in the denial of the unacceptable and the disturbing. Milan Kundera puts it this way: "Kitsch is the absolute denial of shit, in both the literal and the figurative senses of the word; kitsch excludes everything from its purview which is essentially unacceptable in human existence" (248). Kitsch can be understood as having banished hell while refusing "to accept . . . the knowledge that there is no paradise" either, as Yaron Ezrahi, a participant in a symposium on kitsch, put it ("On Kitsch" 309).

Like the myth of utopia, kitsch ultimately attempts to eradicate time and history. Unlike utopia, kitsch is not up to the task. Behind kitsch lies the fear of death. While under Nazism kitsch was heroically glorified in a paradoxical vision of apocalyptic death-in-harmony (see Friedlander), kitsch in the postmodern experience has come down closer to earth, but retains its unease with death. Celeste Olalquiaga suggests that "kitsch is one of the constitutive phenomena of postmodernism." Its "eclectic cannibalism, recycling, rejoicing in surface or allegorical values . . . are those that distinguish contemporary sensibility from the previous belief in authenticity, originality, and symbolic death" (41–42). For Leopoldo Alas Mínguez, kitsch "is the spirit—or the lack of that spirit—of the much celebrated Postmodernity" ("Sinceramente kitsch" 10).[18] He also says that kitsch works "with dead materials, with cadavers" (9).[19] I take this to refer, for example, to recycled materials that figuratively and literally come out of the dustbin or the garbage heap. Paradoxically, however, this "eclectic cannibalism" has the effect of neutralizing the more troublesome aspects of death.

Kitsch as debased utopia is one of those small narratives that has emerged as both a sign and countersign of the master-narrative of utopia. Despite its status as a *petit récit*, it is symbolically central to the post-Franco period under consideration. Kitsch both mimics and parodically subverts the utopian narrative of emancipation and, in its close working relationship to utopia, enables the expression of conflicted, ambivalent feelings toward such master-narratives. Kitsch as debased utopia makes manifest the process of rupture that characterizes this period.

Cursilería in the nineteenth century can be seen as a form of rupture that comes from within the middle-class culture gaining credence, as something produced simultaneously with the culture's historical and economic rise and constituting a sign of the specific culture. In contrast, kitsch in the 1970s and 1980s can be regarded as an index of the *process* of rupture itself and its detachability from concrete, historical origins. I am not aware of any written uses of the word *kitsch* in Spain before the 1970s, although kitsch is first registered in Munich during the 1860s and 1870s.[20] Discussions of kitsch as a mass phenomenon appear in the United States in the late 1930s (Clement Greenberg) and continue in the 1940s and 1950s (e.g. Harold Rosenberg) until the present (see Ross, ch. 2). In Germany Hermann Broch's first notable essay on kitsch appeared in 1933 (with another in 1950–51). In France the topic is hot in the late 1950s and 1960s (see Moles and Wahl); in Italy and Mexico, during the 1960s and early 1970s (Dorfles; Eco; Monsiváis). "Camp" of course surfaces in the 1960s with Susan Sontag's memorable essay.

In Spain, kitsch and camp appear in Castellet's 1970 introduction to his now classic poetry anthology, *Nueve novísimos* [Nine of the newest].[21] There he makes references to Spanish translations of such works as

Umberto Eco's *Apocalípticos e integrados ante la cultura de masas* [Apocalyptics and the integrated in the presence of mass culture] (1968), Gillo Dorfles's *Nuevos ritos, nuevos mitos* [New rites, new myths] (1969), Susan Sontag's *Contra la interpretación* [Against interpretation] (1969), and, in the original French, Barthes's *Mythologies* (1957). In addition, Dorfles's *El kitsch* was published in 1973, and Broch's *Kitsch, vanguardia y el arte por el arte* [Kitsch, vanguard, and art for art's sake] in 1970. It is clear that Barcelona's vanguard originally imported the *theory* of kitsch (and camp) into Spain. In the late 1960s and 1970s, *novísimo* poets like Manuel Vázquez Montalbán, Ana María Moix, Leopoldo María Panero, and Pere Gimferrer exploited camp and kitsch and other mass media effects not only as technical devices, as a reaction to the 1950s social poets, and as commentary on a rapidly changing Spanish society, but also as a personal means of aesthetic liberation and a statement of implicit democratization.[22] In February of 1978, Spain's first sex shop opened in Madrid, only to be closed five months later by the authorities. It was called "Kitsch" (Hooper 155).

By the mid-1980s kitsch and camp were strongly identified with the movida madrileña (which spread to several other Spanish cities). At the same time lo cursi was making an apparent comeback (had it ever disappeared?); it was now being identified with "lo cursi bueno," as Ramón Gómez de la Serna would have said. Leopoldo Alas Mínguez, who dedicates his essay, "Sinceramente kitsch" [Sincerely kitsch], to Gómez de la Serna, "dondequiera que esté" (wherever he may be), attempts to distinguish between kitsch and cursi, resorting to a long list of examples, such as, "Simago is cursi, Corte Inglés is kitsch [both department stores]; life is cursi, death is kitsch; [pop singer] Ana Belén is cursi, Madonna is kitsch," and so on (11).[23] Almodóvar, he says, is "cursi and imagines himself kitsch in his dreams" (10).[24] Finally he notes that kitsch "is insincere, destroying its models by trying to create them through recreation and attempting to fill the void with more void. Lo cursi, on the other hand, treasures and preserves the remains, the crumbs of the kitsch banquet, with a devotion replete with sentimentality, which is therefore not intellectualizable. Lo cursi is lived in secret, it is domestic ecstasy" (12).[25] The Gómez de la Serna influence is palpable, especially in the nostalgia-laden, domestic image of lo cursi; the ironic, tongue-in-cheek inconsistency is all-pervasive. The emphasis on sentimentality is a re-

18. From *Vogue* (Spain), March 1989, an article linking lo cursi and fashion. Courtesy of Ediciones Condé Nast S.A.

minder, too, that lo cursi is, as Ortiz de Montellano put it in 1929, "a nuance of sensibility, never of intelligence, hence its unevenness belongs to [the realm of] taste" (203).[26]

Most astonishing is lo cursi's success in the fashion industry. I was amazed to read in a short, photo-enhanced piece from *Vogue-España* that lo cursi has become the great humanizer of haute couture (see fig. 18).

"Among the new creations," I read, "appears a tendency . . . to recuperate the individual, giving back a sense of identity that seemed lost."[27] How exactly does one give back a sense of identity? By accentuating the details and elevating the accessory to the category of the essential: "being, in a word, cursi." Lo cursi constitutes an alternative to "functional aggressivity or to aggressive functionality, as you prefer,"[28] and makes fashion "something habitable and intimate" (28).

Margarita Rivière's 1992 book on *Lo cursi y el poder de la moda* [Lo cursi and the power of fashion] takes the phenomenon even further, although in a different direction. She says that lo cursi—"pretending to be what one isn't"—is now the norm (85). Bad taste is everywhere, she writes. Any attempt on the part of camp to regenerate or "save" lo cursi in a postindustrial society is a doomed effort (103). Rivière, however, overstates her case, making sweeping generalizations about the norm in social life. Moreover, she takes an essentially nineteenth-century term, lo cursi, which emerges out of a marginalized society in transition toward modernity, and attempts to fit it into a very different cultural context, post-Franco Spain. That pockets of cursilería persist is undeniable; or that the boundaries between lo cursi, kitsch, and camp often become blurred is also part and parcel of shifting categories with contours shaped by protean desire. But lo cursi remains a category of nineteenth-century middle-class marginalization. It is *not* the norm, but rather the antinorm, being unwanted as an attribute, and exists, even when pervasive, as peripheral to the social norm. The threat of lo cursi's contagious social pervasiveness makes it, however, a symbolically central phenomenon for the anxiety-ridden, insecure middle classes of the last century.

This particular kind of class-defined anxiety and insecurity has considerably receded into the background of post-Franco Spain. What lo cursi, kitsch, and camp do share, besides their obvious family relationship, is the marginal. They are narratives of marginality that play a significant role in larger narratives presumably taking center stage. All three categories are closely linked in post-Franco Spain to gays and transvestites. Ana Rossetti makes explicit the connections in her 1988 novel *Plumas de España* [Spanish plumes]. Almodóvar exploits it constantly in his films. Lo cursi in the nineteenth century was attached to the feminine, the provincial, and the inadequate. Kitsch and camp (and, to a lesser extent, lo cursi) in post-Franco Spain often carry attributes of the effeminate or feminizing, the subordinate, and the disempowered. Chroniclers of the movida, however, have recognized the liberating role of homosexuals in creating the conditions for the phenomenon (Gallero 21).

Whether projected onto the gay world, transvestism, or some other cultural image of difference, kitsch—like camp and cursi—constitutes a narrative of exceptionality, in that it points to the empowering difference of marginality, rendering such narratives symbolically significant. But kitsch as debased myth also disempowers, in that it discloses through figures of marginality the inadequacies, betrayed ideals, or impossibility of the master-narrative of utopia. Utopia as a grand narrative of liberation and self-realization goes underground, gets buried when the weight of its metaphorical and symbolic impossibility becomes too much to bear.[29] It gets translated into images of death because feeling itself is also being buried. The fear of death that lies behind kitsch as a powerful cultural metaphor enables kitsch to neutralize deeper, less acceptable feelings. This is what Saul Friedlander calls "affect neutralization," referring to explanations that turn "into rationalization that normalizes, smooths, and neutralizes our vision of the past" (102). Kitsch, taken in its broadest context as debased myth, also neutralizes the present by offering a distancing screen on which to project a protective coating over feeling and the inability to handle it.

Francisco Umbral's *Y Tierno Galván ascendió a los cielos* (1990) is a good example of this fractured or truncated utopian narrative in which large and small narrative units are confused and ultimately fused into one without, however, necessarily creating a unified master-narrative. Umbral begins with Francisco Franco's death in November 1975 and ends with Tierno Galván's in January 1986. Narrative symmetry is not meant, however, to suggest circular repetition so much as to imply difference within sameness. Both deaths for Umbral signal the end of an era. Franco's death means the loss of oppositionality. Tierno's, the loss of utopia. Enrique Tierno Galván's Madrid mayorship was widely regarded as a consolation prize, but Tierno turned it into something else. Along the way, he also turned himself into something else. He more than assumed a new role. José Luis López Aranguren put his finger on it when he spoke of "a veritable *transpersonalización*, or transmutation of person-

ality, the assumption of a different and new personality" (26).[30] In constructing a new persona as mayor of Madrid, Tierno in some ways was a
living enactment of Spanish postmodernity. For many he became identified with la movida, even though some of its participants strongly contested that image. Quico Rivas refers to him as "that cynic Tierno, who is
another of the movida myths . . . A cynic as plain as day, ambitious, a
demagogue and populist. . . . And yes, a great public relations man" (qtd.
in Gallero 91).[31] For others like Juan Luis Cebrián (and Umbral himself),
Tierno represented the revitalization of Madrid and the democratization
of culture and urban life (see Gallero 314).

In Umbral's book, subtitled "Memorias noveladas de la transición"
[Novelized memoirs of the transition], Tierno Galván's mayorship represents the utopian grand narrative; his death and funeral, the literal and
symbolic end of utopia. In fascinating (and at times repulsive) counterpoint we find another narrative: the personal rite de passage of Umbral as
chronicler/character, a narrative that serves as a deliberate debasement
of the utopian ideal. Umbral's experiences revolve around a series of
successively ditched girlfriends, who are, in turn, imaged as either ab-
normal or diseased bodies, as excessive bodies. His first girlfriend, Licaria, possesses a body that is "ephebic and adolescent, as if suffering
from a false adolescence" (23).[32] This same body undergoes an illegal
abortion and later overdoses, along with Sabela, her lesbian lover. Umbral's view of the dead couple is both distanced and intrusively voyeuris-
tic: "Licaria and Sabela weren't stretched out on the bed but seemed
thrown there, naked and drunk. There was nothing pathetic about their
death. They seemed like two plaster molds left over and abandoned on
the debris of the sheets. I thought I saw in them a certain erotic gesture,
the halted or imagined sweep of one last caress" (97).[33]

His second girlfriend, Gualberta, contracts hepatitis B, and Umbral
remarks, "Every great love affair generally ends in hepatitis B. Real or
invented. I dropped Gualberta in a flash" (114).[34] The third, Estebanía—
"postmodern," "Post/Everything"—binges on food and then disgorges
it. At one point Umbral suddenly finds himself cured of his love for her,
"as when, one day, Swann arises and he is cured of Odette. Estebanía
remained, within my amnesia, eternally vomiting her green voracity, her
voracious biography, the young, hungry, barking dog of her scrawny,
pale insides. Eternally" (160).[35]

These overflowing bodies are not alone in their diseased excessiveness. Franco's protracted dying forms the substratum of Umbral's vision of utopia: "Utopia had just been born out of the puddle of blood and shit that Franco's body left beneath the bed" (18).[36] Tierno's triumphant utopian passage through Umbral's book is finally punctured by disease. Like Umbral's ultimate erasure of the female body, Tierno's veiled denial of illness (cancer) negates his body and displaces feeling onto another plane: "Along the Castellana, Tierno and I strolled, and there was so much death in the air that the mayor began to talk to me of his illnesses. Small pains, weakness, that kind of thing" (151). Umbral continues, "Tierno spoke to me of vague discomfort, the doleful demands of one's organism." (152).[37]

The grand narrative of utopia is couched in different terms. "Tierno, when he was mayor," Umbral writes, "did Carrillo [the leader of the Spanish Communist Party] one better in realizing intuitively how to make general Utopia concrete, as a local Utopia of Madrid."[38] He goes on to say, "Tierno Galván made his present utopian, civil, real, collective, spectacular and enlightened, youthfully Jovellanos-like, as though coming from a drugged-out, fucking, incendiary Jovellanos. Tierno would end up becoming [you'll see everything in this book] a Marxist Charles III, a beardless Marx, an unwrinkled Azaña and, I insist on this, a red Jovellanos, postrevolutionary and anarchist, reigning over an immense soirée of chestnut sellers" (43).[39]

Umbral's pervasive irony colors this and other passages in praise of local utopias—a contradiction in terms—but it does not allow readers to dismiss his vision of utopia. When Tierno is ill, the utopian gesture incarnated in the mayor's magical right hand, earlier described as a relic (101), turns eucharistic: "The hermetic thinker had decided to dissipate himself eucharistically among the people" (153).[40] Tierno had become "the inner man who decides to exteriorize himself through a kind of Eucharistic Utopia" (152).[41] The mayor's body is now decorporalized, his "transmutation" as Aranguren saw it, nearly complete.

When Tierno is buried, Umbral equates it with "the end of Utopia." "The Transition has ended and Utopia has died," he writes (165).[42] But utopia is breaking up even before Tierno's death in Umbral's narrative, as when the chronicler views on television Tejero's February 1981 eruption into the parliament, and history once more becomes "mute, annulled, abolished" (82). "Thanks to that unexpected, clandestine, and interrupted filming [of the February event]," he remarks, "we ended up with the live broadcast image of Spain's breakup" (84).[43]

The more profound fracturing of utopia in Umbral's book emerges from the continuing eruption of the body into utopia. Tierno's grand passage through the narration, his peripatetic conversations with Umbral, his funeral coach slowly advancing toward the cemetery, can be seen, literally and figuratively, as a moving metaphor of historic significance.[44] But it is interlaced with smaller narratives that are treated with cynical detachment. Umbral's feelings remain removed from his own life story and displaced or projected onto the grand narrative of utopia, incarnated in Tierno Galván, the master-narrative of emancipation, which at the individual, personal level has been reduced to episodes of hedonistic though ultimately unsatisfying pleasure. Umbral's narrative and metaphorical use of the female body, and of his relationship with women, represents the utopia of emancipation in degraded form. In this sense, his petit récit constitutes a form of kitsch, and the bodies and pleasures recounted therein represent kitschified impersonations and pseudo-experiences. The real failure in this text is not Tierno's or even history's, but Umbral's: it is his failure to come to grips with his own feelings.

What precisely Umbral is mourning or neutralizing through metaphorical displacement and distancing remains, to me at least, unclear. The end of utopia, the fear of death, are themselves screens for something buried more deeply than memory cares to unearth. And what this latest form of cultural subjectivity means for a postmodern or any other kind of society is another story for another time.

Umbral's chronicle is a fractured grand narrative of Madrid, but is it also one of Spain? The question is not easy to answer. Umbral seems almost entirely wrapped up in the life of the capital and his role within it. His view of the televised attempted coup in 1981, for example, which he sees, literally, from between the legs of his lover, that is, in a very concrete, localized fashion, mordantly punctuates his quasi-solipsistic state. On the other hand, Madrid still dominates the rest of Spain, despite the presence of the various regional autonomies. In that sense, Madrid stands in for Spain in Umbral's chronicle, but the vision he gives of both has a strangely hometown air about it. De Certeau argued that city life is "an immense social experience of lacking a place." Pedestrian movements, he said, "are not localized" but, rather, "spatializ[ed]" (97, 103). Yet neither Umbral's perceptions of Madrid nor the context of the movida phenomenon itself seem delocalized. Tierno Galván's remark that to be an effective big city mayor "you have to act like the mayor of a small town" (qtd. in Darnton A2) is apropos here.

Nevertheless, some of the contradictions of a movida both local and postmodern, and of a mayor both small-town and cosmopolitan, are apparent. If you have to act like a small town mayor, you aren't small-town. Similarly, the pervasive use of kitsch by participants of the movida like Almodóvar and Rossetti suggests both a postmodernist self-consciousness (role-playing) and an excess of self-identification with things Spanish (or madrileño), with the local. Movida participants like Umbral almost seem as if they are "playing" at being modern, a condition in which the elements of both the homegrown and the cosmopolitan (read Western or European) share equally. But it is an uneasy mix, just as the relationship between the national and the foreign was in the nineteenth century.

Thus, as I reach the conclusion of this book, there is an odd sense of continuity flowing from the nineteenth to the late twentieth century, which issues out of the experience of uneven modernity.[45] In this regard, it is useful to remember that the phenomenon is not unique to Spain. Raymond Williams observes that

> within Europe itself there was a very marked unevenness of development, both within particular countries, where the distances between capitals and provinces widened, social and culturally, in the uneven developments of industry and agriculture, and of a monetary economy and simple subsistence or market forms. Even more crucial differences emerged between individual countries, which came to compose a new kind of hierarchy, not simply, as in the old terms, of military power, but in terms of development and thence of perceived enlightenment and modernity. (*The Politics of Modernism* 44)

In this, modern Spain has largely found itself to be out of place and out of synch historically and culturally within the European hierarchy noted by

Williams—hence the sense of cultural datedness and inadequacy frequently observed by both Spaniards and non-Spaniards.

Spain's conflicted relationship with modernity can be viewed through the metaphor of identity and change that the phenomenon of cursilería represents. Cursilería, while a sign of marginality, proves central to understanding the process of modernity in nineteenth- and twentieth-century Spain. Michael Holquist points out that "fundamental differences among societies can be grasped only by looking at the stories people tell themselves about themselves—and about others—that define them *as* selves" (10). Lo cursi forms a significant part of that developing narrative of middle-class and national identity in modern Spain. It is symptomatic of how the peripheral and the marginal—starting literally in the provinces (Cádiz)—have been instrumental in creating a larger, at times even national, sense of identity, at once collective and individual, often class- and gender-bound, that has been and become modern despite itself.

Because this book has dealt with both the inner and outer worlds of experiencing modernity, I have at times highlighted personal, concrete experiences, mediated mostly through written and other texts; at other times, I have focused on more publicly historical conditions, as garnered from collectively occurring socioeconomic, cultural changes. In either case, I have tried to situate Spanish middle-class identity within a specific historical and cultural context, but through the use of a loosely fitted structure of feeling in order to indicate incipient change in attitudes and behavior. That structure of feeling is often but not solely manifested in the subjective relationship between persons and things, objects as varied as the language of fans and flowers, albums and poetic homages, society chronicles and poetry recitations, or hairwork and women's fashions. In telling this particular story, I hope that a different, more complex object of study will also have emerged from my analysis: a notion of inner change—which is also historical—that one can see as a kind of narrative object in which narrative—not always written out—is instrumental in shaping experience, transforming feeling, and crystallizing (or rupturing) identities.

These stories of cursilería, which are narratives of identity, in the end have to do primarily with home, with finding a place in a constantly changing world. But home, whatever one calls it—Madrid or Granada,

19. Illustration
by Eusebio Planas
for *El libro de la
familia*, by Juan
Cortada. Barcelona:
Biblioteca Ilustrada de
Espasa Hermanos,
1864.

the local, the feminine, or domestic life itself—ultimately remains something intangible, something that only the imagination and sentiment can
grasp. An illustration like the one adorning *El libro de la familia* [The
book of the family] from 1864 simply reinforces, through its very cursilería, how inadequate most images were as full expressions of this sense
of home (see fig. 19). In this regard, the structures of feeling that have
delicately threaded their way through this book are like the nineteenth-
century phantasmagoria projecting the illusion of shape and story. They
occupy an indefinable middling ground as uncertain and indistinct as the
middle classes themselves. And they have no more—and no less—reality
than the phantasmagoric desire that drives the middle classes toward
realizing their place in the world.

This place, or identity, for the middle classes in Spain has emerged
from the experience and history of local, provincial life. But the relationship between the middle classes and the provinces is not, as we have seen,
a simple one. Cursilería became endemic in nineteenth-century Spain
when local life could no longer be taken as an unchanging given, when

local life was insufficient to define persons or social classes. As lo cursi became identified with the quintessentially provincial, home and identity began to be experienced in forms of increasing displacement, in the stories of cursilería encountered in Galdós, Llanas Aguilaniedo, Valle-Inclán, Lorca, and others. Historically, the movement of more and more people to the cities replicated in physical terms this emotional displacement. Ironically, finding home in the late nineteenth and early twentieth centuries meant reinstituting lo cursi, once seen mostly in a negative light, as a symbolic and nostalgic hominess, brilliantly recreated in Gómez de la Serna's verbal imagination. The Madrid movida, in turn, converted nostalgia for lo cursi into a self-conscious kitsch screen of local identity and culture making. Cursilería had, by then, long achieved visibility in the capital, as Galdós shrewdly analyzes in his middle-class families and characters. By Galdós's time too, the association between Madrid and lo cursi was entrenched, indicating, if not a provincialization of the capital, certainly a nationalization of the phenomenon of cursilería. Thus the provincial character of lo cursi not only forges a link between middle-classness in Spain and national identity, but suggests an odd paradox: the paradox of the provincial as a defining moment in modernity.

A Enrique Tierno Galván, dondequiera que esté.
To Enrique Tierno Galván, wherever he may be.

No es por cierto la tarea más enfadosa ni difícil el buscar *un cursi* por esas calles de Dios, pues que de ellos está plagado mi pueblo, a pesar de su hermoso clima, como dicen que dicen los extranjeros, cuando hablan de Cádiz. ¿Y qué tiene que ver el clima con los cursis? Nada, pero vamos al caso.

Como cada uno pienso que ha de figurarse al *cursi* de su manera; diré yo como me lo presenta la fantasía, por ver si acierto, lo cual en otro caso me es indiferente.

El *cursi* mío es delgado más bien que grueso; su ropa, particularmente el frak o levita siempre le está estrecha, sus toquillas y chalecos los usa de colores fuertes, y en todo su equipaje se notan síntomas de raído, así como en su aire algo de lo que llamamos *recortado*.

El destino de mi *cursi* es el siguiente. Va a un baile, y se pone a *media vela* con viso malo. Disputa con el mozo acerca de la vuelta, y esto a gritos para que se entere el público. Se encara con la orquesta pidiéndole que toque lo contrario a lo que está dispuesta. No pierde nada de lo que se baile, desde el primer wals hasta la greca inclusive. Toca las palmas, en la contradanza española para llevar el compás en ciertas figuras, y en el rigodón para aplaudir a su compañera. Sale del baile con la careta al revés, vestido de trapos y con una máscara del brazo. Al pedir su capa en el guardarropa, empuja a los demás que esperan, y se hace el gracioso. En el teatro principal es siempre de la comisión de aplausos; y en el del Balón se empeña además en disputar con los municipales, por subir a la cazuela y fumar donde está prohibido. En las funciones religiosas, está en la puerta de modo que impida el paso a las señoras al salir de la iglesia, y les dice *bromitas verdes*, siempre de mal gusto y fuera del caso. Está en todas partes donde hay bullas, dispuesto a incomodar lo posible. En la feria es un mueble preciso, y allí suele llevar algunas fraternas, de que él se desentiende para evitar que pasen a vías de hecho. En los toros es de la oposición, y lleva palo grueso para hacer más ruido: pide *caballos*, grita *a la cárcel*, y luego goza contando sus proezas. Generalmente habla mal de las mujeres, y bien de nada ni de nadie. En cuanto apunta el verano se cala las gafas verdes. Es un padrastro para toda reunión, un ente inútil para la buena sociedad.

—"Un cursi," *La estrella* (Cádiz) 25 Dec. 1842: 201.

NOTES

INTRODUCTION

1. See Tarín. For the death and funeral of Tierno Galván, I have relied on accounts from *El país* (Madrid) and *Ya* (Madrid).

2. Francisco Umbral saw it differently; for him, the funeral carriage was "elegant and mysterious" (*Y Tierno Galván* 165).

3. As Tomas Kulka notes, "making use of kitsch is not the same as making kitsch" (9), especially in the arts; see also Santos 209–10.

4. See Botrel and Le Bouil (146), who are unable to date the first hispanized usages of *burguesía* in Spain, but note its appearance (as *burguesia* and *burgeoise*) in Angel Fernández de los Ríos's *Guía de Madrid* (1876) (762–63); also Cavillac, who discusses an 1828 translation of *Gil Blas*, in which "une petite bourgeoise" is turned into "cierta señorita de la clase media" (455).

5. *Clase*, in a meaning close to current usage, does, however, appear in legal documents having to do with sumptuary laws and burial in the eighteenth century. See Goldman 7–16.

6. Original: "una multitud de jóvenes, nacidos en diferentes cunas y provincias."

7. Original: "[el Marqués] sabía de cuánta importancia era para un estado monárquico oponerse a la confusión de las condiciones y las clases."

8. Original: "si hay en España clase media, industrial, fabril y comercial, no se busque en Madrid, sino en Barcelona, en Cádiz."

9. Original: "lo que llamamos *pueblo bajo* ha menguado en calidad y en cantidad, como ha decaído en riqueza y autoridad la aristocracia. Las clases medias absorben visiblemente a las extremas; fenómeno que en parte se debe a los progresos de la civilización, en parte al influjo de las instituciones políticas." See Botrel and Le Bouil 141, for more references.

10. See also Stephanie Sieburth's stimulating analysis of late modernization in Spain in *Inventing High and Low: Literature, Mass Culture, and Uneven Modernity in Spain.*

11. Original: "La cursi por excelencia viste siempre con atraso respectivamente a la moda más generalizada, y nótese que no viste nunca con arreglo a una moda que pasó, sino que se engalana con prendas que pertenecen a distintas épocas, y entre aquellas suele haber una que nunca ha sido moda: creación propia y exclusiva de la persona que la usa."

12. Original: "se ha ido extendiendo por las inferiores primero y por las superiores después . . . la cursi es un producto de la confusión de clases."

13. Original: "una clase de gente fina en la apariencia, y sin duda en el fondo, pero de condición menos noble y de ocupaciones más mecánicas, a quienes se distingue en Andalucía con el raro nombre de *cursis.*"

14. Original: "Somos unas pobres cursis. Las cursis nacen, y no hay fuerza humana que les quite el sello. Nací de esta manera y así moriré. Seré mujer de otro cursi y tendré hijos cursis."

15. As Felski remarks, "the petite bourgeoisie is peculiarly resistant to the romance of marginality" (42).

16. For studies of lo cursi transplanted within the Cuban, Mexican, and Argentinian contexts, see: Ichaso; Monsiváis; Fournier; Roland; Capdevila; Torres Fierro; and Peri Rossi. Also worth noting are Mexican writer José Emilio Pacheco's poem, "Homenaje a la cursilería" (mistranslated, in my view, as "Homage to Kitsch"); novels by Manuel Puig, which explore first-generation, middle-class Argentinians whose immigrant origins and traditions have been replaced by unreal, inappropriate models of culture and behavior (*Boquitas pintadas; La traición de Rita Hayworth*); and Elena Castedo's *Paradise* (1991), in which Spanish Republican exiles come up against the cursilería of 1940s Latin American middle-classness. "*Cursi,*" she writes, "was the worst thing in the world: gold-trimmed figurines of little shepherds; sugary violin music; lots of big words pronounced slowly . . . ; bouquets in your sofas, drapes, pictures, vases and rugs. After meeting cursi people, you laughed at them; they were not to be considered" (126). A belated, self-conscious use of the term *cursi* appears in Felipe Alfau's 1992 *La poesía cursi*, translated in a bilingual edition as *Sentimental Songs*. There are, of course, also related terms, country-specific, to indicate the socially unacceptable, pretentious, or ridiculous, such as *lo picúo* in Cuba and *lo huachafo* in Peru (see Ichaso 148–52; Santos 99–100).

17. See Titus Suck, who remarks: "The *homme civilisé* thus is an expression of a synthesis between older and new social ideals, a symbiosis between a new, economically active bourgeoisie and an enlightened aristocracy, which is itself characteristic of the historically flexible relation between bourgeoisie and dominant aristocracy in France. The practice of *Kultur*, on the other hand, shows different determinations. Above all it shows no continuity with aristocratic values, and expresses the specifically bourgeois sensibilities and culture of a rising, by and large university-educated intelligentsia" (1091–92). An enlightened, courtly society existed in eighteenth-century Spain but does not appear to have caught on or persisted in the next century.

18. See Pereda's satire of the type in his *Los hombres de pro* (1876). The medieval hombre de pro, generally of noble blood, was defined as a man of virtue, loyalty, and courage in battle. The nineteenth-century, middle-class version, however, revealed a significant gap between private virtue (honor) and public virtue (social status) in exploiting privileged circumstances for private gains.

19. Jover, among others, urges caution in the application of this term to nineteenth-century Spain since *bourgeoisie* corresponds to a developed industrial society, not produced in Spain at that time. But as Jover himself says: "Lo más significativo del período es, sin embargo, el auge de las *instituciones bancarias* y *financieras*, a cuya sombra crecerá una de las más típicas *élites* de la España isabelina: la nueva burguesía de negocios" (the most significant thing about the period is, however, the rise of the *financial* and *banking*

institutions, in whose shadow one of the most typical of Isabeline Spain's *elites* will flourish: the new bourgeoisie of business) ("Edad contemporánea" 621). This new class was along the lines of the Second Empire's *bourgeoisie des affaires.*

20. Orig. in *Times Higher Education Supplement* 14 May 1976: 14. Of the lower middle class, Crossick notes that "the absence of dynamic activity, the lack of cohesion and the quest for individual status that is so easy to parody can not themselves justify that neglect [by historians], for it is partly through these weaknesses that the lower middle class has exerted its specific influence upon British social development" (52). Felski, over twenty years later, echoes this position: "It is surely time for scholars to think more carefully about their portrayal of the petite bourgeoisie" (44).

21. See also Jover, "Por una historia" 307–34; and Williams, *Keywords* 87–93, who notes the varied usages of the term *culture* in different intellectual disciplines, stressing that it is "the range and overlap of meanings that is significant." The "many unresolved questions and confused answers," he says, "cannot be resolved by reducing the complexity of actual usage" (91).

22. For a discussion of Corominas and other critics on the etymological origins of the term *cursi,* see chapter 1 of this book.

23. Peter Sahlins stresses that "states did not simply impose their values and boundaries on local society. Rather, local society was a motive force in the formation and consolidation of nationhood and the territorial state" (8). It is useful to bear in mind that even France, traditionally regarded as a strongly defined, centralized nation-state, still had a rich diversity of provincial life and identity in the nineteenth century. See Zeldin's illuminating *France, 1848–1945,* vol. 2, ch. 2.

24. Original: "Ahora existe lo cursi; que no es lo bueno ni lo malo, ni lo que divierte ni lo que aburre; es . . . una negación: lo contrario de lo distinguido."

25. See Ringrose 55–80, for an excellent synthesis of nineteenth-century Spain's economic development.

26. Spain is not unique in this regard. Theodore Zeldin observes that "the inferiority complex of provincials in this period is one of the most important and deceptive factors in the image that France had as a nation" (29).

I. ON ORIGINS

1. For the various accounts of lo cursi, see Silvela and Liniers, Ichaso, Anderson Imbert, Roland, Fernández Almagro, and Tierno Galván's brilliant sociological analysis of the phenomenon. Ramón Gómez de la Serna's wonderfully personal essay on lo cursi deserves special attention, which I give in chapter 7. Recent interpretations include Margarita Rivière's *Lo cursi y el poder de la moda* (1992) and Carlos Moreno Hernández's *Literatura y cursilería* (1995). After I finished this book, I ran across Andrés Holguín's insightful remarks on lo cursi, in which he notes that "no hay ningún concepto unívoco que, aislado, sirva para definir *lo cursi*. Ninguna palabra es sinónima suya" (there is

no single concept which, by itself, serves to define *lo cursi*. No word is synonymous with it) (131).

2. For anthropological work on the "structure of feeling," see the studies by James W. Fernandez, Michelle Rosaldo, David Gilmore, and Stanley Brandes cited in my bibliography.

3. See note 2 above; also, Lutz; S. Stewart; Lakoff and Johnson, for examples.

4. "We will never find an adequate fit between the anthropologist's text and the literary critics', between a contemporary culture that has been the subject of anthropological study and a cultural artifact" (Greenblatt, "The Eating of the Soul" 97).

5. "If the referent of a narrative is indeed the tropological structure of its discourse, then the narrative will be the attempt to account for this fact" (de Man 22). To be fair, White's claims only presume to apply to Freud.

6. "Tropes, as their name implies," de Man writes, "[are] always on the move" (16).

7. See Derrida's "Le retrait de la métaphore" and "White Mythology."

8. It is difficult if not impossible in ordinary parlance to distinguish to anyone's satisfaction between *feeling* and *emotion* (*sentimiento* and *emoción* are also similar in Spanish). Although Ricoeur attempts to do so by contrasting "poetic feelings" with "bodily emotions," even he ultimately collapses the two in conceiving of feeling as metamorphosed emotion ("The Metaphorical Process" 155).

9. See the analysis of Heidegger's metaphorically embedded language in Derrida's "Le retrait de la métaphore."

10. Felipe Picatoste in "¡Pobres burgueses!" (1892) energetically defends the Spanish middle classes who he says are constantly being attacked and satirized by the lowest kind of journalism and literature (165). Carlos Frontaura's feeling of sympathy for individuals and families who have come down in the world ("Tipos madrileños: Las señoritas cursis," 1886) is preceded by similar sentiments in Roberto Robert's costumbrista sketch of 1871 ("La señorita cursi") and even earlier in F. de Paula Madrazo (*Dos meses en Andalucía*, 1849).

11. Original: "la extraña poesía de las cosas vulgares . . . ¡Oh modestos acordeones! Vosotros sois de nuestra época: humildes, sinceros, dulcemente plebeyos, quizá ridículamente plebeyos; pero vosotros decís de la vida lo que quizá la vida es en realidad: una melodía vulgar, monótona, ramplona ante el horizonte ilimitado."

12. Original: "Al revés que la ternura es la nostalgia hacia dentro, dolor, y hacia fuera, placer."

13. Original: "A mí me encantan los perros. Yo soy un cursi. Esta facilidad que poseo de encogérseme el corazón ante cosas que a muchas personas les dejan indiferentes, es una cursilería. . . . Yo pertenezco a la clase de los insignificantes, de los cursis."

14. Original: "un perro cursi, pero muy satisfecho de la existencia, canelo, insignificante [que] pasó por allí" (Alas, "Superchería" 92).

15. Original: "la pista del perro canelo, que tomaba los *fenómenos* como lo que eran, como una . . . superchería" (Alas, "Superchería" 94).

16. I refer to the character Santos Barinaga in *La Regenta* who dies of hunger and neglect amid a stream of banalities and clichés from fellow Vetustans who do nothing to help him. Clarín turns the cliché, "moría como un perro" (he died like a dog), into a literal one of Darwinistic significance, when not only Santos but also an old dog dies.

17. Original: "¡Pues, sí, soy español, español de nacimiento, de educación, de cuerpo, de espíritu, de lengua y hasta de profesión y oficio; español sobre todo y ante todo, y el españolismo es mi religión, y el cielo en que quiero creer es una España celestial y eterna, y mi Dios un Dios español, el de Nuestro Señor Don Quijote; un Dios que piensa en español y en español dijo: ¡sea la luz!, y su verbo fue verbo español."

18. Original: "Esta mi vida mansa, rutinaria, humilde, es una oda pindárica tejida con las mil pequeñeces de lo cotidiano. ¡Lo cotidiano! ¡El pan nuestro de cada día dánosle hoy!"

19. Original: "una inmensa niebla de pequeños incidentes. Y la vida es esto, la niebla. La vida es una nebulosa."

20. Original: "En ella [la clase media] se engendran los talentos sin fortuna, los hombres sin nombre, los apellidos *originales;* apellidos que hay que hacer, porque los ascendientes, que no leían periódicos, no se cuidaban de semejante cosa."

21. See Adrian Shubert's introduction to his *Social History of Spain* for an overview.

22. See Bretón de los Herreros's social satire, *A Madrid me vuelvo,* for an 1828 reference to the Old Christian lineage of the character Esteban: "muy rico, / de esclarecido linaje, / cristiano viejo" (very rich, / of illustrious lineage, / an Old Christian) (33). I came across prescriptions of blood purity in a text published as late as 1853. The book, *Instructorio espiritual de los Terceros, Terceras y Beatas de Ntra. Señora del Carmen,* by Fr. Manuel de Santa Teresa, was published in Mexico, but is clearly a Spanish text written in an earlier period. Chapter 11 contains a series of questions seeking information on the background of candidates to this religious order, such as: "Si saben que los Padres, Abuelos o Visabuelos del Pretendiente, no descienden de Judíos, Moros, Cismáticos, Herejes, ni de Penitenciados por el Santo Oficio de la Inquisición, o por otros Jueces públicamente afrentados" (If they know whether the parents, grandparents or great grandparents of the candidate descend from Jews, Moors, Schismatics, Heretics, or Penitents publicly condemned by the Holy Inquisition or by other Tribunals) (86).

23. See Bourdieu. José Martí comments on a similar situation in Cuba in his 1885 novel, *Lucía Jerez [Amistad funesta]*. There is now, he writes, an "aristocracia del espíritu" (an aristocracy of the spirit) with social pretensions that include dressing their children well so as to reveal "la distinción del alma" (the distinction of the soul) (111).

24. I am relying here on distinctions and categories that Pierre Bourdieu, Tom Lutz, and Kathleen Stewart discuss in their cultural analyses of distinction, American nervousness, and postmodern nostalgia, respectively.

25. Observers of the current Spanish scene informally suggest that the word *hortera* (with roots in the nineteenth century) may be replacing *cursi.* In Antonio Flores's 1843 satiric sketch "El hortera," an ambitious *hortera,* or store clerk, aspires to being a "new capitalist" and has aristocratic social pretensions.

26. Original: "El gabinete [de Agripina] . . . sería hoy *cursi* seguramente, ante el de la esposa de cualquier director de un *crédito mobiliario.*"

27. Original: "Carretela, / mamá: la berlina es cúrsi; / . . . ¡berlina con una yegua!" I am grateful to José Manuel González Herrán for providing me with a copy of this play, privately printed in 1869.

28. Original: "Esto es contra la liturgia del buen tono. Una dama elegante podrá prodigar todos sus favores a un caballero; pero no bailará con él cinco veces. Hacerlo así le parecería soberanamente ridículo, o *cursi.*" The anonymous review appeared in *El contemporáneo* (Madrid) (22 Dec. 1861). My thanks to David Gies for pointing out this reference to me. See also Gies's impressively researched *The Theatre in Nineteenth-Century Spain*, 274–75, for more on *La cruz del matrimonio*.

29. In the same year Silvela, who later earned the nickname "Cursilvela," also published *Los neo-cultos*, an attack on various kinds of pretentious and mannered writings, ranging from academic discourses to low-brow journalism: "La moda, tal como existe ya, nos parece fea, y además, como todos los colorines brillantes y baratos, lleva consigo el peligro inevitable de hacerse *cursi* en muy pocos días" (This fashion, such as it is now, is in my view an unattractive one, and besides, like all things colored cheaply brilliant, carries with it the inevitable risk of becoming *cursi* in very short order) (26). See also Zamora Vicente's edition of Valle-Inclán's *Luces de bohemia* (76, n.17).

30. Original: "Aunque entre los revolucionarios de septiembre hay muchos de buena fe, pero alucinados sin linaje de duda, no cabe en lo posible negar, que la revolución a quien sirven, es impía, y además es *CURSI.*" The article from which I cite and which appeared in the neo-Catholic, absolutist newspaper, *La regeneración* (Madrid) in 1870, repeats the word *cursi* eight times, always in capital letters.

31. See Robert, "La señorita cursi"; Prugent, "La cursi"; C. Gil, "El sastre" 331; Moreno Godino, "La modista" 318; and, from the collection *Madrid por dentro y por fuera*, Asmodeo, "Un gran baile" 146–47; 149; Corzuelo, "La misa de una" 251; Moja y Bolívar, "La romería de San Isidro" 163; de Cortázar, "El Cotillon" 350; Robert, "El Suizo viejo" 15; 21; de Lustonó, "El lipendi" 224.

32. In *El escándalo* Alarcón observes that the *Diccionario de la Real Academia Española* has included the term in its 1869 edition (2:91–92). See also *Nuevo manual de urbanidad*, citing from "María de la Peña": " 'Hija de la fortuna la palabra *cursi*, ha subido uno a uno los peldaños de la escala social, hasta ocupar puesto de honor en el Diccionario de la lengua. Como obscura mujercilla llega a las alturas de la grandeza por su natural donaire y la flaqueza del hombre' " (A daughter of fortune, the word *cursi* has climbed one by one the steps of the social ladder, until it now occupies a place of honor in the Dictionary of the Royal Academy. Like a woman of obscure origins, it has reached the pinnacle of greatness through its natural grace and the weakness of men) (96). The reference clearly marks an updating to the original 1850 edition.

33. See Boloix; González López; Larrubiera Crespo; and Taboada. Illustrators like Ramón Cilla and Angel Pons brought cursilería to graphic light; see Fernández Almagro,

"Las ilustraciones." Other examples of lo cursi may be found in: Segovia 227; Matoses; de la Torre 206; Frontaura; Valero de Tornos; and Sánchez Pérez. Marta Palenque (*Gusto poético*) observes that frequent mention of lo cursi is made in the popular *Ilustración española y americana* (151, n.146). David Gies has pointed out to me as well a reference to cursi in Luis Mariano de Larra's play, *Los corazones de oro* 22.

34. See Solís, "El romanticismo gaditano"; *Historia del periodismo gaditano 1800–1850;* and "La burguesía gaditana y el romanticismo."

35. J. M. Iribarren, *El porqué de los dichos;* Pedro M. Payán Sotomayor, *El habla de Cádiz;* and "Cursi," *Diccionario enciclopédico ilustrado de la provincia de Cádiz* 2 (1985) are the only sources—all of them meant for popular consumption—that cite Solís's discovery, but they do not study its implications and significance.

36. Millán Contreras (1946) appears to be the first to mention F. de Paula Madrazo's book. Margarita Rivière (1992) also refers to it (89), but notes merely that Madrazo's description has "an undoubted sociological interest" while suggesting possible "desclasamiento" (declassing). She makes no mention of the 1842 article in *La estrella*.

37. Madrazo says in his brief introduction to *Dos meses en Andalucía* that the articles comprising his book appeared in *La España* (Madrid) and were reprinted in *El comercio* (Cádiz) (9). Madrazo, who was born in Barcelona in 1817 and died in Madrid in 1868, was a stenography expert and author of a *Manual de administración* (1857).

38. Original: "Cubren con sus largos mantos las averías de su traje, que embellecido por tres volantes parece otra cosa de lo que realmente es."

39. Original: "las protagonistas de esos dramas de amor que se representan a la sombra del follaje."

40. Sánchez Guerrero's reply to Sbarbi, titled "Cursi," appeared in volume 2 of *El averiguador universal* (1880). I have not been able to locate this publication. Sbarbi's own *Florilegio o ramillete alfabético de refranes* (1873) (in which cursi appears) is also reprinted in *El averiguador universal* (1880).

41. See the article by de Luna; and Iribarren 523. Corominas skeptically wonders whether the Tessi Curt (or Court) aren't "a mere pseudoetymological myth" (2:301).

42. An embryonic version of J. de Burgos's *La familia de Sicur* (1899) first appeared in his *Las cursis burladas*, which played in Madrid and Cádiz in 1881. See also references in Mariano Barranco's *Los martes de las de Gómez* (1885) (6; 17); and, in a work I have not been able to see, Juan José Herranz y Gonzalo's *Los cursis*.

43. The distinguished physician Federico Rubio, who grew up in Cádiz, in *La mujer gaditana* (1902) also attributes the invention of the word *cursi* to the same Asturian medical student, "Zarandeses" (56). On the family name "Sarandeses" and connection with medicine, see Sarandeses Pérez; Suárez, 7; 83–84; and Tolivar Faes 209; 213.

44. Personal communication with Milad Doueihi (12 Mar. 1994), who notes that the surnames "Secour/Secourt/Secours" and "Sicour/Sicourt/Sicours" can be found in France. Haphazard Spanish pronunciation of French words could easily shift the "e" and "i" sounds around.

45. Original: "¡*Curr . . . sii!* (que fue como se pronunció en su origen y en mis tiempos, prolongando mucho la *r* de la primera sílaba y la *i* de la segunda)."

46. Under the entry for "dandi," Corominas (2:423) notes that he has heard the word pronounced "dandí" in Spain, which indicates to him that French mediated between the Spanish and the original English term.

47. Like *cursi, miau* has closely related phonetic connotations, as Pérez Galdós saw with devastating clarity in his 1888 novel of the same name.

48. This is also an example of what Hermann Broch calls the "non-style" of the late nineteenth century, an eclectic heaping together of styles, which for him represented the bourgeois mask of rationalization erasing the ugliness and horror of historical and social reality ("El arte").

49. Original: "combinaciones ingeniosas, hacían que dos solos vestidos pareciesen cuatro. Empleáronse a estilar entonces los boas de pieles, y ellas pusieron una trampa en el tejido y con ella cogieron suficiente número de gatos para fabricarse con sus pieles tres de aquellos adornos, que parecían de martas cibelinas."

50. Original: "creación propia y exclusiva de la persona que la usa . . . Esa prenda es una revelación; es el sello individual de cada una; ninguna cursi la copia de otra."

51. Roberto Robert notes: "Hay en toda cursi, hasta en la menos cursi, algo de origi-nalidad, si no en ideas, en aspiraciones y sentimientos, y no puede ser cursi la señorita que carezca de imaginación por completo" (There is in every cursi, even in the least cursi, an element of originality, if not in ideas, in aspirations and feelings; a young woman completely lacking in imagination cannot be considered *cursi*) ("La señorita cursi" 84).

52. For example, Schuchardt, who first noted the 1865 reference, rejects Lafuente's thesis as unfounded (265).

53. Original: "¿Por qué la palabra *cursi* no había de venir de cualquiera de estas islas, pueblos y colonias? Pero al mismo tiempo, ¿Por qué de estas y no de otras? ¿Y por qué no de ninguna? Este es el resultado práctico que se saca de todas las etimologías." *Coryce:* a promontory in Greece; *corucayos:* inhabitants of Coryce, known for their curiosity; *corosuna:* lively, gay youth; *Cursianum:* a fortress in Asia Minor; *Corsiae:* a Mediterranean island near Samos; *Corsia:* Corsica; *Cursus:* a village in Roman Iberia (see Liniers and Silvela 25).

54. Original: "¡Mal año para los etimologistas! Echense a revolver raíces y desinencias, barajen cuanto quieran copto y sánscrito, griego y hebreo, a ver si sacan en limpio de dónde nos vino el vocablo."

55. In a personal communication (29 Dec. 1989), Manuel García Castellón has noted a similar meaning for the Arabic word *kursî:* a small seat, often overdecorated in bad taste, designed for guests, and found in homes of modest means.

56. Original: "casi lindas, casi feas, saliendo del tiempo, como lentas serpientes." Ander-son Imbert, like Ichaso (159) before him, situates the Sicur family in Madrid, not in Cádiz (120). This change in locale may have occurred because, by the twentieth century, the

image of nineteenth-century cursilería had become strongly identified with the Spanish capital.

57. Original: "vocablos no cultos, formados por una concreción verbal, a veces caprichosa, del vulgo; pero casi siempre cargada de sentido común y de sorna."

58. See Lloréns 45–56. Raymond Williams in *Keywords* notes that the term *liberal* was "given, by its enemies, a foreign flavour" (180) in England, but he appears unaware of its earlier usage as a political party and ideological position in Spain.

59. Original: "El hijo del comerciante no hereda bienes sino créditos y posibilidades de comerciar."

60. See Castañeda y Alcover for more examples of handwriting manuals.

61. Original: "¿Y sabéis por qué era esa escuela [the Colegio de S. Felipe Neri] la mejor? Porque en ella se enseñaba el carácter de letra inglesa y además los quebrados comunes y las fracciones decimales."

62. Original: "Permitía a títulos y caballeros comerciar sin desdoro de su clase, pero invitaba también a los verdaderos burgueses a buscar las formas de vida propias del aristócrata."

63. I have not been able to find out where *piri* comes from. A local term, it appears to have died out sometime before the 1850s, although de Castro cites it in his 1857 "Diccionario de voces gaditanas."

64. Original: "Son los Piris, bien pintados, / Un compuesto de dos sexos."

65. A suspect term, the piri is related to two other social types, *el elegante* and *el flamante*. Rámon de Navarrete, in "El elegante" (1843), sees the type as a "ser indefinible" (an undefinable being) (403); and El-Modhafer, in *Diccionario de los flamantes* (1843), equates "flamante" with "elegante," "pedante e ignorante," as well as "marica," or effeminate, noting that such men wear corsets (qtd. in Castañeda y Alcover 241–42). All of these types have an antecedent in the eighteenth-century petimetre. See, for example, Ramón de la Cruz's *El petimetre;* and Rebecca Haidt's discussion of the figure in *Embodying Enlightenment* (ch.3) and in "Fashion, Effeminacy, and Homoerotic Desire."

66. Unfortunately, Solís only reprints part of the article, which has become blurred over time and nearly impossible to read in the yellowing, disintegrating pages of *ABC*. After completing this book, I did find another copy of "Un cursi," but once again, only the first page was available. I have marked the author as anonymous, but it is quite possible that the second, missing page indicates authorship. My heartfelt thanks go to David Herzberger for providing me with a copy of this reference. Because of its rarity and significance, I have reproduced the extant fragment of "Un cursi" in an appendix.

67. Original: "Cádiz fue en sus felices tiempos, cuando entraban en su puerto las flotas cargadas del oro de América, la cuna del lujo. . . . Hoy no es lo que fue un día. Han mudado mucho los tiempos; se han transformado las familias; han desaparecido algunos capitales. . . . una vida modesta y retirada ha sucedido en innumerables casas a una existencia de ostentación y de goces."

68. Original: "L'explication la plus plausible de cet anéantissement progressif du com-

merce de Cadix se trouve d'abord dans l'affaiblissement de son crédit. . . . on ne peut pas se le dissimuler, notre place est en Espagne même, la plus mal notée de toutes celles de la Péninsule. Son papier est le plus discrédité à la bourse de Madrid, et peu de personnes se hasardent aujourd'hui à l'accepter."

2. ADORNING THE FEMININE, OR THE LANGUAGE OF FANS

1. Original: "[La literata] aprende a escribir letra inglesa, porque es de forma más distinguida que la de las muestras de Iturzaeta."

2. Cotarelo y Mori, however, calls Naharro's penmanship style a "derivation" of the English hand (2:109).

3. Original: "la UNIFORMIDAD de un Caracter nacional distintivo, como le tienen las demás Naciones, y teníamos nosotros antes."

4. Original: "Razón por la que no se usa en escrituras, ni en protocolos que haya necesidad imperante de conservar en los archivos, siendo los comerciantes los que más la practican, por lo que puede considerarse su carácter de letra oficial en esta clase social."

5. At the 1867 Universal Exposition in Paris, Antonio Bastinos saw several Spanish calligraphy exhibits, singling out Castilla Benavides's collection of penmanship "que no ha obtenido premio y bien lo merecía, por haber hallado el medio de hacer más fácil la escritura española con una pequeña transacción con la inglesa" (which obtained no prize but richly deserved it, for having discovered a way to make the Spanish hand easier by adapting it to the English pen) (1:102).

6. My thanks to Dolores O'Connor for bringing this article to my attention.

7. Original: "muebles de lujo cursi y barato en una de esas solitarias calles de nuestras ciudades."

8. Original: "Adiós, castiza y grave letra española; pronto desaparecerás hasta de la valija de los carteros si continúa el insensible descastamiento de esta nación, que cada día se deja borrar alguno de los rasgos con que fue más conocida en el mundo."

9. Original: "En cuanto él veía en el papel de su propiedad los párrafos que iba copiando con aquella letra inglesa esbelta y pulcra que Dios le había dado, ya se le antojaba obra suya todo aquello" (*La Regenta* 1:260–61).

10. Original: "La esencia de lo cursi estaba en el excesivo temor de parecerlo." Clarín mistakenly identifies the Valera text as *Pepita Jiménez*. The source is actually *Las ilusiones del doctor Faustino.*

11. Santiago de Liniers is responsible for the first part of the *Filocalia*, which is dated 24 April 1868. Francisco Silvela wrote the "Reglamento instructivo para la constitución del Club de los Filócalos."

12. Original: "¿Qué es la *cursería*? ¿hasta dónde llegan las fronteras de ese poderosísimo imperio de la *Corsia*, cuyas invasiones crecen de día en día . . . ? ¿De dónde nace el mal? ¿cómo se comunica y cunde su contagio?"

13. Original: "El imperio de la *cursería* es uno de los peligros de la revolución. Significa la invasión por las masas del terreno artístico, poético, monumental e indumentario."

14. The classic modern statement on this subject is Walter Benjamin's "The Work of Art in the Age of Mechanical Reproduction."

15. Original: "Y es que todo se sabe, todo se ve, todo se desea, y hay la fantasmagoría de poseerlo todo: solo que la piedra es cartón, el diamante straus, el oro doublé y el roble pino pintado. . . . artistas de catálogo, literatos de sección amena, graciosos de gacetilla, elegantes de prendería, sois unos *cursis*."

16. Original: "cualidad derivada, una idea de relación que varía según los términos con que se compare."

17. I am indebted to Susan Stewart's stimulating approach to the narrative of objects as "a structure of desire . . . that both invents and distances its object and thereby inscribes again and again the gap between signifier and signified that is the place of generation for the symbolic" (*On Longing* ix).

18. Original: "tan vago e indefinible que depende casi siempre del criterio de las personas el hallarle o no hallarle en otros. Lo que sí ocurre por lo común es que las acusaciones son mutuas."

19. The hair picture is also, of course, as Hazel Gold observes in "Francisco's Folly: Picturing Reality in Galdós' *La de Bringas*," "an image of other images, a . . . pastiche of fanciful Romantic engravings, statues and paintings" (65). See chapter 4 of this book for a detailed analysis of the novel.

20. See Schor, *Reading in Detail*, for the relationship between ornament, detail, and the feminine; also, Gordon; Gold, "Small Talk: Towards a Poetics of the Detail in Galdós" 34; and Delgado, *La imagen elusiva* 56.

21. The familial resemblance between lo cursi and kitsch is evident here. As Milan Kundera writes in *The Unbearable Lightness of Being:* the "aesthetic ideal of the categorical agreement with being is a world in which shit is denied and everyone acts as though it did not exist. This aesthetic ideal is called *kitsch*." He also says: "kitsch is a folding screen set up to curtain off death" (248; 253). See also Merlino 38–42 (my thanks to Maite Zubiaurre for pointing out this reference to me).

22. Ichaso writes: "Lo cursi es lo *casi* bello y lo *casi* feo" (lo cursi is the *almost* beautiful and the *almost* ugly) (128).

23. Original: "El escritor de costumbres no escribe exclusivamente para esta o aquella clase de la sociedad."

24. Original: "Debe de estar como la mayor parte de los hombres, por de fuera encuadernado con un lujo asiático, y por dentro en blanco . . . lo más caro, lo más inglés, eso es lo mejor."

25. Original: "Es bueno advertir que una de las circunstancias que debe tener es que se pueda decir de él: 'Ya me han traído el *álbum* que encargué a Londres.' También se puede decir en lugar de Londres, París; pero es más vulgar, más trivial. Por lo tanto, nosotros

asconsejamos a nuestras lectoras que digan *Londres:* lo mismo cuesta una palabra que otra."

26. Original: "Ese librote es, como el abanico, como la sombrilla, como la tarjetera, un mueble enteramente de uso de señora, y una elegante sin *álbum* sería ya en el día un cuerpo sin alma, un río sin agua, en una palabra, una especie de Manzanares."

27. Original: "En su verdadero objeto es un repertorio de la vanidad."

28. Original: "son distintas fuentes donde se mira y se refleja un solo Narciso."

29. It should be pointed out, however, that even aristocrats possessed albums. One example listed as "Album de curiosidades" in the Biblioteca Nacional (Madrid) contains, for instance, watercolors by Vicente López and A. Gemoles (1850) and poems by J. Heriberto García de Quevedo ("A Helena," 1855), Ventura de la Vega ("Una cita en el campo"), Ramón de Navarrete ("A una rosa," 1855), the Duque de Rivas ("Lo pasado nada es ya"), and Pedro Madrazo ("Lamentación política de este álbum, dirigiéndose a su dueña," 1874). In "Soneto," Ramón Ceruti begins by saying: "Elenita: Aunque no soi [sic] poeta he querido consignar en este Album algo por lo que me recuerde V. mientras viva." He then copies a sonnet by the recipient's grandfather, Pedro Valencia (the Conde de Casa Valencia), who is also his friend. Here, the album appears both to symbolize the distinction of class and to confer distinction on its owner by conflating object (both the album and the poem) and person (Elena and her grandfather). The copyist also seems to derive some sort of vicarious distinction through the act of writing out the sonnet in Elena's album. See also Romero Tobar for other examples of aristocrats' albums ("Los álbumes de las románticas" 85).

30. Original: "El valor . . . de un *álbum* puede ser considerable; una pincelada de Goya, un capricho de David, o de Vernet, un trozo de Chateaubriand, o de lord Byron, la firma de Napoleón, todo esto puede llegar a hacer de un *álbum* un mayorazgo para una familia."

31. Original: "El *álbum* no se lleva en la mano, pero se transporta en el coche; el *álbum* y el *coche* se necesitan mutuamente . . . el *álbum* se envía además con el lacayo de una parte a otra. Y como siempre está yendo y viniendo, hay un lacayo destinado a sacarlo; el lacayo y el *álbum* es el ayo y el niño."

32. Even so, poet Manuel del Palacio at the end of the century would write nostalgically about how his own personal album dating from the 1850s was now in pieces or probably in the hands of autograph collectors ("Hojas de un álbum" 235). Larra appears to be the first in Spain to talk at length about the album fad, as Romero Tobar notes in his excellent study, "Los álbumes de las románticas" 76. See also Puyol; Esquer Torres; and Romero Tobar, "Manuscritos poéticos." An album held by the Díaz-Pérez family, which I examined, is typically leather-bound, with decorative metal clasps (4.5" × 6"), containing contributions from a Professor Mellado, Manuel del Palacio, Maestro Tomás Martín, and others, dried flowers sent by Tristán Medina from Switzerland in 1867, and sixteen photographs. It was compiled between the 1860s and 1890s. I am grateful to Rodrigo Díaz-Pérez for generously allowing me access to the album.

In America, Edgar Allan Poe popularized autograph collecting in a series of articles on literary autographs in 1836 and 1841–42. See Thornton's *Handwriting in America* for an engaging account of the autograph album (77; 86–88; 114–15).

The album craze had not completely faded away even in the 1930s. Lorca was feted, his autograph pursued for young girls' albums during his Montevideo visit in 1934 (see Anderson, "García Lorca en Montevideo" 176). Other examples of Lorca's album verses can be found in *Federico García Lorca: Trece de Nieve* 24; *Antología poética* 123; Forradellas 3; and Prieto 58. The poem in Prieto, "Balada del pastor sin rebaño," was probably written around 1921–22, but it appeared in María Asunción ("Chunchita") del Río's album in 1928 (personal communication from Christopher Maurer to Andrew Anderson; and from Anderson to me [5 Nov. 1990]). Lorca also poked fun at album verses. See "Baladilla de Eloísa muerta" (1921) ("Album blanco" 5). Closely related in spirit are the cursi postcards Dalí and his sister Ana María sent Lorca in 1927 (Santos Torroella 48–49; 63; 134; 137). Grateful thanks go to Andrew Anderson for providing and sorting out all these references.

33. Original: "Como el caso es tener un recuerdo, propio, intrínsecamente de la persona misma, es indispensable que lo que se estampe vaya de puño y letra del autor."

34. Original: "Un *álbum*, pues, viene a ser un *panteón* donde vienen a enterrarse en calidad de préstamos adelantados hechos a la posteridad una porción de notabilidades."

35. Original: "¿Qué es una bella sino un *álbum*, a cuyos pies todo el que pasa deposita su tributo de admiración? ¿Qué es su corazón muchas veces sino *álbum?* Perdónennos la atrevida comparación, pero ¡dichoso el que encuentra en esta especie de *álbum* todas las hojas en blanco! ¡Dichoso el que no pudiendo ser el primero (no pende siempre de uno el madrugar) puede ser siquiera el último!"

36. Original: "*¿De qué trata?* No trata de nada; es un libro en blanco."

37. Original: "colgado todo de sus trofeos; es su *lista civil*, su presupuesto, o por lo menos el de su amor propio."

38. Original: "Hemos reparado que todas las dueñas de *álbum* son hermosas, graciosas, de gran virtud y talento y amabilísimas."

39. Original: "Por el tiempo en que comienza esta fiel historia de sucesos reales, ya el álbum de versos y dibujos era cosa bastante desacreditada, y el abanico convertido en álbum, el colmo de lo cursi."

40. Original: "Lo que Julita Frondoso, anciana respetable, muy bien conservada, le pedía [al poeta] Ibáñez era, efectivamente, unos versos para un abanico de Luz. Luz tenía también álbum-abanico, o mejor, lo tenía su madre a nombre de Luz."

41. A. Escobar 263; Zozaya 45–46. See also Marrasquino; *Los abanicos: Su lenguaje expresivo. Con detalles de los alfabetos dactilológico y campilológico*, a compilation taken from the lengthy entry on fans in the *Diccionario enciclopédico hispano-americano* (1887); Almela Mengot; *Abanicos: La colección del Museo Municipal de Madrid;* and *Otros abanicos*, this last a catalogue of an exhibit that provoked criticism for being considered a frivolous misuse of government funds (see Sánchez Ferlosio 11–12; and Angeles García 34).

42. Original: "No se ha desterrado el vicio todavía; pero ya pasó aquel furor por recoger firmas de autores."

43. Original: "Debo recordar que los abanicos generalmente son de papel, y este papel por uno de los lados suele estar pintarrajeado con asuntos campestres, y por el otro queda en blanco."

44. Original: "Mientras el álbum ha pasado a ser una prenda *cursi*, el abanico es y seguirá siendo el más afortunado de los objetos."

45. Original: "álbum flotante del bello sexo, tarjeta que usa el genio para presentarse al mundo, el abanico brinda al vate desconocido perenne gloria y regalado aplauso."

46. Original: "En pintura [Julita] entró por el naturalismo primero que en literatura. En la época de los últimos resplandores de la hermosura de esta señora, empezaba el realismo a estar de moda en España."

47. Original: "*pedazos de la realidad* puestos en el lienzo. Daban ganas de ordeñarlas."

48. Original: "un molino cansado de moler, en ruinas por fuera y por dentro; la molinera vieja, la cítola gastada."

49. Original: "Aquel registro de notabilidades más o menos pasajeras siguió siendo la manía de Julita; los amantes variaban; la manía siempre era la misma."

50. Original: "Ibáñez estaba de moda, era entre místico y diabólico y con las señoras tenía mucho más partido que Trabanco había tenido en sus mejores tiempos. Además, vivía casi siempre en París o en Londres, y esto le refrescaba la fama como si fuera sal."

51. Original: "tal prenda no es / Sólo un artístico objeto, / Sino breve parapeto / O biombo japonés, / Donde se oculta el rubor, / Que es de la virgen divisa, / Y se esconde la sonrisa, / Que es un destello de amor."

52. Original: "Todo abanico es bello, porque siempre conserva huellas, perfumes, recuerdos de su dueña. Si el arte le hermosea, el abanico entonces es el consorcio de la belleza material y moral."

53. For examples, see Aza 11; Cano, "En el abanico de Concha" 82; Vidart 14; Sepúlveda 27; Urbano 136; Ossorio y Gallardo, "En el abanico de mi bella amiga" 192; Pérez Zúñiga 346.

54. Original: "La mujer andaluza necesita tanto el abanico como la lengua. Además, el abanico tiene una gran ventaja sobre el órgano natural del habla: la de transmitir el pensamiento a larga distancia."

55. Original: "Y el ser hechos a puño—los manuscritos o cursivos—y el ser hechos con pluma, y de acero, les ha dado su carácter, su estilo. Los mecanografiados, los de máquina, lo mismo que los de imprenta, son ya de imitación, carecen de estilo. Los grafólogos nada tienen que hacer con ellos. ¿Es que no hay también entre los hombres unos que tienen carácter mayúsculo, rectilíneo, grabado, y otros que tienen carácter minúsculo, curvilíneo, pintado?"

Shakespeare made the correspondences even more literal in his *Comedy of Errors:* "Say what you will, sir, but I know what I know. / That you beat me at the mart, I have your hand to show. / If the skin were parchment, and the blows you gave were ink, / Your own handwriting would tell you what I think" (279).

56. In a provocative study, Hazel Gold develops the museum mentality of collecting and exhibiting evident in several of Galdós's novels. See "A Tomb with a View" 312–34.

57. For further analogies between gossip and narrative, see Patricia Meyer Spacks's intriguing study, *Gossip*. Gossip also plays a pivotal role in Galdós's *Cánovas* (see chapter 5 of this book).

58. "Las dos o tres hojas de *La Época* se doblaban, primero, por la mitad en sentido de la latitud, y después, otra vez, formando ángulo recto con el pliegue anterior, de manera que parecía un folleto en un cuarto muy ampliado. *El Imparcial, El Liberal* y *El País* se doblaban dos veces en su anchura, formando una faja" (the two or three sheets of *La Época* were folded, first, in half and horizontally, and then again, forming a right angle to the first fold, so that it seemed like an enlarged quarto feuilleton. *El Imparcial, El Liberal,* and *El País* were folded two times widthwise, like a wrapper) (Araujo-Costa 187). Format aside, *La época* also weighed more than other papers, causing its price to go up since the state imposed a tax based on paper weight (*los derechos de timbre*) (Utt 15–16).

59. Original: "las descripciones de un novelista en el género de Flaubert y de Zola que fuera anotando con todo pormenor un atavío, un peinado, un maquillaje de mujer."

60. Original: "no según las cualidades que las personas mencionadas reunan verdaderamente, sino por aquellas otras que convenga atribuirles."

61. I have since run across a fictionalized reading experience of *La época* (Madrid) in Antonio de Hoyos y Vinent's first novel, *Cuestión de ambiente* (1903), which begins with these words: "Cogió con mano febril *La época*, que en blasonada bandeja de plata la ofrecía un criado. . . . desplegó el periódico húmedo aún, aspirando con fruición el acre olor a tinta de imprenta que exhalaba." (He anxiously picked up *La época*, which a servant offered him on an emblazoned silver tray. . . . Unfolding the slightly damp newspaper, he breathed with pleasure the acrid smell of printer's ink that the paper still exuded) (19). What the protagonist impatiently searches for is the society column.

62. Original: "¿Qué se ha figurado, que nos va a gustar ahora menos que antes, por lo del naturalismo y el idealismo, y por lo del *documento humano* y la fotografía, y el arte por el arte, y toda esa conversación?"

63. Compare this to Luis Buñuel's late twentieth-century fascination with a fin de siglo fan "on which many of the greatest writers and musicians of the age had scribbled a few words or notes. Side by side on this frivolous article were inscriptions from Massenet, Gounod, Mistral, Alphonse Daudet, Heredia, Banville, Mallarmé, Zola, Octave Mirbeau, Pierre Loti, Huysmans, and Rodin; together, they summed up the spirit of an era" (80–81).

64. Original: "Se miraban y se sonreían, como dos antiguos conocidos que nada recordaban de intimidades y ternezas. . . . Aún Trabanco, como poeta, daba cierto tinte de filosófica *añoranza* a las reminiscencias comunes . . . pero la de Frondoso, nada absolutamente, nada parecía recordar; es decir, se acordaba de todo, pero como si no."

65. In another take on the relationship fan / feminine, Emilia Pardo Bazán uses the object to symbolize her protagonist Bertina's lack of sensibility and blindness to harsh social realities. In "El abanico" (1908), the fan serves as a screen covering reality: "La sociedad esgrime un abanico inmenso" (society flourishes an immense fan) (1639). Pardo Bazán had her own collection of fans and lectured and wrote about them as well. See her "Abanicos"; "La vida contemporánea"; and Enrique Casal's commentary on her 1914 Ateneo talk about fans, an event he viewed as having more social than intellectual interest (125–28).

66. The fan, of course, can express much more than I have suggested here. For example, in an excellent study of Juan Meléndez Valdés's eighteenth-century poem, "El abanico," Monroe Hafter explores the fan as not only a sign of privilege and authority but a "game of social power." "'El abanico' . . . is not about love, or even eroticism," he remarks. "Its playful tone and artful construction make a delightful game out of the serious struggle for power. This is the ultimate game. A rising bourgeois and professional class contests superiority with certain ranks of the nobility" (197).

3. SALON POETS, THE BÉCQUER CRAZE, AND ROMANTICISM

1. I am reminded of Larra's conflicted self, as he vacillates between an intellectually critical, culturally refined "Frenchness" and attraction for his rough-hewn yet good-hearted compatriot Braulio in "El castellano viejo."

2. Along these lines, we can also see Virgil Nemoianu's notion of a later, tamed romanticism rooted in middle-class values and culture, which he calls Biedermeier in his excellent study *The Taming of Romanticism* (4; 29), as a kind of cultural practice.

3. Arno J. Mayer would argue, however, that the artifacts of culture in middle-class society are part and parcel of a stable, hierarchical society since, for him, the middle classes, in emulating the aristocracy, essentially prolonged the old regime (*The Persistence of the Old Regime* 14).

4. In what follows, I am indebted to the work of Marta Palenque, Joaquín Criado Costa, and Eleazar Huerta. See also Titus Suck, who discusses the role of French salons and German reading clubs in "the formation of a genuinely bourgeois cultural identity" (1095).

5. For more details, see my "Romanticism, Realism, and the Presence of the Word" 330. The discussion on Zorrilla and Pardo Bazán's *El cisne de Vilamorta* first appeared, in different form, in passages from "Romanticism, Realism, and the Presence of the Word" and "Pardo Bazán's *El Cisne de Vilamorta* and the Romantic Reader."

6. Original: "Era una composición de allí, de aquel poeta, de aquel momento, de aquella escena, para nosotros, en nuestra lengua, en nuestra poesía, en poesía que nos arrebató, que nos electrizó . . . Si a solas también la hubiera leído a cada uno de sus oyentes, ¿hubiera producido el mismo efecto? ¿La hubieran hallado tan ideal, tan bella, tan original y tan espontánea? No seguramente."

7. Original: "El silencio era absoluto: el público, el más a propósito y el mejor preparado; la escena solemne y la ocasión sin par. Tenía yo entonces una voz juvenil, fresca y argentinamente timbrada, y una manera nunca oída de recitar, y rompí a leer . . . pero según iba leyendo . . . iba leyendo en los semblantes de los que absortos me rodeaban, el asombro que mi aparición y mi voz les causaba."

8. For a detailed analysis of Pardo Bazán's novel *El cisne de Vilamorta*, see my article.

Becquermania inspired both imitations and parodies of the *Rimas*. From the deluge of imitations, see: Gassó y Ortiz 78; de las Heras 366; Mediano 288; Mayorga 15; Jiménez de Quirós 8; Sánchez de León 11; Martín Orozco 79; Sepúlveda, "Rima" 389; and Avilés 5. Parodies—both poetic and political—abounded well into the twentieth century. See, for examples, Estévanez 12; Vallejo 1–2; "Imitación de Becker" 1; López Valdemoro 13; "No volverán" [1]; Acho-Cam [1]; "Becqueriana" 3; Creso 3; Pizarroso 12; de la Guardia 118; "Becqueriana" 4; J. A. Goytisolo, qtd. in García Nieto 27; and González 178. Clarín took wickedly cruel potshots at Bécquer imitators and other second- and third-rate poets in his "El poeta-búho: Historia natural" and "Los grafómanos"; see also "Tú y yo" 6, for satiric comments on the "tú y yo" (you and I) school of poetry. The Alvarez Quintero brothers milked both Bécquer and sentimentality in *La rima eterna* (1914), a two-act play inspired by a Bécquer poem; they also turned it into a zarzuela called *Becqueriana* in 1915. Poet Concha Méndez recalled an aunt who loved Bécquer's verses: "la oía decir que estaba enamorada de él, como si fuera un ser presente" (I used to hear her say that she was in love with him, as though he were present in the flesh) (Ulacia Altolaguirre 50). (My thanks to Curtis Wasson for providing this reference.) During the Franco regime, Bécquer was extremely popular among adolescents (see Martín Gaite 37; and Amorós 67; 89). Ana María Moix satirized the romantic female adolescent, equally enamored of Bécquer and the martyred fascist José Antonio Primo de Rivera, in her 1973 novel *Walter, ¿por qué te fuiste?* 97; 123–25.

9. Original: "Por los tenebrosos rincones de mi cerebro acurrucados y desnudos, duermen los extravagantes hijos de mi fantasía, esperando en silencio que el arte los vista de la palabra."

10. Original: "Yo sé un himno gigante y extraño / que anuncia en la noche del alma una aurora."

11. Original: "Yo he pasado muchas noches leyendo sus rimas y al leerlas mi espíritu se sentía trasportado a otra atmósfera."

12. Original: "Leyendo las *Rimas* nos identificamos con él [el poeta] . . . nos admiramos al sorprender en el vate sentimientos que creíamos pura y exclusivamente nuestros."

13. Original: "Amamos la memoria del poeta con una adoración fervorosa; con una especie de culto idolátrico; como amamos los recuerdos queridos."

14. Original: "Emocionarnos y hacernos sentir de una manera tan intensa es privilegio exclusivo de los genios."

15. Original: "Yo que supe todo esto, no dije siquiera esta boca es mía, convencido de que por la boca muere el pez; temeroso de disgustar con mis réplicas al amigo íntimo de las

nueve hermanas . . ., y deseando no incurrir en el olímpico desprecio de una autoridad literaria de tan alta representación en la república de las letras."

16. Original: "porque ni ha escrito nada ni sabe escribir, reservando sus pujos de literato para cuando va a mi pueblo, donde contrajo matrimonio con una aristócrata."

17. See Chichón 125–26, on Bécquer's popularity in 1875; also Díez Taboada 81–126. Pío Baroja (born 1872), on the other hand, had less positive memories of the poet at the turn of the century: "A Bécquer, cuando yo era estudiante, se le consideraba como un sensiblero y como un cursi; pero, a pesar de esta opinión generalizada, se ha sostenido y ha quedado a flote con motivo" (In my student days, we considered Bécquer soppy and even cursi; but, despite prevailing opinion, the poet has endured and, with good reason, prospered) (*Memorias* 866).

18. Original: "Inútilmente he buscado muchas veces juicios críticos sobre el poeta hispalense," he writes, "pues nada he visto en este sentido . . . ¿A qué obedece este profundo silencio?"

19. Original: "En suma; esta clase de representaciones no son más que un pretexto para que media docena de bacantes impúdicas y lujuriosas, luzcan las pantorrillas y las protuberancias maxilares."

20. Original: "Hay en Bécquer mucha melancolía, algo de histerismo, algo de fiebre y sobre todo una sensibilidad exagerada que le convierte en juguete de sus emociones. Es un hipocondriaco incurable. . . . unido a una voluptuosidad dulce, a una delicadeza extraordinaria y a una sensibilidad puramente femenina, late el amor vehemente."

21. See Benítez; Sebold, Introduction 9–19; Gamallo Fierros 431–37; López Estrada, *Poética* 71–75; and Bécquer, "Revista de salones," "El Carnaval," "Bailes y bailes," and "Gacetilla de la capital," all in his *Obras completas*. The romantic legend of Bécquer as a frail and melancholy dreamer, initially propagated by his friends and colleagues after his death, has been significantly modified with the discovery of an enterprising Bécquer, interested in moneymaking schemes and, evidently, in pornographic projects as well, judging from the 1991 appearance of *Sem*. Bécquer was also an active participant in the political life of the nation, according to Estruch Tobella, who does not, however, believe the Bécquer brothers had anything to do with the creation of *Sem* (303–4; 315). See also Brown on "the nebularization of the 'Bécquer legend' " (16); and Díez Taboada 91.

22. Original: "tomos pequeñitos, con un lujo desconocido. Encuadernados en oro, con cantoneras de plata, registros de seda y una cajita donde meterlos, también en forma de libro. Para las mujeres aristócratas—novelitas originales de barba de pavo—, para formar una colección y ponerla en los tocadores elegantes en un pequeño mueble de ébano. Cada uno, una lámina en acero. Dedicados a diferentes mujeres visibles por su belleza y su posición. Se publicará por tomos mensuales o quincenales. Caro, bastante caro. La cuestión es hacerlos objetos de moda y lujo."

23. Original: "La idea es formar una biblioteca de obras sólo de mujeres de todas las épocas y las naciones. Edición bonita, ni cara ni barata, que comenzará desde Safo. Halagar la vanidad de las mujeres. Incluir las obras de las poetisas indias y árabes;

en fin, mucho oropel. Debe tener aceptación escribiendo un gran prospecto adulando a las mujeres y suscitando la curiosidad de las lectoras con un gran número de nombres."

24. Original: "una obra toda de autógrafos en forma de álbum, en la cual se pondrán poesías buenas y originales de los mejores poetas contemporáneos españoles."

25. Original: "El cronista de la sociedad es un tipo particular, especialísimo, *sui generis:* no es ni hombre ni mujer, vive en dos elementos, y tiene por consiguiente algo de anfibio . . . las mujeres lo miran como hombre, los hombres lo consideran como mujer."

26. Original: "Nace de padres pobres . . . pero generalmente en los países en que el hombre se parece a la mujer. Tiene ambición a su modo: la ambición de la mujer que luce el aderezo o el zapato de seda en los salones, y por esta causa toca a su meta no bien llega a la posición social de *poeta de salón.* Porque se dice que todos los hombres tienen algo de poetas; pero el poeta de salón tiene poco de hombre; es el verdadero poeta lo que el gorila es al hombre; el segundo una mueca de la naturaleza humana; el primero una mueca de la poesía."

27. Original: "La base de su poesía es la trampa, está lleno de deudas. Pugna por ser amable; lee en los salones los versos de sus compañeros con la insidiosa complacencia de la muchacha casadera que viste a una novia; pero ¡los lee tan bien! . . . ¡es tan tierno, tan oportuno, tan *local!* ¡Tan local! ¡Ya lo creo! Esta localidad se revela en su vida íntima."

28. Original: "El poeta de salón en su cualidad de sirena-macho, encanta a las damas."

29. Original: "Grilo es un poeta tan malo, que si no hubiera Velardes en el mundo, podría pasar por el peor poeta."

30. Original: "En resumen, esta poesía *inédito* de Grilo parece uno de eso perritos de lanas, con ojos de cristal, que tienen las viudas de intendentes que reciben caballeros solos; perritos que son restos de un mal entendido romanticismo de sus tiernos abriles."

31. "Eso no es ser poeta, Grilo, eso es ser modisto." Similarly, Salvador Granés's satiric epigram reads: "Es el señor de Grilo / poeta de algodón, con vistas de hilo" (Señor Grilo is a poet / made of cotton, with threads as vistas) (*Calabazas y cabezas* 171). The association made between cursilería and dressmakers was not only applied to poets, but to politicians as well. Tomás Tuero said that liberal Segismundo Moret's political success was "el triunfo de la *cursilería* en la política española" (the triumph of *cursilería* in Spanish politics) and that he was an "orador para uso de modistas" (an orator fit for dressmakers) (90–91).

32. Original: "¡Versos de Grilo! ¡Más versos de Grilo! ¡Gran rebaja en los precios!"

33. Original: "Grilo cuando lee, lee refritos."

34. Emilio Bobadilla cites the "Grilo-types," as well as Emilio Ferrari, Narciso Campillo, and Carlos Fernández Shaw, as examples in "Ripios en prosa y verso."

35. Original: "Es más bien que Grilo, *grillo;* siempre canta al mismo son."

36. Original: "Grilo, qué sé yo . . . Goza de simpatías allá entre las damas de alto copete, y le imprime sus poesías la reina madre, que, por lo visto, está en fondos . . . ninguno medrará gran cosa por el camino del Parnaso."

37. The autograph of the letter is reproduced in Grilo's collection, *Ideales,* which is dedicated to his daughter Magdalena.

38. Sanz Cuadrado 68, n.3. To get the flavor of "Las ermitas de Córdoba," here is the opening stanza: "Hay de mi alegre sierra / Sobre las lomas, / Unas casitas blancas / Como palomas" (On the slopes / of my happy hills, / there are little houses, / white like doves) (3).

39. Original: "Soy demasiado sentimental, demasiado romántico, demasiado *cursi* para el ejercicio permanente del consuelo del dolor ajeno, para resignarme al papel de *imperme-able,* que deje correr sin empaparle la lluvia de las lágrimas de los demás."

40. For other favorable views of Grilo, see Sanz Cuadrado; Alcalá Galiano; A. G.; and J. Navarrete.

41. Original: "Ya entonces, sin poder darme cuenta del por qué, se verificaba en mi interior algo extraño al escucharlas." Díaz Martín in 1886 expressed the broad appeal of Bécquer in these terms: "El que mejor sepa *pinchar* lo que siente el pueblo y sus inagotables maneras de expresarse, ese será el mejor poeta" (he who knows best how *to tap into* what the people feel and their myriad ways of expressing themselves, will be the best poet) (368).

42. Original: "de todas clases, edades y tipos, a quienes infaliblemente tutea y le tutean, pues el *tú* parece ser el tratamiento oficial de este lírico magnate."

43. Ricardo Gullón recalled that his generation heard actors like Ricardo Calvo recite "con estilo de dicción hoy perdido, tal *Oriental* o *Leyenda,* de Zorrilla, que en sus labios resultaba impresionante" (with a kind of stylized diction now lost, an *Oriental* or a *Legend* by Zorrilla, which on his lips sounded impressive) (*Direcciones del modernismo* 153).

44. See López Martín. Azorín tried to imagine in 1934 how the poetry of another salon poet, José Selgas, would have been recited: "No sabemos cómo un recitante público habría de declamar estos versos. Si los declamaba con voz recia y engolada, los versos no resistirían a la recia entonación. Se quebrarían como un sutil cristal de Venecia. La voz apropiada para Selgas habría de ser quedita, casi apagada, susurrante, levísima. Con esa voz habría que recitar la maravillosa poesía 'Chist,' esa poesía en que se pinta a un niño dormido en su cuna y en que el poeta a cada momento pide que no se haga ruido para que no se despierte. Y con esa voz habría que recitar también a los versos dedicados a las auras nocturnas, a la lluvia, a la niebla" (We don't know how a public reciter would have declaimed these verses. If he had declaimed them with bombast and a full-throated voice, the verses would not have withstood the effects of such a harsh intonation. They would have broken like fragile Venetian glass. The appropriate voice for Selgas's poetry would have to be quiet, almost muted, whispering, very light. With that voice you would recite the marvelous poem, "Chist," that poem which paints the picture of a child asleep in his cradle and in which the poet at every moment asks us not to make a sound so as not to wake him. And with that voice you would recite as well the verses dedicated to the coming dawn, to the rain, to the mist) (Martínez Ruiz, "Las obras de Selgas" n.pag.).

45. An example of how private expression of the self could be translated into the public

domain in the nineteenth century is found in the varied uses of the album, which was not only produced privately in its usual unpublished, domestic form (see chapter 2), but also commercially. For examples, see *Album poético español; Album poético,* which was a gift to subscribers of *La ilustración ibérica; El Album de Madrid,* a short-lived journal with the format of an album; and *Album de "Blanco y negro": Españoles ilustres de principios del siglo XX,* containing photos, short biographies and autographs, published by the popular illustrated weekly, *Blanco y negro.* Other albums that saw publication appear not to have been commercially motivated. See, for example, *Album poético dedicado a S. M. El Rey D. Alfonso XII y al Ejército con motivo de su triunfal entrada en la capital de la Monarquía,* giving hosannas for the end of the Carlist War (although I note that the staff of the *Gaceta de Madrid* cooked this one up) and *Album que dedican a S. M. la reina doña Isabel II los profesores de educación primaria.* Also, Entrambasaguas, "Una olvidada antología poética."

4. TEXTUAL ECONOMIES: THE EMBELLISHMENT OF CREDIT

1. See Rivière and Moreno Hernández for recent attempts at understanding cursilería.
2. See, for example, Sánchez-Albornoz,"El trasfondo económico de la revolución" and his *España hace un siglo: Una economía dual;* Bahamonde Magro and Toro Mérida 24–33; and Carr 264–77.
3. I am indebted to John Sekora's work for this understanding of the concept of luxury. For Sekora, "the changes in meaning of the concept of luxury represent nothing less than the movement from the classical world to the modern" (1).
4. "Por do quiera que tendamos la vista," he writes, "vemos la práctica contrariando las teorías de la sociedad moderna: esta ha proclamado la igualdad, y jamás se ha pretendido con más empeño el distinguirse unos de otros" (Wherever we look, we see practice contradicting the theory of modern society: we have proclaimed equality, in the midst of increasing efforts to distinguish ourselves from one another) (Castellanos de Losada, "El siglo XIX" 671). See also J. Bustillo 200–205; and Pareja Serrada 185.
5. Original: "¡El lujo de las mujeres! Esa no es más que una manera capciosa de presentarnos la cuestión, porque las mujeres no han venido a ser más que el lujo de los hombres."
6. Moral condemnation of luxury as a feminine weakness also appears during the Franco regime. The Infanta Eulalia de Borbón felt compelled in 1946 to defend luxury as a necessity for women, adding that luxury was now a generalized phenomenon in all social classes. (Could this possibly be true in the harsh post–Spanish civil war period of restrictions and shortages?) But several pages later she comes round to the traditional view, saying that a woman's "lujo verdadero . . . está en ella misma, en su distinción" (true luxury . . . resides in herself, in her distinction) (79; 87).
7. Original: "No condenamos absolutamente el lujo; él fomenta las artes, y es bueno que la dama de elevada condición, vistiéndose con la elegancia y riqueza que le corresponde,

dé lucro al comerciante, al platero, al joyero y demás industriales . . . y porque nosotros que hemos declamado con todas nuestras fuerzas contra la detestable pasión de la avaricia, deseamos que el dinero circule."

8. See Palenque, *Gusto poético* 13–35, for more details on the *Ilustración española y americana* and its founder-entrepreneur, Cádiz-born Abelardo de Carlos. The prospectus for the *Ilustración* promised that every number would be "tan lujosa como la de los periódicos de esta clase que se publican en el extranjero" (as luxurious as that of the magazines of this kind published abroad) (Palenque 22).

9. For two excellent analyses of Spain's middle classes and modernization, see Ringrose and Cruz.

10. Original: "¿Qué otra cosa es la Bolsa de los fondos públicos sino el escaparate del crédito nacional? ¿Y no es el periodismo un vidrio, y vidrio de aumento, de ese armario exquisito llamado opinión pública?"

11. Original: "Pues negar que el estómago tiene su vidrio en los banquetes patrióticos, la conciencia el suyo en los casinos y en los clubs, la cabeza sus andenes en los ateneos y en las tertulias públicas, y que la sociedad toda no vive dentro de un escaparate de cristal, sería lo mismo que negar nuestra existencia y decir que la publicidad no era el alma de esta generación." See also Flores's "Los gritos de Madrid o la publicidad en 1850" (*La sociedad de 1850*), which is actually about printed advertising. Modern advertising agencies, which were established in the United States and France in 1841 and 1845, appeared in Barcelona in 1870. By 1879 there were three in Madrid alone (see Palenque, *Gusto poético* 21). This and other Flores quotations are taken from *La sociedad de 1850*, an anthology of his articles more accessible than *Ayer, hoy y mañana*, in which these pieces first appeared in 1853 (with subsequent editions in 1857, 1863–64, and later, the last in 1892–93). Flores died in 1865.

12. Eagleton comments that "structures of power must become structures of feeling, and the name for this mediation from property to propriety is the aesthetic" ("The Ideology of the Aesthetic" 21).

13. See Kagan, *Students and Society in Early Modern Spain;* Amelang; and Cruz.

14. This dominance of a ruling class in nineteenth-century politics and commerce can be seen in other European national cultures as well. See Mayer, *The Persistence of the Old Regime;* and Colley, ch. 4, for the specific example of Great Britain.

15. It is also worth noting that *La de Bringas* (1884) appeared after a banking crisis in 1882 and Spain's de facto abandonment of the gold standard in 1883, thus moving to a fiduciary, or largely paper money, economy. See Tortella Casares, "Las magnitudes monetarias" 460; 474; and his "Estimación del stock" 126–27.

16. I will be citing from Alda Blanco and Carlos Blanco Aguinaga's excellent edition of *La de Bringas;* and the equally fine English translation of Catherine Jagoe, entitled *That Bringas Woman*.

17. The hair picture has received some notable critical analysis, among them, those of Bly, Gold ("Francisco's Folly"), A. Ramírez, Bergmann, Lopes, Labanyi ("Problem of Fram-

ing"), and Franz, to whom I am indebted for their insights into this text. See also Ynduráin for an overview of lo cursi in Galdós's novels.

I have found an equally grotesque example of a cursi object in Eduardo López Bago's *El cura (caso de incesto)* (1885), in which a Christ Child figure, replete with artificial flowers, blessed medals, a cross made of paper, the Virgin Mary, and the like, encased in a bell glass (or *fanal*), is prolixly—and parodically—described. Could López Bago have been thinking of Galdós's hair picture in *La de Bringas?*

18. Original: "un delicado obsequio con el cual quería nuestro buen Thiers [Francisco Bringas] pagar diferentes deudas de gratitud a su insigne amigo don Manuel María José del Pez" (57).

19. For more information on hair pictures and hair jewelry, see Armstrong 39–40; 72–80; Carlisle 416–17; Campbell; and Bell.

20. Original: "Lo que sí espero. . . . es que por ningún caso introduzca en la obra cabello que no sea nuestro. Todo se ha de hacer con pelo de la familia" (60).

21. Laurence Lerner also discusses the question of the male sentimentalist (197). For representative poems (and poets) in Spanish, see as examples: Alarcón y Meléndez; E. Bustillo 178; Cano, "La niña muerta" 4; Fernández Grilo; R. Gil 383–85; Guijarro 66; Pascual y C. 63; Querol; Ruiz Aguilera; Selgas, "La cuna vacía" 41; and Soravilla 366.

22. See Lopes's excellent discussion: "the collage technique used in the long description of the cenotaph is a pattern upon which the whole novel is generated" (75). Gold also offers a perceptive analysis of Galdós's descriptive techniques and effects displayed in the hair picture ("Francisco's Folly" 55–58).

23. See Bell 39–40, for a description of the tomb and willow tree design. Buñuel recalled seeing in the 1920s a hair picture "made entirely of hair, right down to the tombs and the cypresses," in a blind man's home in Toledo (73).

24. Original: "Lo que la señora de Pez quería era . . . algo como poner en verso una cosa poética que está en prosa . . . Quería la madre que aquello fuera bonito y que hablara lenguaje semejante al que hablan los versos comunes, la escayola, las flores de trapo, la purpurina y los *Nocturnos*, fáciles para piano" (58).

25. Original: "Serena y un tanto majestuosa . . . [y] de sus ojos elocuentes se desprendía una convicción orgullosa, la conciencia de su papel de piedra angular de la casa en tan aflictivas circunstancias" (305).

26. My sources for these details on the historical Bringas family come from Cruz 39–40; and Ortiz Armengol 241–51.

27. See Blanco and Blanco Aguinaga; Aldaraca; and Varey, "Francisco Bringas," for examples. Nicholas Round, in one of the few commentaries on the Bringas children, notes how Alfonsín (a spendthrift) and Isabelita (a hoarder and collector) echo their parents "as a 'living metaphor' of the characters and ways of life of Rosalía and Don Francisco" (45).

28. Original: "[Francisco] tenía la enfermedad epiléptica de la gestación artística. La obra, recién encarnada en su mente, anunciaba ya con íntimos rebullicios que era un ser vivo . . . Al mismo tiempo, su fantasía se regalaba de antemano con la imagen de la obra,

figurándosela ya parida y palpitante, completa, acabada, con la forma del molde en que estuviera. Otras veces veíala nacer por partes, asomando ahora un miembro, luego otro, hasta que toda entera aparecía en el reino de la luz" (60–61).

29. See David Simpson's discussion of the powers of fetishes and fetishism and the fundamental phallicism informing them (20–21).

30. Labanyi ("Problem of Framing" 26) points out that there are actually two narrative beginnings in *La de Bringas:* the description of the hair picture (which she considers a false start) and the narrator's entrance into the labyrinthine world of the Royal Palace.

31. Original: "Llameaban en el cerebro del artista, al modo de fuegos fatuos . . . ciertas ideas atañederas al presupuesto de la obra. Bringas las acariciaba, prestándoles aquella atención de hombre práctico que no excluía en él las desazones espasmódicas de la creación genial. Contando mentalmente, decía" (61).

32. Original: "Goma laca: *dos reales y medio.* A todo tirar gastaré *cinco reales* . . . Unas tenacillas de florista, pues las que tengo son un poco gruesas: *tres reales* . . . etc." (62).

33. "Money is the perfect image of desire," writes David Simpson, " 'being' nothing, and promising everything, forever. It is a fetish that it is therefore all the more difficult to disassemble" (38). See also Marx 1:71–72; 74.

34. Original: "contemplando en éxtasis lo que aún no es más que una abstracción" (95).

35. Original: "En esto la pobre niña, llegando al período culminante de su delirio, sintió que dentro de su cuerpo se oprimían extraños objetos y personas. Todo lo tenía ella en sí misma, cual si se hubiera tragado medio mundo" (124).

36. Original: "Los pedacitos de lana de bordar y de sedas y trapo llenaban un cajón. Los botones, las etiquetas de perfumería, las cintas de cigarros, los sellos de correo, las plumas de acero usadas, las cajas de cerillas vacías, las mil cosas informes, fragmentos sin uso ni aplicación, rayaban en lo incalculable" (253).

37. Original: "el efecto de un fluido miasmático que se filtraba en ella" (132).

38. Original: "Esta pasión mujeril . . . hace en el mundo más estragos que las revoluciones" (94).

39. See also Delgado, " 'El derecho de revisión': *La de Bringas* y el discurso de la alienación femenina," which has since been revised and incorporated into her book, *La imagen elusiva: Lenguaje y representación en la narrativa de Galdós.*

40. Silvia Tubert has perceptively noted a libidinal economy at work in *La de Bringas:* "Si los trapos son objeto erótico para Rosalía, el pelo con que elabora su cenotafio no lo es menos para Bringas" (if clothes are an erotic object for Rosalía, the hair with which [Francisco] Bringas creates his cenotaph is no less so for him) (376). See also Gold, "Francisco's Folly" (64).

41. Original: "fueron la fruta cuya dulzura le quitó la inocencia y por culpa de ellos un ángel con espada de raso me la echó de aquel Paraíso en que su Bringas la tenía tan sujeta. Nada, nada . . . , cuesta trabajo creer que aquello de doña Eva sea tan remoto. Digan lo que quieran, debió de pasar ayer, según está de fresquito y palpitante el tal suceso. Parece que lo han traído los periódicos de anoche" (93).

42. The same humorous image reoccurs when Rosalía spots a very expensive shawl (*manteleta*) for the first time: "¡Qué pieza, qué manzana de Eva!" (98) (It was a lovely thing, an apple fit for Eve!) (33).

43. Original: "Me falta considerar esto bajo el aspecto económico . . . Muchos censuran estas fiestas por el dineral que se gasta en ellas inútilmente, dinero que aplicado a objetos de mayor interés sería reproductivo. En un millón de pesetas calculan algunos el gasto de anoche, y creo que se han quedado cortos. Pero cualquiera que sea la cifra, paréceme fuera de lugar los aspavientos sentimentales que hacen a propósito de ella . . . Fuera de que es imposible y económicamente absurdo reglamentar el empleo que cada cual quiera dar a su peculio, las artes e industrias suntuarias, que dan circulación y vida a inmensos capitales, no existirían sin estas demandas constantes del capricho y de la frivolidad, elemento fatal, imprescindible de toda sociedad, y que lejos de ser privativo de la nuestra, parece menos avasallador en esta generación que en las precedentes. La prensa inglesa se queja un día y otro de que el retraimiento y perpetuo luto en que vive la corte de la Reina Victoria paraliza ciertas industrias de mucha importancia en la vastísima metrópoli."

44. Peter Bly's point that "it would be dangerous to conclude that Galdós-the-newspaper-columnist was always candid in his articles" is well taken ("From Disorder to Order" 405, n.20). But I think the ambiguity is present in both his newspaper article and the novel.

45. See Hemingway 20; 23; and 26–27; also Miller.

46. It is evident, however, that Galdós's views on the use of French phrases in Spanish were also subject to change, depending on the context. In a *La prensa* article, he wrote this about the language of society reporters: ". . . la necesidad de introducir en su lenguaje mil terminachos franceses, convierte su estilo en una jerga insufrible" (the need to introduce into their writing slews of French monstrosities converts their style into an insufferable gibberish) ("Carta" 68).

47. The notion of *bricolage* comes from Lévi-Strauss (16–33). Lopes uses the related term *collage* in his analysis of *La de Bringas*.

48. See Lévi-Strauss's perceptive comments on Mr. Wemmick's suburban castle (17; 150).

49. Original: " 'Te voy a hacer un armario para la ropa, tan bueno y tan famoso, que la gente pedirá papeleta para verlo, como la Historia Natural y Caballerizas. El arrendatario de las cortas de Balsaín me da cuanta madera de pino me haga falta . . . En los sótanos de esta casa hay un depósito de caobas que se están pudriendo, y Su Majestad me permitirá sacar una piececita . . . El contratista del panteón de Infantes, de El Escorial, me ha ofrecido todo el mármol que quiera' " (175).

50. Original: "simbolizan que aquella casa, que aquel jardín se ha construido con parte de la fortuna que el autor del *Diccionario* ha adquirido con la publicación de su obra."

51. In Paredes Alonso's informative biography of Pascual Madoz, there is no mention of Francisca Madoz; and her death is confused with that of another daughter (400, n.7).

52. Joaquín de Entrambasaguas gives a useful description of this and other nineteenth-century coronas poéticas ("Coronas poéticas"). The Madoz corona, he says, had to have

been a very limited edition and is considered rare (15). The copy I consulted is from the Biblioteca Nacional (Madrid).

53. There were, of course, exceptions worthy of mention, such as Carolina Coronado's *octava*, "Tú pensaste que el mar era tu cuna," which later appeared in her *Poesías* (1852 edition). In the *Corona poética*, her poem is the lead-in, coming immediately after Fernando Madoz's introduction.

54. Sáez de Melgar's simultaneous defense of women writers and praise of the precocious fourteen-year-old Alejandra Argüelles Toral y Hevía should be compared to Rubén Darío's likening of the *niña-prodigio* (the female child prodigy) to a form of prostitution in 1906 ("Niñas prodigios" 320–21).

55. See Sebold's "Galdós y el 'bello monstruo' Rodríguez Cao," for parallels between Cao and Galdós's fictional creation Valentín in *Torquemada en la hoguera* (1889).

56. Fittingly, three of the four volumes of Rodríguez Cao's *obras* are prefaced with prologues, each one from a different pen.

57. For these details on Pascual Madoz as benefactor of Zarauz, I have relied on Madoz's own remarks ("Zarauz," *Diccionario*, vol. 16) and José Mugica's "Madoz, bienhechor de Zarauz."

58. Original: "Hemos creído conveniente traer aguas a esta posesión: afortunadamente pudieron nuestros intereses conciliarse con los de la v. del modo siguiente: carecía el ayunt. de fondos suficientes para proporcionar a la pobl. esta importante mejora."

59. Original: "una pobl. de mucha concurrencia en la época de los baños que alcanzará mucha vida, mucha animación, muchos beneficios."

60. Original: "Zarauz, llorará eternamente, no lo dudamos, la pérdida de una niña, que hubiera completado más tarde las ideas benéficas de sus padres, el sistema marcado de protección con que estos miran los intereses de pueblo tan agradecido . . . ¡aquel día de triste memoria, en que todo un pueblo esperaba con mayor ansiedad la sentencia para el de vida o muerte; la sentencia de su porvenir; una comisión se había presentado reclamando la posesión de un *cadáver!!*

"En su dolor, en su desesperación se había persuadido el pueblo de Zarauz que era este el medio de obligar a sus protectores a que no abandonasen aquella residencia; y olvidaba sin duda que en el sensible corazón de aquellos hablaban muy alto estas pruebas de sentimiento, estas manifestaciones de pública gratitud, esta triste y dolorosa ovación. *El cadáver pertenece al panteón de mi familia; mi familia pertenecerá siempre a la desconsolada población de Zarauz.*"

61. Laurence Lerner notes that " 'angel' is a figure for bestowing status on the loveliness of the dead child." In the nineteenth century, "angels have now become symbols of the emotional life, above all of grief and hope" (102).

62. Original: "La hermosa criatura . . . no podía persuadirse de que siendo ella feliz, fueran los otros seres, desgraciados; y si momentos tuvo en que miró con ceño torvo a los autores de sus días, fue sólo cuando estos resistían los caprichos de su hija en exigencias de caridad y beneficencia."

63. Patronage was present in Jesús Rodríguez Cao's case when Carolina Coronado provided him an initial entrée, with a public reading (and homage), into La Infantil, a literary academy geared toward children. See Rivera y Delgado 24–25.

64. Original: "La inagotable caridad de aquella criatura angelical hizo doblemente sentida su muerte, llorada en tiernas composiciones por algunos poetas, formando con todas una corona fúnebre que, como viva expresión de su pena y de la amistad que a los mismos unía con el padre de la niña, D. Pascual Madoz, campeón infatigable de la libertad, publicaron en un elegante opúsculo. Jamás olvidaré que él y el difunto Conde de las Navas fueron las primeras personas que me favorecieron y alentaron con su generosa protección, recién llegado yo a Madrid, completamente desconocido y sin apoyo."

65. Original: "Zarauz es la playa aristocrática, numerosas familias de lo que pudiéramos llamar nuestro *Faubourg,* poseen allí casas de campo y palacios magníficos, y otros se instalan en el *Grand-Hotel* y en el de la *Terrasse;* allí todo el mundo se conoce, casi todos se *tutean.*"

66. Original: "casas feas, cursis, presuntuosas, un *quiero y no puedo,* que ni eran villas, ni *chalets,* ni casasas: que eran . . . una caricatura y una mixtificación. Porque en Zarauz, antes refugio de paz veraniega para las gentes aristocráticas, cayeron muchos cursis, entrometidos y trepadores."

67. Already in the 1840s the intimacy of spas and bathing resorts in general was promoting the illusion that social categories had disappeared. See Madrazo, *Una espedición a Guipúzcoa* 20; 27.

68. Paredes Alonso also remarks that Pascual Madoz was typical of the "nueva aristocracia," or new aristocracy, which was a product of the "aburguesamiento de la nobleza de sangre y del ennoblecimiento de la burguesía" (embourgeoisement of the nobility of blood and the ennobling of the bourgeoisie) (201). See Paredes Alonso 24–26 on Madoz's family origins.

Madrazo in 1849 also made note of changing attitudes of the aristocracy toward commerce and material progress, citing the example of a Basque nobleman, José María de Araquistain, who removed the family shield from his house to make room for a window and better ventilation (*Una espedición a Guipúzcoa* 52).

5. FABRICATING HISTORY

1. Original: "Yo, que ya me siento demasiado clásica, me aburro . . . me duermo."

2. Cánovas himself was solidly middle-class. "A self-made provincial" (Carr 348), he married well, especially the second time, with Joaquina Osma, the daughter of a well-known Madrid banker who was also a cofounder of the Northern railroad company and director of Crédito Mobiliario (Espadas Burgos 18). See also Fernández Almagro, *Cánovas* (12–13; 27; 132–34; 431–39).

3. See his *Historia de la decadencia de España* xix, xxvi; and "Discusión del proyecto de contestación al discurso de la Corona" 216; also *Velada* 6.

4. "El primer Cánovas es el de los apologistas inmoderados e hiperbólicos; el segundo, el de Pi y Margall; el tercero, el de 'Clarín'; el cuarto, el de Campoamor; el quinto—reciente, flamante—, el de Galdós" (The first Cánovas belongs to the immoderate, hyperbolic apologists; the second, is Pi y Margall's; the third, 'Clarín's'; the fourth, Campoamor's; the fifth—recent, brilliant—Galdós's) (Martínez Ruiz, "Los cinco Cánovas" 49).

5. Original: "Pues los admiradores de Cánovas son como el franchute del cuento; como él, miden a su hombre con el paraguas, y resulta que es un monumento de muchos paraguas cuadrados. Pero yo . . . le mido como Herodoto medía la torre de Belo; le mido . . . por estadios. Y Cánovas, amigo mío, tendrá todos los cientos de paraguas . . . que se quiera; pero lo que es estadios, no mide ni siquiera uno."

6. Original: "y si la vida fuese una vida no sólo privada, sino pública; si su historia llegase a ser tanto la historia de la nación como la del individuo . . . hay algo como de duelo en la atmósfera, algo así como de orfandad en la sociedad contemporánea; se palpa el vacío de una gran personalidad . . . sentimos que empieza una nueva era en la historia de nuestros días."

7. Original: "como si la Providencia enlazase la muerte de un hombre con los problemas más pavorosos de la sociedad y de la patria para dar mayor realce a sus funerales."

8. Original: "Me pareció como un rapto, llevado a cabo a espaldas de la humanidad por espíritus fantásticos y malignos."

9. Original: "Y después, si se cierra el libro, y se acuesta uno y sueña, se ven flotar en la fantasía, no los personajes de la historia, ni los parajes por donde han pasado, sino los pujos arcaicos y castizos de Cánovas, sus muletillas adverbiales, los *estos, aquellos, últimos, dichos, propios,* etc., a que se agarra; conjunciones sueltas, y, en fin, una *Valpurgis* de palabras abstractas, un aquelarre de ripios en prosa."

10. Original: "Cánovas *ripia* la vida como los versos . . . *Ripiar* la vida es llenar el alma de cascajo para hacerse hombre de peso."

11. Original: "grandes ripios de la prosa de su existencia."

12. A "ripio" is defined as "toda palabra o frase superflua que se pone en el verso para rellenarlo, y así darle el número necesario de sílabas; o para satisfacer a la ley de la rima (perfecta o imperfecta)" (any superfluous word or phrase that is placed in a line of verse to pad it, hence to give it the necessary number of syllables; or to satisfy rules of rhyme (assonance or consonance) (Bartina 64). Bartina divides ripios into three groups: *ripios de pensamiento* (clichés, commonplaces), *ripios centrales o de relleno* (superfluous words in the middle of a line); and *ripios de rima* (words used to force a rhyme scheme) (65). In architecture, *ripiar* is to fill with rubble. A *ripio* is rubbish, debris, riprap. Tomás Tuero called liberal politician Segismundo Moret "el cursi cultivador del ripio" (the cursi cultivator of the superfluous) (92).

13. Original: "Con Cánovas principié este libro, con Cánovas le demedié y con Cánovas quiero concluirle."

14. Original: "A orillas de la Isuela hallé esta crónica: en una de aquellas huertas de suelo

verde, y pobladas de árboles frutales, cuyas bardas y setos se sustentan en las piedras robadas a los muros de Huesca."

15. Original: "Los moderados y los conservadores, sus hijos, son los que han solido sustentarse en las piedras robadas, o de las piedras robadas a las iglesias y a los conventos, pero no vale confundir las especies."

16. Fray Mortero's real name was Juan Fraile Miguélez, according to Martínez Cachero (97). It is of interest to note that the fourth edition (1913) of Valbuena's *Ripios vulgares* was dedicated to the memory of Leopoldo Alas. Oddly, the republican Clarín liked Valbuena's rough and ready satire. See, for example, his palique (1885) on *Ripios aristocráticos* (in *Mezclilla* 291–95); and *Apolo en Pafos* 38–41.

17. In a letter to his publisher Manuel Fernández Lasanta on 20 August 1886, Alas writes that "el folleto se titula *Cánovas y su tiempo* por aquello del *Solitario y su tiempo*" (the pamphlet is called *Cánovas and his time*, echoing *The solitary one and his time*) (Blanquat and Botrel 27). I strongly suspect he had also read Campoamor's 1884 *folleto*, in which the same proposed title appears.

18. Original: "Con lo que he dicho he concluido de tejer el cordón que ha de sostener el cuadro y el marco que ahora vais a ver fabricar. . . . Tosca es su fabricación por las condiciones del fabricante, pero de gran solidez."

19. Original: "¿No entiendes esto, historiador travieso y chiquitín? . . . Vístate bien, ahora que tienes dinerito fresco, y no busques tu sastre entre los de medio pelo. Reanuda y cultiva tus antiguas amistades y disponte a estrechar las nuevas relaciones que te salgan al paso. No desdeñes a los hombres de pro. . . . El pro se acerca taconeando recio. . . . La pobretería se aleja pisando con el contrafuerte. . . . Adiós, hijo. . . . Si sientes apetito de lecturas, pon a un lado al amigo Saavedra Fajardo, y entretente con el *Manual del perfecto caballero en sociedad*, consagrando algunos ratos a la *Moda Elegante*."

20. Ironically, Cánovas himself was hardly elegant: "Unprepossessing in appearance—with his squint, nervous tic, and appalling clothes, he looked like 'a subaltern on half-pay'" (Carr 348).

21. Original: "*Pardon, mon ami*. Me sé de memoria a todo el señorío de Madrid, lo que llamamos *gens du monde*."

22. Original: "*le grand critique de société*, por mal nombre *Asmodeo*."

23. Original: "las interesantes novedades políticas que, según ella, conocía mejor que nadie en Madrid."

24. All the titles of rare books given as gifts by García Fajardo's socially ambitious mother to Cánovas (234) actually belonged to the statesman's library. See Pérez de Guzmán 79; 87–88. In addition, Fr. Hernando de Talavera's "De murmurar o mal decir" and "De vestir y de calzar" had just appeared in 1911 in the NBAE (Nueva Biblioteca de Autores Españoles) series. Pérez de Guzmán says, however, that only a very small portion of the 30,000 volumes were gifts, contrary to rumor that Cánovas's library was largely built on such donations (61; 68). I suspect Galdós used Pérez de Guzmán as a source.

25. Original: "A mí me llegan diversos papeles interesantes, trozos de la Historia viva que

aún destilan sangre al ser arrancados del cuerpo de la Humanidad. Yo los leo con toda avidez; los ordeno, los colecciono."

26. Original: "Yo . . . resumo y sintetizo [la información *efeméridea*] agregando otras noticias y datos que nos dieron las vagarosas hijas del viento."

27. Original: "Ya le conocía y le admiraba como historiógrafo eminente. Yo también soy aficionado a la Historia, y en el nuevo Colegio de Chamartín tendré a mi cargo esa importante asignatura."

28. Original: "por su afán de traerme noticias que, a mi parecer eran más que Historia, chismografía."

29. Original: "Los que le tratan íntimamente dicen que el Sr. Cánovas es un murmurador a la manera de Tácito. Esto no es cierto."

30. Original: "A pesar de ser poco calumniable, no he conocido, sin embargo, un hombre de quien más nos guste murmurar a todos."

31. Kathleen Vernon skillfully analyzes the role of gossip in *Realidad* and *La incógnita*.

32. Original: "Aquí tiene que haber una gran catástrofe o esto desaparece por putrefacción. Esto está muerto, muerto, muerto."

33. Original: "pero, entiéndase bien, en los anales *del ser interno* de la nación. Demasiado sabes tú que la vida externa y superficial no merece ser perpetuada en letras de molde."

34. Original: "Elena Sanz *rayó a gran altura* en el *racconto* del primer acto y en el brindis del tercero."

35. Original: "Elena Sanz nació en Castellón de la Plana por los años 1852 o 53, y no doy más porque ello ni quita ni pone un ardite en el valor documental de esta verídica historia."

36. Felipe Trigo in *El semental* also exploits the word *conspicuous* in a similar context.

37. Original: "En uso del sagrado derecho de preterición me callo lo que importa poco a mis fines."

38. Original: "He sido recibido y oído con gratitud y amabilidad inexplicables, cuyo jubilo particular le comunico *por orden expresa*, a la par que con toda mi espontaneidad."

39. Original: "una política de inercia, de ficciones y de fórmulas mentirosas. . . . Todo esto va *decorado* con el profuso reparto de honores, distinciones y títulos nobiliarios."

40. Original: "Sigo creyendo que la llamada *gente cursi* es el verdadero estado llano de los tiempos modernos, por la extensión que ocupa en el censo y la mansedumbre pecuaria con que contribuye a las cargas del Estado."

41. Original: "Atención, caballeros. Mi Casiana era su propia modista. Juntos íbamos los dos a comprar las telas."

42. The bustle came in with a change of regime, when Amadeo de Saboya's wife introduced it in 1870 (Soldevila 44). Of this strange artifact Cánovas is reputed to have said: "Es un artificio que contiene un fondo de verdad" (It's an artifice which contains at bottom some truth) (Soldevila 52).

43. See also Quinn 22. The opposition called Cánovas a "zurcidor de voluntades" (a weaver of minds and wills). See his "Discusión de proyecto de contestación" 219.

44. See Ross Chambers's illuminating comments on oppositionality.

45. Original: "Reconozco que en los países definitivamente constituidos, la presencia mía es casi un estorbo. . . . no me resigno al tristísimo papel de una sombra vana."

46. Interestingly enough, this phrase seems to echo similar concerns in the writings of Cánovas. Thus, in *Historia de la decadencia de España*, he says: "la decadencia de España coincidió desgraciadamente con la constitución definitiva de la Europa" (Spain's decadence coincided unfortunately with the definitive constitution of Europe) (757). Related to this is the idea of the *"ser interno de la nación"* in *Cánovas* (203), which also reverberates in the pages of the Málaga-born historian: "las naciones tienen siempre una Constitución interna" (nations always have an internal Constitution) (qtd. in *Acto solemne* 13). See also Cánovas's "Discusión del proyecto de contestación" (215).

6. THE DREAM OF NEGATION

1. The concept of negation has a long history of intellectual permutations. *Webster's Third New International Dictionary* gives these definitions: "1a: the act of negating: denial, contradiction; the operation of forming a negation. b: an instance of negating a negative doctrine or statement or proposition or judgment; spec. a statement that is true provided the unqualified original statement is false. c: a negating particle (as *not*): negative. 2a: something that is merely the absence of something actual: something without real existence of its own: nonentity. b: something that is the negative opposite of something positive." See Richard Gale on the "horror of negative events" that some philosophers express (2). Kurrik in *Literature and Negation* gives an excellent account of negation from Genesis to Lacan, passing by way of Kant, Hegel, Nietzsche, Freud, and the modern novel; there is, however, a curious omission: Sartre's theory of imagination, the condition and power of imagining unreality, with its freedom to negate (*L'Imaginaire*, 1940). My debt to Nietzsche and Freud will become evident in these pages.

2. For other forms of negating negation, see Marcuse on negating capitalism ("thought in contradiction must become more negative and more utopian in opposition to the status quo," xxvi); and JanMohamed, on "Negating the Negation as a Form of Affirmation in Minority Discourse." The negating of negation should be distinguished from the notion of negativity, which Sanford Budick and Wolfgang Iser explain in this way: "The modern coinage *negativity* . . . becomes inevitable when we consider the implications, omissions, or cancellations that are necessarily part of any writing or speaking. These lacunae indicate that practically all formulations . . . contain a tacit dimension, so that each manifest text has a kind of latent double. Thus, unlike negation, which must be distinguished from negativity, this inherent doubling in language defies verbalization. It forms the unwritten and unwritable—unsaid and unsayable—base of the utterance. But it does not therefore negate the formulations of the text or saying. Rather, it conditions them through blanks and negations" (xii). See also Iser, *The Act of Reading*, for the relationship between negation and literary blanks produced by negation (217).

3. The modern invention of the highlander as a national symbol of Scottishness readily comes to mind; see Trevor-Roper.

4. A modern, annotated edition, with a useful study by Angel Isac, appeared in 1996. I discuss *Granada la bella* more fully in chapter 8.

5. Original: "Sostiene la clase propietaria y capitalista luchas enconadas entre sí por las creencias religiosas, por las doctrinas filosóficas, por los sistemas económicos, por egoísmos de bandería, sin norte que le guíe y sin una aspiración común a que enderece sus pasos; parece un organismo que se disgrega y camina derechamente a su disolución. En cambio el proletariado, desechando de sí cuanto desune y divide, y atento sólo a lo que aproxima y asocia, no tiene más que un ideal inmediato, *la conquista del poder político.*"

6. Original: "Nace y tiene su raíz en la aspiración general de todos los seres y especialmente del hombre, ya individualmente, ya como ser colectivo, a distinguirse, a sobresalir, a dominar, a dirigir, a mandar."

7. Original: "privilegio y . . . fuerza que por ley natural de su esencia tiende[n] a sobresalir, a distinguirse, a imponerse."

8. Original: "Actualmente, en Madrid, la palabra negadora de moda, es, *cursi.* Hoy todo es aquí cursi; pocos son los cuadros de la Exposición que se han librado del epíteto y poquísimas las obras literarias de la temporada, o de otras anteriores, a cuyo asunto haya dejado de aplicarse el sambenito de esa palabreja semi-inglesa y semi-tonta, que no obstante decir muy poco o nada, constituye hoy por hoy en la corte la fórmula inevitable y compendiada de todo juico crítico en materia de arte."

9. Original: "El elogio neutraliza y embrutece; la negación es la única que puede producir el desequilibrio necesario para que las ideas sigan brotando."

10. Original: "Sin diferencia de nivel, sin oposición no puede haber dinamismo, ni exteriorización de energía."

11. Original: "Por eso, cuando mi mala fortuna me lleva a presenciar cómo tiran del pellejo del ausente los *habitués* a tal o cual congregación de gente del oficio, pienso que era caso de contárselo al interesado y darle la enhorabuena encima."

12. Original: "Despreciar todo lo que no existe en el momento actual. Eternizar lo efímero, fijar lo fugitivo, engrandecer lo diminuto. Eso debe ser el arte, el arte nuestro; el actualismo; no hay otro arte posible."

13. Original: "Somos colaboradores [Félix y yo]. Yo vivo, él escribe . . . Lo curioso es que he tomado tan en serio mi papel de experimentador que ya en las cosas más sencillas veo asunto novelable, y ya no sé si él escribe lo que yo vivo o si yo vivo lo que él escribe."

14. Original: "Y como tú dices, que las modistas no saben dar estilo, y el estilo debe ser cosa propia de uno, que sin estilo no hay distinción posible."

15. Original: "Aquello sí que tenía estilo; allí, ni luz eléctrica, ni timbres, ni teléfonos; nada de esta ferretería progresista tan antipática y tan cursi."

16. Original: "Ahora dices eso, y otras veces reniegas de todo lo antiguo; dices que estamos en un país atrasadísimo. . . . si a cada instante varía lo distinguido."

17. Original: "por eso dicen que la vida moderna no tiene carácter; como si el no tenerlo no fuera un carácter como otro cualquiera."

18. Original: "La invención de la palabra 'cursi' complicó horriblemente la vida. Antes existía lo bueno y lo malo, lo divertido y lo aburrido, y a ello se ajustaba nuestra conducta. Ahora existe lo cursi, que no es lo bueno ni lo malo, ni lo que divierte ni lo que aburre; es . . . una negación: lo contrario de lo distinguido; es decir, una cosa cada día; porque en cuanto hay seis personas que piensan o hacen lo mismo, ya es preciso pensar y hacer otra cosa para ser distinguido; y por huir de lo cursi se hacen tonterías, extravagancias . . . , hasta maldades."

19. Original: "Los espíritus escogidos . . . huyendo de la multitud; la multitud siguién-doles por donde vayan. Unos, cursis por el afán de imitar a otros; otros, más cursis por el afán de distinguirse de todos." Sharply experienced social separation is notable in the incomprehension and indifference of the upper classes toward the lower orders, as this comment from one character reveals: "como veníamos a pie y la gente baja, hija, está cada día más insolente. . . . Como si el gastar dinero en caprichos no fuera en beneficio de los que trabajan, y como si una no socorriera a mucha gente. Un dineral pago yo todos los meses de suscripciones benéficas" (as we were coming on foot and the lower classes, needless to say, are getting more insolent every day. . . . As if spending money on little luxuries weren't doing a favor to the working classes, and as if one didn't do one's bit to help so many people. I pay out huge sums every month to charities) (Benavente, *Lo cursi* 90).

20. Original: "Maldad es disfrazar los sentimientos, y por no parecer cursis los dis-frazamos muchas veces y obligamos a los demás a disfrazarlos."

21. Original: "[Rosario] ha oído decir que los celos no se llevan; es una cursilería tener celos de su marido. ¡Oh! El miedo a lo cursi es mi cómplice. . . . Para Agustín no hay bueno ni malo. Todo es cursi o es distinguido. Es cursi tener celos; es cursi alarmarse porque su mujer se muestre amable conmigo; es cursi desconfiar de mí, su mejor amigo."

22. See Ara Torralba; Mainer; Broto Salanova, *Un olvidado;* and his annotated edition of *Alma contemporánea*, for a much needed reevaluation of Llanas Aguilaniedo and his times.

23. Original: "Una generación de viejos y agotados, de psicasténicos, de impotentes, de analistas y atormentadores de su yo, desfila por el teatro, por la novela, por las diversas manifestaciones del arte de nuestros días."

24. See Cardwell for the proliferation of the "degenerate artist" as a social redemptive (115). Llanas Aguilaniedo's aesthetic elitism is of course also part of a larger cultural phenomenon, that of modernism and the avant-garde. As Poggioli observes, "in the face of society and especially official society, the avant-garde looks and works like a culture of negation" (107). Gabriel Alomar, in 1905, talks of "iperestetici, posseduti, ispirati. La loro opera comincia da una grande negazione" (the hyperaesthetics, the possessed, the divinely inspired. Their work begins with a great negation) (33). For negation as a literary theme, see Barrow.

25. Original: "La apacible belleza, la tranquilidad y el fino encanto de aquella Naturaleza resignada que caía con su Sol, contrastando con el ruido de coches y los murmullos del paseo, despertaba en el alma complicada armonía de sentimientos, estados de vibración particulares, parecidos a los que en nosotros provocan algunas composiciones de Chopin, las que parecen contarnos la extinción de una raza, aquellas en que llora el gran compositor las desgracias de los suyos, las poéticas tristezas . . . de la vencida Polonia. . . . Hermoso cuadro aquel que tan bien simbolizaba el espíritu de nuestro tiempo."

26. Original: "como todo lo incompleto, hacía soñar; soñar con el complemento."

27. Original: "Siempre ha sido la obra de arte un reflejo de la emoción experimentada por el artista; pero dando mayor amplitud al concepto de esa emoción, y exagerándola como base de toda producción, se obtiene una literatura de *emotivos*."

28. See Felipe Trigo, "El emotivismo," for a sharp contemporary critique of the inconsistencies and contradictions found in Llanas.

29. Llanas himself saw male hysteria in the Galdosian character Federico from *Realidad* (*Alma* 239).

30. Original: "la adaptación progresiva de los inadaptables, la vuelta a lo sencillo de los desengañados de la complicación y del análisis; la congregación de las almas crepusculares de nuestra época que buscan juntas en el olvido de todo, el reposo absoluto del espíritu."

31. Original: "Es el anuncio de la noche de la inteligencia con que ha de renacer para vivir el nuevo día."

32. Original: "esa especial aristocracia de espíritus que han alcanzado el grado máximo de diferenciación de su tiempo."

33. It would be stretching things to see in Llanas the same kind of conclusion Maurice Blanchot arrives at, that "negation is tied to language . . . [and] is the achievement of this negation" (43, 45). Departing from a Nietzschean creativity through destruction, Blanchot goes on to say that "language can only begin with the void: no fullness, no certainty can even speak; something essential is lacking in anyone who expresses himself" (43).

34. This use of the emotions as something intrinsically modern, as something to be employed in modern ways, is visible even in scientific discourse. In an early text of the histologist Ramón y Cajal, who received the Nobel Prize in 1906, aimed at forming the minds of young researchers in the sciences, he writes: "impregnemos de emoción y simpatía las cosas observadas; hagámoslas nuestras, tanto por el corazón como por la inteligencia" (let us bathe with emotion and sympathy the things we observe; let us make them ours, as much through the heart as through the intellect) (117). My thanks to Lincoln Lambeth for referring me to this text, which was originally published in 1899.

The discussion of nostalgia in Galdós's *Discurso* and Llanas Aguilaniedo's *Alma contemporánea* first appeared, in different form, in a section of my "Nostalgia and Exile."

7. THE MARGINS OF HOME: MODERNIST CURSILERÍA

1. Also pertinent here is Ross Chambers's understanding of ironic "appropriation" within the system of canonicity in order to "change the products of the system." And he continues: "The irony of appropriation . . . negates, or can negate, the system without denying its own involvement in that system" (21).

2. Original: "estilista original y al mismo tiempo adorador de la lengua patria, adorador hasta el fetichismo."

3. Original: "Querer como te quiero / querida mía, / cifrando en ti del alma / la dicha toda, / me dicen que es solemne cursilería, / pues querer de tal modo / ya no es de moda."

4. Original: "una violenta diatriba, una sátira punzante y cruel contra todos los *modernismos* sociales, políticos, literarios, hasta religiosos."

5. Original: "había tenido la desgracia de construir buena parte del Ensanche al compás del llamado 'modernismo'. "

6. Original: "todos los remates y las tribunas y a rascar las artísticas fachadas de sus casas *modern styl,* suprimiendo toda la hojarasca y la ornamentación que traba y suplanta la arquitectura del edificio."

7. Gómez de la Serna expanded his original 1934 essay in 1943. I will be citing from the later edition, which includes more examples of cursilería, but the text remains in essence unchanged in spirit and tone from first publication. The only noticeable modification comes in Ramón's attitude toward Juan Ramón Jiménez, whom he lambasts even more in 1943 for being cursi, comparing *Platero y yo* to Martínez Sierra's *Canción de cuna* (49).

8. Original: "Así como lo barroco tiene su última explicación en lo cursi, lo cursi tiene su primera explicación y antecedente en lo barroco."

9. Original: "los extravagantes callejeros, sin hogar seguro, sin academicidad posible."

10. Original: "se pliega hacia la conciencia interior del que ha de vivir dentro de ella como si intentase ser su concha sinuosa, el revés de su mascarilla total."

11. Original: "el arte *vermicelle* [que] está en la calle."

12. Original: "Se pierde la cabeza pensando en las cosas del género Nouveau Style, o del género Atelier d'Artiste o del género Demi-Mondaine, los pendentif Lalique, el Bar Maxim's o la Sala Aeolian de París."

13. Original: "¡Qué sex-appeal el de todas esas cosas y esas bombas eléctricas! Se dedicaba galantería a los objetos, mirando biombos y mamparas."

14. Original: "Las mujeres parecían pantallas, y las pantallas mujeres. Porque todo lo presidía el culto a la mujer."

15. Original: "En el Modern Style llegó a su apoteosis el triunfo de la mujer y su larga cabellera. Todo lo que hay en ella de curvo y ondulante, de plástico y de blando, fue el oleaje de las nuevas formas."

16. Original: "apliqué casero, invención de señoritas."

17. Original: "Es algo privado y es sólo gracia personal y casera."

18. Original: "otra manera de adornar el gabinete santuario de la casa, armonía de la familia."

19. Original: "lámpara que quiere ser flor, otra cosa que lámpara, la gran voluntad de ser aparece integral. Tampoco había abandonado esta lámpara su deseo de ser joya, ni dejó de pensar en las modas femeninas de su época y en el dibujo de los adornos de los trajes o de los sombreros."

20. Original: "Esta lámpara quería pensar y alentar conversaciones adornadas, pensamientos con rimbombancias, pasiones con fervores líricos."

21. In another vanguardist, epigrammatic piece on lo cursi, Ortiz de Montellano writes in *Contemporáneos* that "el buen arte cursi forma la estética de los sentimientos humanos conmovedores" (good cursi art shapes the aesthetic of poignant human feelings) (201).

22. Original: "Me vengaba en la destrucción de la absurda canéfora o de la musmé lampadarizada o del niño golfo en yeso mal pintado."

23. Original: "prepara panales de mimos al tiempo que revolotea, que quiere anidar, que pide resquicios, que quiere desmelenamientos y minuciosas trazas."

24. Original: "chineros de corazonadas, bomberas de presagios, jarrones llenos como de bolitas de ojos muertos, espejos con marco de traje de baile, consolas funambúlicas."

25. See César Nicolás's excellent study of "metáforas metonímicas" and "metonimias metafóricas," 129–51.

26. Original: "Los de la época cursi panteonizaban sus cosas, las cuidaban de la pulmonía del tiempo y por eso inventaron los fanales en que se solidificó la cascada del tiempo en su caer de concha en concha."

27. This image recalls Larra's metaphor of the album as a "pantheon" of signatures (see chapter 2).

28. Original: "Somos humo, delicuescentes, blandos, perezosos, languidecientes, agónicos y entonces tenemos que propender a lo nalgado, a lo caderudo, a lo sinuoso."

29. Original: "¿Es que convertida en cosa suelta la tráquea y los pulmones no son uno de esos objetos [cursis]?"

30. Original: "Lo que se estiliza sin incurrir en la filigrana y el firulete no tiene la venosidad que hace vivir lo inguinal. Todo debe tener manojos de vísceras, raíces curvas y enrevesadas, tendencias a la hidrografía y la complejidad del sistema nervioso."

31. Original: "Lo entrañable, las entrañas, tienen algo de lo que se aglomera en lo cursi."

32. Original: "Lo cursi está creado por el deseo de abrigar bien la vida y consagrar su contoneo."

33. Original: "No se descansa sino en lo cursi y todos sentimos el deseo de esa regresión, que es regresión hacia el pasado y hacia el futuro, pues lo más grato del porvenir es que tendrá sus formas nuevas de cursilería."

34. Original: "adornística espontánea, ingenua, que quiere mimarnos frente al vacío . . . esa deseada habitación cursi."

35. Original: "En la exclamación espontánea es difícil hacer distinciones, pero para eso sirve el *Ensayo*, con su politubería de cristal para los cultivos diferentes."

36. Original: "Pero acabemos aquí este ensayo sobre lo cursi que podría apoyarse en tantas razones y tantas cosas, hasta llegar a ser interminable." The 1934 version of the essay ends with these words: "Este ensayo sobre lo cursi podría apoyarse en tantas razones y tantas cosas, que llegaría a ser interminable. Para acabarlo sólo pido una viñeta cursi" (This essay on lo cursi could be based on even more reasons and examples, but then it would end up being interminable. To finish it off, I ask for just one cursi vignette) (38). A drawing by Bores of a cupid in a curlicued cloud, not included in the 1943 edition, follows.

37. Original: "Las cosas nos salvan . . . [las cosas] son como nosotros . . . ¿Que no somos la cosa? Somos cosa, cosa blanda, con circulación asesinante, con digestión apurada."

38. Original: "El cuello [de Concha] florecía de los hombros como un lirio enfermo, los senos eran dos rosas blancas aromando un altar, y los brazos, de una esbeltez delicada y frágil, parecían las asas del ánfora rodeando su cabeza."

39. Original: "con el cuidado religioso y amante que visten las señoras devotas a las imágenes de que son camaristas."

40. Original: "la miniatura, el bibelot esbozado de la mujer desnuda."

41. Original: "Lo bonito impera sobre lo hermoso; hoy, el *bibelot* vive sobre la estatua, y la Venus de Milo retrocede ante la bayadera moderna."

42. Original: "Las dos niñas se aplicaron a deshilar el lenzuelo, lanzándose miradas furtivas, para ver cuál adelantaba más en su tarea. Concha e Isabel secreteaban. Daba las diez un reloj, y sobre los regazos infantiles, en el círculo luminoso de la lámpara, iban formando lentamente las hilas, un cándido manojo."

43. Original: "La niña de porcelana que enhebra un aguja debajo de la pantalla de la lámpara."

8. THE CULTURE OF NOSTALGIA, OR
THE LANGUAGE OF FLOWERS

1. A point also made by Howard Young (137), who looks at nostalgia in poetic texts by T. S. Eliot, Pedro Salinas, and Lorca.

2. Original: "roja por la mañana, a la tarde se pone blanca y se deshoja por la noche" (76). I will be citing from the Martínez Cuitiño edition, along with the Gwynne Edwards translation of *Doña Rosita*. All remaining translations, unless otherwise noted, are my own.

3. "Sentimentality is the strong tendency in modern literature (from the eighteenth century to the present) to dwell upon the emotional aspects of human life, but to dwell upon them not by representing or investigating fresh and authentic emotional experience, but by conventionalizing and reifying such experience, often in terms of a supposed

relationship to a nostalgic past. Sentimentality is therefore the inauthentic manipulation of emotion as an object of worship" (Fulweiler 6).

4. Original: "Es un drama para familias que yo titulo, el gran drama poético de la cursilería."

5. Original: "Mejor sería decir el drama de la cursilería española, de la mojigatería española, del ansia de gozar que las mujeres han de reprimir, por fuerza en lo más hondo de su entraña enfebrecida."

6. See note 13 of chapter 2 for the twentieth-century persistence of such cursi objects as album verses, even in Lorca. Lorca's brother discusses the intentionally cursi element in *Doña Rosita la soltera* (228–29). After I had finished this study, Mario Hernández's edition of *Doña Rosita la soltera* appeared, with an excellent introduction (and valuable appendices). He, too, notes that "lo cursi resucita como condena y como rara apoteosis estética" (lo cursi is both condemned and revived in a rare aesthetic apotheosis) in the play (55). In the same time period as Lorca's *Doña Rosita*, works like Pedro Muñoz Seca and Pedro Pérez Fernández's *La cursilona* (a zarzuela, adapted from the comedy *La pluma verde*, 1922) (1930) and Luis de Vargas's *La cursi del hongo* (1933), a comedy, were also being produced. The sense of lo cursi as outdated (and out of place in 1930s Spain) is echoed in these lines from *La cursi del hongo:* "Ya no se ven por el mundo esas señoritas cursis, venidas a menos, que sólo viven del recuerdo de sus apellidos ilustres. Estamos en tiempos más positivos. Ahora el que no trabaja no come" (You no longer see around here those cursi misses, who've come down in the world, living off the memory of their illustrious name. We are living in more practical times. Now, if you don't work, you don't eat) (9).

7. Original: "poema granadino del novecientos, dividido en varios jardines con escenas de canto y baile."

8. For comments on the historic-cultural dimensions of the Granadine reality reflected in *Doña Rosita*, see Rodrigo, "*Doña Rosita la soltera:* Crónica de una ciudad" and "*Doña Rosita la soltera:* Teatro y realidad"; Morris 120–33; and Martín Recuerda 22–40.

9. Christopher Soufas suggests that *Doña Rosita* is related to the "idea of theater as a confrontation between private and public domains" (109). He focuses more on the theatrical strategies and the theater practices which allow the play of public versus private than I do.

10. Original: "una Torre Eiffel de nácar sobre dos palomas que llevan en sus picos la rueda de la industria."

11. In discussing some of the weaknesses of New Historicism, Vincent Pecora singles out the example of Walter Benn Michaels's work. "For Michaels and a number of younger Americanists, since everything is always already 'representation,' representation is where all the 'real' action has been all along" (244).

12. Geertz appears, however, more aware of the limitations of a purely internal approach to culture in his later work: "We need . . . something rather more than local knowledge. We need a way of turning its varieties into commentaries one upon another, the one lighting what the other darkens" (*Local Knowledge* 233).

13. Martínez Cuitiño points to even earlier "pre-texts" of *Doña Rosita*, such as the unpublished story "Mazurka" (1917) (55–56). See also Hernández 247–58.

14. Original: "Es que todo lo quiere volando. Hoy ya quisiera que fuese pasado mañana. Se echa a volar y se nos pierde de las manos" (73).

15. Original: "He aquí la vida de mi doña Rosita. Mansa, sin fruto, sin objeto, cursi. . . . ¿Hasta cuándo seguirán así todas las doñas Rositas de España?"

16. Original: "Viene pálida, vestida de blanco, con un abrigo hasta el filo del vestido" (185).

17. Original: "Y cuando llega la noche / se comienza a deshojar" (186).

18. Andreas Huyssen discusses nostalgia "as a form of memory" that is "always implicated, even productive in [utopia]" (88). The implication to me is, then, that nostalgia is "historical."

19. Or as Ricoeur puts it, "to figure is always to see as, but not always *to see* or *to make visible*" (*The Rule of Metaphor* 61).

20. For example, see Gimeno, ch. 14; Jazmín, *El lenguaje de las flores* 9; 28; Pareja Serrada 119 (on "la niña y la flor"); Ossorio y Gallardo, "Mujeres y flores" 50–51; and Camprodón, *¡Flor de un día!*, this last another probable nineteenth-century source for Lorca's play, for the combined *brevitas* of life and love-woman theme in flower imagery. Women of the working classes and flowers were also associated economically, particularly in the artificial flower business. See Sergeant 94–116; and Boxer 401–23. As a hobby, artificial flower making appealed to middle-class women throughout Europe and the Americas. Carmen de Burgos devotes five chapters, fully one-third of her early twentieth-century book, *Las artes de la mujer*, to the craft.

21. Original: "'Sólo en ti pongo mis ojos,' / el heliotropo expresaba. / 'No te querré mientras viva,' / dice la flor de la albahaca. / 'Soy tímida,' la violeta. / 'Soy fría,' la rosa blanca. / Dice el jazmín: 'Seré fiel'; / y el clavel: '¡Apasionada!'" (13).

22. Original: "¿Y qué os voy a decir? Hay cosas que no se pueden decir porque no hay palabras para decirlas; y si las hubiera, nadie entendería su significado" (176).

23. See Daniel Devoto's classic source study of *Doña Rosita la soltera* for the "rosa mutabile" and flower language texts; also Anderson, "More Sources for García Lorca's *Doña Rosita la soltera*," 149–64; Laffranque 279–300; Rees 81–92; Jiménez-Vera 127–37; Francisco García Lorca 229–31; Morris 122; Salazar Rincón, ch. 5; and Hernández 47–55. The choral opening to Bécquer's 1860 zarzuela *La cruz del valle* also exploits the language of flowers: "La camelia / es la hermosura, / el clavel es el afán, / la violeta / es la ternura / y el orgullo el tulipán. / Son los mirtos / la armonía, / los laureles el valor, / y en sus himnos / de alegría / es un verso cada flor" (The camellia / is beauty, / the carnation is desire, / the violet / is tenderness / and the tulip pride. / Myrtles are / harmony, / laurels valor, / and in its hymns / of joy / every line of verse is a flower) (222). My thanks to David Gies for this last reference.

24. An example of this universalizing tendency in presenting the language of flowers, which is taken to reductive extremes, can be found in "El sentido de las flores" by La

Condesa X (*Caridad española* 60–63). Here all flowers are essentially the same because they suggest the same unequivocal content: "son nuestras ilusiones, nuestros anhelos, / son nuestras esperanzas, son nuestro encanto" ([flowers] are our illusions, our desires, / our hopes, our delight) (60).

Although Beverly Seaton found only three Spanish-language texts in the Americas (New York, San José, and Lima) and one published by Garnier in Paris (78–79), versions of the language of flowers also appeared in books, almanacs, and magazines in Spain. See, for example, Florencio Jazmín, *El lenguaje de las flores*, which enjoyed great success, the first two editions being quickly sold out (Castañeda y Alcover 295); José Anselmo Clavé, "El lenguaje de las flores," 95–96; "Lenguaje de las flores," 62–68; Eusebio Blasco, "El lenguaje de las flores," 420–22, a send-up of the fad; *La rueda del amor y de la fortuna, con cien preguntas diferentes y el Lenguaje de las Flores;* and "El lenguaje de las flores," which consists of a series of photos of a young woman holding a daisy. Castañeda y Alcover also lists a *Telegrafía amorosa*, by Mariano del Castillo, which includes the languages of flowers, fans, colors, and hands, from the mid-nineteenth century (139). In *El amor en los tiempos del cólera* [Love in the time of cholera] (1985), Colombian novelist Gabriel García Márquez recreated the era of flower language in his character Florentino Areza, who composes a *Secretario de los enamorados*. See also Sebold, "García Márquez y lo cursi" 145–49.

25. Original: "Lo que es difícil de retener en la memoria es el sentido simbólico apropiado a cada flor."

26. Roberto Sánchez perceptively comments that "la verdadera emoción, parecen [los objetos] decirnos, se esconde tras lo superficial, lo falso; tras fórmulas hechas: el lenguaje del abanico, el lenguaje de los guantes, el lenguaje de los sellos y el lenguaje de las horas. El artificio mata todo aliento humano" (real emotion, [objects] seem to say to us, is hidden behind the superficial, the false: behind ready-made formulas: the language of fans, the language of gloves, stamps, and hours. Artifice kills all human breath) (335). Sánchez's last sentence, however, not only undercuts his point, but cannot be sustained textually, since *Doña Rosita* is all about the supreme humanness of artifice.

27. That Lorca was familiar with Freud's texts, and in particular with *The Interpretation of Dreams*, seems quite certain. See Huélamo Kosma; and Paul Julian Smith's excellent study, *The Theatre of García Lorca* 72. Like Smith, however, I am less interested in proving Freud's influence on the playwright than in exploring the complex relationship between individual psyche and collective social body.

28. Original: "La estética genuinamente granadina es la estética del diminutivo, la estética de las cosas diminutas."

29. Original: "Diminutivo asustado como un pájaro, que abre secretas cámaras de sentimiento y revela el más definido matiz de la ciudad. El diminutivo no tiene más misión que la de limitar, ceñir, traer a la habitación y poner en nuestra mano los objetos o ideas de gran perspectiva."

30. Original: "Hay que hurgar y explorar nuestra propia intimidad y secreto."

31. Original: "Todo tiene por fuerza un dulce aire doméstico; pero, verdaderamente, ¿quién penetra esta intimidad?"

32. See Handley; Morris 41; 71–72; and Mitchell, ch. 11, for more discussion of the andalucismo movement and debate.

33. Praz offers a delicious parody of the tourist in love with "romantic Spain": "The tendency to pan-taurism is early apprehended through a violent pro-Spanish feeling. The subject begins by experiencing an irrepressible craving to appear Spanish, and to this effect he combs his hair with a lead comb in order to make it look darker, adopts a Cordovan felt hat for his head-dress, covers his fingers with diamond rings, has his boots polished at every step, drinks Anís del Mono, and, whenever it is on, goes to hear the opera of *Carmen*, whose overture makes him beside himself. All these fixed ideas belong to the symptomatological equipment of pan-taurism. The very sound of the Spanish language acts on the subject as the sight of a desirable courtesan" (*Unromantic Spain* 76). Praz's book evidently was not translated into Spanish. See Francesco Fiumara's informative analysis of the changes Praz made in the English translation and the 1955 Italian edition of *Penisola pentagonale* (orginally published in 1928).

34. Significantly, ambivalence over provincial life and provincialism is also found in more centralized nation-states like France. See Zeldin 2:29.

35. Original: "Elemento que llaman elegante y que algunos, tratándose de esta clase de fiestas, se atreverían a calificar de cursi."

36. *O'Shea's Guide to Spain and Portugal,* originally published in 1865, went through thirteen editions. The tenth edition, which I used, dates from 1895.

37. For more information on modern Granadine history and economy, see Gay Armenteros and Viñes Millet; Díaz Lobón; Morilla Critz; and Arcas Cubero. The need to improve Granada's commercial and industrial base, to bring the province and city out of their backwardness, poverty, and isolation, becomes a nineteenth- and twentieth-century *cri de guerre* among the local notables. See, for example, Montells y Nadal who, as a liberal progressive, espoused the oft heard idea that "la felicidad fundada en el trabajo es indestructible y de naturaleza siempre progresiva" (happiness founded on work is indestructible and always progressive in nature) (xi).

38. See Varela Ortega for a richly detailed history of Restoration politics.

39. Original: "Madrid se había olvidado de las provincias, y, como España *era* pura provincia, tenía por fuerza que resultar, en vez de una política 'nacional,' una política provinciana, localista y rural en el peor sentido de estos vocablos."

40. Morilla Critz, for example, calls Andalusia a "colonia interna" within Spain (114). See also Acosta Sánchez (232); and Juan Goytisolo (289). Goytisolo—inter alia—stresses the close connection between the rising economic fortunes of Catalan industry and protectionism and the socioeconomic hardship of the South.

41. The "Polos de Desarrollo," or regional growth poles, were a feature of the Franco regime's economic policy up to 1975 (Hadjimichalis 22; 156).

42. For this account of political and cultural andalucismo, see Acosta Sánchez; Ar-

cas Cubero 91–93; Handley, "Federico García Lorca and the 98 Generation" 51–52; Mitchell, ch. 11; and Ruiz Lagos, "La atracción del sur" 9–38.

43. This Granadine modernization—and destruction of the old city—continues relentlessly, according to Ian Gibson in 1992 (*Lorca's Granada* xv–xvi). See also Alejandro V. García's "El múltiple abandono de la historia urbana de Granada."

44. Original: "Esta ramplonería arquitectónica vino a Europa de rechazo y fue del gusto de los hombres de negocios, de los mangoneadores de terrenos y solares, y de los fabricantes de casas baratas; cundió el amor a la línea recta, y llegó el momento de que los hombres no pudieran dormir tranquilos mientras su calle no estuviera tirada a cordel. Donde las condiciones de las ciudades exigían estos ensanches, la sacrificada fue la estética, y donde los ensanches no estaban justificados, se procuró al mismo tiempo afear las poblaciones y hacerlas inhabitables."

45. Original: "No hay duda que aquí existe un *esquema de nostalgia* que es antieuropeo, pero que no es oriental. Andalucía."

46. The evidence by association that Eisenberg gives to prove Martínez Sierra's homosexuality or bisexuality includes the following: Gregorio Martínez Sierra was a protegé of Jacinto Benavente; he published works by Benavente and other homosexuals such as Antonio de Hoyos y Vinent and Pedro de Répide, and translated Oscar Wilde; he helped García Lorca in his career; he was a friend and collaborator of Manuel de Falla; he had a summer house in Morocco (much frequented by homosexuals). Gregorio also wrote an unproduced (and unpublished) play, *Sortilegio*, with a married homosexual as protagonist (Eisenberg, "Guía *gay*" 115). Martínez Sierra may very well have been a homosexual (or bisexual), but, in my view, Eisenberg hasn't presented a strong enough case, either biographically or textually. He also fails to point out that Martínez Sierra eventually separated from his wife (and collaborator) María, to live with the actress Catalina Bárcena, whom he had met in 1906 and with whom he had a child in 1922.

47. Baedeker lists two locations for an "R. Garzón" photography studio in Granada (330). The photographs in *Granada: Guía emocional* are not at all suggestive but simply the usual touristy views of the city and environs. The 1931 edition, which I also consulted, does not reproduce the photographs, or, interestingly enough, the subtitle, "Guía emocional."

48. Original: "el involuntario artificio de mi maraña."

49. Original: "que no sea un hombre ni mujer—ya que hombres y mujeres nos habremos destrozado la vida—un ser espiritual, refrigerante, consolador, maternal, pueril."

50. Original: "Hablar de flores es comprometido pues que de ellas se salta a las estrellas."

51. Original: "El alma que en esta poesía se expresa no es espiritual; es más bien el alma de un cuerpo que fuera vegetal."

52. Martínez Sierra's words were: "y hay una monarquía, y un gobierno que llaman conservador, y reglamentos pueriles, y fusilamientos absurdos. . . . Y España calla" (And there's a monarchy, and a government they call conservative, and puerile regulations, and absurd executions. . . . Yet Spain says nothing) (*Granada* 309). Martínez Sierra is

evidently referring to, among other things, the working-class, anticlerical, and anti-government rioting and violence of Barcelona's Tragic Week and subsequent execution of the anarchist schoolteacher Ferrer, in 1909, events which occurred under the ministry of conservative politician Antonio Maura. These words still appear in the 1931 edition.

53. In a different but related context, Paul Julian Smith also stresses "the fragility of the boundary between literal and symbolic" (102). Smith's study, *The Theatre of García Lorca*, covers *Yerma*, *Bodas de sangre*, *Así que pasen cinco años*, and *El público*, but does not include *Doña Rosita la soltera*.

54. Sahuquillo suggests that the image of the dahlias trampled into the ground in the opening scene of *Doña Rosita* may be related to Lorca's experience and literary imagining of homosexuality (172). He also notes that flower imagery in general is often associated with homosexual experience in poets like Lorca, Cernuda, Gil-Albert, and Prados (299).

55. Original: "Ayer me encontré las semillas de dalias pisoteadas por el suelo" (70). For the connection between flowers and death, see Bonaparte 231–35, who remarks that a flower placed on the death bed or tomb "a pour fonction de nier la mort" (functions as a denial of death) (233–34); and Bataille 173–78, who notes that "l'amour a l'odeur de la mort" (love has the odor of death) (177). Derrida also picks up on this association (*Glas* 22). Peter Sacks points out that "flowers, like the poetic language to which they are so often compared, serve not only as offerings or as gestures for respite but also as demarcations separating the living from the dead" (19).

56. Enright points out another usage for the language of flowers in the example of the "professional lady who wore a camellia, either white or red, depending" (8).

57. The "old maid" is a type found in many national literatures. Marina Warner remarks that "in Catholic countries the unmarried woman who has not taken the veil is a pathetic figure of fun—the *zitella*, the old maid ridiculed in popular Italian songs" (235). One of Lorca's probable sources for Doña Rosita was Mobellán de Casafiel's costumbrista sketch "Rosa la solterona." For a late nineteenth-century theatrical example, see Luis Cocat and Heliodoro Criado's *Las solteronas* from 1894.

58. Original: "feria de las flores, semanal alcahuetería filantrópica."

59. Original: "En cierto modo el *Libro de Granada* viene a ser un mapa de la soltería granadina."

60. Moreno Hernández (135) unfortunately conflates kitsch with lo cursi in categorizing *Canción de cuna* and other late modernist texts of the period. See my review of *Literatura y cursilería*.

61. Patricia O'Connor has convincingly demonstrated that María Martínez Sierra at the very least co-authored *Canción de cuna* (54).

62. Original: "El poeta querría / háberosle sabido contar día por día / con toda su emoción; mas fuera empeño vano. / ¡Quién hará la comedia del vivir cotidiano! / La vida va tejiéndose con ritmo tan igual, / que el tiempo se ha dormido en la quietud fragante; / ¡quién sabe si pasó un siglo o un instante!"

63. Original: "Yo, siempre que comulgo, me figuro que recibo al Señor en figura de niño, y así le aprieto contra el corazón."

64. Original: "Coge un rayo de sol en el espejo y le pasea por entre las ramas y por el techo de la celda y por las paredes de enfrente, y con eso se consuela, pensando que es una mariposa o un pájaro y que va donde al pensamiento se le antoja."

65. Original: "Se oyen dentro los cascabeles del coche. Las monjas desfilan. El telón empieza a bajar lentamente al empezar a desfilar las monjas. Sor Juana de la Cruz queda sola en escena y se deja caer en un sillón, llorando acongojada."

66. Original: "Salen [Doña Rosita, la Tía, el Ama] y a su mutis queda la escena sola. Se oye golpear la puerta. De pronto se abre un balcón del fondo y las blancas cortinas oscilan con el viento" (186).

67. The earlier *¡Flor de un día!* by Camprodón (1851) also centers on the much used figure of a female orphan, squeezing as much sentimentality as possible out of the topos. See the actor Chicote's comments on this play (167–70). In her memoirs, María Martínez Sierra remarked that she liked seeing men weep at performances of *Canción de cuna*. The play's success was, she wrote, akin to a "fiesta de familia" in mood (277–78).

68. See Anderson on the importance of familial relationships in *Doña Rosita* ("Las relaciones familiares").

69. Original: "Quiero huir, quiero no ver, quiero quedarme serena, vacía" (174).

70. Original: "Soy como soy y no me puedo cambiar. Ahora lo único que me queda es mi dignidad. Lo que tengo por dentro lo guardo para mí sola" (175).

71. "Es querer y no encontrar el cuerpo" (157); for the purposes of my analysis, I have translated this phrase literally ("wanting and not finding the body"), whereas the published English translation reads, "It's like loving someone and not being able to find him" (140).

72. Original: "Cada año que pasaba era como una prenda íntima que arrancaran de mi cuerpo" (173).

73. The banging door refers to death, according to Francisco García Lorca, who cites one of his brother's poems: "Una puerta / no es puerta / hasta que un muerto / sale por ella. / Rosa de dos pétalos / que el aire abre y cierra" (A door / is not a door / until a death / passes through it. / A rose of two petals / that the air opens and closes) (241). The ending of *Doña Rosita* also draws on the conventions of sentimental melodrama, as Morris points out (127).

74. While nineteenth-century cities turned increasingly into stone, cemeteries took on more of the appearance of gardens. Celestino Barallat y Falguera, for example, looked to the burying grounds of Baltimore (Greenmount), Philadelphia, and Boston as models arranged around the idea of a sacred woods and garden. See his *Principios de botánica funeraria*, which Jaume Bover calls a "manual de jardinería modernista" (a manual of modernist gardening) (foreword xii). Lorca reverses the fin de siglo funerary site by turning Doña Rosita's garden into a symbolic cemetery.

75. My thanks to the graduate seminar, "Metaphor and Identity in Modern Spain," given

at Emory University in September 1996, in which I benefited greatly from the lively exchanges between students and myself; and to Andrew Anderson and Francesco Fiumara, for their bibliographical help.

9. CODA: THE METAPHOR OF CULTURE
IN POST-FRANCO SPAIN

1. Original: "No puede una mujer sentirse placenteramente feliz si no es bajo el cobijo de una sombra más fuerte. Más fuerte en todo: en lo sentido y en lo imaginado. Precisa nuestra feminidad sentirse frágil y protegida." "Consúltame," *Medina* 13 June 1943, qtd. in Martín Gaite 50.

2. Original: "aquel fascismo trasnochado y ridículo que se nos imponía en nuestra infancia con recitados, lecturas y una buena dosis de palmetazos mientras nos suplementaban la escasa dieta con leche en polvo y queso de los americanos, tiene mucho que ver con las mentalidades y actitudes que hoy componen el mosaico macro y microfísico de los diversos poderes y formas de vida hispanos."

3. See Stephanie Sieburth's excellent discussion of this issue within the Spanish context in her *Inventing High and Low* 1–26.

4. See Susan Stewart ("Cultural Theory") for an incisive critique of the problem of organicist, functionalist models.

5. Original: "Nace la posmodernidad. Hay una generación que sabe que la dictadura es una cuestión de esperar, que ya no hay que luchar contra ella, que el viejecito camp se morirá solo o le mataremos de muerte natural."

6. Eduardo Subirats contends that postmodernism signifies the obsolescence of modernism: "en su vacío cultural, estilístico y artístico, la ruptura, la protesta y la superación vanguardista que representa el *Postmodern* pone de manifiesto la obsolescencia de la vanguardia misma, es decir, su muerte" (in its cultural, stylistic and artistic emptiness, the rupture, protest, and transcendence of the vanguard that the *Postmodern* represents demonstrates the obsolescence of the vanguard itself, that is, its death) (*La crisis de las vanguardias* 161–62).

7. I take the notion of "structures of the imagination" from Friedlander's *Reflections of Nazism* (19), an eloquent, suggestive meditation on the paradoxical and powerful conjunction of death-and-harmony images in Nazism.

8. Original: "La cultura marca el signo de los ochenta. Hay que reciclarse para estar de actualidad. Todo se hace en nombre de la cultura y, como el nivel de vida ha aumentado, todo el mundo quiere resultar lo más sofisticado posible, lanzándose a devorar la cultura que arrojan las instituciones continuamente . . . Lo que lleve el sello cultural es incuestionable, como antes lo era lo que venía de fuera."

9. Original: "¿Hasta qué punto están imbricados el poder y la cultura?"

10. Original: "En cuanto oigo la palabra *cultura* extiendo un cheque en blanco al portador."

11. Original: "*Light* es no mezclarse, no involucrarse, quedarse al margen manteniendo la figura."

12. Original: "Problemas, ninguno. . . . Sin disonancias. . . . Sea todo benévolo. Todo blando. Todo light."

13. Original: "La primera norma . . . consiste en anularse como individuo bajo un disfraz desenvuelto de personalidad arrolladora."

14. Original: "Lo más desalentador de todo proyecto de furiosa individualidad es que se construye con los restos de múltiples identidades. Ser diferente no es que sea un pecado, como dijo el filósofo, sino que es imposible."

15. Original: "La pasión por lo apócrifo lleva al posmoderno a admirar locamente a los travestís, aunque él no sea una loca. . . . El travestí es posmoderno sin saberlo."

16. Friedlander writes that "kitsch is a debased form of myth, but nevertheless draws from the mythic substance" (49).

17. Calinescu notes the "open-ended indeterminacy" of kitsch (228).

18. Original: "es el espíritu—o la falta de espíritu—de esa famosa Posmodernidad."

19. Original: "con materiales muertos, con cadáveres." He also says that "el campo en el que germinan las semillas de esas dos plantas que son lo cursi y lo kitsch es la muerte" (the field in which the seeds of these two plants we call lo cursi and kitsch germinate is death) (Alas Mínguez, "Sinceramente kitsch" 9).

20. Virginia Gibbs employs the term *kitsch* incorrectly when she applies it to late nineteenth-century Madrid, Restoration Spain, and Valle-Inclán's *Sonatas*. Not only does the category not appear in Spain then (as far as I can ascertain) but, more importantly, the highly industrialized, consumer-oriented society in which kitsch thrives does not yet exist in Spain then.

21. The words *camp* and *kitsch* do not appear in the latest edition I consulted of the *DRAE* (1992). However, I recently came across Celeste Olalquiaga's suggestive book, *The Artificial Kingdom: A Treasury of Kitsch Experience* (New York: Pantheon, 1998).

22. Ellen Marson sums up some of the sociopolitical elements of 1960s Spain that the novísimos would have experienced: "the 1966 Ley de Prensa, relaxation of social customs, industrialization and urbanization, university unrest and rebellion, easy access to foreign works, foreign travel, and with this a marked fascination for alternate cultural forms (television, radio, movies, comics, jazz)" (191).

23. Original: "Simago es cursi, el Corte Inglés es kitsch; la vida es cursi, la muerte es kitsch; Ana Belén es cursi, Madonna es kitsch."

24. Original: "cursi y se sueña kitsch en un sueño."

25. Original: "es insincero, destruye sus modelos tratando de crearlos al recrearlos, intenta llenar el vacío con vacío. Lo cursi en cambio atesora y preserva los restos, las migajas del banquete kitsch, con una devoción repleta de sentimentalismo y por tanto no intelectualizable. Lo cursi se habita en secreto, es un éxtasis casero."

26. Original: "un matiz de la sensibilidad, nunca de la inteligencia, entonces su desequilibrio pertenece al gusto."

27. Original: "Entre las nuevas creaciones aparece una tendencia . . . a recuperar al individuo y a devolverle un sentimiento de identidad que parecía perdido."

28. Original: "la agresividad funcional o de la funcionalidad agresiva—como se prefiera."

29. Vilarós offers another kind of utopia: "la adicción como metáfora para la utopía más o menos marxista que alimentó a la izquierda española desde el final de la guerra civil. La utopía fue la droga de adicción de las generaciones que vivieron el franquismo" (addiction as a metaphor for the more or less Marxist utopia that nurtured the Spanish left since the end of the civil war. Utopia was the drug of choice for the generations living under the Franco regime) ("Los monos del desencanto español" 221). This notion is further elaborated in her provocative book, *Los monos del desencanto*.

30. Original: "verdadera *transpersonalización* o transmutación de personalidad, asunción de una personalidad distinta y nueva."

31. Original: "el cínico de Tierno que es otro de los mitos de la movida. . . . Un cínico como la copa de un pino, ambicioso, demagogo, populista. . . . y eso sí, un gran relaciones públicas."

32. Original: "efébico y adolescente de una falsa adolescencia."

33. Original: "Licaria y Sabela estaban no tendidas sobre el lecho, sino como arrojadas, desnudas y borrachas. No había nada patético en su muerte. Parecían dos escayolas sobrantes y abandonadas sobre los escombros de las sábanas. Me pareció como ver en ellas un cierto ademán erótico, el vuelo parado e imaginado de una penúltima caricia."

34. Original: "Todos los grandes amores suelen acabar en una hepatitis B. Real o inventada. De Gualberta, no volví a acordarme."

35. Original: "como cuando, un día, Swann se levanta curado de Odette. Estebanía quedó, en mi olvido, vomitando eternamente su voracidad verde, su biografía voraz, el perro joven, hambriento y ladrante de su delgada y rubia tripa. Eternamente."

36. Original: "La Utopía acababa de nacer del charco de sangre y mierda que había dejado el cuerpo de Franco debajo de la cama."

37. Original: "En la Castellana, paseábamos Tierno y yo, y había tanta muerte en el oxígeno que el alcalde empezó a hablarme de sus enfermedades. Molestias, debilidad, cosas. . . . Tierno me hablaba de dolencias vagas, de las tristes exigencias del organismo."

38. Original: "Tierno, cuando alcalde, tuvo sobre [Santiago] Carrillo la intuición de concretar la Utopía general en Utopía local, madrileña."

39. Original: "Tierno Galván hizo su presente utópico, ciudadano, real, colectivo, espectacular e ilustrado, juvenil y jovellanista, como de un Jovellanos drogado, follador e incendiario. Tierno llegaría a ser (todo se verá en este libro) un Carlos III marxista, un Marx afeitado, un Azaña sin verrugas e, insisto, un Jovellanos rojo, posrevolucionario y ácrata, reinando en un inmenso sarao de castañeras."

40. Original: "El pensador hermético había decidido disiparse eucarísticamente en los demás."

41. Original: "el hombre interior que decide exteriorizarse mediante la Utopía/Eucaristía."

42. Original: "La transición ha terminado y la Utopía ha muerto."

43. Original: "Gracias a aquella filmación casual, clandestina e interrumpida tuvimos la imagen viva y directa de la fragmentación de España."

44. Within the context of modern Hungarian history, Istvān Rev talks about attending funerals as a "therapy of closeness, of taking part, being present at the historical occasion" (28). In an excellent article, Paul Julian Smith sees in Umbral's chronicles of the period "the twin stories of the nation and the body" ("Modern Times" 329).

45. In *The Moderns*, Paul Julian Smith notes the "problematic and fluid cohabitation of the modern and postmodern" in post-Franco society (46).

Los abanicos. Su lenguaje expresivo. Con detalles de los alfabetos dactilológico y cam-pilológico. (Biblioteca del Diccionario Enciclopédico Hispano-Americano). 1887. Valencia: Librerías París-Valencia, 1992.

Abanicos: La colección del Museo Municipal de Madrid: Museo Municipal, diciembre 1995–febrero 1996. Madrid: Ayuntamiento, 1995.

Abu-Lughod, Lila, and Catherine A. Lutz. "Introduction: Emotion, Discourse, and the Politics of Everyday Life." *Language and the Politics of Emotion.* Ed. Lutz and Abu-Lughod. Cambridge: Cambridge University Press, 1990. 1–23.

Acho-Cam [Tomás Camacho?]. "Becqueriana." *La mosca roja* (Barcelona), la época, No. 33 (12 Nov. 1882): [1].

Acosta Sánchez, José. *Andalucía: Reconstrucción de una identidad y la lucha contra el centralismo.* Barcelona: Anagrama, 1978.

Acto solemne en honor de Don Antonio Cánovas del Castillo para conmemorar el Centenario de su nacimiento. Celebrado por las Reales Academias Española, de la Historia, de Bellas Artes y de Ciencias Morales y Políticas, en el Salón de Actos Públicos de la Primera, el día 5 de marzo de 1928. (Discursos de Gabriel Maura Gamazo, el marqués de Lema, el conde de Romanones, Joaquín Sánchez de Toca, Miguel Primo de Rivera.)

A. G. "Antonio Grilo." *La ilustración española y americana* 50.7 (22 Feb. 1906): 108.

Aladro, Carlos Luis. *La tía Norica de Cádiz.* Madrid: Editora Nacional, 1975.

Alarcón, Pedro Antonio de. *El escándalo.* 1875. 2 vols. Ed. Mariano Baquero Goyanes. Madrid: Espasa-Calpe, 1973.

Alarcón y Meléndez, Julio. *Sentimientos.* Prol. Vicente Barrantes. Madrid: Imprenta de R. Labajos, 1865.

Alas, Leopoldo. "Album-abanico." 1898. *Doctor Sutilis.* Madrid: Renacimiento, 1916. 257–67.

———. *Apolo en Pafos.* 1887. Ed. Adolfo Sotelo Vázquez. Barcelona: PPU, 1989.

———. *Cánovas y su tiempo.* Madrid: Fernando Fe, 1887.

———. "Los grafómanos." *Nueva campaña.* 1887. Foreword. Antonio Vilanova. Barcelona: Editorial Lumen, 1990. 93–102.

———. *A Hoax / Superchería.* Trans. Michael Nimetz. Lewiston, N.Y.: Edwin Mellen Press, 1995.

———. *Mezclilla.* 1889. Foreword. Antonio Vilanova. Barcelona: Editorial Lumen, 1987.

———. "El poeta-búho: Historia natural." 1885. *Cuentos.* Ed. Angeles Ezama. Barcelona: Crítica, 1997. 71–75.

——. "¿Por qué no escribe Alarcón? (Palique tal vez indiscreto)." 1885. *Obra olvidada: Artículos de crítica.* Ed. Antonio Ramos-Gascón. Madrid: Ediciones Júcar, 1973. 51–57.

——. "*La Pródiga:* Novela de Alarcón." 1882. *Obra olvidada: Artículos de crítica.* Ed. Antonio Ramos-Gascón. Madrid: Ediciones Júcar, 1973. 44–46.

——. *La Regenta.* 1884–85. 2 vols. Ed. Gonzalo Sobejano. Madrid: Castalia, 1981.

——. *La Regenta.* 1884–85. Trans. John Rutherford. New York: Penguin, 1984.

——. *Su único hijo.* 1891. Ed. Carolyn Richmond. 2d ed. Madrid: Espasa-Calpe, 1990.

——. *Superchería. Cuervo. Doña Berta.* 1889–90. Foreword. Ramón Pérez de Ayala. Madrid: Taurus, 1970.

——. "Versicultura: Grilus Vastatrix." *La literatura en 1881.* By Armando Palacio Valdés and Alas. Madrid: Alfredo de Carlos Hierro, 1882. 93–97.

Alas [Mínguez], Leopoldo. *La orgía de los cultos: Viaje crítico por las ciénagas de la cultura española.* Madrid: Temas de Hoy, 1989.

——. "Sinceramente kitsch." *El kitsch español.* Ed. Sánchez Casado. Madrid: Temas de Hoy, 1988. 9–12.

Album Familia Díaz-Pérez, n.d. Ann Arbor, Mich.

Album de "Blanco y Negro": Españoles ilustres de principios del siglo XX. Madrid: Blanco y Negro, n.d. [Dec. 1903–Nov. 1904].

Album de curiosidades. (Biblioteca Nacional, Madrid) (ca. 1850–90). 22 leaves.

El album de Madrid (14 Apr.–6 Oct. 1899).

Album poético. Barcelona: Establecimiento Editorial de Ramón Molinas, 1890.

Album poético dedicado a S. M. El Rey D. Alfonso XII y al Ejército con motivo de su triunfal entrada en la capital de la Monarquía. Madrid: Imprenta Nacional, 1876.

Album poético español. Madrid: A. de Carlos e Hijo, 1874.

Album que dedican a S. M. la reina doña Isabel II los profesores de educación primaria. Madrid: Imp. a cargo de Gabriel Díaz, 1860.

Alcalá Galiano, José. "El poeta Grilo." *La ilustración española y americana* 21. 47 (22 Dec. 1877): 394–95, 398.

Alcántara, Francisco. "Descastamiento." *El imparcial* (Madrid) 24 Mar. 1896: n. pag.

Aldaraca, Bridget A. *El Angel del Hogar: Galdós and the Ideology of Domesticity in Spain.* Chapel Hill: North Carolina Studies in the Romance Languages and Literatures, 1991.

Alfau, Felipe. *Sentimental Songs/La poesía cursi.* Trans. Ilan Stavans. Elmwood Park, Ill.: Dalkey Archive Press, 1992.

Almagro San Martín, Melchor de. *Biografía del 1900.* Madrid: Revista de Occidente, 1943.

Almela Mengot, Vicente. *Los abanicos de Valencia.* Madrid: Publicaciones de la Escuela de Artes y Oficios Artísticos de Madrid, No. 13, 1943.

Almodóvar, Pedro. *The Patty Diphusa Stories and Other Writings.* Trans. Kirk Anderson. London: Faber & Faber, 1993.

Bibliography

Alomar, Gabriel. *Il futurismo.* 1905. Ed. M. Caterina Ruta. Introd. Giuseppe Grilli. Palermo: Edizioni Novecento, 1990.

Alvarez Quintero, Serafín and Joaquín. *Becqueriana.* Madrid: Imprenta de Regino Velasco, 1915.

——. *La rima eterna: Comedia en dos actos, inspirada en una rima de Bécquer.* Madrid: Imprenta de Regino Velasco, 1914.

Amelang, James S. *Honored Citizens of Barcelona: Patrician Culture and Class Relations, 1490–1714.* Princeton, N.J.: Princeton University Press, 1986.

Amicis, Edmundo de. *Spain and the Spaniards.* Trans. Wilhelmina W. Cady. New York: Putnam's Sons, 1881.

Amorós, Andrés. *Subliteraturas.* Esplugues de Llobregat: Editorial Ariel, 1974.

Anderson, Andrew A. "García Lorca en Montevideo: Una cronología provisional." *Bulletin hispanique* 87 (1985): 167–79.

——. "More Sources for García Lorca's *Doña Rosita la soltera.*" *The Discerning Eye: Studies Presented to Robert Pring-Mill on his Seventieth Birthday.* Ed. Nigel Griffin et al. Llangrannog, U.K.: Dolphin, 1994. 149–64.

——. "Las relaciones familiares y el compás del vals: Dos facetas desapercibidas de *Doña Rosita la soltera.*" *El teatro de Lorca: Tragedia, drama y farsa.* Ed. Cristóbal Cuevas García. Málaga: Publicaciones del Congreso de Literatura Española Contemporánea, 1996. 199–215.

Anderson Imbert, Enrique. "Crónica. Papeles. Cursi." *Sur* 224 (1953): 119–20.

Aparisi y Guijarro, Antonio. "Carta primera." 1870. *Obras.* Vol. 3. Madrid: Impr. de La Regeneración, a cargo de D. R. Ramírez, 1873. 250–56.

Appadurai, Arjun. "Introduction: Commodities and the Politics of Value." *The Social Life of Things: Commodities in Cultural Perspective.* Ed. Appadurai. Cambridge: Cambridge University Press, 1986. 3–63.

Apter, Emily. "Splitting Hairs: Female Fetishism and Postpartum Sentimentality in the Fin de Siècle." *Eroticism and the Body Politic.* Ed. Lynn Hunt. Baltimore: Johns Hopkins University Press, 1991. 164–90.

Ara Torralba, Juan Carlos. "El alma contemporánea de *Alma contemporánea,* claves ideológicas para un libro y un cambio de siglo." *Alazet* 2 (1990): 9–54.

Aramburu y Pacheco, Alfonso de. *La ciudad de Hércules.* Cádiz: Librería Cerón y Cervantes, 1945.

Aranda, Eusebio. *José Selgas.* Murcia: Academia Alfonso X el Sabio, 1982.

Araujo-Costa, Luis. *Biografía de "La Época."* Madrid: Libros y Revistas, 1946.

Arcas Cubero, Fernando. "Aspectos de la trayectoria histórica del andalucismo." *Nacionalismo y regionalismo en España.* Córdoba: Excma. Diputación Provincial de Córdoba, 1985. 91–93.

Arconada, César M. "Quince años de literatura española." 1933. *La vanguardia y la República.* Ed. Jaime Brihuega. Madrid: Cátedra, 1982. 325–36.

Bibliography

Argüelles Toral y Hevía, Alejandrina. *Ensayos poéticos.* Irún: Imprenta de la Elegancia, a cargo de Antonio Atienza, 1862.

Arias de Velasco y Sarandeses, Francisco. "El origen de la voz *cursi.*" *El español* 5.181 (13 Apr. 1946): 1+.

Ariès, Philippe. *Western Attitudes toward Death: From the Middle Ages to the Present.* Trans. Patricia M. Ranum. Baltimore: Johns Hopkins University Press, 1975.

Armstrong, Nancy. *Victorian Jewelry.* New York: Macmillan, 1976.

Armstrong, Nancy, and Leonard Tennenhouse, eds. *The Ideology of Conduct: Essays in Literature and the History of Sexuality.* New York: Methuen, 1987.

Arrieta, Rafael Alberto. "Becqueriana." *La prensa* (Buenos Aires) 16 Feb. 1936: n. pag.

Asmodeo [Ramón de Navarrete]. "Un gran baile." *Madrid por dentro y por fuera.* 1873. Ed. Eusebio Blasco. Madrid: Asociación de Libreros de Lance de Madrid, 1996. 145–56.

Auerbach, Erich. " 'Figura.' " *Scenes from the Drama of European Literature: Six Essays.* 1959. Gloucester, Mass.: Peter Smith, 1973. 11–76.

Austin, J. L. *How to Do Things with Words.* 1962. Cambridge: Harvard University Press, 1975.

Avilés, Angel. "Becqueriana." *Gente vieja* (Madrid) 3.54 (10 June 1902): 5.

Aza, Vital. "En el abanico de Emilia A. . . ." *Día de moda* (Madrid) 1.19 (14 June 1880): 11.

Babbit, Irving. "On Being Original." *Literature and the American College: Essays in Defense of the Humanities.* 1908. Washington, D.C.: National Humanities Institute, 1986. 186–201.

Baedeker, Karl. *Spain and Portugal: Handbook for Travellers.* 3d ed. Leipzig: Baedeker, 1908.

Bahamonde Magro, Angel. "Crisis de la nobleza de cuna y consolidación burguesa (1840–1880)." *Madrid en la sociedad del siglo XIX.* Vol. 1. Ed. Luis E. Otero Carvajal and Bahamonde. Madrid: Comunidad de Madrid, 1986. 325–75.

Bahamonde Magro, Angel, and Julián Toro Mérida. *Burguesía, especulación y cuestión social en el Madrid del siglo XIX.* Madrid: Siglo Veintiuno, 1978.

Barallat y Falguera, Celestino. *Principios de botánica funeraria.* 1885. Presentación by Jaume Bover. Barcelona: Editorial Alta Fulla, 1984.

Barbany, J. "Cursilería." *La vida moderna* (Barcelona) 2.10 (7 Jan. 1892): 146.

Barnstone, Willis. "Antonio Machado and Rubén Darío: A Failure of Literary Assassination, or the Persistence of Modernism in the Poetry of Antonio Machado." *Hispanic Review* 57 (1989): 281–306.

Baroja, Pío. *Memorias. Obras completas.* Vol. 7. Madrid: Biblioteca Nueva, 1949.

——. "Elogio sentimental del acordeón." *Paradox, rey.* 5th ed. Madrid: Espasa-Calpe, 1970.

Barranco, Mariano. *Los martes de las de Gómez: Caricatura en un acto y en prosa.* 1885. Mexico City: Eusebio Sánchez, 1894.

Barrera, Pedro María. "La literata." *Los españoles de ogaño.* Vol. 2. Madrid: Librería de Victoriano Suárez, 1872. 359–70.

Barrero Amador, Valeriano. "Gustavo A. Bécquer: Estudio crítico biográfico." *Revista de España* 138 (Feb. 1892): 276–93; 139 (Mar.–Apr. 1892): 432–44; 141 (July–Aug. 1892): 187–206; 149 (Nov.–Dec. 1894): 273–96.

Barrow, Leo L. *Negation in Baroja: A Key to His Novelistic Creativity.* Tucson: University of Arizona Press, 1971.

Barthes, Roland. *Mythologies.* 1957. Trans. Annette Lavers. New York: Hill and Wang, 1972.

——. *S/Z.* 1970. Trans. Richard Miller. New York: Hill and Wang, 1974.

Bartina, Sebastián. *Verso y versificación: Tratado de métrica castellana.* 2d ed. Barcelona: Dalmau y Jover, 1955.

Bastinos, Antonio J. *Hojas secas.* 2 vols. Barcelona: Imprenta de Jaime Jepús y Roviralta, 1894.

Bataille, Georges. "Le langage des fleurs." *Oeuvres complètes.* Vol. 1. Paris: Gallimard, 1970. 173–78.

Baudrillard, Jean. "The Ecstasy of Communication." Trans. John Johnston. *The Anti-aesthetic: Essays on Postmodern Culture.* 5th printing. Ed. Hal Foster. 1983; Seattle: Bay Press, 1987. 126–34.

——. "Simulacra and Simulations." Trans. Paul Foss, Paul Patton, and Philip Beitchman. *Selected Writings.* Ed. Mark Poster. Stanford, Calif.: Stanford University Press, 1988. 166–84.

——. "Symbolic Exchange and Death." Trans. Charles Levin. *Selected Writings.* Ed. Mark Poster. Stanford, Calif.: Stanford University Press, 1988. 119–48.

——. *Le système des objets.* Paris: Gallimard, 1968.

Bécquer, Gustavo Adolfo. *La cruz del valle.* 1860. *Teatro.* Ed. Juan Antonio Tamayo. Madrid: Consejo Superior de Investigaciones Científicas, 1949.

——. "La feria de Sevilla." 1869. Bécquer, *Obras completas* 1231–41.

——. *Obras completas.* 11th ed. Madrid: Aguilar, 1964.

——. "La Pereza." Bécquer, *Obras completas* 690–95.

——. *Rimas y declaraciones poéticas.* 2d ed. Ed. Francisco López Estrada and María Teresa López García-Berday. Madrid: Espasa-Calpe, 1986.

Bécquer, Valeriano, and Gustavo Adolfo Bécquer. *Sem: Los Borbones en pelota.* Ed. Robert Pageard, Lee Fontanella, and María Dolores Cabra Loredo. Madrid: Ediciones El Museo Universal, 1991.

"Becqueriana." *Chorizos y polacos* 1.3 (30 June 1901): 4.

"Becqueriana." *Los desheredados* (Sabadell) (2 Dec. 1885): 3.

Bell, C. Jeanenne. *Collector's Encyclopedia of Hairwork Jewelry.* Paducah, Ky.: Collector Books, 1998.

Benavente, Jacinto. *Lo cursi.* 1901. *La fuerza bruta. Lo cursi.* 5th ed. Madrid: Espasa-Calpe, 1966.

——. *Modas.* 1901. *Teatro.* Vol. 4. 4th ed. Madrid: Librería de los Sucesores de Hernando, 1922.

Benítez, Rubén. "Bécquer y la Marquesa del Sauce." *Anales de literatura española* 5 (1986–87): 13–24.

Benjamin, Walter. "On Language as Such and on the Language of Man." *Reflections.* Ed. Peter Demetz. Trans. Edmund Jephcott. New York: Schocken, 1986. 314–32.

——. "Paris, Capital of the Nineteenth Century." *Reflections.* Ed. Peter Demetz. Trans. Edmund Jephcott. New York: Schocken, 1986. 146–62.

——. "The Work of Art in the Age of Mechanical Reproduction." *Illuminations.* Ed. Hannah Arendt. Trans. Harry Zohn. 1969. New York: Schocken, 1985. 217–51.

Bennett, Anna Gray. *Unfolding Beauty: The Art of the Fan.* New York: Thames and Hudson, 1988.

Bensusan, S[amuel] L[evy]. *Home Life in Spain.* New York: Macmillan, 1910.

Bergmann, Emilie. "'Los sauces llorando a moco y baba': Ekphrasis in Galdós's *La de Bringas.*" *Anales galdosianos* 20.1 (1985): 75–82.

Berman, Marshall. *All That Is Solid Melts into Air: The Experience of Modernity.* 1982. New York: Penguin, 1988.

Bewell, Alan. *Wordsworth and the Enlightenment: Nature, Man, and Society in the Experimental Poetry.* New Haven, Conn.: Yale University Press, 1989.

Bhabha, Homi K. "Introduction: Narrating the Nation." *Nation and Narration.* Ed. Bhabha. London: Routledge, 1990. 1–7.

Blanchot, Maurice. "Literature and the Right to Death." 1949. *The Gaze of Orpheus and Other Literary Essays.* Ed. P. Adams Sitney. Trans. Lydia Davis. Barrytown, N.Y.: Station Hill, 1981. 21–62.

Blanco, Alda, and Carlos Blanco Aguinaga. Introduction to *La de Bringas.* By Benito Pérez Galdós. Madrid: Ediciones Cátedra, 1985. 11–45.

Blanco White, José. *Cartas de España.* Trans. Antonio Garnica. Madrid: Alianza, 1972.

Blanquat, Josette. "Documentos galdosianos: 1912." *Anales galdosianos* 3 (1968): 143–50.

Blanquat, Josette, and Jean-François Botrel, eds. *Clarín y sus editores: 65 cartas inéditas de Leopoldo Alas a Fernando Fe y Manuel Fernández Lasanta, 1884–1893.* Rennes: Université de Haute-Bretagne, 1981.

Blasco, Eusebio. "Cursinópolis." *Cuentos.* Primera serie. Madrid: Fernando Fe, 1899. 169–75.

——. "El lenguaje de las flores." *Del amor . . . y otros excesos: Obras festivas en prosa (de 1865 a 1869).* Madrid: Administración, 1873. 420–22.

——, ed. *Madrid por dentro y por fuera.* 1873. Madrid: Asociación de Libreros de Lance de Madrid, 1996.

Bly, Peter. "From Disorder to Order: The Pattern of *Arreglar* References in Galdós' *Tormento* and *La de Bringas.*" *Neophilologus* 62 (1978): 392–405.

Bibliography

——. *Pérez Galdós: La de Bringas*. London: Grant and Cutler, 1981.

Bobadilla, Emilio. "Ripios en prosa y verso." *Triquitraques*. Madrid: Fernando Fe, 1892. 101–7.

Boloix, Antonio. "Monólogos eternos." *El mundo cómico* 4.120 (14 Feb. 1875): 7–8.

Bonaparte, Marie. "De la mort et des fleurs." 1933. *Revue française de psychanalyse* 51.1 (1987): 231–35.

Borbón, Eulalia de. *Para la mujer*. Barcelona: Hispano Americana de Ediciones, 1946.

Borrow, George. *The Bible in Spain*. 1842. London: John Murray, 1899.

Botrel, Jean-François. "Antonio de Valbuena y la novela de edificación (1870–1903)." *Tierras de León* no.55 (1984): 131–44.

Botrel, Jean-François, and J. Le Bouil. "Sur le concept de 'clase media' dans la pensée bourgeoise en Espagne au XIXe siècle." *La question de la "bourgeoisie" dans le monde hispanique au XIXe siècle*. Bordeaux: Editions Bière, 1973. 137–60.

Bourdieu, Pierre. *Distinction: A Social Critique of the Judgement of Taste*. Trans. Richard Nice. Cambridge, Mass.: Harvard University Press, 1984.

Bover, Jaume. Foreword. Barallat y Falguera. vii–xiv.

Bowlby, Rachel. "Modes of Modern Shopping: Mallarmé at the *Bon Marché*." Armstrong and Tennenhouse. 185–205.

Boxer, Marilyn J. "Women in Industrial Homework: The Flowermakers of Paris in the Belle Epoque." *French Historical Studies* 12 (1982): 401–23.

Brandes, Stanley. *Metaphors of Masculinity: Sex and Status in Andalusian Folklore*. 1980. Philadelphia: University of Pennsylvania Press, 1986.

Bredin, Hugh. "Metonymy." *Poetics Today* 5.1 (1984): 45–58.

Bretón de los Herreros, Manuel. *A Madrid me vuelvo*. 1828. *Obras*. Vol. 1. Madrid: Imprenta de Miguel Ginesta, 1883.

——. "La castañera." 1843. *Obras*. Vol. 5. Madrid: Imprenta de Miguel Ginesta, 1884. 501–8.

Brihuega, Jaime, ed. *La vanguardia y la República*. Madrid: Cátedra, 1982.

Brinkley, Robert, and Michael Deneen. "Towards an Indexical Criticism: On Coleridge, de Man, and the Materiality of the Sign." *Revolution and English Romanticism: Politics and Rhetoric*. Ed. Keith Hanley and Raman Selden. Hemel Hemstead, U.K.: Harvester Wheatsheaf; New York: St. Martin's, 1990. 277–302.

Broch, Hermann. "El arte a fines del siglo XIX y su no-estilo." *Kitsch, vanguardia y el arte por el arte*. Trans. Margarita Muñoa. Barcelona: Tusquets, 1970. 63–80.

——. "Kitsch and 'Art with a Message.'" 1933. Dorfles 68–76.

——. "Notes on the Problem of Kitsch." 1950–51. Dorfles 49–67.

Broto Salanova, Justo. *Un olvidado: José María Llanas Aguilaniedo (estudio biográfico y crítico)*. Huesca: Instituto de Estudios Altoaragoneses, 1992.

Brown, Rica. "The Bécquer Legend." *Bulletin of Spanish Studies* 18 (1941): 4–18.

Budick, Sanford, and Wolfgang Iser. Introduction to *Languages of the Unsayable: The*

Play of Negativity in Literature and Literary Theory. Ed. Budick and Iser. New York: Columbia University Press, 1989. xi–xxi.

Buñuel, Luis. *My Last Sigh.* 1982. Trans. Abigail Israel. New York: Vintage, 1984.

Burgos, Carmen de. *Las artes de la mujer.* Valencia: Prometeo, n.d.

Burgos, Javier de. *Las cursis burladas.* Madrid: Enrique Arregui, 1882.

——. *La familia de Sicur: Sainete lírico en verso.* Music by Gerónimo Giménez. Madrid: R. Velasco, 1899.

Bustillo, Eduardo. "La muerte en la cuna." *Album poético.* Barcelona: Establecimiento Editorial de Ramón Molinas, 1884. 178.

Bustillo, José. "Las mujeres pintadas por sí mismas." *Album de la prensa.* By Bustillo et al. Madrid: Imprenta de los Señores Rojas, 1870. 200–5.

Calinescu, Matei. *Five Faces of Modernity: Modernism, Avant-Garde, Decadence, Kitsch, Postmodernism.* Durham, N.C.: Duke University Press, 1987.

Cámara Villar, Gregorio. Prologue. Sopeña Monsalve. 13–22.

Campbell, Mark. *The Art of Hair Work.* 1875. Ed. Jules and Kaethe Kliot. Berkeley, Calif.: LACIS, 1989.

Campoamor, Ramón de. *Cánovas: Estudio biográfico.* 1884. Madrid: Imp. de la Comp. de Impresores y Libreros, n.d.

Camprodón, Francisco. *¡Flor de un día!* 1851. *Teatro moderno español.* Leipzig: Brockhaus, 1885. 105–66.

Cano, Carlos. "En el abanico de Concha." *La vida literaria* 5 (4 Feb. 1899): 82.

——. "La niña muerta (de una corona fúnebre)." *Día de moda* 1.27 (9 Aug. 1880): 4.

Cánovas del Castillo, Antonio. 1852. *La campana de Huesca.* Mexico City: Porrúa, 1984.

——. "Discusión del proyecto de contestación al discurso de la Corona." 1876. *Discursos parlamentarios.* Ed. Diego López Garrido. Madrid: Centro de Estudios Constitucionales, 1987. 195–238.

——. *Historia de la decadencia de España, desde el advenimiento de Felipe III al trono hasta la muerte de Carlos II.* 2d ed. Madrid: Librería Gutenberg de José Ruiz, 1910.

——. *Problemas contemporáneos.* Vol. 1. Madrid: Imprenta de A. Pérez Dubrull, 1884.

Cantor, Paul. "Friedrich Nietzsche: The Use and Abuse of Metaphor." *Metaphor: Problems and Perspectives.* Ed. Davis S. Miall. Brighton, U.K.: Harvester, 1982. 71–88.

Capdevila, Arturo. *Despeñaderos del habla: Negligencia—Cursilería—Tuntún.* Buenos Aires: Losada, 1952.

Cardona, Rodolfo, ed. Introduction to *La viuda blanca y negra.* By Ramón Gómez de la Serna. Madrid: Cátedra, 1988. 11–63.

Cardwell, Richard A. "Médicos chiflados: Medicina y literatura en la España de fin de siglo." *Siglo diecinueve* 1 (1995): 91–116.

Carlisle, Lillian Baker. "Hair Work Jewelry." *The Spinning Wheel's Complete Book of Antiques.* Ed. Albert Christian Revi. New York: Grosset and Dunlap, 1972. 416–17.

Carnero, Guillermo. *Los Orígenes del romanticismo reaccionario: El matrimonio Böhl de Faber.* Valencia: Universidad de Valencia, 1978.

Bibliography

Carr, Raymond. *Spain: 1808–1939.* Oxford: Clarendon, 1966.

Carretero, Tomás. "Mis vates." *Miscelánea* 1.44 (16 Sept. 1900): 465–68.

——. "La vida literaria." *Arte y letras* 2.18 (5 May 1901): 249–50.

Casal, Enrique. *Fiestas aristocráticas, 1913–1914.* Madrid: Administración, 1914.

Castañeda y Alcover, Vicente. *Ensayo de una bibliografía comentada de manuales de artes, ciencias, oficios, costumbres públicas y privadas de España (siglos XVI al XIX).* Madrid: Maestre, 1955.

Castedo, Elena. *Paradise.* New York: Warner Books, 1991.

Castellanos de Losada, Basilio Sebastián. "De la escritura en general, y en particular de la española." *Album de Ajara: Corona científica, literaria, artística y política.* Ed. Castellanos de Losada. Madrid: Imprenta de D. Alejandro Fuentenebro, 1856, 182–210.

——. "El siglo XIX: Discurso histórico-arqueológico." *Album de Ajara: Corona científica, literaria, artística y política.* Ed. Castellanos de Losada. Madrid: Imprenta de D. Alejandro Fuentenebro, 1856. 547–683.

Castellet, José María, ed. *Nueve novísimos poetas españoles.* Barcelona: Barral, 1970.

Castle, Terry. "Phantasmagoria: Spectral Technology and the Metaphorics of Modern Reverie." *Critical Inquiry* 15 (1988): 26–61.

Castro, Adolfo de. "Diccionario de voces gaditanas." *Nombres antiguos de las calles y plazas de Cádiz.* Cádiz: Revista Médica, 1857. i–xviii.

——. "Historia e importancia de una palabra." *El imparcial* (Madrid) 12 June 1882: 3–4.

Castro y Serrano, José de. *Cartas trascendentales escritas a un amigo de confianza.* 1862. Primera y segunda serie. Madrid: Imprenta de Fortanet, 1887.

Cate-Arries, Francie. "The Discourse of Desire in the Language of Flowers: Lorca, Freud, and *Doña Rosita.*" *South Atlantic Review* 57 (1992): 53–68.

Cavillac, Cécile. "Les équivalents du mot *bourgeois* dans la traduction espagnole de *Gil Blas.*" *Revue de littérature comparée* 43 (1969): 449–58.

Caws, Peter. "What is Structuralism?" *Claude Lévi-Strauss: The Anthropologist as Hero.* Ed. E. Nelson Hayes and Tanya Hayes. Cambridge, Mass.: MIT Press, 1970. 197–214.

Certeau, Michel de. *The Practice of Everyday Life.* Trans. Steven Rendall. Berkeley: University of California Press, 1988.

Chambers, Ross. "Irony and the Canon." *Profession* 90 (1990): 18–24.

Chichón, Rafael. "Un pensamiento de Bécquer." *El bazar* 4.8 (21 Nov. 1875): 125–26.

Chicote, Enrique. *La Loreto y este humilde servidor (recuerdos de la vida de dos comediantes madrileños).* Madrid: Aguilar, 1944?

Choay, Françoise. *The Modern City: Planning in the 19th Century.* Trans. Marguerite Hugo and George R. Collins. New York: George Braziller, 1969.

Cirici Narváez, Juan Ramón. "Cádiz en la visita de Isabel II." *El Casino y la ciudad de Cádiz: Política, sociedad y cultura en el Cádiz del siglo XIX.* Ed. José Luis Millán-Chivite. Cádiz: Caja de Ahorros, 1986. 41–55.

Bibliography

Clark, William George. *Gazpacho: Or, Summer Months in Spain*. London: John W. Parker, 1850.

Clavé, José Antonio. "El lenguaje de las flores." 1859. *Flores de estío: Poesías*. 3d ed. Barcelona: López, Editor, Librería Española, 1893. 95–96.

Clementa Millán, María. "García Lorca y la ciudad." *Lecciones sobre Federico García Lorca: Granada, mayo de 1986*. Ed. Andrés Soria Olmedo. Granada: Comisión Nacional del Cincuentenario, 1986. 253–63.

Cocat, Luis, and Heliodoro Criado. *Las solteronas: Juguete cómico en un acto y en prosa*. 1894. *Tres comedias modernas: En un acto y en prosa*. Ed. Frederic William Morrison. New York: Henry Holt, 1909.

Cohen, Anthony P. "Culture as Identity: An Anthropologist's View." *New Literary History* 24 (1993): 195–209.

Colley, Linda. *Britons: Forging the Nation, 1707–1837*. New Haven, Conn.: Yale University Press, 1992.

Collini, Stefan. "Badly Connected: The Passionate Intensity of Cultural Studies." *Victorian Studies* 36 (1993): 455–60.

Comellas García-Llera, José Luis. "Dinámica y mentalidad de la burguesía gaditana en el siglo XVIII." *La burguesía mercantil gaditana (1650–1868)*. Cádiz: Instituto de Estudios Gaditanos, 1976. 13–40.

"La Condesa X." *Caridad española: "Mi alma" (Poesías)*. Madrid: Imprenta de Antonio Marzo, 1914.

Conte, Augusto. *Recuerdos de un diplomático*. Vol. 1. Madrid: Imprenta de J. Góngora y Alvarez, 1901.

Contreras, Jaime. "Family and Patronage: The Judeo-Converso Minority in Spain." *Cultural Encounters: The Impact of the Inquisition in Spain and the New World*. Ed. Mary Elizabeth Perry and Anne J. Cruz. Berkeley: University of California Press, 1991. 127–45.

Corominas, Joan. *Diccionario crítico-etimológico castellano e hispánico*. Vol. 2. Madrid: Gredos, 1980.

Corona fúnebre a la memoria de la señorita doña Alejandra Argüelles Toral y Hevía. Madrid: Imprenta de D. José Cuesta, 1861.

Corona poética dedicada a la me moria de la malograda señorita Francisca Madoz y Rojas. Madrid: Imprenta de T. Fortanet, 1850.

Coronado, Carolina. *Poesías*. Ed. Noël Valis. Madrid: Castalia / Instituto de la Mujer, 1991.

Cortázar, Eduardo de. "El Cotillon." *Madrid por dentro y por fuera*. Ed. Blasco. 349–58.

Cortezo, Carlos María. *Paseos de un solitario*. Madrid: Ruiz Hermanos, 1923.

Corzuelo, Andrés. "La misa de una." *Madrid por dentro y por fuera*. Ed. Blasco. 247–54.

Cossío, José María de. *Cincuenta años de poesía española, 1850–1900*. 2 vols. Madrid: Espasa-Calpe, 1960.

Cotarelo y Mori, Emilio. *Diccionario biográfico y bibliográfico de calígrafos españoles*. 2 vols. Madrid: Tip. de la "Revista de Arch., Bibl. y Museos," 1913–16.

Creso. "Los golondrinos." *La chispa* 1.17 (21 Aug. 1890): 3.

Criado Costa, Joaquín. *Vida y creación poética de Antonio Fernández Grilo.* Córdoba: Real Academia de Córdoba / Consejo Superior de Investigaciones Científicas, 1975.

Crossick, Geoffrey. "The Emergence of the Lower Middle Class in Britain: A Discussion." *The Lower Middle Class in Britain, 1870–1914.* Ed. Crossick. London: Croom Helm, 1977. 11–60.

Cruz, Jesús. *Gentlemen, Bourgeois, and Revolutionaries: Political Change and Cultural Persistence among the Spanish Dominant Groups, 1750–1850.* Cambridge: Cambridge University Press, 1996.

Cruz, Ramón de la. "El petimetre." *Sainetes.* Ed. Emiliano M. Aguilera. Barcelona: Editorial Iberia, 1959. 131–50.

"Cursi." *Diccionario enciclopédico ilustrado de la provincia de Cádiz.* Vol. 2. Cádiz: Caja de Ahorros de Jerez, 1985. 108–9.

"Un cursi." *La estrella* (Cádiz) (25 Dec. 1842): 201.

Curtius, Ernst Robert. *European Literature and the Latin Middle Ages.* 1948. Trans. Willard R. Trask. New York: Harper and Row, 1963.

Darío, Rubén. *España contemporánea.* 1901. Barcelona: Editorial Lumen, 1987.

——. "Niñas prodigios." *Obras completas.* Vol. 1. Madrid: Afrodisio Aguado, 1950. 309–21.

——. *Prosas profanas y otros poemas.* Ed. Ignacio M. Zuleta. Madrid: Editorial Castalia, 1983.

Darnton, John. " 'Old Professor' Governs Madrid Like an Old Pro." *New York Times* 3 May 1983: A2.

Delbanco, Andrew. *The Puritan Ordeal.* Cambridge, Mass.: Harvard University Press, 1989.

Delgado, Luisa Elena. " 'El derecho de revisión': *La de Bringas* y el discurso de la alienación femenina." *Romance Languages Annual* 4 (1992): 427–30.

——. *La imagen elusiva: Lenguaje y representación en la narrativa de Galdós.* Amsterdam: Rodopi, 2000.

de Man, Paul. "The Epistemology of Metaphor." *On Metaphor.* Ed. Sheldon Sacks. Chicago: University of Chicago Press, 1981. 11–28.

Dendle, Brian J. *Galdós: The Mature Thought.* Lexington: University Press of Kentucky, 1980.

Derrida, Jacques. *Glas.* Trans. John P. Leavey Jr. and Richard Rand. Lincoln: University of Nebraska Press, 1986.

——. "Le retrait de la métaphore." *Psyche: Inventions de l'autre.* Paris: Galilée, 1987. 63–93.

——. "White Mythology: Metaphor in the Text of Philosophy." *Margins of Philosophy.* Trans. Alan Bass. Chicago: University of Chicago Press, 1982. 207–71.

Descuret, J.-B.-F. *La médecine des passions: ou, le passions considérées dans leurs rapports avec les maladies, les lois et la religion.* 1841. 2 vols. 3d ed. Paris: Labé, 1860.

Bibliography

Devoto, Daniel. "*Doña Rosita la soltera:* Estructura y fuentes." *Bulletin hispanique* 69 (1967): 407–35.

Díaz Lobón, Eduardo. "Notas acerca de la economía granadina a principios del siglo XIX." *Andalucía contemporánea (Siglos XIX y XX)*. Vol. 1. Córdoba: Monte de Piedad y Caja de Ahorros de Córdoba, 1979. 57–65.

Díaz Martín, Manuel. "Bécquer y la poesía popular." *La ilustración artística* 5.261 (27 Dec. 1886): 368.

Díez Taboada, Juan María. "Eduardo de Lustonó, curioso editor de Bécquer." *Revista de literatura* 47.94 (1985): 81–126.

Diego, Estrella de. *La mujer y la pintura del XIX español: Cuatrocientas olvidadas y algunas más*. Madrid: Cátedra, 1987. 138–45.

——. "Prototipos y anti-prototipos de comportamiento femenino a través de las escritoras españolas del último tercio del siglo XIX." *Literatura y vida cotidiana: Actas de las Cuartas Jornadas de Investigación Interdisciplinaria: Seminario de Estudios de la Mujer*. Zaragoza / Madrid: Universidad de Zaragoza / Universidad Autónoma de Madrid, 1987. 233–50.

Domínguez Ortiz, Antonio. "Cádiz en la historia moderna de Andalucía." *Cádiz en su historia: I Jornadas de Historia de Cádiz*. Cádiz: Caja de Ahorros, 1982. 7–25.

Dorfles, Gillo, ed. *Kitsch: The World of Bad Taste*. New York: Universe, 1969.

Douglas, Ann. *The Feminization of American Culture*. New York: Avon, 1978.

Drozdiak, William. "Unity Eludes Germans of East, West." *Washington Post* 27 Oct. 1996: A29.

Eagleton, Terry. "The Ideology of the Aesthetic." *The Politics of Pleasure: Aesthetics and Cultural Theory*. Ed. Stephen Regan. Buckingham, U.K.: Open University Press, 1992. 17–31.

——. *Literary Theory: An Introduction*. Minneapolis: University of Minnesota Press, 1983.

Eco, Umberto. "La struttura del cattivo gusto." *Apocalittici e integrati*. Milan: Bompiani, 1965. 67–131.

Eisenberg, Daniel. "Granada." *Encyclopedia of Homosexuality*. Ed. Wayne R. Dynes. New York: Garland, 1990. 489–90.

——. "Judaism, Sephardic." *Encyclopedia of Homosexuality*. Ed. Wayne R. Dynes. New York: Garland, 1990. 644–48.

——. "Una temprana guía *gay: Granada (Guía emocional)*, de Gregorio Martínez Sierra (1911)." *Erotismo en las letras hispánicas*. Ed. Luce López-Baralt and Francisco Márquez Villanueva. Mexico City: El Colegio de México, 1995. 111–20.

Elliot, Frances. *Diary of an Idle Woman in Spain*. Vol. 2. 1884. Leipzig: Tauchnitz, 1913.

Enciso Recio, Luis Miguel. "Actividades de los franceses en Cádiz (1789–1790)." *Hispania* 19 (1959): 251–86.

Engelberg, Edward. *Elegiac Fictions: The Motif of the Unlived Life*. University Park: Pennsylvania State University Press, 1989.

Bibliography

Enright, D. J. *Fair of Speech: The Uses of Euphemism.* Oxford: Oxford University Press, 1985.

Entrambasaguas, Joaquín de. "Coronas poéticas del siglo XIX." *El libro español* 14 (May 1971): 9–21.

———. "Una olvidada antología poética." *Homenaje a don Agustín Millares Carlo.* Vol. 2. El Fondo para la Investigación Económica y Social de la Confederación Española de Cajas de Ahorros. Las Palmas de Gran Canaria: Caja Insular de Ahorros de Gran Canaria, 1975. 475–95.

Escobar, Alfredo. *La sociedad española vista por el marqués de Valdeiglesias, 1875–1949.* Ed. Mercedes Escobar y Kirkpatrick. Madrid: Biblioteca Nueva, 1957.

Escobar, José. "El sombrero y la mantilla: moda e ideología en el costumbrismo romántico español." *Revisión de Larra: ¿Protesta o revolución?* By Jean-René Aymes et al. Paris: Les Belles Lettres, 1983. 161–65.

Espadas Burgos, Manuel. "La Restauración y la España posible de 1875." *La Restauración monárquica de 1875 y la España de la Restauración.* By J. A. Cánovas del Castillo et al. Madrid: Biblioteca "La Ciudad de Dios," 1978. 7–20.

Espy, Willard R. *The Garden of Eloquence: A Rhetorical Bestiary.* New York: Harper and Row, 1983.

Esquer Torres, Ramón. "Dos álbumes inéditos del romanticismo." *Revista de literatura* 28.55–56 (1965): 163–227.

Estévanez, Nicolás. "3 de enero." 1873. *Mis memorias.* 1899. Madrid: Tebas, 1975.

"Los estrenos. Zarzuela. *Becqueriana.*" *ABC* (Madrid) 10 Apr. 1915: 15.

Estruch Tobella, Joan. "Bécquer, autor de *Doña Manuela.*" *Spain and its Literature: Essays in Memory of E. Allison Peers.* Ed. Ann L. Mackenzie. Liverpool: Liverpool University Press, 1997. 303–15.

Ezama Gil, Angeles. "La ilustración de relatos breves en la revista *La Vida Galante.*" *Boletín del Museo e Instituto "Camón Aznar"* 34 (1988): 73–96.

Fairbank, Alfred. *A Book of Scripts.* 1949. London: Faber and Faber, 1977.

"The Fan." *Godey's Lady's Book and Magazine* 71 (Sept. 1865): 253–54.

Felski, Rita. "Nothing to Declare: Identity, Shame, and the Lower Middle Class." *PMLA* 115 (2000): 33–45.

Ferguson, Priscilla Parkhurst. "The *Flâneur:* Urbanization and Its Discontents." *Home and Its Dislocations in Nineteenth-Century France.* Ed. Suzanne Nash. Albany: State University of New York Press, 1993. 45–61.

Fernandez, James W. *Persuasions and Performances: The Play of Tropes in Culture.* Bloomington: Indiana University Press, 1986.

Fernández Almagro, Melchor. *Cánovas: Su vida y su política.* 2d ed. Madrid: Tebas, 1972.

———. "Las ilustraciones de *Blanco y Negro* y la emoción histórica." 1955. *Las terceras de "ABC."* Ed. Luisa Rojas. Madrid: Prensa Española, 1976. 82–85.

———. "¿Qué es lo cursi . . . ?" *ABC* (Madrid) (2 Jan. 1951): n. pag.

Fernández Cifuentes, Luis. *"Doña Rosita la soltera o el lenguaje de las flores." Cuadernos hispanoamericanos* Nos. 433–34 (July–Aug. 1986): 319–40.

——. Introduction to *Los majos de Cádiz*. By Armando Palacio Valdés. Cádiz: Universidad de Cádiz, 1998. 7–65.

Fernández Grilo, Antonio. "Antonio Grilo: Poetas del siglo XIX." *Lecturas* 8.86 (1928): 775–77.

——. "En el álbum de la esposa de Revilla." *Día de moda* 1.18 (7 June 1880): 15.

——. "Las ermitas de Córdoba." *Ideales*. Paris: Sánchez y Cía, 1891. 3–10.

Fernández de Moratín, Nicolás. *La Petimetra. Desengaños al teatro español. Sátiras.* 1762. Ed. David T. Gies and Miguel Angel Lama. Madrid: Editorial Castalia, 1996.

Fernández Pérez, Paloma. *El rostro familiar de la metrópoli: Redes de parentesco y lazos mercantiles en Cádiz, 1700–1812.* Madrid: Siglo Veintiuno, 1997.

Fernández de los Ríos, Angel. *Guía de Madrid: Manual del madrileño y del forastero.* 1876. Madrid: Monterrey, 1982.

Fineman, Joel. "The History of the Anecdote: Fiction and Fiction." *The New Historicism*. Ed. H. Aram Veeser. New York: Routledge, 1989. 49–76.

Fiumara, Francesco. "Traducirse a sí mismo: Alteraciones, adiciones y omisiones en el capítulo inicial de las diferentes versiones de *Penisola pentagonale* de Mario Praz." *Romance Languages Annual 1999*. West Lafayette, Indiana: Purdue Research Foundation, 2000. 456–60.

Flitter, Derek. *Spanish Romantic Literary Theory and Criticism*. Cambridge: Cambridge University Press, 1992.

Flores, Antonio. "El hortera." *Los españoles pintados por sí mismos.* 1843. Ed. Agustín Criado Becerro. Madrid: Dossat, 1992. 178–84.

——. *La sociedad de 1850*. Ed. Jorge Campos. Madrid: Alianza, 1968.

Flory, M. A. *A Book about Fans: The History of Fans and Fan-Painting*. New York: Macmillan, 1895.

Ford, Richard. *A Hand-Book for Travellers in Spain, and Readers at Home.* Vol. 1. 1845. Ed. Ian Robertson. Carbondale: Southern Illinois University Press, 1966.

Forradellas, Joaquín. "Un poema desconocido de García Lorca." *Insula* 290 (Jan. 1971): 3.

Fortes, José Antonio. "Hoy, literatura light." *República de las letras* 15 (Mar. 1986): 17–21.

Foucault, Michel. "What is Enlightenment?" *Postmodernism: A Reader*. Ed. Patricia Waugh. Trans. C. Porter. London: Edward Arnold, 1992. 96–108.

Fournier, Raoul. *El cristal con que se mira. La cursilería y padecimientos afines.* Mexico City: Editorial Diana, 1980.

Fraile Miguélez, Juan. *Cascotes y machaqueos: Pulverizaciones a Balbuena* [sic] *y Clarín.* 2d ed. 1892. Madrid: Viuda de Hernando y Compañía, 1898.

Franz, Thomas R. "Don Francisco as Fate: The Construction of the Cenotaph in *La de Bringas*." *Neophilologus* 80 (1996): 259–67.

Bibliography

Freud, Sigmund. "Fetishism." 1927. *The Standard Edition of the Complete Psychological Works of Sigmund Freud*. Vol. 21. Trans. and ed. James Strachey. London: Hogarth, 1961. 149–57.

———. *The Interpretation of Dreams*. 1900. *The Standard Edition of the Complete Psychological Works of Sigmund Freud*. Vols. 4 and 5. Trans. and ed. James Strachey. London: Hogarth, 1966.

———. "Mourning and Melancholia." 1917. *The Standard Edition of the Complete Psychological Works of Sigmund Freud*. Vol. 14. Trans. and ed. James Strachey. London: Hogarth, 1966. 239–58.

———. "Negation." 1925. *The Standard Edition of the Complete Psychological Works of Sigmund Freud*. Vol. 19. Trans. and ed. James Strachey. London: Hogarth, 1966. 234–39.

Friedländer, Saul. *Reflections of Nazism: An Essay on Kitsch and Death*. Trans. Thomas Weyr. 1984; Bloomington: Indiana University Press, 1993.

"Frida." "Cursis." *La nueva España* (Oviedo) 21 Jan. 1962: 21.

Frigolé, Joan. *Un etnólogo en el teatro: Ensayo antropológico sobre Federico García Lorca*. Barcelona: Muchnik Editores, 1995.

Frontaura, Carlos. "Tipos madrileños: La señoritas cursis." *La ilustración española y americana*, 30.44 (Nov. 1886): 326–27.

Fulweiler, Howard W. *"Here a Captive Heart Busted": Studies in the Sentimental Journey of Modern Literature*. New York: Fordham University Press, 1993.

Gale, Richard M. *Negation and Non-Being*. Oxford: Blackwell, 1976.

Gallero, José Luis. *Sólo se vive una vez: Esplendor y ruina de la movida madrileña*. Madrid: Ediciones Ardora, 1991.

Gamallo Fierros, Dionisio, ed. *Páginas abandonadas: Del olvido en el ángulo oscuro*. By G. A. Bécquer. Madrid: Editorial Valera, 1948.

Ganivet, Angel. *Granada la bella*. 1896. Ed. Fernando García Lara. Granada: Diputación Provincial de Granada, 1996.

García, Alejandro V. "El múltiple abandono de la historia urbana de Granada." *El país* (Madrid) 22 Mar. 1985: 31.

García, Angeles. "El abanico, soporte común de una exposición de 28 pintores." *El país* (Madrid) 30 Apr. 1985: 34.

García Lorca, Federico. "Album blanco." Ed. Miguel García-Posada. *Los Domingos de ABC* (Madrid) (17 Aug. 1986): 4–6.

———. "Alocución primera." 1935. *Alocuciones argentinas*. Madrid: Fundación Federico García Lorca, 1985. 13–15.

———. *Antología poética*. Ed. Mario Hernández. 2d. ed. Madrid: Alce, 1978.

———. *Doña Rosita la soltera, o El lenguaje de las flores*. 1935. Ed. Luis Martínez Cuitiño. 5th ed. Madrid: Espasa-Calpe, 1995.

———. *Federico García Lorca: Trece de Nieve* Nos. 1–2 (1976).

——. "Granada (paraíso cerrado para muchos)." 1926. *Obras completas*. Vol. 3. Ed. Arturo del Hoyo. Madrid: Aguilar, 1986. 132–36.

——. *Plays: One. "Blood Wedding," "Doña Rosita the Spinster," "Yerma."* Trans. Gwynne Edwards and Peter Luke. 1987. London: Methuen, 1994.

——. *"Romancero gitano."* 1926. *Obras completas*. Vol. 3. Ed. Arturo del Hoyo. Madrid: Aguilar, 1986. 339–46.

García Lorca, Francisco. *In the Green Morning: Memories of Federico.* Trans. Christopher Maurer. New York: New Directions, 1986.

García Márquez, Gabriel. *El amor en los tiempos del cólera.* 1985; Buenos Aires: Editorial Sudamericana, 1991.

García Montero, Luis. "Andalucía como imagen literaria." *Literaturas regionales en España: Historia y crítica.* Ed. José María Enguita and José-Carlos Mainer. Zaragoza: Institución "Fernando el Católico," 1994. 101–15.

García Nieto, José. " 'Poesía eres tú' y una feliz parodia escrita en nuestros días." *Boletín de la Real Academia Española* 67 (1987): 21–28.

Gassó y Ortiz, Blanca de. "La poesía." *El bazar* 4.5 (31 Oct. 1875): 78.

Gay, Peter. *The Bourgeois Experience: Victoria to Freud.* Vol. 1. *Education of the Senses.* New York: Oxford University Press, 1984.

Gay Armenteros, Juan, and Cristina Viñes Millet. *Historia de Granada.* Vol. 4. *La época contemporánea. Siglos XIX y XX.* Granada: Editorial Don Quijote, 1982.

Geertz, Clifford. *The Interpretation of Cultures: Selected Essays.* New York: Basic Books, 1973.

——. *Local Knowledge: Further Essays in Interpretive Anthropology.* New York: Basic Books, 1983.

Gerigonza liberalesca. Madrid: E. Aguado, 1823.

Gibson, Ian. *Federico García Lorca: A Life.* New York: Pantheon, 1989.

——. *Lorca's Granada: A Practical Guide.* London: Faber and Faber, 1992.

Gibbs, Virginia. *Las "Sonatas" de Valle-Inclán: Kitsch, sexualidad, satanismo, historia.* Madrid: Editorial Pliegos, 1991.

Gies, David Thatcher. *The Theatre in Nineteenth-Century Spain.* Cambridge: Cambridge University Press, 1994.

Gil, Constantino. "El sastre." *Los españoles de ogaño.* Vol. 2. Madrid: Librería de Victoriano Suárez, 1872. 325–35.

Gil, Ricardo. "El último juguete." *Tesoro poético del siglo XIX.* Vol. 5. *Poetas independientes* (Primera Parte). Ed. Vicente Gómez-Bravo. Madrid: Jubera Hermanos, Editores, 1902. 383–85.

Gilmore, David D. *Aggression and Community: Paradoxes of Andalusian Culture.* New Haven, Conn.: Yale University Press, 1987.

Gimeno, María Concepción. *La mujer española.* Madrid: Bailly Baillière, 1877.

Gold, Hazel. "Francisco's Folly: Picturing Reality in Galdós' *La de Bringas.*" *Hispanic Review* 54 (1986): 47–66.

Bibliography

———. *The Reframing of Realism: Galdós and the Discourses of the Nineteenth-Century Spanish Novel.* Durham, N.C.: Duke University Press, 1993.

———. "Small Talk: Towards a Poetics of the Detail in Galdós." *Revista hispánica moderna* 47 (1994): 30–46.

———. "A Tomb with a View: The Museum in Galdós' *Novelas contemporáneas.*" *MLN* 103 (1988): 312–34.

Goldman, Peter B. "What's in a Word? 'Class' and Its Evolution in the Eighteenth Century." *Romance Quarterly* 29.1 (1992): 7–16.

Gómez de la Serna, Ramón. "Las cosas y 'el ello.'" *Revista de occidente* 134 (Aug. 1934): 190–208.

———. "Lo cursi." *Lo cursi y otros ensayos.* Buenos Aires: Editorial Sudamericana, [1943]. 7–54.

———. "Ensayo sobre lo cursi." *Cruz y raya* 16 (July 1934): 9–38.

———. "Prólogo a las novelas de la nebulosa." *El hombre perdido.* Buenos Aires: Editorial Poseidón, 1947. 7–19.

———. *La viuda blanca y negra.* 1917/1918. Ed. Rodolfo Cardona. Madrid: Cátedra, 1988.

Gómez Marín, Manuel. Prologue to *Obras literarias.* Vol. 1. By J. Rodríguez Cao. Madrid: Imprenta de R. Labajos, 1869. i–vii.

Gómez-Moreno, Manuel. *Guía de Granada.* 1892. Granada: Universidad de Granada, Instituto Gómez-Moreno de la Fundación Rodríguez-Acosta, 1982.

González, Angel. "Poética No. 4." *Angel González.* Ed. Andrew P. Debicki. Madrid: Ediciones Júcar, 1989. 178.

González Gil, Luis. "La niña cursi." *Blanco y negro* 594 (20 Sept. 1902): n. pag.

González López, Luis. "A una cursi." *La chispa* 2.69 (20 Aug. 1891): 8–9.

González Troyano, Alberto. "El Cádiz romántico: Coyunturas y divagaciones." *El Casino y la ciudad de Cádiz: Política, sociedad y cultura en el Cádiz del siglo XIX.* Ed. José Luis Millán-Chivite. Cádiz: Caja de Ahorros de Cádiz, 1986. 31–39.

Goody, Jack. *The Culture of Flowers.* Cambridge: Cambridge University Press, 1993.

Gordon, Rae Beth. *Ornament, Fantasy, and Desire in Nineteenth-Century French Literature.* Princeton, N.J.: Princeton University Press, 1992.

Goytisolo, Juan. "Tierras del sur." *El furgón de cola.* 1967. Barcelona: Seix Barral, 1976. 273–94.

Granés, Salvador M. *Calabazas y cabezas.* Madrid: M. Romero, 1880.

Grassi, Angela. *La gota de agua.* Madrid: Tipografía de Gregorio Estrada, Compañía, 1875.

Greenberg, Clement. "The Avant-Garde and Kitsch." 1939. Dorfles 116–26.

Greenblatt, Stephen. "The Eating of the Soul." *Representations* 48 (1994): 97–116.

———. *Shakespearean Negotiations: The Circulation of Social Energy in Renaissance England.* Berkeley: University of California Press, 1988.

Guardia, Angel de la. "Becquerianas." *El album ibero americano,* 10.10 (14 Sept. 1892): 118.

Gubar, Susan. "'The Blank Page' and the Issues of Female Creativity." *The New Feminist Criticism: Essays on Women, Literature, and Theory.* Ed. Elaine Showalter. New York: Pantheon, 1985. 292–313.

Guijarro, Ricardo. ["No lloréis por la niña que muere"]. *Album poético.* Barcelona: Est. Editorial de Ramón Molinas, 1885. 66.

Gullón, Ricardo. *Direcciones del modernismo.* 2d ed. Madrid: Gredos, 1971.

——. "La Historia como materia novelable." *Anales galdosianos* 5 (1970): 23–37.

Gutiérrez Girardot, Rafael. *Modernismo.* Barcelona: Montesinos, 1983.

Hadjimichalis, Costis. *Uneven Development and Regionalism: State, Territory, and Class in Southern Europe.* London: Croom Helm, 1987.

Hafter, Monroe Z. "The Deceptive Slightness of Meléndez's 'El abanico.'" *Pen and Peruke: Spanish Literature of the Eighteenth Century.* Ed. Hafter. Ann Arbor: Michigan Romance Studies, University of Michigan, vol. 12, 1992. 185–201.

Hagen, Oskar. *Patterns and Principles of Spanish Art.* 1943; Madison: University of Wisconsin Press, 1948.

Haidt, Rebecca. *Embodying Enlightenment: Knowing the Body in Eighteenth-Century Spanish Literature and Culture.* New York: St. Martin's, 1998.

——. "Fashion, Effeminacy, and Homoerotic Desire (?): The Question of the *Petimetres.*" *Letras peninsulares* 12.1 (1999): 65–80.

Haig, Elizabeth. *The Floral Symbolism of the Great Masters.* London: Kegan Paul, Trench, and Trübner, 1913.

Handley, Sharon. "Federico García Lorca and the 98 Generation: The *Andalucismo* Debate." *Anales de literatura española contemporánea* 21 (1996): 41–58.

——. "*Romancero gitano* and the *Quincalla meridional.*" *Anales de literatura española contemporánea* 20 (1995): 127–37.

Harries, Karsten. "Metaphor and Transcendence." *On Metaphor.* Ed. Sheldon Sacks. Chicago: University of Chicago Press, 1981. 71–88.

Hemingway, Maurice. "Narrative Ambiguity and Situational Ethics in *La de Bringas.*" *Galdós' House of Fiction: Papers Given at the Birmingham Galdós Colloquium.* Ed. A. H. Clarke and E. J. Rodgers. Llangrannog, U.K.: Dolphin, 1991. 15–27.

Heras, Dionisio de las. "Tú y yo." *El bazar* 3.23 (5 Sept. 1875): 366.

Hernández, Mario. Introduction to *Doña Rosita la soltera, o El lenguaje de las flores. Los sueños de mi prima Aurelia.* Madrid: Alianza, 1998. 7–56.

Herzog, Tamar. "Municipal Citizenship and Empire: Communal Definition in Eighteenth-Century Spain and Spanish America." *Privileges and Rights of Citizenship: Law and the Juridical Construction of Civil Society.* Ed. Julius Kirshner and Laurent Mayali. Berkeley: University of California Press, 2002. 147–67.

Hobsbawm, Eric, and Terence Ranger, eds. *The Invention of Tradition.* Cambridge: Cambridge University Press, 1983.

Holguín, Andrés. "Lo cursi." *Las formas del silencio y otros ensayos.* Caracas: Monte Avila, 1969. 131–39.

Holquist, Michael. "A New Tour of Babel: Recent Trends Linking Comparative Literature Departments, Foreign Language Departments, and Area Studies Programs." *ADFL Bulletin* 27.1 (1995): 6–12.

Homans, Peter. *The Ability to Mourn: Disillusionment and the Social Origins of Psychoanalysis.* Chicago: University of Chicago Press, 1989.

Hooper, John. *The New Spaniards.* London: Penguin, 1995.

Hoyos y Vinent, Antonio. *Cuestión de ambiente.* Madrid: Establecimiento Tipográfico de Idamor Moreno, 1903.

———. *El primer estado (actuación de la aristocracia antes de la revolución, en la revolución y después de ella).* Madrid: Renacimiento, 1931.

Huélamo Kosma, Julio. "La influencia de Freud en el teatro de García Lorca." *Boletín de la Fundación Federico García Lorca* 6 (1989): 59–83.

Huerta, Eleazar. *El simbolismo de la mano en Bécquer.* Albacete: Diputación, 1990.

Hume, David. "Of Refinement in the Arts." 1752. *Essays Moral, Political, and Literary.* Vol. 1. London: Longmans, Green, 1875. 299–309.

Hutcheon, Linda. "Metafictional Implications for Novelistic Reference." *On Referring in Literature.* Ed. Anna Whiteside and Michael Issacharoff. Bloomington: Indiana University Press, 1987. 1–13.

Huyssen, Andreas. "Memories of Utopia." *Twilight Memories: Marking Time in a Culture of Amnesia.* New York: Routledge, 1995. 85–101.

Ichaso, Francisco. "Crisis de lo cursi." *Defensa del hombre.* La Habana: Trópico, 1937. 126–82.

"Imitación de Becker." *Jacque-Mate* (Madrid) 13 Mar. 1873: 1.

Iribarren, José María. *El porqué de los dichos: Sentido, origen y anécdota de los dichos, modismos y frases proverbiales de España con otras muchas curiosidades.* 4th ed. Madrid: Aguilar, 1974.

Isac, Angel. "Ganivet y la crítica de la ciudad moderna." Ganivet 11–52.

Iser, Wolfgang. *The Act of Reading.* Baltimore: Johns Hopkins University Press, 1978.

Jagoe, Catherine. *Ambiguous Angels: Gender in the Novels of Galdós.* Berkeley: University of California Press, 1994.

James, Elsa Nitzche. "Commemorative and Dated Fans." *The Spinning Wheel's Complete Book of Antiques.* Ed. Albert Christian Revi. New York: Grosset and Dunlap, 1972. 218–19.

Jameson, Fredric. Foreword to *The Postmodern Condition: A Report on Knowledge.* By Lyotard. vii–xxi.

———. "Postmodernism and Consumer Society." *The Anti-aesthetic: Essays on Postmodern Culture.* 1983. Ed. Hal Foster. Seattle, Wash.: Bay Press, 1987. 111–25.

JanMohamed, Abdul R. "Negating the Negation as a Form of Affirmation in Minority Discourse: The Construction of Richard Wright as Subject." *The Nature and Context of Minority Discourse.* Ed. JanMohamed and David Lloyd. New York: Oxford University Press, 1990. 102–23.

Bibliography

Jazmín, Florencio. *El lenguaje de las flores.* Exp. ed. Barcelona: Manuel Saurí, 1878.

Jed, Stephanie H. *Chaste Thinking: The Rape of Lucretia and the Birth of Humanism.* Bloomington: Indiana University Press, 1989.

Jiménez de Quirós, Enrique. "Becquerianas." *La semana madrileña* 3.58 (26 Jan. 1885): 8.

Jiménez-Vera, Arturo. "The Rose Symbolism and the Social Message in *Doña Rosita la soltera.*" *García Lorca Review* 6 (1978): 127–37.

Jovellanos, Gaspar Melchor de. "Elogio fúnebre del señor Marqués de los Llanos de Alguazas, leído en la Sociedad Económica de Madrid el día 5 de agosto de 1780." *Obras.* Ed. Cándido Nocedal. *BAE* 1. Madrid: Rivadeneyra, 1858. 283–87.

Jover Zamora, José María. "Edad contemporánea." *Introducción a la historia de España.* By Antonio Ubieto et al. 14th ed. Barcelona: Teide, 1983. 507–927.

——. "Por una historia de la civilización española." *La civilización española a mediados del s. XIX.* Madrid: Espasa-Calpe, 1991. 307–87.

Kagan, Richard L. "Prescott's Paradigm: American Historical Scholarship and the Decline of Spain." *American Historical Review* 101 (1996): 423–46.

——. *Students and Society in Early Modern Spain.* Baltimore: Johns Hopkins University Press, 1974.

Kant, Immanuel. "An Answer to the Question: What is Enlightenment?" Trans. Lewis White Beck. *Postmodernism: A Reader.* Ed. Patricia Waugh. London: Edward Arnold, 1992. 89–95.

Kirkpatrick, Susan. "The Ideology of *Costumbrismo.*" *Ideologies and Literature* 2.7 (1978): 28–44.

Kopytoff, Igor. "The Cultural Biography of Things: Commoditization as Process." *The Social Life of Things: Commodities in Cultural Perspective.* Ed. Arjun Appadurai. Cambridge: Cambridge University Press, 1986. 64–91.

Kulka, Tomas. *Kitsch and Art.* University Park: Pennsylvania State University Press, 1996.

Kundera, Milan. *The Unbearable Lightness of Being.* Trans. Michael Henry Heim. New York: Harper and Row, 1984.

Kurrik, Maire Jaanus. *Literature and Negation.* New York: Columbia University Press, 1979.

Labanyi, Jo. "Adultery and the Exchange Economy." *Scarlet Letters: Fictions of Adultery from Antiquity to the 1990s.* Ed. Nicholas White and Naomi Segal. New York: St. Martin's, 1997. 98–108.

——. *Myth and History in the Contemporary Spanish Novel.* Cambridge: Cambridge University Press, 1989.

——. "Nation, Narration, Naturalization: A Barthesian Critique of the 1898 Generation." *New Hispanisms: Literature, Culture, Theory.* Ed. Mark I. Millington and Paul Julian Smith. Ottawa: Dovehouse, 1994. 127–49.

——. "Postmodernism and the Problem of Cultural Identity." *Spanish Cultural Studies.
An Introduction: The Struggle for Modernity.* Ed. Helen Graham and Labanyi.
Oxford: Oxford University Press, 1995. 396–406.

——. "The Problem of Framing in *La de Bringas.*" *Anales galdosianos* 25 (1990):
25–34.

Laffranque, Marie. "Federico García Lorca, de 'Rosa Mudable' a la 'Casida de la
Rosa.' " *Lecciones sobre Federico García Lorca: Granada, mayo de 1986.* Ed. Andrés
Soria Olmedo. Granada: Comisión Nacional del Cincuentenario, 1986. 279–300.

Lafuente y Alcántara, Emilio. *Cancionero popular.* 2 vols. Madrid: Carlos Bailly-
Baillière, 1865.

Lakoff, George, and Mark Johnson. *Metaphors We Live By.* Chicago: University of Chicago Press, 1980.

Lara y Pedrajas, Antonio de. *D. Antonio Cánovas del Castillo: Estudio crítico.* Madrid:
Imprenta de los Hijos de M. G. Hernández, 1901.

Larra, Luis Mariano de. *Los corazones de oro.* Madrid: Imprenta de José Rodríguez, 1875.

Larra, Mariano José de. "El álbum." 1835. *Artículos varios.* Ed. Evaristo Correa Calderón. Madrid: Editorial Castalia, 1976. 494–501.

——. "El castellano viejo." 1832. *Artículos de costumbres.* Vol. 1. Ed. José R. Lomba y
Pedraja. Madrid: Espasa-Calpe, 1965. 74–90.

——. "Jardines públicos." 1834. *Artículos de costumbres.* Vol. 1. Ed. José R. Lomba y
Pedraja. Madrid: Espasa-Calpe, 1965. 160–67.

Larrubiera Crespo, A. "Cursilerías." *La risa* 1.38 (16 Sept. 1888): 11–13.

Laserna, José de. "Los teatros. Comedia. *Lo cursi,* comedia en tres actos y en prosa por
D. Jacinto Benavente." *El imparcial* (Madrid) 20 Jan. 1901: 3.

——. "Los teatros. Lara. *Modas,* sainete en un acto y en prosa por D. Jacinto Benavente." *El imparcial* (Madrid) 19 Jan. 1901: 1.

Lavaur, Luis. "Ganivet en la encrucijada turística de su tiempo." *Estudios turísticos* 9
(Jan.–Mar. 1966): 27–51.

"Lenguaje de las flores." *Almanaque del maestro.* Barcelona: Juan Bastinos e Hijos, 1872.
62–68.

"El lenguaje de las flores." *Blanco y negro* 9 Apr. 1910: n. pag.

León y Domínguez, José María. *Recuerdos gaditanos.* Cádiz, 1897.

Lerner, Laurence. *Angels and Absences: Child Deaths in the Nineteenth Century.*
Nashville, Tenn.: Vanderbilt University Press, 1997.

Leverenz, David. *Manhood and the American Renaissance.* Ithaca, N.Y.: Cornell University Press, 1989.

Lévi-Strauss, Claude. *The Savage Mind.* 1962. Chicago: University of Chicago Press,
1966.

Levine, Lawrence W. *Highbrow/Lowbrow: The Emergence of Cultural Hierarchy in America.* Cambridge, Mass.: Harvard University Press, 1988.

Lewis, Tom. "Afterword: Aesthetics and Politics." *Critical Practices in Post-Franco Spain.* Ed. Silvia L. López, Jenaro Talens, and Darío Villanueva. Minneapolis: University of Minnesota Press, 1994. 160–82.

Lida, Clara E. "Literatura anarquista y anarquismo literario." *Nueva revista de filología hispánica* 19 (1970): 360–81.

Liern, Rafael María. "El álbum de Rosalía." *La risa* 1.11 (11 Mar. 1888): 12–13.

Liniers, Santiago de, and Francisco Silvela. *La filocalia o arte de distinguir a los cursis de los que no lo son, seguido de un proyecto de bases para la formación de una hermandad o club con que se remedie dicha plaga.* Madrid: Imprenta de Tomás Fortanet, 1868.

Litvak, Lily. *A Dream of Arcadia: Anti-industrialism in Spanish Literature, 1895–1905.* Austin: University of Texas Press, 1975.

——. *Erotismo fin de siglo.* Barcelona: Antoni Bosch, 1979.

Liu, Alan. "Local Transcendence: Cultural Criticism, Postmodernism, and the Romanticism of Detail." *Representations* 32 (fall 1990): 75–113.

Llanas Aguilaniedo, José María. *Alma contemporánea: Estudio de estética.* 1899. Ed. Justo Broto Salanova. Huesca: Instituto de Estudios Altoaragoneses, 1991.

——. "Los negadores en el arte." 1899. *La novela aragonesa en el siglo XIX.* Ed. Rosa-María Andrés Alonso and José-Luis Calvo Carilla. Zaragoza: Guara, 1984. 174–76.

Lloréns Castillon, Vicente. "Sobre la aparición de 'Liberal.'" *Literatura, historia, política: Ensayos.* Madrid: Revista de Occidente, 1967. 45–56.

Lomas, John, ed. *O'Shea's Guide to Spain and Portugal.* 10th ed. 1865. London: Adam and Charles Black, 1895.

Lopes, José Manuel. "The Sarcastic Descriptor: Satire and Parody in Benito Pérez Galdós' *La de Bringas.*" *Foregrounded Description in Prose Fiction: Five Cross-literary Studies.* Toronto: University of Toronto Press, 1995. 68–90.

López Aranguren, José Luis. "La vida como conducta y como función." *El país* (Madrid) 20 Jan. 1986: 26.

López Bago, Eduardo. *El cura (caso de incesto).* Madrid: Juan Muñoz y Cía, [1885].

López Estrada, Francisco. Introduction to *Rimas y declaraciones poéticas.* By Bécquer. 9–64.

——. *Poética para un poeta: Las "Cartas literarias a una mujer" de Bécquer.* Madrid: Gredos, 1972.

López Valdemoro, J. "¡Me caso! (imitación de Bécquer)." *Día de moda* 1.23 (17 June 1883): 6.

Lorenzo-Rivero, Luis. *Estudios literarios sobre Mariano J. de Larra.* Madrid: José Porrúa Turanzas, 1986.

Loughran, David K. "F. García Lorca y Granada: La geografía de una estética." *MLN* 89 (1974): 289–97.

Lukács, John. "The Bourgeois Interior." *American Scholar* 39 (1970): 616–30.

Luna, José Carlos de. "Cursi." *ABC* (Madrid) 26 June 1953: n. pag.

Lustonó, Eduardo de. "El lipendi." *Madrid por dentro y por fuera.* Ed. Blasco. 221–28.

Lutz, Tom. *American Nervousness, 1903: An Anecdotal History*. Ithaca, N.Y.: Cornell University Press, 1991.

Lyotard, Jean-François. *The Postmodern Condition: A Report on Knowledge*. Trans. Geoff Bennington and Brian Massumi. Minneapolis: University of Minnesota Press, 1988.

Lyu, Claire. " 'High' Poetics: Baudelaire's *Le Poème du hachisch*." *MLN* 109 (1994): 698–740.

MacCannell, Dean. "Introduction to the 1989 Edition." *The Tourist: A New Theory of the Leisure Class*. 1976. New York: Schocken, 1989. ix–xx.

Machado, Antonio. *Poesías completas*. Ed. Manuel Alvar. Madrid: Espasa-Calpe, 1987.

Madoz, Pascual. *Diccionario geográfico-estadístico-histórico de España y sus posesiones de Ultramar*. 16 vols. Madrid: Establecimiento Literario-Tipográfico de Pascual Madoz y L. Sagasti, 1845–50.

Madrazo, Francisco de Paula. *Dos meses en Andalucía en el verano de 1849*. Madrid: Imprenta de la Biblioteca del Siglo, 1849.

———. *Una espedición a Guipúzcoa, en el verano de 1848*. Madrid: Imprenta de Don Gabriel Gil, 1849.

Magnien, Brigitte. "Cultura urbana." *1900 en España*. Ed. Serge Salaün and Carlos Serrano. Madrid: Espasa-Calpe, 1991. 107–29.

Mainer, José-Carlos. "La crisis de fin de siglo a la luz del 'emotivismo': Sobre *Alma contemporánea* (1899), de Llanas Aguilaniedo." *¿Qué es el modernismo? Nueva encuesta, nuevas lecturas*. Ed. Richard A. Cardwell and Bernard McGuirk. Boulder, Colo.: Society of Spanish and Spanish-American Studies, 1993. 147–64.

Mandrell, James. " 'Poesía . . . eres tú,' or the Construction of Bécquer and the Sign of Woman." *Culture and Gender in Nineteenth-Century Spain*. Ed. Lou Charnon-Deutsch and Jo Labanyi. Oxford: Oxford University Press, 1995. 53–73.

"Manual del perfecto modernista." 1898. *Las vanguardias del siglo XIX*. Ed. Mireia Freixa. Barcelona: Gustavo Gili, 1982. 394–99.

Maravall, José Antonio. *Culture of the Baroque: Analysis of a Historical Structure*. Trans. Terry Cochran. Minneapolis: University of Minnesota Press, 1986.

———. "Ganivet y el tema de la autenticidad nacional." *Revista de occidente* 11 (1965): 389–409.

———. "La imagen de la sociedad arcaica en Valle-Inclán." *Revista de occidente*, 2a época, 44–45 (1966): 225–56.

Marcus, Steven. "Freud and Dora: Story, History, Case History." *In Dora's Case: Freud—Hysteria—Feminism*. Ed. Charles Bernheimer and Claire Kahane. 2d ed. 1985. New York: Columbia University Press, 1990. 56–91.

Marcuse, Herbert. *Negations: Essays in Critical Theory*. Trans. Jeremy J. Shapiro. London: Free Association Books, 1988.

Marrasquino. "En la Exposición artística: Abanicos, miniaturas y encajes." *La época* (Madrid) 2 June 1895.

Marson, Ellen Engelson. "Mae West, Superman, and the Spanish Poets of the Seventies." *Literature and Popular Culture in the Hispanic World: A Symposium*. Ed. Rose S. Minc. Gaithersburg, Md.: Hispamérica, 1981. 191–98.

Martí, José. *Lucía Jerez* [*Amistad funesta*]. 1885. Ed. Manuel Pedro González. Madrid: Gredos, 1969.

Martín Gaite, Carmen. *Usos amorosos de la postguerra española*. Barcelona: Anagrama, 1987.

Martín Orozco, J. "En el álbum de una niña: Imitación a Bécquer." *La ilustración ibérica* 10.161 (30 Jan. 1886): 79.

Martín Recuerda, José. *Análisis de "Doña Rosita la soltera o el Lenguaje de las flores" (de Federico García Lorca): Tragedia sin sangre*. Salamanca: Universidad de Salamanca, 1979.

Martínez Cachero, José María. "Polémicas y ataques del 'Clarín' crítico." *Clarín y su obra: En el centenario de "La Regenta." Actas del Simposio Internacional Celebrado en Barcelona del 20 al 24 de Marzo de 1984*. Ed. Antonio Vilanova. Barcelona: Universidad, 1985. 83–102.

Martínez Cuitiño, Luis. Introduction to *Doña Rosita la soltera*. By Federico García Lorca. 9–60.

Martínez López, Enrique. Introduction to *Granada, paraíso cerrado, y otras páginas granadinas*. By Federico García Lorca. Granada: Miguel Sánchez, 1971. 15–69.

Martínez Montávez, Pedro. "Al-Andalus: La alter-identidad." *Revista de occidente* 140 (1993): 86–97.

Martínez Olmedilla, Augusto. *Periódicos de Madrid: Anecdotario*. Madrid: Aumarol, 1956.

Martínez Ruiz, José (Azorín). "Los cinco Cánovas." 1912. *Escritores*. Madrid: Biblioteca Nueva, 1956. 49–56.

——. "Las obras de Selgas." *La prensa* (Buenos Aires) 23 Dec. 1934: n. pag.

Martínez Sierra, Gregorio. *Granada: Guía emocional*. Paris: Garnier Hermanos, [1911].

——. *Granada*. Madrid: Renacimiento, 1931.

Martínez Sierra, Gregorio, and María Martínez Sierra. *Canción de cuna. Primavera en otoño. La suerte de Isabelita. Lirio entre espinas*. Madrid: Renacimiento, 1915.

Martínez Sierra, María. *Gregorio y yo: Medio siglo de colaboración*. Mexico City: Biografías Gandesa, 1953.

Marx, Karl. *Capital: A Critical Analysis of Capitalist Production*. 1867. 3 vols. Ed. Frederick Engels. Trans. Samuel Moore and Edward Aveling. New York: International Publishers, 1979.

Massa, Pedro. "Estreno de *Doña Rosita la soltera*." *Obras completas*. Vol. 3. By Federico García Lorca. Madrid: Aguilar, 1986. 667–68.

Matoses, Manuel (Andrés Corzuelo). *Loza ordinaria: Apuntes de la vida cursi. Obras*. Madrid: Librería de la Viuda de Hernando y Compañía, 1888.

Mauss, Marcel. *The Gift: Forms and Functions of Exchange in Archaic Societies*. Trans. Ian Cunnison. 1925. New York: Norton, 1967.

Mayer, Arno J. "The Lower Middle Class as Historical Problem." *Journal of Modern History* 47 (1975): 409–36.

——. *The Persistence of the Old Regime: Europe to the Great War*. New York: Pantheon, 1981.

McFarland, Thomas. *Shapes of Culture*. Iowa City: University of Iowa Press, 1987.

McInnis, Judy B. "The Psychological Map of García Lorca's Aesthetics: Granada as Universal Image." *The Comparatist* 8 (1984): 33–42.

Mayorga, Ventura. "Rimas." *Día de moda* 1.27 (9 Aug. 1880): 15.

Mediano, Baldomero. "Rimas." *Revista de Aragón* 2.36 (17 Sept. 1879): 288.

Mendoza, Cristina, and Eduardo Mendoza. *Barcelona modernista*. Barcelona: Planeta, 1989.

Merlino, Mario. "Notas, citas y perlas de lo cursi." *Letra* 8 (1987/88): 38–42.

Millán Contreras, Donato. "Una palabra busca su origen—¿Cómo nació el vocablo cursi?" *El español* 5.174 (23 Feb. 1946): 16.

Miller, Stephen. "*La de Bringas* as *Bildungsroman:* A Feminist Reading." *Romance Quarterly* 34 (1987): 189–99.

Mitchell, Timothy. *Flamenco Deep Song*. New Haven, Conn.: Yale University Press, 1994.

Mobellán de Casafiel, S[ebastián] de. "Rosa la solterona." *Las españolas pintadas por los españoles*. Vol. 1. Ed. Roberto Robert. Madrid: Imprenta a cargo de J. E. Morete, 1871. 93–104.

"El modernismo." *Miscelánea* 1.14 (18 Feb. 1900): 108.

"Modismos." *Vogue* (Spain) Mar. 1989: 28.

Moix, Ana María. *Walter, ¿por qué te fuiste?* Barcelona: Barral, 1973.

Moja y Bolívar, F. "Los cursis literarios." *Jaque-Mate* 2.59 (23 Mar. 1873): 2–4; 61 (30 Mar. 1873): 2–4; 62 (6 Apr. 1873): 2; 4; 63 (13 Apr. 1873): 2–3; 64 (20 Apr. 1873): 2; 67 (11 May 1873): 3–4.

——. "La romería de San Isidro." *Madrid por dentro y por fuera*. Ed. Blasco. 155–66.

Moles, Abraham A. *Le Kitsch: L'art du bonheur*. Paris: Maison Mame, 1971.

Moles, Abraham A., and Eberhard Wahl. "Kitsch et objet." *Communications* 13 (1969): 105–29.

Molinas, César, and Leandro Prados de la Escosura. "Was Spain Different? Spanish Historical Backwardness Revisited." *Explorations in Economic History* 26 (1989): 385–402.

Monlau, Pedro Felipe. *Higiene del matrimonio*. 1853. 13th ed. Paris: Garnier Hermanos, [1865].

Monsiváis, Carlos. *Días de guardar*. 1970. Mexico City: Era, 1989.

——. "Instituciones: La cursilería." *Escenas de pudor y liviandad*. 9th ed. 1981. Barcelona: Grijalbo, 1988. 171–87.

Monte-Cristo (Eugenio Rodríguez Ruiz de la Escalera). "Madrid elegante: Veraneo aristocrático." *Album Salón* 3.48 (16 Aug. 1899): 192.

Montells y Nadal, Francisco de Paula. *Proyecto para la ejecución de un ferro-carril que desde Granada vaya a empalmar con el que se está ejecutando de Málaga a Córdoba.* 1854. Granada. Universidad de Granada, 1993.

Mora Guarnido, José. *Federico García Lorca y su mundo.* Buenos Aires: Losada, 1958.

Moreno Godino, F. "La modista." *Los españoles de ogaño.* Vol. 2. Madrid: Librería de Victoriano Suárez, 1872. 314–24.

——. "El poeta de salón." *La risa* 1.25 (17 June 1888): 5–7; 10.

Moreno Hernández, Carlos. *Literatura y cursilería.* Valladolid: Universidad de Valladolid, 1995.

Morilla Critz, José. "La teoría de la dependencia económica en el estudio del siglo XIX andaluz." *Andalucía contemporánea (Siglos XIX y XX).* Vol. 2. Córdoba: Monte de Piedad y Caja de Ahorros de Córdoba, 1979. 113–25.

Morris, C. B. *Son of Andalusia: The Lyrical Landscapes of Federico García Lorca.* Nashville, Tenn.: Vanderbilt University Press, 1997.

M[ugica], J[osé]. "Madoz, bienhechor de Zarauz." *Boletín de la Real Sociedad Vascongada de los Amigos del País* 3 (1947): 117–19.

Muñoz Seca, Pedro, and Pedro Pérez Fernández. *La cursilona: Zarzuela en un acto.* Alcalá de Henares: Imprenta de la Escuela de Reforma, 1930.

Naharro, Vicente. *Arte de enseñar a escribir cursivo y liberal.* Madrid: Imprenta de Vega y Compañía, 1820.

Nash, Suzanne. Introduction to *Home and Its Dislocations in Nineteenth-Century France.* Ed. Nash. Albany: State University of New York Press, 1993. 1–21.

Naval, María Angeles. "Becquerianismo y becquerianos aragoneses." *Actas del Congreso "Los Bécquer y el Moncayo" celebrado en Tarazona y Veruela septiembre 1990.* Ed. Jesús Rubio Jiménez. Zaragoza: Centro de Estudios Turiasonenses, 1992. 423–35.

Navarrete, José. "Zorrilla y Grilo." *La ilustración española y americana* 38.111 (22 Jan. 1894): 46–47.

Navarrete, Ramón de. "El elegante." *Los españoles pintados por sí mismos.* 1843. Ed. Agustín Criado Becerro. Madrid: Dossat, 1992. 397–404.

Nemoianu, Virgil. *The Taming of Romanticism: European Literature and the Age of Biedermeier.* Cambridge, Mass.: Harvard University Press, 1984.

Nickel, Catherine. "The Function of Language in García Lorca's *Doña Rosita la soltera.*" *Hispania* 66 (1983): 522–31.

Nicolás, César. "Imagen y estilo en Ramón Gómez de la Serna." *Studies on Ramón Gómez de la Serna.* Ed. Nigel Dennis. Ottawa: Dovehouse, 1988. 129–51.

Nietzsche, Friedrich. *Thus Spoke Zarathustra. The Portable Nietzsche.* Ed. and Trans. Walter Kaufmann. New York: Viking, 1972.

Nora, Pierre. "Between Memory and History: *Les Lieux de Mémoire.*" *Representations* 26 (spring 1989): 7–25.

"No volverán." *La mosca* 1.1 (9 Apr. 1881): [1].

Nuevo manual de urbanidad, cortesía, decoro y etiqueta o El hombre fino. 1850. Valencia: Librerías París-Valencia, 1993.

O'Connor, Patricia W. *Gregorio and María Martínez Sierra.* Boston: Twayne, 1977.

Olalquiaga, Celeste. *Megalopolis: Contemporary Cultural Sensibilities.* Minneapolis: University of Minnesota Press, 1992.

Olózaga, José de. "Una nueva aplicación de las lecturas en alta voz." *Album de la prensa: Colección de artículos, poesías, cuentos, epigramas, etc., etc.* Madrid: Imprenta de los Señores Rojas, 1870. 237–41.

Ong, Walter J. *Orality and Literacy: The Technologizing of the Word.* London: Methuen, 1982.

"On Kitsch: A Symposium." *Salmagundi* 85–86 (1990): 197–312.

Ortega y Frías, Ramón. *La gente cursi: Novela de costumbres ridículas.* Madrid: Urbano Manini, 1872.

Ortega y Gasset, José. "Azorín: Primores de lo vulgar." 1917. *El espectador.* Vol. 2. *Obras completas.* Madrid: Revista de Occidente, 1946. 157–91.

——. *La deshumanización del arte.* 9th ed. 1925. Madrid: Revista de Occidente, 1967.

——. "Intimidades." 1929. *El espectador.* Vol. 2. *Obras completas.* Madrid: Revista de Occidente, 1946. 629–57.

——. *Meditaciones del Quijote.* 1914. Ed. Julián Marías. Madrid: Cátedra, 1985.

——. "La poesía de Ana de Noailles." *Revista de Occidente* 1 (1923): 29–41.

——. *La redención de las provincias.* 1927–1928. *Obras completas.* Vol. 11. Madrid: Revista de Occidente, 1969.

——. "Sentido del preciosismo (la *Sonata de estío*)." 1904. *Ramón del Valle-Inclán: An Appraisal of his Life and Works.* Ed. Anthony Zahareas, Rodolfo Cardona and Sumner Greenfield. New York: Las Américas, 1968. 48–56.

——. "Teoría de Andalucía." *Notas de andar y ver (viajes, gentes y países).* 1927. Madrid: Revista de Occidente, 1988. 173–85.

Ortiz Armengol, Pedro. "Tres apuntes hacia temas de *Fortunata y Jacinta.*" *Letras de Deusto* 4.8 (1974): 241–51.

Ortiz de Montellano, Bernardo. "Definiciones para la estética de. . . ." *Contemporáneos* 3.10 (1929): 199–205.

Ortner, Sherry B., and Harriet Whitehead. Introduction to *Sexual Meanings: The Cultural Construction of Gender and Sexuality.* Ed. Ortner and Whitehead. Cambridge: Cambridge University Press, 1981. 1–27.

Orwell, George. "Inside the Whale." 1940. *A Collection of Essays.* Garden City, N.Y.: Doubleday, 1954. 215–56.

Oslé, Julián. *Cádiz 1900 en las fotografías de Ramón Muñoz.* [Madrid]: Sílex, 1991.

Ossorio y Gallardo, Carlos. "En el abanico de mi bella amiga." *Album poético.* Barcelona: Establecimiento Editorial de Ramón Molinas, 1885. 192.

——. "Mujeres y flores." *Album poético.* Barcelona: Establecimiento Tipolitográfico Editorial de Ramón Molinas, 1890. 50–51.

Otero Carvajal, Luis Enrique. "El proceso de formación de la nueva élite de poder local en la provincia de Madrid. 1836–1874." *Madrid en la sociedad del siglo XIX.* Vol. 1. Ed. Otero Carvajal and Angel Bahamonde. Madrid: Comunidad de Madrid, 1986. 377–451.

Otros abanicos. Madrid: Banco Exterior de España, 1985.

Pacheco, José Emilio. "Homenaje a la cursilería / Homage to Kitsch." *Don't Ask Me How the Time Goes By: Poems. 1964–1968.* Trans. Alastair Reid. New York: Columbia University Press, 1978. 32–33.

El país (Madrid) 20–21 Jan. 1986.

Palacio, Eduardo de. "Abanicos." *Madrid cómico* 5.130 (15 August 1885): 3; 6.

Palacio, Manuel del. "Hojas de un álbum." [1904]. *Mi vida en prosa: Crónicas íntimas.* Madrid: Librería General de Victoriano Suárez, n.d. [1934?]. 234–38.

——. "El modernismo (fábula)." *Blanco y negro* 573 (26 Apr. 1902): n. pag.

Palacio Valdés, Armando. "Don Antonio F. Grilo." *Nuevo viaje al Parnaso.* 1879. *Obras.* Vol. 2. Madrid: Aguilar, 1965. 1226–31.

——. *La hermana San Sulpicio.* 1889. Mexico City: Porrúa, 1972.

——. *El señorito Octavio.* 1881. *Obras.* Vol. 2. Madrid: Aguilar, 1965.

Palenque, Marta. *Gusto poético y difusión literaria en el realismo español: "La Ilustración Española y Americana," 1869–1905.* Sevilla: Alfar, 1990.

——. *El poeta y el burgués (poesía y público, 1850–1900).* Sevilla: Alfar, 1990.

Pardo Bazán, Emilia. "El abanico." 1908. *Obras completas.* Vol. 1. Ed. Federico Carlos Sainz de Robles. 3d ed. Madrid: Aguilar, 1973. 1637–39.

——. "Abanicos." *La época* (Madrid) 8 June 1895.

——. *El cisne de Vilamorta.* 1885. *Obras completas.* Vol. 2. Ed. Federico Carlos Sainz de Robles. 3d ed. Madrid: Aguilar, 1973.

——. "La vida contemporánea." *La ilustración artística* 33.1671 (5 Jan. 1914): 30.

Paredes Alonso, Francisco Javier. *Pascual Madoz, 1805–1870: Libertad y progreso en la monarquía isabelina.* 2d ed. 1982. Pamplona: Ediciones Universidad de Navarra, 1991.

Pareja Serrada, Antonio. *Influencia de la mujer en la regeneración social: Estudio crítico.* Guadalajara: Establecimiento Editorial de D. Antero Concha, 1880.

Pascual y C., Eduardo. "¡Llora! A una huérfana." *El bazar* 3.4 (Apr. 1875): 63.

Pastor Díaz, Nicomedes. Prologue to *Obras completas.* By José Zorrilla. Ed. Narciso Alonso Cortés. Valladolid: Librería Santarén, 1943. 13–24.

Payán Sotomayor, Pedro M. *El habla de Cádiz.* Cádiz: Fundación Municipal de Cultura, 1983.

Pecora, Vicent P. "The Limits of Local Knowledge." *The New Historicism.* Ed. H. Aram Veeser. New York: Routledge, 1989. 243–76.

Percival, MacIver. *The Fan Book.* New York: Frederick A. Stokes, 1921.

Pereda, José María de. *Los hombres de pro.* 1876. *Obras completas.* Vol. 3. Ed. Noël Valis. Santander: Tantín, 1990.

——. *Tanto tienes, tanto vales.* 1861. *Ensayos dramáticos.* Santander: Privately printed, 1869.

Pérez de Guzmán, Juan. "Cánovas del Castillo juzgado por sus libros." *La España moderna* 19.226 (Oct. 1907): 60–92.

Pérez Firmat, Gustavo. *Idle Fictions: The Hispanic Vanguard Novel, 1926–1934.* Durham, N.C.: Duke University Press, 1982.

Pérez Galdós, Benito. *Cánovas.* 1912. Madrid: Hernando, 1973.

——. "Carta (26 Feb. 1884)." *Las cartas desconocidas de Galdós en "La Prensa" de Buenos Aires.* Ed. William Shoemaker. Madrid: Ediciones Cultura Hispánica, 1973. 63–71.

——. *La de Bringas.* 1884. Ed. Alda Blanco and Carlos Blanco Aguinaga. Madrid: Cátedra, 1985.

——. *La desheredada.* 1881. 2d ed. Madrid: Alianza, 1970.

——. *Discurso.* Menéndez y Pelayo-Pereda-Pérez Galdós. *Discursos leídos ante la Real Academia Española.* Madrid: Est. Tip. de La Viuda e Hijos de Tello, 1897.

——. *La familia de León Roch.* 1878. *Obras completas.* Vol. 4. Ed. Federico Carlos Sainz de Robles. 7th ed. Madrid: Aguilar, 1969.

——. *Fortunata y Jacinta.* 1885–86. 2 vols. Ed. Francisco Caudet. Madrid: Cátedra, 1985.

——. *Miau.* 1888. Ed. Ricardo Gullón. Madrid: Revista de Occidente, 1957.

——. *That Bringas Woman.* Ed. and Trans. Catherine Jagoe. London: Everyman, 1996.

Pérez Zúñiga, Juan. "En varios abanicos." *La gran vía,* 2.49 (3 June 1894): 346.

Peri Rossi, Cristina. "Apoteosis de lo cursi." *Marcha* 7 Nov. 1969: 29.

Perriam, Chris. *Desire and Dissent: An Introduction to Luis Antonio de Villena.* Oxford: Berg, 1995.

Petrey, Sandy. *Realism and Revolution: Balzac, Stendhal, Zola, and the Performances of History.* Ithaca, N.Y.: Cornell University Press, 1988.

Picatoste, Felipe. "¡Pobres burgueses!" *Ultimos escritos de Felipe Picatoste.* Madrid: Miguel Romero, 1892. 161–65.

Pizarroso, A. "Becqueriana." *Barcelona cómica* 16 Feb. 1892: 12.

Pocock, J. G. A. *Virtue, Commerce, and History: Essays on Political Thought and History, Chiefly in the Eighteenth Century.* Cambridge: Cambridge University Press, 1985.

Poggioli, Renato. *The Theory of the Avant-Garde.* Trans. Gerald Fitzgerald. Cambridge, Mass.: Harvard University Press, 1968.

Poster, Mark. Introduction to *Selected Writings.* By Jean Baudrillard. Stanford: Stanford University Press, 1988. 1–9.

Praz, Mario. *An Illustrated History of Interior Decoration.* New York: Thames and Hudson, 1983.

——. *Unromantic Spain.* New York: Knopf, 1929.

Predmore, Michael. "Satire in the *Sonata de primavera.*" *Hispanic Review* 56 (1988): 307–17.

Prieto, Gregorio, ed. *Lorca y la generación del 27.* Madrid: Biblioteca Nueva, 1977.

Bibliography

Prieto-Moreno, Francisco. *Granada.* 1954. Trans. John Forrester. 9th ed. Barcelona: Noguer, 1965.

Probyn, Elspeth. "Travels in the Postmodern: Making Sense of the Local." *Feminism/Postmodernism.* Ed. Linda J. Nicholson. New York: Routledge, 1990. 176–89.

Prugent, Enrique. "La cursi." *Los españoles de ogaño.* Vol. 1. Madrid: Librería de Victoriano Suárez, 1872. 256–58.

Puig, Manuel. *Boquitas pintadas.* 1969. Barcelona: Seix Barral, 1986.

——. *La traición de Rita Hayworth.* 4th ed. Buenos Aires: Editorial Sudamericana, 1970.

Puyol, Julio. "Un álbum romántico." *Revista Crítica Hispano-Americana* 1.1 (1915): 20–29.

Querol, Vicente W. *Poesías.* 1877; 1891. Ed. Luis Guarner. Madrid: Espasa-Calpe, 1964.

Quinn, David. "Cánovas y el historicismo." *Hispanófila* 72 (May 1981): 19–30.

Ramírez, Angel E. *José Zorrilla: Biografía anecdótica.* Madrid: Mundo Latino, n.d. [1915?].

Ramírez, Arthur. "The Heraldic Emblematic Image in Galdós' *La de Bringas.*" *Revista de estudios hispánicos* 14.1 (1980): 65–74.

Ramón y Cajal, Santiago. *Los tónicos de la voluntad: Reglas y consejos sobre investigación científica.* 1899. Madrid: Espasa-Calpe, 1981.

Rees, Margaret A. " 'Rosa y jazmín de Granada': The Role of Flowers in Lorca's Plays and Poetry." *Leeds Papers on Lorca and on Civil War Verse.* Ed. Rees. Leeds: Trinity and All Saints' College, 1988. 81–92.

Reher, David Sven. *Town and Country in Pre-industrial Spain: Cuenca, 1550–1870.* Cambridge: Cambridge University Press, 1990.

——. "Urban Growth and Population Development in Spain, 1787–1930." *Urban Population Development in Western Europe from the Late-Eighteenth to the Early-Twentieth Century.* Ed. Richard Lawton and Robert Lee. Liverpool: Liverpool University Press, 1989. 190–219.

Rev, Istvān. "Parallel Autopsies." *Representations* 49 (winter 1995): 15–39.

Review of *La cruz del matrimonio,* by Luis de Eguilaz. *El contemporáneo.* 22 Dec. 1861.

Rheims, Maurice. *La vie étrange des objets: Histoire de la curiosité.* Paris: 10/18, 1963.

Ribbans, Geoffrey. "Galdós's View of the Bourbon Restoration in *Cánovas.*" *Studies in Honor of Bruce W. Wardropper.* Ed. Dian Fox, Harry Sieber, and Robert ter Horst. Newark, Del.: Juan de la Cuesta, 1989. 221–36.

Ricoeur, Paul. "The Metaphorical Process as Cognition, Imagination, and Feeling." *On Metaphor.* Ed. Sheldon Sacks. Chicago: University of Chicago Press, 1981. 141–57.

——. *The Rule of Metaphor.* Trans. Robert Czerny. Toronto: University of Toronto Press, 1993.

Riffaterre, Michael. *Semiotics of Poetry.* 1978. Bloomington: Indiana University Press, 1984.

Ringrose, David. *Spain, Europe and the "Spanish Miracle" 1700–1900.* Cambridge: Cambridge University Press, 1996.

Rivera y Delgado, M. de. *Biografía de D. Jesús Rodríguez Cao. Obras literarias.* Vol. 1. By Rodríguez Cao. Madrid: Imprenta de R. Labajos, 1869.

Rivière, Margarita. *Lo cursi y el poder de la moda.* Madrid: Espasa-Calpe, 1992.

Robert, Roberto. "La señorita cursi." *Las españolas pintadas por los españoles.* Vol. 1. Ed. Robert. Madrid: Imprenta a cargo de J. E. Morete, 1871. 83–91.

——. "El Suizo viejo." *Madrid por dentro y por fuera.* Ed. Blasco. 15–21.

Rodrigo, Antonina. "*Doña Rosita la soltera:* Crónica de una ciudad." *ABC* (Madrid) 17 Aug. 1986: 49–50.

——. "*Doña Rosita la soltera:* Teatro y realidad." *Lecciones sobre Federico García Lorca: Granada, mayo de 1986.* Ed. Andrés Soria Olmedo. Granada: Comisión Nacional del Cincuentenario, 1986. 117–28.

Rodríguez, Rodney T. "El trasfondo económico y moral de *La de Bringas.*" *Letras de Deusto* 15.33 (1985): 165–73.

Rodríguez Cao, Jesús. *Obras literarias.* 4 vols. Madrid: Imprenta de R. Labajos, 1869–70.

Rodríguez-Puértolas, Julio. "A Comprehensive View of Medieval Spain." *Américo Castro and the Meaning of Spanish Civilization.* Ed. José Rubia Barcia. Berkeley: University of California Press, 1976. 113–34.

Roland, Alfredo E. "Lo cursi, el estilo finisecular y el 900." *Imago mundi* 2.7 (1955): 42–53.

Roldán, Antonio. "Cómo caen las niñas cursis." *El cuento semanal* 5.243 (25 Aug. 1911): n. pag.

Romero Tobar, Leonardo. "Los álbumes de las románticas." *Escritoras románticas españolas.* Ed. Marina Mayoral. Madrid: Fundación Banco Exterior, 1990. 73–93.

——. "En los orígenes de la bohemia: Bécquer, *Pedro Sánchez* y la revolución de 1854." *Bohemia y literatura (de Bécquer al modernismo).* Ed. Pedro M. Piñero and Rogelio Reyes. Sevilla: Universidad de Sevilla, 1993. 27–49.

——. "Manuscritos poéticos del siglo XIX: Indice de doce álbumes." *Trabajos de la Asociación Española de Bibliografía.* Madrid: Ministerio de Cultura, 1993. 275–310.

Rosaldo, Michelle Z. "Toward an Anthropology of Self and Feeling." *Culture Theory: Essays on Mind, Self, and Emotion.* Ed. Richard A. Schweder and Robert A. LeVine. 1984. Cambridge: Cambridge University Press, 1989. 137–57.

Rose, Hugh James. *Among the Spanish People.* 2 vols. London: Richard Bentley & Son, 1877.

——. *Untrodden Spain, and Her Black Country.* 2 vols. 2d ed. London: Samuel Tinsley, 1875.

Rosenberg, Harold. "Pop Culture: Kitsch Criticism." *The Tradition of the New.* 1959. New York: McGraw-Hill, 1965. 259–68.

Ross, Andrew. *No Respect: Intellectuals and Popular Culture.* New York: Routledge, 1989.

Rossetti, Ana. *Plumas de España.* Barcelona: Seix Barral, 1988.

Roth, Michael S. "Returning to Nostalgia." *Home and Its Dislocations in Nineteenth-Century France.* Ed. Suzanne Nash. Albany: State University of New York Press, 1993. 25–43.

Round, Nicholas G. "Rosalía Bringas' Children." *Anales galdosianos* 6 (1971): 43–50.

Rubio y Galí, Federico (El Doctor Ruderico). *Mis maestros y mi educación: Memorias de niñez y juventud.* Madrid: Imprenta y encuadernación de V. Tordesillas, 1912.

———. *La mujer gaditana: Apuntes de economía social.* Madrid: Idamor Moreno, 1902.

Rubert de Ventós, Xavier. *Teoría de la sensibilidad.* 2d ed. 1969. Barcelona: Ediciones Península, 1973.

La rueda del amor y de la fortuna, con cien preguntas diferentes y el Lenguaje de las Flores. n.d. Valencia: Librerías, París-Valencia, 1992.

Ruiz Aguilera, Ventura. *Elegías y armonías: Rimas varias.* 3d ed. Madrid: Imprenta, Estereotipia y Galvanoplastia de Aribau y Cía, 1873.

Ruiz Lagos, Manuel. "La atracción del sur." *La atracción del sur.* Sevilla: Universidad de Sevilla, 1988. 9–38.

———. *Ensayos de la revolución: Andalucía en llamas, 1868–1875.* Madrid: Editora Nacional, 1977.

Rybczynski, Witold. *Home: A Short History of an Idea.* New York: Viking, 1986.

Sacks, Peter. *The English Elegy: Studies in the Genre from Spenser to Yeats.* Baltimore: Johns Hopkins University Press, 1985.

Saglia, Diego. " 'The True Essence of Romanticism': Romantic Theories of Spain and the Question of Spanish Romanticism." *Journal of Iberian and Latin American Studies* 3.2 (1997): 127–45.

Sahlins, Marshall. *Historical Metaphors and Mythical Realities: Structure in the Early History of the Sandwich Islands Kingdom.* Ann Arbor: University of Michigan Press, 1981.

Sahlins, Peter. *Boundaries: The Making of France and Spain in the Pyrenees.* Berkeley: University of California Press, 1989.

Sahuquillo, Angel. *Federico García Lorca y la cultura de la homosexualidad.* Stockholm: University of Stockholm, 1986.

Saisselin, Rémy G. *The Bourgeois and the Bibelot.* New Brunswick, N.J.: Rutgers University Press, 1984.

Salarich, Joaquim. *Higiene del tejedor.* 1858. *Condiciones de vida y trabajo obrero en España a mediados del siglo XIX.* Ed. Antoni Jutglar. Barcelona: Anthropos, 1984.

Salazar Rincón, Javier. *"Rosas y mirtos de luna . . .": Naturaleza y símbolo en la obra de Federico García Lorca.* Madrid: Universidad Nacional de Educación a Distancia, 1999.

Salvany, Juan Tomás. "El abanico." *Almanaque de la Lira para 1883.* Madrid: Establecimiento Tipográfico de Alfredo Alonso, 1883. 56–58.

Sánchez, Roberto. "García Lorca y la literatura del siglo XIX: Apuntes sobre *Doña Rosita la soltera*." *Federico García Lorca.* Ed. Ildefonso-Manuel Gil. Madrid: Taurus, 1973. 323–36.

Sánchez-Albornoz, Nicolás. "Cádiz, capital revolucionaria, en la encrucijada económica." *La revolución de 1868: Historia, pensamiento, literatura.* Ed. Clara E. Lida and Iris M. Zavala. New York: Las Américas, 1970. 80–108.

——. *España hace un siglo: Una economía dual.* Madrid: Alianza, 1988.

——. "El trasfondo económico de la revolución." *La revolución de 1868: Historia, pensamiento, literatura.* Ed. Clara E. Lida and Iris M. Zavala. New York: Las Américas, 1970. 64–79.

Sánchez Casado, Antonio. "El característico estilo del kitsch español." *El kitsch español.* Ed. Sánchez Casado. Madrid: Temas de Hoy, 1988. 13–17.

Sánchez de León, Enrique. "Imitación de Bécquer." *Día de moda* 1.29 (22 Aug. 1880): 11.

Sánchez Ferlosio, Rafael. "La cultura, ese invento del Gobierno." *El país* (Madrid) 22 Nov. 1984: 11–12.

Sánchez Pérez, Antonio. "Cursilerías." *La ilustración española y americana* 34 (15 Sept. 1893): 154–55.

——. "La venganza de 'Juan Cursi.'" *La ilustración española y americana* 46 (15 Jan. 1902): 32; 34; (30 Jan. 1902): 58–59.

Santa Teresa, Fr. Manuel de. *Instructorio espiritual de los Terceros, Terceras y Beatas de Ntra. Señora del Carmen.* Mexico City: Reimpreso por V. García Torres, Ex-Convento del Espíritu Santo, 1853.

Santiago y Palomares, Francisco Javier de. *Selected Writings, 1776–95.* Ed. Dennis P. Seniff. Exeter, U.K.: University of Exeter, 1984.

Santos, Lidia. *Kitsch tropical: Los medios en la literatura y el arte en América Latina.* Madrid: Iberoamericana, 2001.

Santos Torroella, Rafael. "Salvador Dalí escribe a Federico García Lorca." *Poesía* 27–28 (14 Apr. 1987).

Sanz Cuadrado, María Antonia. "Grilo y la crítica." *Cuadernos de literatura* 6.16–18 (July–Dec. 1949): 67–103.

Sarandeses Pérez, Francisco. *Heráldica de los apellidos asturianos.* Oviedo: Instituto de Estudios Asturianos, 1966.

Sarduy, Severo. *Written on a Body.* Trans. Carol Maier. New York: Lumen, 1989.

Sarmiento, Ramón. "*Ideales:* El libro de Grilo." *La ilustración española y americana,* 39.13 (8 Apr. 1895): 222.

Sartiliot, Claudette. *Herbarium-Verbarium: The Discourse of Flowers.* Lincoln: University of Nebraska Press, 1993.

Sartre, Jean-Paul. *L'Imaginaire: Psychologie phénoménologique de l'imagination.* 1940. Paris: Gallimard, 1971.

Sbarbi y Osuna, José María. *Florilegio o ramillete alfabético de refranes y modismos.* Madrid: Imp. de A. Gómez Fuentenebro, 1873.

——. "Rectificación literaria: Cur-si. (artículo inodoro)." *El imparcial* (Madrid) 19 June 1882: [4].

Scarry, Elaine. "Imagining Flowers: Perceptual Mimesis (Particularly Delphinium)." *Representations* 57 (winter 1997): 90–115.

Schor, Naomi. "Female Fetishism: The Case of George Sand." *The Female Body in*

Western Culture. Ed. Susan Rubin Suleiman. Cambridge, Mass.: Harvard University Press, 1986. 363–72.

——. *Reading in Detail: Aesthetics and the Feminine.* New York: Methuen, 1987.

Schuchardt, H[ugo]. "Die *Cantes Flamencos.*" *Zeitschrift für romanische Philologie* 5 (1881): 249–322.

Searle, John. *Speech Acts: An Essay in the Philosophy of Language.* Cambridge: Cambridge University Press, 1969.

Seaton, Beverly. *The Language of Flowers: A History.* Charlottesville: University Press of Virginia, 1995.

Sebold, Russell P. "Galdós y el 'bello monstruo' Rodríguez Cao." *De ilustrados y románticos.* Madrid: El Museo Universal, 1992. 139–43.

——. "García Márquez y lo cursi." *De ilustrados y románticos.* Madrid: El Museo Universal, 1992. 145–49.

——. Introduction to *Rimas.* By Bécquer. Madrid: Espasa-Calpe, 1989. 9–157.

Seco de Lucena Vázquez de Gardner, María Encarnación. *La estética de lo pequeño y la reducción espacial en la obra de Federico García Lorca.* Granada: Universidad de Granada, 1990.

Segovia, Angel María. *Melonar de Madrid.* Madrid: Imp. a cargo de A. Florenciano, 1876.

Seigel, Jerrold. *Bohemian Paris: Culture, Politics, and the Boundaries of Bourgeois Life, 1830–1930.* New York: Penguin, 1987.

Sekora, John. *Luxury: The Concept in Western Thought, Eden to Smollett.* Baltimore: Johns Hopkins University Press, 1997.

Selgas, José. "La cuna vacía." *Tesoro poético del siglo XIX.* Vol. 5. *Poetas independientes* (Primera Parte). Ed. Vicente Gómez-Bravo. Madrid: Jubera Hermanos, 1902. 41.

——. "El lujo de las mujeres." *Delicias del nuevo paraíso: Recogidas al vapor en el siglo de la electricidad.* Madrid: Administración de La Moda Elegante, 1871. 129–36.

Sepúlveda, Ricardo. "En un abanico." *Cádiz* 1.4 (10 June 1877): 27.

——. "Rima (de un libro inédito)." *La gran vía* 1.25 (17 Dec. 1893): 389.

Sergeant, Elizabeth Shepley. "The Other Side of the Door." *French Perspectives.* New York: Houghton Mifflin, 1916. 94–116.

Shakespeare, William. *The Comedy of Errors. Complete Works.* Ed. G. B. Harrison. New York: Harcourt, Brace and World, 1952.

Sheriff, John K. *The Fate of Meaning: Charles Peirce, Structuralism, and Literature.* Princeton, N.J.: Princeton University Press, 1989.

Shubert, Adrian. *A Social History of Modern Spain.* London: Unwin Hyman, 1990.

Sieburth, Stephanie. *Inventing High and Low: Literature, Mass Culture, and Uneven Modernity in Spain.* Durham, N.C.: Duke University Press, 1994.

Sigourney, Mrs. L. H. *Letters of Life.* New York: Appleton, 1866.

Silvela, Francisco. *Los Neo-cultos.* Madrid: Imprenta de El Imparcial, 1868.

Bibliography

Simón Palmer, María del Carmen. *Escritoras españolas del siglo XIX: Manual bio-bibliográfico.* Madrid: Castalia, 1991.

Simpson, David. *Fetishism and Imagination: Dickens, Melville, Conrad.* Baltimore: Johns Hopkins University Press, 1982.

Sinués de Marco, María del Pilar. *El Angel del hogar: Estudios morales acerca de la mujer.* 1859. 2 vols. Mexico City: Imprenta de J. R. Barbedillo y Compañía, 1876.

Smith, Paul Julian. *The Body Hispanic.* Oxford: Clarendon, 1989.

———. *The Moderns: Time, Space, and Subjectivity in Contemporary Spanish Culture.* Oxford: Oxford University Press, 2000.

———. "Modern Times: Francisco Umbral's Chronicle of Distinction." *MLN* 113 (1998): 324–38.

———. *The Theatre of García Lorca: Text, Performance, Psychoanalysis.* Cambridge: Cambridge University Press, 1998.

Soldevila, Carles. *La moda ochocentista.* Barcelona: Argos, 1950.

Solís, Ramón. "La burguesía gaditana y el romanticismo." *La burguesía mercantil gaditana, 1650–1868.* Cádiz: Instituto de Estudios Gaditanos-Excma. Diputación Provincial de Cádiz, 1976. 79–107.

———. "La cursilería y las niñas de Sicur." *ABC* (Madrid) 21 Oct. 1962: n. pag.

———. *Historia del periodismo gaditano, 1800–1850.* Cádiz: Instituto de Estudios Gaditanos-Excma. Diputación Provincial de Cádiz, 1971.

———. "El romanticismo gaditano." *Revista de occidente* 97 (Apr. 1971): 48–72.

Solsona, Conrado. "Mi clase." *Notas humorísticas.* Madrid: Luis Navarro, 1882. 145–48.

Sommer, Doris. *Foundational Fictions: The National Romances of Latin America.* Berkeley: University of California Press, 1991.

Sontag, Susan. "Notes on 'Camp.'" 1964. *Against Interpretation.* 1966. New York: Farrar, Straus, Giroux, 1986. 275–92.

Sopeña Monsalve, Andrés. *El florido pensil: Memoria de la escuela nacionalcatólica.* Barcelona: Grijalbo Mondadori, 1994.

Soravilla, Javier. "¡Vuelve al cielo!" *El bazar* 3.23 (5 Sept. 1875): 366.

Soufas, C. Christopher. *Audience and Authority in the Modernist Theater of Federico García Lorca.* Tuscaloosa: University of Alabama Press, 1996.

Spacks, Patricia Meyer. *Gossip.* Chicago: University of Chicago Press, 1986.

Spitzer, Leo. "A New Spanish Etymological Dictionary." *Modern Language Notes* 71 (1956): 271–83.

Starobinski, Jean. "The Idea of Nostalgia." *Diogenes* 54 (1966): 81–103.

Stewart, Kathleen. "Nostalgia—A Polemic." *Cultural Anthropology* 3 (1988): 227–41.

Stewart, Susan. *On Longing: Narratives of the Miniature, the Gigantic, the Souvenir, the Collection.* Baltimore: Johns Hopkins University Press, 1984.

———. "The State of Cultural Theory and the Future of Literary Form." *Profession 93* (1993): 12–15.

Bibliography

Suárez, Constantino. *Escritores y artistas asturianos: Indice bio-bibliográfico.* Vol. 7. Ed. José María Martínez Cachero. Oviedo: Instituto de Estudios Asturianos, 1959.

Subirats, Eduardo. *La crisis de las vanguardias y la cultura moderna.* Madrid: Ediciones Libertarias, 1985.

——. *Después de la lluvia: Sobre la ambigua modernidad española.* Madrid: Temas de Hoy, 1993.

Suck, Titus. "Bourgeois Class Position and the Esthetic Representation of Class Interest: The Social Determination of Taste." *MLN* 102 (1987): 1090–1121.

Taboada, Luis. *Cursilones.* Madrid: Librería de San Martín, n.d.

——. *Los cursis.* Madrid: Casa Editorial, Viuda de Rodríguez Serra, [1903].

——. "Fragmentos de la vida de un cursi." *El mundo cómico* 3.104 (25 Oct. 1874): 2–3.

——. *Los ridículos.* Madrid: Librería de Angel de San Martín, n.d.

——. *La vida cursi.* Madrid: Fernando Fe, 1891–92.

Talavera, Fr. Hernando de. *Escritores místicos españoles.* Vol. 1. Ed. Miguel Mir. NBAE, 16. Madrid: Bailly Baillière, 1911.

Tarín, Santiago. "La carroza no salía a la calle desde 1970." *Ya* (Madrid) 22 Jan. 1986: 17.

Thornton, Tamara Plakins. *Handwriting in America: A Cultural History.* New Haven, Conn.: Yale University Press, 1996.

Tierno Galván, Enrique. "Aparición y desarrollo de nuevas perspectivas de valoración social en el siglo XIX: Lo cursi." 1952. *Desde el espectáculo a la trivialización.* Madrid: Taurus, 1961. 79–106.

Tolivar Faes, José. *Historia de la medicina en Asturias.* Salinas: Ayalga, 1976.

Tolosa Hernández, J. "Cursilería." *Miscelánea* 1.46 (30 Sept. 1900): 487.

Torre, José María. "Dolora cursi." *La ilustración ibérica* 8.378 (29 Mar. 1890): 206.

Torrecilla, Jesús. *La imitación colectiva: Modernidad vs. autenticidad en la literatura española.* Madrid: Gredos, 1996.

——. *El tiempo y los márgenes: Europa como utopía y como amenaza en la literatura española.* Chapel Hill: North Carolina Studies in the Romance Languages and Literatures, 1996.

Torres Fierro, Danubio. "Conversación con Manuel Puig: La redención de la cursilería." *Eco* 173 (Mar. 1975): 507–15.

Tortella Casares, Gabriel. "Estimación del *stock* de oro en España (1874–1914)." *La Banca española en la Restauración.* Vol. 2. Madrid: Banco de España, 1974. 117–39.

——. "Las magnitudes monetarias y sus determinantes." *La Banca española en la Restauración.* Vol. 1. Madrid: Banco de España, 1974. 457–521.

Trevor-Roper, Hugh. "The Invention of Tradition: The Highland Tradition of Scotland." Hobsbawm and Ranger. 15–41.

Trigo, Felipe. "El emotivismo: I." *Revista nueva* 28 (15 Nov. 1899): 219–24.

——. "El emotivismo: II." *Revista nueva* 30 (5 Dec. 1899): 291–98.

——. *El Semental.* 2d ed. Madrid: Renacimiento, 1931.

Tsuchiya, Akiko. "The Construction of the Female Body in Galdós's *La de Bringas*." *Romance Quarterly* 40 (1993): 35–47.

"Tú y yo." *La chispa* 1.16 (14 Aug. 1890): 6.

Tubert, Silvia. "Rosalía de Bringas: El erotismo de los trapos." *Bulletin of Hispanic Studies* (Glasgow) 74 (1997): 371–87.

Tuero, Tomás. "D. Segismundo Moret." *Tomás Tuero (la leyenda de un periodista)*. By Manuel Fernández Rodríguez Avello. Oviedo: Instituto de Estudios Asturianos, 1958. 89–93.

Tuñón de Lara, Manuel. *Estudios sobre el siglo XIX español*. Madrid: Siglo Veintiuno, 1973.

Ulacia Altolaguirre, Paloma. *Concha Méndez: Memorias habladas, memorias armadas*. Madrid: Mondadori, 1990.

Umbral, Francisco. *Guía de la posmodernidad*. Madrid: Temas de Hoy, 1987.

———. *Y Tierno Galván ascendió a los cielos: Memorias noveladas de la transición*. Barcelona: Seix Barral, 1990.

Unamuno, Miguel de. "Estilo y carácter." 1924. *De esto y de aquello*. Vol. 4. Ed. Manuel García Blanco. Buenos Aires: Editorial Sudamericana, 1954. 581–83.

———. *Niebla*. 1914. Ed. Mario J. Valdés. Madrid: Cátedra, 1983.

Urbano, Ramón A. "El abanico de Concha." *La gran vía* 2.36 (4 Mar. 1894): 136.

Urey, Diane Faye. *The Novel Histories of Galdós*. Princeton, N.J.: Princeton University Press, 1989.

Utt, Roger L. *Textos y con-textos de Clarín*. Madrid: Istmo, 1988.

Uzanne, Octave. *L'éventail*. Paris: A. Quantin, 1882.

Valbuena, Antonio de (Venancio González; Miguel de la Escalada). *Ripios Académicos*. Madrid: La España Editorial, 1890.

———. *Ripios vulgares*. 1891. 4th ed. Madrid: Est. Tip. de los Hijos de Tello, 1913.

Valera, Juan. *Obras completas*. Vol. 1. Ed. Luis Araujo Costa. 5th ed. Madrid: Aguilar, 1968.

Valero de Tornos, J. "Cursis alevosos." *La ilustración española y americana* 27.23 (22 June 1883): 385; 388.

Valis, Noël. "Fabricating Culture in Galdós's *Cánovas*." *MLN* 107 (1992): 250–73.

———. "Nostalgia and Exile." *Journal of Spanish Cultural Studies* 1.2 (2000): 117–33.

———. "Pardo Bazán's *El Cisne de Vilamorta* and the Romantic Reader." *MLN* 101 (1986): 298–324.

———. Review of *Literatura y cursilería*. By Carlos Moreno Hernández. *Anales galdosianos* 31–32 (1996–97): 143–45.

———. "Romanticism, Realism, and the Presence of the Word." *Letras peninsulares* 3.2–3 (fall / winter 1990): 321–39.

———. "Two Ramóns: A View from the Margins of Modernist *Cursilería*." *Anales de la literatura española contemporánea* 17.3 (1992): 325–45.

Valle-Inclán, Ramón del. *Luces de bohemia*. Ed. Alonso Zamora Vicente. 5th ed. Madrid: Espasa-Calpe, 1985.

———. *Sonata de otoño. Sonata de invierno.* 12th ed. Madrid: Espasa-Calpe, 1985.

———. *Sonata de primavera. Sonata de estío.* 13th ed. Madrid: Espasa-Calpe, 1984.

Vallejo, G. "Imitación de Becker." *Jaque-Mate* 2.42 (23 Jan. 1873): 1–2.

Varela Ortega, José. *Los amigos políticos: Partidos, elecciones y caciquismo en la Restauración (1875–1900).* Madrid: Alianza, 1977.

Varey, John. "Francisco Bringas: *Nuestro buen Thiers.*" *Anales galdosianos* 1 (1966): 63–69.

———. "Popular Entertainments in Madrid, 1758–1859: A Survey." *Renaissance and Modern Studies* 22 (1978): 26–44.

Vargas, Luis de. *La cursi del hongo. La farsa* No. 310 (19 Aug. 1933).

Vázquez Montalbán, Manuel. *Crónica sentimental de España.* Barcelona: Lumen, 1971.

———. *Crónica sentimental de la transición.* Barcelona: Planeta, 1985.

———. *Panfleto desde el planeta de los simios.* Barcelona: Grijalbo Mondadori, 1995.

Vega, José Blas. "La novela corta erótica española: Noticia bibliográfica." *El bosque* 10–11 (1995): 35–45.

Velada en memoria de D. Antonio Cánovas del Castillo. Discurso de D. Alejandro Pidal. Extracto de los discursos de los Sres. D. Gumersindo de Azcárate y D. Segismundo Moret. Madrid: Hijos de M. G. Hernández, 1897.

Vernon, Kathleen M. "Chismografía en las novelas de Galdós: *La incógnita* y *Realidad.*" *La torre* 3.10 (1989): 205–19.

Vidart, Luis. "En un abanico." *Día de moda* 1.29 (22 August 1880): 14.

Vilanova, Antonio. "El tradicionalismo anticastizo, universal y cosmopolita de las *Sonatas* de Valle-Inclán." *Homenaje a Antonio Sánchez Barbudo: Ensayos de literatura española moderna.* Ed. Benito Brancaforte, Edward R. Mulvihill, and Roberto G. Sánchez. Madison: Department of Spanish and Portuguese, University of Wisconsin, 1981. 353–94.

Vilarós, Teresa. *El mono del desencanto: Una crítica cultural de la transición española, 1973–1993.* Madrid: Siglo Veintiuno, 1998.

———. "Los monos del desencanto español." *MLN* 109 (1994): 217–35.

———. "Revuelo de plumas en la España de la transición." *Revista de crítica cultural* 8 (May 1994): 20–25.

Walsh, John. "Las mujeres en el teatro de Lorca." *Estelas, laberintos, nuevas sendas: Unamuno, Valle-Inclán, García Lorca, la guerra civil.* Ed. Angel G. Loureiro. Barcelona: Anthropos, 1988. 279–95.

Walsh, Peter. "Wild from Seclusion: Art and Locality in Baltimore, Maryland, USA." *Link* 1 (1996): 8–29.

Warner, Marina. *Alone of All Her Sex: The Myth and the Cult of the Virgin Mary.* 1976. New York: Pocket Books, 1978.

Westmacott, Mary (Agatha Christie). *The Rose and the Yew Tree.* 1947. New York: Dell, 1975.

White, Deborah Elise. "*Studies on Hysteria:* Case Histories and the Case against History." *MLN* 104 (1989): 1035–49.

White, Hayden. "The Fictions of Factual Representation." *The Literature of Fact.* Ed. Angus Fletcher. New York: Columbia University Press, 1976. 21–44.

——. *Metahistory: The Historical Imagination in Nineteenth-Century Europe.* Baltimore: Johns Hopkins University Press, 1973.

Williams, William Carlos. "Introduction to Charles Sheeler—Paintings—Drawings—Photographs (1939)." *Selected Essays.* New York: Random House, 1954. 231–34.

Williams, Raymond. *Keywords: A Vocabulary of Culture and Society.* 1976. New York: Oxford University Press, 1983.

——. *Marxism and Literature.* Oxford: Oxford University Press, 1977.

——. *The Politics of Modernism: Against the New Conformists.* Ed. Tony Pinkney. London: Verso, 1989.

Ya (Madrid) 22 Jan. 1986.

Ynduráin, Francisco. "Lo 'cursi' en la obra de Galdós." *Actas del Segundo Congreso Internacional de Estudios Galdosianos.* Vol. 1. Las Palmas: Excmo. Cabildo Insular de Gran Canaria, 1979. 266–82.

Young, Howard T. "Bridges to Romance: Nostalgia in Eliot, Salinas, and Lorca." *The Spanish Avant-Garde.* Ed. Derek Harris. Manchester: Manchester University Press, 1995. 136–48.

Zeldin, Theodore. *France, 1848–1945.* 2 vols. Oxford: Clarendon Press, 1973–1977.

Zorrilla, José. *Recuerdos del tiempo viejo.* Vol. 1. Madrid: Publicaciones Españolas, 1961.

Zozaya, Antonio (Carlos Christian Federico Schüler). "Abanico." *Instantáneas.* Barcelona: Antonio López, n.d. 45–46.

Zuleta, Ignacio. *La polémica modernista: El modernismo de mar a mar (1898–1902).* Bogotá: Instituto Caro y Cuervo, 1988.

Zumthor, Paul. "The Text and the Voice." *New Literary History* 16 (1984): 67–92.

Index

cultural anthropology and, 20; Raymond Williams and, 20, 35
Style pompier, 15
Subirats, Eduardo, 349 n.6
Suck, Titus, 306 n.17, 320 n.4

Taboada, Luis, 55, 56
Talavera, Hernando de, 194, 333 n.24
Tertulias, 122, 130
Tessi Curt, 59–60, 64
Things. *See* Objects
Thornton, Tamara Plakins, 81, 317 n.32
Tierno Galván, Enrique, 1–2, 21, 22, 29, 30, 71, 77, 81, 82, 87, 97, 200, 231, 295–99, 302, 307 n.1; death of, 1, 295, 305 n.1; funeral of, 2–3, 305 n.1; opposition to Franco, 2–3; tradition and, 3
Tolosa Hernández, J., 228
Transition, 279, 296, 297
Transvestites, 289, 294–95
Trevor-Roper, Hugh, 336 n.3
Trigo, Felipe, 334 n.36, 338 n.28
Tsuchiya, Akiko, 161
Tubert, Silvia, 161, 167, 328 n.40
Tuero, Tomás, 323 n.31, 332 n.12

Umbral, Francisco, 29, 281–82, 289, 290, 295–99, 305 n.2, 352 n.44; *Y Tierno Galván ascendió a los cielos* and, 29, 295–99
Unamuno, Miguel de, 8, 48, 109; *Niebla* and, 45–47, 67, 204, 205, 231
Urbanization, 265, 266, 302
Urey, Diane Faye, 179, 180, 199
Utopia: motif of, 29, 290, 291, 295, 297–98, 351 n.29
Uzanne, Octave, 102

Valbuena, Antonio de, 134, 186–87, 333 n.16
Valencia, Elena, 316 n.29
Valencia, Pedro (Conde), 316 n.29

Valera, Juan, 56, 83, 87
Valle-Inclán, Ramón del, 24, 44, 275, 302; *Femeninas* and, 225; *La lámpara maravillosa* and, 268; *Sonatas* and, 27, 225, 226, 227, 230, 238, 239–43, 350 n.20
Varela Ortega, José, 345 n.38
Vargas, Luis de, 342 n.6
Vázquez Montalbán, Manuel, 292
Vega, Ventura de la, 316 n.29
Ventín, Ramón, 240
Verlaine, Paul, 221
Vernon, Kathleen M., 334 n.31
Vilanova, Antonio, 225
Vilarós, Teresa, 279, 282, 351 n.29
Viñes Millet, Cristina, 262

Wahl, Eberhard, 291
Warner, Marina, 347 n.57
War of 1898, 26, 202, 203
Wasson, Curtis, 321 n.8
Welles, Orson, 227
Westmacott, Mary, 118, 119
White, Deborah Elise, 37, 308 n.5
White, Hayden, 38, 189
Wilde, Oscar, 271, 346 n.46
Williams, Raymond, 20, 35, 36, 221, 299–300, 307 n.21, 313 n.58. *See also* Structure of feeling
Williams, William Carlos, 251
Women: luxury and, 142, 144–46, 162–63, 240; role of, 130, 277

Ynduráin, Francisco, 327 n.17
Young, Howard T., 341 n.1

Zarauz, 149, 171, 172, 174–78, 330 n.57
Zea, Francisco, 172
Zeldin, Theodore, 18, 20, 307 nn.23, 26
Zola, Emile, 105
Zorrilla, José, 123–24, 133, 134, 320 n.5
Zubiaurre, María Teresa, 315 n.21

Noël Valis is Professor of Spanish at Yale
University. She has authored and edited the
following books: *The Novels of Jacinto Octavio
Picón; The Decadent Vision in Leopoldo Alas: A Study
of "La Regenta" and "Su Unico Hijo"; "Malevolent
Insemination" and Other Essays on Clarín;* (with
Carol Maier) *In the Feminine Mode: Essays on
Hispanic Women Writers and Other Studies.* She
also translated *The Poetry of Julia Uceda.*

Library of Congress Cataloging-in-Publication Data
Valis, Noël.
The culture of cursilería:
bad taste, kitsch, and class in modern Spain / Noël Valis.
p. cm.   Includes bibliographical references and index.
ISBN 0-8223-3000-8 (cloth : alk. paper)
ISBN 0-8223-2997-2 (pbk. : alk. paper)
1. Kitsch—Spain—History—19th century. 2. Middle Class—
Spain—History—19th century. 3. Popular culture—Spain—
History—19th century. 4. Kitsch—Spain—History—20th
century. 5. Middle Class—Spain—History—20th century.
6. Popular culture—Spain—History—20th century.
7. Spain—Social life and customs. I. Title.
BH301.K5 V35 2002   306'.0946—dc21   2002008829